ECONOMIC ISSUES, PROBLEMS AND PERSPECTIVES

# MODELLING MULTIDISCIPLINARY CAUSES OF THE GREEK CRISIS

## A CONCEPTUAL ANALYSIS

# Economic Issues, Problems and Perspectives

Additional books and e-books in this series can be found on Nova's website under the Series tab.

ECONOMIC ISSUES, PROBLEMS AND PERSPECTIVES

# MODELLING MULTIDISCIPLINARY CAUSES OF THE GREEK CRISIS

## A CONCEPTUAL ANALYSIS

JANINE MUKUDDEM-PETERSEN
AND
DAWIE SCHOLTZ

nova science publishers
New York

**Library of Congress Cataloging-in-Publication Data**

Names: Mukuddem-Petersen, J., author.

Title: Modelling multidisciplinary causes of the Greek crisis : a conceptual analysis / Janine Mukuddem-Petersen (Chair, UCT GSB Postgraduate Committee, Graduate School of Business, University of Cape Town, Cape Town, South Africa) and Dawie Scholtz (Boston Consulting Group).

Description: Hauppauge, New York : Nova Science Publishers, Inc., [2019] | Series: Economic issues, problems and perspectives

Identifiers: LCCN 2018060121| ISBN 9781536135473 (hardcover) | ISBN 9781536148411 (eISBN)

Subjects: LCSH: Financial crises--Greece. | Greece--Economic policy--1974- | Greece--Economic conditions--21st century.

Classification: LCC HB3807.5 M85 2019 | DDC 330.9595/076--dc23 LC record available at https://lccn.loc.gov/2018060121

*Published by Nova Science Publishers, Inc. † New York*

Janine Mukuddem-Petersen

*To my beloved daughters Daena Blythe Kendra Petersen and Jenna Erin Dae Petersen*

Dawie Scholtz

*For Mopo, without whom none of this would be possible*

# CONTENTS

# LIST OF FIGURES

# List of Tables

# List of Abbreviations

| | |
|---|---|
| EC | European Commission |
| ECB | European Central Bank |
| EMU | European Monetary Union |
| GDP | Gross Domestic Product |
| IMF | International Monetary Fund |
| ND | New Democracy (centre-right Greek political party) |
| OECD | The Organisation for Economic Development and Cooperation |
| PASOK | Pan-Hellenic Socialist Movement (centre-left Greek political party) |
| SGP | The European Stability and Growth Pact |
| SYRIZA | Coalition of the Radical Left (far-left Greek political party, translated from Greek) |
| VAT | Value-Added Tax |

# PREFACE

The ongoing Greek crisis has been the subject of immense scholarly interest and debate since it erupted in 2009. Vast amounts of research from a number of disciplines have attempted to explain the causes of the crisis, with a great variety of approaches adopted in doing so. Unfortunately, there has been little effort to develop a comprehensive cross-disciplinary framework for understanding how the crisis came about. This study has 'bridged the divide' by developing such a cross-disciplinary conceptual model for the causes of the Greek crisis.

The literature review process revealed that studies from the political science, public administration, economics, financial economics and monetary economics disciplines contained a range of explanations for the occurrence of the Greek crisis. Qualitative content analysis techniques were used to synthesise the findings from these five fields into a cross-disciplinary conceptual model.

By integrating the findings from the five disciplines above, a number of new insights were generated. Firstly, it was found that the crisis manifested primarily as a collapse of confidence in the ability of the Greek state to pay its debts. Secondly, that high sovereign debt levels, internal political opposition to reform, a deterioration of competitiveness of the Greek economy, the existence of destructive political institutions and the possibility of an exit from the European Monetary Union acted as key causes (amongst others) for the collapse of confidence in Greek sovereign bonds. Finally, a number of implications for policy makers in Greece and elsewhere were found and elaborated upon.

*Chapter 1*

# INTRODUCTION

On 14 August 2015, Greece's Parliament voted to accept the country's third bailout in five years – securing €86 billion from the European Central Bank (ECB), the International Monetary Fund (IMF) and the European Commission (EC) in order to avoid the imminent insolvency of the Greek state. The third bailout package, as with the two before, is contingent upon stringent economic reforms that will affect every aspect of Greek public policy and public life (The Guardian Newspaper, 2015).

Since the eruption of the Greek crisis in 2009 (Polito & Wickens, 2014), it has dominated world headlines and has done untold damage to the Greek economy and the lives of the Greek people (Krugman, 2014). It has had numerous social and political implications given that it has necessitated a fundamental rethinking of the Greek social contract (Sakellaropoulos & Sotiris, 2014).

Naturally, there has been significant interest in understanding the causes of the Greek crisis and distilling the lessons to be learnt from it. Deepening the collective understanding of what went wrong in Greece, and how to avoid such crises in future, is clearly a valuable scholarly endeavour that can help to improve public policy in future.

Significant work has been done in this regard. There now exists a plethora of research on numerous aspects of the crisis. Early attempts at sketching the causes and their implications (Nelson, Belkin, & Mix, 2010; Kouretas & Vlamis, 2010; Kokkoris, Olivares-Caminal, & Papadakis, 2010; Arghyrou & Tsoukalas, 2011) provide valuable context and varying explanations of the causes of the crisis. Since then, a large number of studies have been conducted looking into different root causes of the crisis. A number of studies focus on the role played by Greece's Euro membership (Krugman, 2014; Robbins, 2015; De Grauwe, 2011; Arghyrou & Tsoukalas, 2011; Arghyrou & Tsoukalas, 2010; Fouskas & Dimoulas, 2012; Dellas & Tavlas, 2013), on the role of Greece's fiscal policies in the 2000s (Zettelmeyer, Trebesch, & Gulati, 2013; Kaplanoglou & Rapanos, 2013; Kokkoris, Olivares-Caminal, & Papadakis, 2010; Georganta, 2011; Featherstone,

2011) and the role of ineffective Greek institutions (Kaplanoglou & Rapanos, 2013; Featherstone, 2011; Yfantopoulos, 2013) in precipitating the crisis. There are also a myriad studies on the social and political background to the crisis (Sakellaropoulos & Sotiris, 2014; Vasilopoulou & Halikiopoulou, 2013; Dobrescu & Durach, 2014; Karyotis & Rudig, 2015).

It is important to note that these studies are derived from multiple theoretical and ideological perspectives, and originate from a variety of disciplines. An extensive survey of existing academic literature indicates that research on the causes of the crisis can be found in five academic disciplines: financial economics, political science, monetary economics, public administration and economics. Each discipline provides unique insights and perspectives of the crisis, its causes and its implications. But unfortunately, very little work has been done to integrate the research outcomes concerning the Greek crisis into one, holistic whole.

Indeed, several scholars (Malakos, 2013; Sklias & Maris, 2013; Robbins, 2015) have already suggested that such an integration is required. The literature is replete with studies that, for example, recommend harsh wage deflation and austerity measures in Greece (Antzoulatos, 2011; Papanikos, 2014; Creighton, 2011) without examining Greece's political and institutional realities, undermining the credibility of such recommendations (Karyotis & Rudig, 2015).

This book addresses this shortcoming by developing a conceptual model of the causes of the Greek crisis, drawing from each of the various disciplines mentioned above. This is the first study on this topic to produce such an integrative conceptual model. It therefore adds significant value to the existing knowledge base on the Greek crisis, given that it creates a single, comprehensive summation of the causes of the crisis (and their interrelationships). Shirazi (2015) outlines how integration of existing knowledge from diverse fields can create new insights, suggesting that such studies add value to existing research.

The study utilised qualitative content analysis techniques (Krippendorf, 1989) on literature spanning monetary economics, financial economics, economics, political science and public administration in order to construct a descriptive conceptual model. The study is therefore explicitly descriptive (Elo & Kyngas, 2007) in nature.

The book thus aimed to overcome the existing challenge of 'research silos' on the Greek crisis, thereby contributing to the collective knowledge base on the topic by providing an effective cross-disciplinary integration of knowledge.

## 1.1. Research Aims and Objectives

Given that an enormous amount of qualitative and quantitative research has already been conducted on the Greek crisis (Fouskas & Dimoulas, 2012), this research will focus on synthesising the content from existing studies. Special focus will be given to integrating the contributions from different fields on this topic, enabling the creation of a cross-disciplinary conceptual model of the causes of the crisis.

The primary goals/corresponding objectives strived for in this book are described below:

**1. Literature review of the Greek crisis**

*Goal:* To describe the existing literature on the crisis, incorporating studies from a variety of theoretical perspectives and disciplines.

*Objective:* Uncover as much literature on the crisis as possible from a variety of databases (e.g., Ebscohost, Econlit, Science Direct, Jstor and Emerald) and from a variety of disciplines (financial economics, monetary economics, economics, political science and public administration) and begin to develop a preliminary understanding of the factors contributing to the crisis.

**2. Apply qualitative content analysis techniques on the literature**

*Goal:* To discover the most prevalent concepts that are identified as causes of the Greek crisis.

*Objective:* Use qualitative content analysis methods (Krippendorf, 1989) on selected literature to condense the literature into concepts that will enable synthesis of the different academic disciplines.

**3. A conceptual model**

*Goal:* To construct a conceptual model of the causes of the Greek crisis.

*Objective:* Construct a conceptual model using qualitative content analysis outcomes. The model should provide causal relationships between key factors that drove the emergence of the Greek crisis and will be mapped out visually and explained in narrative style with the use of supporting literature.

**4. Greek politics**

*Goal:* To understand what role the Greek political environment played in the development of the crisis.

*Objective:* Use the constructed conceptual model to understand whether and how Greek political preferences contributed to the crisis. This involves understanding the role of politics in two time-periods: Firstly, the pre-crisis democratic period, which can be defined as 1981-2009 (Vasilopoulou, Halikiopoulou, & Exadaktylos, 2014) and secondly, the crisis period (from 2009 onwards).

**5. Greek debt**

*Goal:* To understand how and why the Greek government accumulated excessive debt.

*Objective:* Use the constructed conceptual model to deduce a framework for the root causes of Greek debt accumulation.

**6. Greece and global financial markets**

*Goal:* To understand how and why Greek government bonds lost credibility in the global financial markets.

*Objective:* Greece and global financial markets: Use the constructed conceptual model to understand which factors eroded the global financial markets' confidence in Greek sovereign bonds.

**7. Greece and the Eurozone**

*Goal:* To understand whether, and if so, how, Greece's membership of the European Monetary Union contributed to the crisis.

*Objective:* Greece and the Eurozone: Use the constructed conceptual model to deduce a framework to understand if Greece's Eurozone membership contributed to the Greek crisis; and if so, how it contributed to the crisis.

## 1.2. Research Questions

The following research questions are posed with regards to each of the aims and objectives that have been identified:

**Question 1. Literature review of the Greek crisis:**

- What literature is available on the Greek crisis?
- What academic discipline does each study fall under?
- What literature pertaining to the Greek crisis will be helpful to this study, and what inclusion criteria should be utilised?

**Question 2. Qualitative content analysis:**

- What are the dominant concepts identified in the qualitative content analysis process?
- What are the relationships between those concepts?
- What degree of conceptual overlap exists between the different disciplines?

**Question 3. Conceptual model of the causes of the Greek crisis:**

- How can a conceptual model be constructed to summarise and integrate the content of the literature?

**Question 4. Greek politics:**

- What role did public opinion play in the build-up to the crisis?
- What role did public opinion play during the crisis?
- Are there particular political institutions that contributed to the crisis?

**Question 5. Greek debt:**

- How much debt did Greece accumulate before the crisis?
- Why did the market provide Greece with so much debt for so long?
- Why did the Greek government accumulate so much debt?

**Question 6. Greece and the global financial markets:**

- Why did the global financial markets lose faith in Greek sovereign bonds?
- What internal and external shocks affected market confidence in Greece?

**Question 7. Greece and the Eurozone:** Did Eurozone membership help or hinder Greece in the build-up to and during the crisis?

There are two important issues to note at this point: Firstly, the questions exclude the social underpinnings of the crisis. This has been a deliberate choice given that the literature suggests that social factors are much more associated with the implications of the crisis (Petmesidou, 2013; Sakellaropoulos & Sotiris, 2014) as opposed to the causes of the crisis. The social factors that contributed to the crisis – such as reliance on the social welfare system – are adequately captured in the political science literature on the topic, as it manifested itself in the form of a powerful anti-austerity and anti-social welfare reform political lobby in the period before the crisis (Fouskas & Dimoulas, 2012). The social *implications* of the crisis are however immense and is likely to receive significant attention as the crisis continues to unfold (Matsaganis, 2011).

Secondly, it should be noted that no particular hypotheses have been developed for this study. It has been designed as a purely descriptive inductive qualitative content analysis. Cho and Lee (2014) suggest that inductive qualitative content analysis studies approach the unit of analysis without pre-conceived notions of theory or hypotheses, and that the content of the texts should guide the analysis.

## 1.3. Research Limitations, Delimitations and Assumptions

The research in this book has purposefully been limited to the *causes* of the Greek crisis, given that there is a significant, yet fractured, literature on the causes of the crisis (Gibson, Palivos, & Tavlas, 2014) that is readily available for analysis. The implications of the crisis are however still unfolding, with the literature still catching up to the latest developments.

An important limitation is therefore the availability of scientific literature on the latest developments of the crisis, but the chosen delimitation is simply to limit the study to the causes of the crisis, which are more comprehensively covered given that the crisis erupted in 2009 already (Nelson, Belkin, & Mix, 2010).

The accessibility of literature is an additional limitation. There is a significant literature readily available on the accessible databases, but a number of articles are available for purchase only. Unfortunately no budget has been allocated to this study, meaning that the only feasible delimitation is to add 'freely accessible' as an inclusion criteria for articles to be included in the study.

The only significant assumption that was identified at the outset, was that the various disciplines have produced research on Greece that is sufficiently-alike to be integrated into a single conceptual model. If this assumption was not met, it would have made integration between the various disciplines challenging, with a possible alternative approach being the creation of multiple conceptual models for the different disciplines. The study has however indicated that the research on the Greek crisis is sufficiently-alike across the different disciplines to be effectively integrated into a single conceptual model. The assumption was therefore met.

## 1.4. Ethical Considerations

Given that the study is based on secondary data, there are no major ethical considerations. Schreier (2012) suggests that unobtrusiveness and the use of secondary data are two major advantages of qualitative content analysis given that it simplifies the ethical considerations in the research. Also note that the appropriate ethics documentation have been completed and submitted.

*Chapter 2*

# LITERATURE REVIEW

Since the Greek crisis broke out in earnest in 2009, the Greek experience has influenced debates and discussions on economic policy the world over. Numerous countries are engaged in conversations on how 'not to become the next Greece'. Turley (2014) for example details how a recent spate of elections in the United Kingdom, United States and Europe have all been dominated by issues of fiscal reform and austerity, with direct references to the Greek experience featuring prominently in most election campaigns.

Krugman (2014) calls this the '*Hellenization*' of the fiscal debate, wherein the Greek experience has framed numerous countries' moves towards austerity. But Krugman and others (see Arghyrou & Tsoukalas, 2011; Featherstone, 2011; Fouskas, 2013) raise an important point: The Greek crisis was a result of a large number of political, economic and external factors that are unique to Greece in some cases. Observers should therefore be careful not to draw conclusions and lessons from the Greek experience without considering all of these contextual factors. Indeed, without understanding the complexity of the Greek context, one cannot learn from the Greek experience. This review will therefore assess the existing academic literature on the Greek crisis and the relevant underlying theory to develop a sufficiently-nuanced view of how the crisis came about. It includes literature from the political science perspective, from economics, from monetary economics, from public administration and from financial economics. The discussion will be guided by the following issues: 1) The build-up of Greek debt; 2) Greece's ascension to the European Monetary Union; 3) The deterioration of Greek competitiveness; 4) The unfolding of the crisis; 5) Methodology and 6) Conclusion. The headings and subheadings have been numbered for reference in later sections.

# 1. THE BUILD-UP OF GREEK DEBT

The literature provides little consensus for a singular starting point from which the manifestation of the Greek crisis can be understood. But given that the Greek crisis manifested as a sovereign debt crisis, Kouretas and Vlamis (2010) suggest a sensible first step: Start by looking at the evolution of Greek public debt since 1970.

## 1.1. The Greek Welfare State

The political science literature provides an important insight relating to this graph. The rapid increase in Greek public debt relative to GDP coincided with the formation of the Greek welfare state, which began in 1981 after the election of Andreas Papandreou as Greece's first socialist Prime Minister (Matsaganis, 2011; Kouretas & Vlamis, 2010). Papandreou's Panhellenic Socialist Movement (PASOK) governed Greece from 1981 to 2004 (Hembruff, 2013) and prioritised the creation of an extensive Greek social welfare system.

The formation of the Greek social welfare system, which is considered one of the most generous social welfare systems in Europe (O'Donnel & Tinios, 2003), clearly had a significant impact on Greece's public finances.

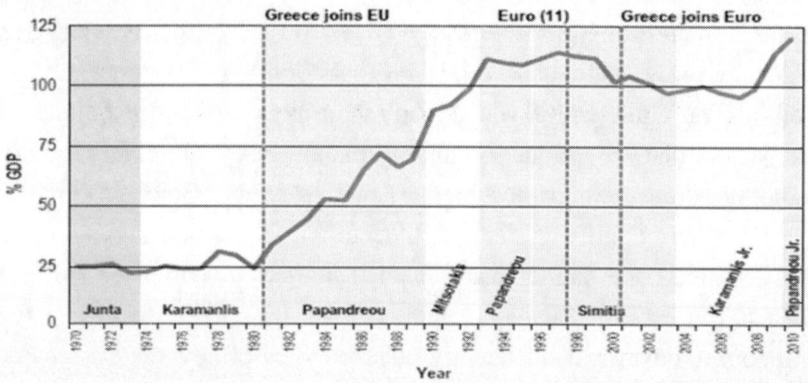


Source: Kouretas and Vlamis (2010).

Figure 1. Greek public debt-to-GDP ratio 1970-2010.

As Figure 1 indicates, Greece rapidly accumulated a significant stock of public debt in the period after 1981, reaching 100% of GDP in the early nineties. Krajewska (2014) finds that the formation of the welfare state was the primary driver of the increased debt burden as it necessitated an expensive, debt-fueled expansion of the Greek public service. This meant that by 2009, the Greek state employed 650 000 out of a total Greek population of 11 million people. The IMF has warned that this is an excessive number of public employees, proposing that Greece reduce the number by 23%, or 150 000 (Kot, 2013, as cited by Krajewska, 2014). The problem is underlined by the fact that Greece spends 13.5% of its GDP on public sector wages, as opposed to an EU average of 10%.

At the same time Reddy (2011) indicates that by 2008, the Greek pension 'replacement rate' – that is, the size of average pension payments as a percentage of pre-retirement salaries – was by far the highest in Europe at between 70 and 80 percent, with Zartaloudis (2014) finding that Greece gave particularly generous pension benefits to public sector employees. Zartaloudis additionally finds that Greece provided, on average, significant and above-inflation pay increases to public sector employees in the period between 1980-2008. Christopoulou and Monastiriotis (2014) finds that the public sector wage premium stood at an enormous 32% by 2008, implying that public sector jobs paid 32% more than comparable private sector jobs at the time. This meant that personnel payments (in the form of both high pensions and high salaries) became the single highest expenditure item in the Greek national budget by the mid-1990s and continued to grow as a percentage of the total budget until the crisis in 2009. Zartaloudis (2014), Katsimi and Moutos (2010), Michaelides, Papageorgiou and Vouldis (2013) and Mitsopoulos and Pelagidis (2014) (and many others) argue that the large, expensive and inefficient Greek public service was a primary driver of high and unsustainable fiscal deficits.

Reddy (2011) raises an additional important point: the rising age of the Greek population – and by definition the rising age of Greek government employees – meant that the country was facing ever-escalating pension payments for the growing number of retirees.

## 1.2. Poor Governance

As discussed in the previous section, the build-up of debt did not occur overnight. The problem developed over many years and a number of Greek governments attempted to 'modernise' the Greek state during 90s and 2000s to reduce expenditure and improve fiscal sustainability (Reddy, 2011; Hembruff, 2013; Finger, 2015). Modernisation attempts were however mostly unsuccessful and failed to significantly reduce the country's debt burden. This failure is particularly problematic given that the country experienced significant economic growth of 3.9% per year between 2001 and 2008, second only to Ireland in the Eurozone (Gibson, Hall, & Tavlas, 2010); and yet despite this growth it could not reduce its overall debt burden as a percentage of GDP.

Fouskas and Dimoulas (2012) argue that Greece was unable to reduce its debt as a percentage of GDP during the 1990s and 2000s due to a number of irresponsible spending decisions and governance challenges. They cite excessive military expenditure as a prime example. In the period 2006 – 2010, Greece ranked as the fifth largest weapons importer in the world and, bizarrely, at the beginning of the crisis in 2010, the country ordered six warships from France (€2.5 billion) and six submarines from Germany (€5 billion) despite its ongoing fiscal crisis (Fouskas, 2013; Fouskas & Dimoulas, 2012). Featherstone (2011) also points to weak governance as the central reason behind Greece's inability to address deficits in the 2000s. In particular, Featherstone cites ineffective public budget management and weak implementation capabilities as key problems. The Greek budget before 2010 for example consisted of 14 000 separate line items, each representing grouped items of expenditure, obscuring details of public spending on particular items and making it impossible to assess the efficacy of spending on particular items.

The public administration and political science literature includes a plethora of studies that identify a number of other governance-related issues that contributed to the Greek government's deficits, including widespread corruption (Sakellaropoulos & Sotiris, 2014; Featherstone, 2011; Neslon, Belkin, & Mix, 2010; Sklias & Maris, 2013), ineffective revenue collection (Featherstone, 2011; Kaplanoglou & Rapanos, 2013; Olivares-Caminal & Papadakis, 2010; Yfantopoulos, 2013; Fouskas, 2012) and the inefficacy of Greece's statistical services, making it difficult to manage government expenditure accurately (Georganta, 2011; Kaplanoglou & Rapanos, 2013).

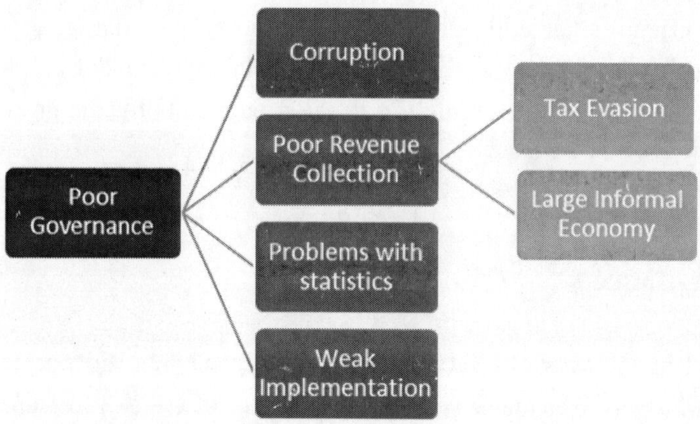


Figure 2. Visual representation of poor governance and related issues.

Ineffective revenue collection in particular has received significant attention. Yfantopoulos (2013) estimates that between 25% and 30% of the Greek economy operates informally, and without being taxed, leading to an estimated loss to the Greek state of €261 billion between 2003 and 2011. This is an enormous amount in the Greek context, given that the total value of IMF, EC and ECB bailouts between 2010 and 2015 has amounted to €305 billion. Williams and Renooy (2008) find that Greece's losses to undeclared income and other fraudulent activities are by far the largest in Europe, whilst the European Commission (as cited by Featherstone, 2011) indicates that 30% of potential revenues are not collected due to tax evasion and other fraudulent activities.

Krajewska (2014) concludes that ineffective Greek tax collection lead Greek tax revenues to be the smallest in relation to GDP in Europe in 2009 at 30.5% of GDP, as opposed to the weighted European average of 39.1%. Ultimately this issue is perhaps best-illustrated by the infamous 2059-strong list of IMF-identified wealthy Greek industrialists, politicians, bankers and ship-owners who had collectively evaded €13 billion in taxes between 1998 and 2007 (Fouskas, 2013).

The literature therefore paints a grim picture of the Greek state in the decade before the crisis erupted in 2009, suggesting that successive Greek governments had contributed to the country's debt problems through ineffective governance. Clearly, ineffective public administration played a role. Greek governments were unable to reign in corruption, unable to collect taxes effectively, unable to manage budgets and financial statistics effectively, unable to contain the public sector wage bill and unable to reform a very expensive social welfare system. Ultimately, this meant it was unable to contain its fiscal deficits and the build-up of debt that lead to the crisis.

## 1.3. The Politics of Debt

Interestingly, a number of studies focusing purely on the economics of the crisis (for examples see: Dellas & Tavlas, 2013; Arghyrou & Tsoukalas, 2011) rightfully point to government's failures in addressing Greece's fiscal imbalances; yet provide no analysis of the political context that fuelled the situation. This is a problematic omission, as the political context was an important driver of the governance issues in Greece (Sklias & Maris, 2013).

A number of studies by Greek political science scholars has been assessed to address this shortcoming. Featherstone and Papadimitriou (2008) for example extensively analysed the opposition to health care, pension and labour market reforms proposed by Prime Minister Simitis during his tenure (1996-2000), indicating that meaningful reform efforts were aggressively opposed by influential public sector unions and other left-leaning movements. Featherstone and Papadimitriou conclude that reform aimed at cutting fiscal expenditure was simply not politically or legislatively viable at the time. Petmesidou (2013) and O'Donnel and Tinios (2003) also outline how influential public sector unions have played a significant part in blocking pension reform and public sector modernisation throughout the last decade. Karyotis and Rudig (2013), Vasilopoulou and Halikiopoulou (2013), Psitimis (2011) and Dobrescu and Durach (2014) also find strong evidence of public opinion opposing austerity measures in Greece; therefore supporting the thesis that political pressures were at least partly responsible for motivating Greek governments to spend excessively. Numerous other scholars have also made the case that successive Greek governments chose to accumulate debt instead of engaging in 'politically-unpopular' reforms, thereby choosing the politically expedient option and leaving higher and higher debt for future governments to deal with (Kokkoris, Olivares-Caminal, & Papadakis, 2010; Baltas & Chair, 2013; Featherstone, 2011; Schimmer & Kunisch, 2011).

It must be noted however that the political science studies on political opposition to reform (see: Petmesidou, 2013; O'Donnel & Tinios, 2003; Kovras, 2010; Karyotis & Rudig, 2015; Sklias & Maris, 2013) all rely on either polling and other survey information, or election results, which captures opinion at particular moments in time, and which is therefore not generalizable. Dobrescu and Durach (2014) for example find strong anti-austerity opinion in 2012, but are quick to point out that findings are not generalizable for other periods of time. We can therefore conclude that there was strong opposition to austerity measures and economic reforms at *certain points in time* during the 2000s, based on the existing research. But despite an extensive search, no formal academic evidence could be found to suggest widespread public support for austerity measures in Greece, *at any point in time*. Anti-austerity sentiments have also been confirmed in the recent referendum in Greece, where voters rejected the latest round of austerity measures by landslide margins (Huffington Post, 2015). Interestingly, the Greek government opted to accept the austerity measures in any event, perhaps indicating that the need for reform has become desperate enough to defy the apparent traditional political gravity opposing austerity measures in Greece. From a political perspective, it may also be easier to implement unpopular measures if they are enforced by vilified outsiders such as the 'Troika' (Karyotis & Rudig, 2015).

A number of the surveyed studies have gone further and developed sociological theories to explain Greeks' political opposition to reducing government expenditure. Although the theoretical sociological aspects of Greek political opposition to reform has been judged to not be relevant to the study (and therefore won't be included in this discussion), it is useful to understand the public attitudes that shapes Greeks' political preferences in relation to national debt and fiscal policy. Theodossopoulos (2013) suggests widespread support for the idea that 'Europe must help pay the debt', given that Greeks believe that joining the European Monetary Union has come at great expense, and has benefited other European countries – such as Germany – more than it benefitted Greece. Hembruff (2013) and Streeck (2012) find slightly different underpinnings for the opposition to reduced spending. They suggest that Greeks blame the 'foreign bankers' who triggered the global financial crisis and the traditional Greek governing parties (PASOK and New Democracy (ND)), who they see as corrupt and ineffective. Despite these nuanced differences, the political science and sociological research on Greece suggest that the Greek people see the current crisis as caused by external players (with the research differing on which players are the primary culprits), or a few corrupt local elites. The Greeks therefore see no need why they, as the perceived victims of the crisis, should be made to suffer or repay the debts. This rationale appears to be a widespread belief that underpins mass opposition to the current reform efforts and other reform efforts during the 1990s and 2000s.

There is one final point to be made on the tension within the political science literature on the Greek crisis: Political science scholars who openly identify as leftist, such as Sakellaropoulos and Sotiris (2014), Petmesidou (2013) or Fouskas and Dimoulas (2012) primarily assign the blame for Greece's escalating debt burden on ineffective government leadership and a lax tax regime which enabled the wealthy to avoid taxation. For these scholars, the welfare state in its original form is sustainable, but only if managed effectively and thus they do not see the need for structural reform of the Greek social welfare system. Other, more conservative, scholars such as O'Donnel and Tinios (2003) or Kouretas and Vlamis (2010) however contend that the Greek welfare state as originally envisioned by Papandreou is inherently unsustainable and unaffordable, especially considering the ageing nature of Greece's population. This difference belies the potential for ideological bias in the political science studies on this topic. In order to overcome the risk of biased results in the eventual content analysis and conceptual mapping stage, this book included contributions from both sides of the ideological spectrum to ensure that a balanced and nuanced outcome is ensured.

## 1.4. Greece's Debt Compared to Others

Greece had clearly accumulated large amounts of debt, and we have now established some preliminary underpinnings of the debt. But Krugman (2014) also raises (and answers) an important question about Greek debt: Why is it that Greece is experiencing a sovereign debt crisis when there are other countries with similar amounts or more debt than Greece? Consider, by way of explanation, the graph below:

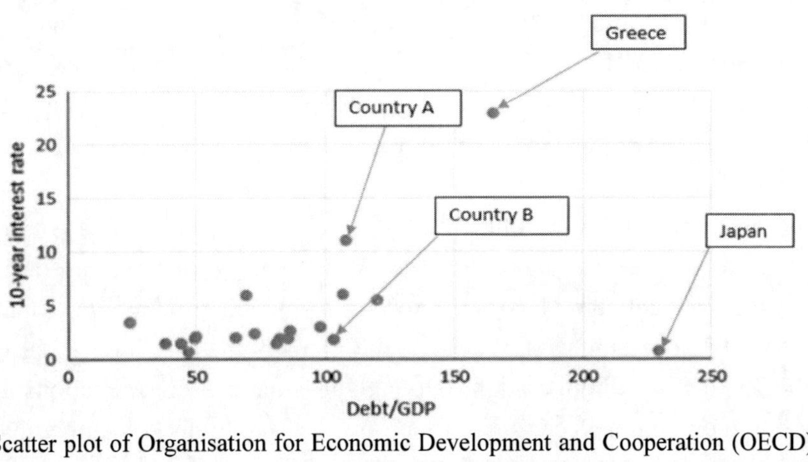


Figure 3. Scatter plot of Organisation for Economic Development and Cooperation (OECD) countries' debt-to-GDP ratios and 10 year interest rates on sovereign bonds at the end of 2012. Source: Adapted from Krugman (2014) (Lines and labels added).

Krugman uses this graph to make a very important point – perceived country default risk (as expressed through higher interest rates on sovereign bonds) is not just a function of the amount of debt a country has. Krugman argues that those in the UK, US and elsewhere who are engaging in political debates about 'not becoming the next Greece' as a motivation for austerity measures are making a significant mistake given that debt levels alone are not indicative of a country's default risk. A number of monetary economics scholars (Krugman, 2014; De Grauwe, 2011; Dellas & Tavlas, 2013; Eichengreen, 2003) argue that currency regimes and domestic regulation play an enormous role in determining country default risk, and that it is in fact impossible to 'become the next Greece' if a country has a free floating exchange rate.

The graph above strongly supports this argument, and the juxtaposition between Greece and Japan in particular provides a powerful example of how debt levels are not necessarily indicative of default risk. Japan had the most government debt of any OECD country in 2012 at 240% of GDP, yet the interest rates on its 10 year government bonds remained astonishingly low. Greece on the other hand had far less debt at the time (160% of GDP), but was perceived as being extremely risky, with investors demanding exorbitant interest rates beyond 20% to justify any investment in Greek government debt. Krugman (2014) argues that the different currency regime choices between the two countries is the root cause. The Japanese have control over their own currency, issue debt in their own currency, have access to seigniorage revenues and have the ability to deflate their own currency if need be. Greece, which is a member of the European Monetary Union (EMU), has no such freedom and Krugman argues this is why Greece is different. This issue will be discussed in greater depth in the section on European Monetary Union membership.

For now though, it is important to note that the monetarists' (Krugman, 2014; De Grauwe, 2011; Dellas & Tavlas, 2013) arguments about the difference between Greece and Japan provide a powerful rationale in support of this study: A comprehensive understanding of all interrelated factors is required to truly understand why particular countries have different risk profiles, and why some countries experience crises whilst others are stable. The point is that one cannot look at one particular variable to understand why and how the Greek crisis came about; or in fact to understand any country's risk profile.

Consider, as an additional example, the difference between countries A and B in the graph above. Both have a little more than 100% of GDP in government debt. Both are OECD countries. Yet country A is perceived as much more risky, with much higher interest rates on its sovereign bonds. Again, the point is that a complex set of factors spanning politics, public administration, international financial considerations, economic issues and currency regimes combine to produce a particular outcome that is less favourable for country A than for country B.

And that is why this study will aim to integrate the existing knowledge on Greece to introduce as many factors as possible to understand the causes of the Greek crisis. A simple like-for-like comparison of debt levels between countries provides only a very limited insight into those countries' potential default risk.

### 1.5. Section Summary

- In the period between 1981 and 2010, Greece built up a significant stock of debt, consistently in excess of 100% of GDP.
- Despite attempts at modernisation and rapid economic growth in the 2000s, Greece was unable to reduce its debt burden as a % of GDP.
- The Greek debt burden has its roots in the formation of a large welfare state and has been exacerbated by endemic corruption, weak revenue collection, governance challenges and an internal political atmosphere opposed to fiscal reform.
- Greece's debt burden is significant, but the size of debt alone does not explain why Greece experienced a sovereign debt crisis. Other factors must be taken into account as well.

## 2. The European Monetary Union

Having established the roots of Greek debt accumulation, the logical next step is to explore how it is that Greece was able to sustain so much debt for so long. Indeed, it is extraordinary that Greece was able to sustain its expansionary, deficit-driven fiscal policy for so long (Evangelopoulos, 2012). Numerous scholars (Zettelmeyer, Trebesch, & Gulati, 2013; Gibson, Hall, & Tavlas, 2010; Major, 2014) argue that Greece's EMU membership enabled it to do so. Consider Figure 4 below.

### 2.1. Non-Enforcement of EMU Treaties

Dellas and Tavlas (2013), Lianou (2012) and Martin and Waller (2012) raise two important points about the relationship between Greek deficits and Greece's European Monetary Union (EMU) membership in the 2000s: Firstly, deficits were consistently, and significantly, above the 3% annual deficit-to-GDP ratio limit agreed upon in the European Stability and Growth Pact (SGP). All countries wanting to join the EMU had to agree to the SGP, and Greece therefore became a signatory when it became a member of the European Monetary Union in 2001 (De Grauwe, 2011). Greek total debt-to-GDP was also consistently above the 60% limit prescribed in the SGP (Dellas & Tavlas, 2013; Martin & Waller, 2012), raising significant questions about the enforcement of the SGP in the decade preceding the crisis. The SGP explicitly requires the European Union to intervene when 'excessive deficits' are incurred (an excessive deficit being defined as any deficit above 3%), with numerous clauses in the SGP allowing for fines and other penalties on countries that exceed the prescribed deficit limits. Nelson, Belkin and Mix (2010) however find that no fines have ever been imposed since the formation of the SGP, despite the fact that 20 of the 27 signatories violated the deficit regulations in 2010 alone; and Greece clearly violated the requirements during its entire time as an EMU member. Martin and Waller (2010), Nelson, Belkin and Mix (2010), Dellas and Tavlas (2013), Kouretas and Vlamis (2010), Featherstone (2011), Verney and Bosco (2013), Lianou (2012) and many others point to non-enforcement of the EMU treaties as a major amplifier of the crisis. These authors all suggest that the lack of political will by European authorities to enforce the fiscal discipline that was originally envisaged in the EMU treaties signalled to both the Greek government and the financial markets that Greek debt accumulation was acceptable and sustainable, providing a de facto endorsement of Greek fiscal policy in the 2000s. Some scholars (Arghyrou & Tsoukalas, 2011; Dellas & Tavlas, 2013) have also argued that the EU's unwillingness to intervene in member countries' fiscal policies signalled a willingness to bail out indebted countries at some future date, reinforcing these countries' access to easy credit from the global financial markets. The first point is therefore that Greece violated the deficit limits in the SGP, and that EU enforcement of the deficit limit could have potentially staved off the crisis by cutting off Greece's access to debt.

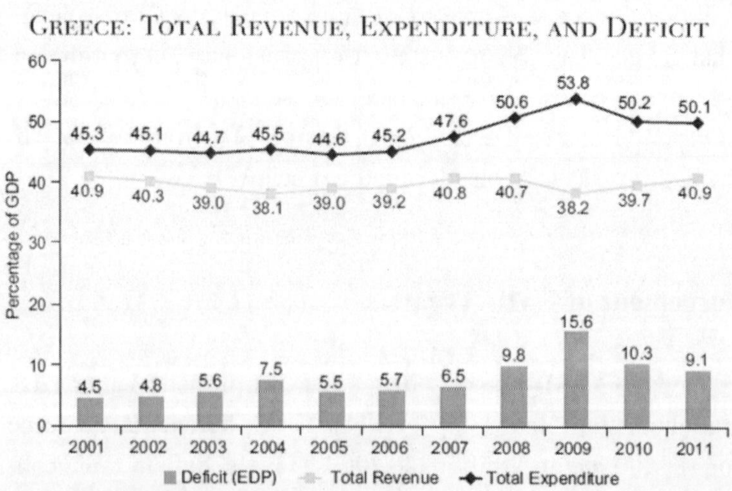


Source: Dellas and Tavlas (2013).

Figure 4. Greek government deficit, revenue and expenditure: 2001-2011.

## 2.2. Access to Cheap Credit

Secondly, a number of scholars have argued that Greece's EMU membership helped to fuel the country's debt-driven growth-path in the 2000s given that its new-found EMU membership status secured it cheap and easy access to global capital markets (Krugman, 2014; De Grauwe, 2011; Zettelmeyer, Trebesch, & Gulati, 2013; Major, 2014; Pappas, 2011; Arghyrou & Tsoukalas, 2011; Nelson, Belkin, & Mix, 2010; Kouretas & Vlamis, 2010; Antzoulatos, 2011; Gibson, Hall, & Tavlas, 2010). Antzoulatos (2011) goes so far as to suggest that easy access to cheap credit actively encouraged successive Greek governments to fuel growth with increased government spending and debt. This is supported by Rajan (2010), who suggests that cheap credit can motivate governments to support heightened levels of consumption in order to secure political support. The argument therefore goes that the Greek political preference for significant government expenditure, combined with easy access to cheap debt, resulted in expansionary, debt-fuelled Greek fiscal policy in the 2000s.

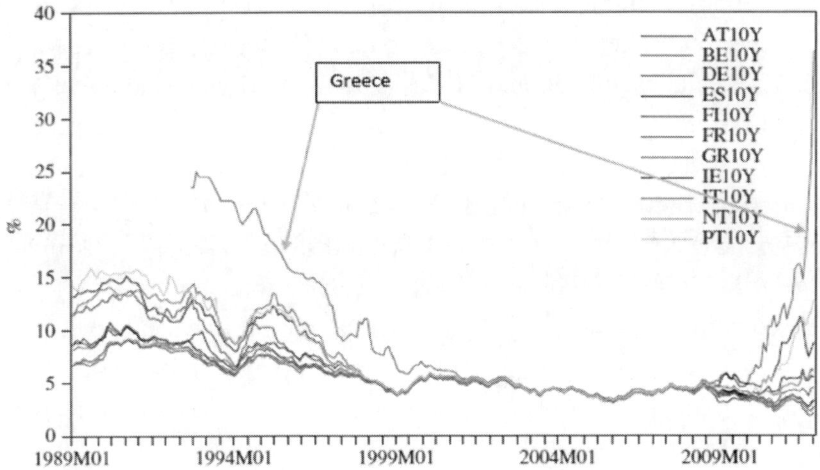


Figure 5. European 10-year sovereign bond yields per country: 1989-2011. Source: Adapted from Tamakoshi and Hamori (2013), lines and label added.

Figure 5 makes it clear that EMU membership temporarily increased the credibility of the Greek state as a debtor (De Grauwe, 2011), thereby lowering the yields on its sovereign bonds in the period leading up to and after it joined the EMU (Baele et al., 2004; Georgoutsos & Migiakis, 2013; Pagano & Von Thadden, 2004). There is a significant literature on why this occurred. In short, by joining the EMU and adopting the Euro, Greece gave up monetary independence and with it the ability to print its own currency and set its own interest rates (Martin & Waller, 2012). Greece therefore gave up the ability to devalue its currency, in effect providing strong assurance to bond holders that Greek debt would not be devalued through monetary mechanisms (Krugman, 2014;

De Grauwe, 2011; Arghyrou & Tsoukalas, 2011). Oliveira, Curto and Nunes (2012) additionally indicate that investors began treating all Eurozone government bonds as if they had no country-specific risks given the credibility of the European Central Bank, and the implicit belief that any Eurozone country facing fiscal difficulties would be assisted by the European authorities. The result was therefore a lowering of the risk premium on Greek sovereign bonds and thus a lowering of yields on Greek sovereign bonds (Tamakoshi & Hamori, 2013), making Greek government debt cheaper.

Figure 5 illustrates this effect very clearly. The Greek 10 year bond yield (the green line labelled GR10Y above) was dramatically reduced in the period leading up to Greece joining the EMU, after which it remained low, and in touch with other EMU countries until the crisis erupted in 2009. Balcerowicz (2014) suggests that EMU membership 'excessively supressed' the risk premium on Greek debt, creating artificially low sovereign bond yields and creating new space for the Greek government to use debt to finance its activities (Georgoutsos & Migiakis, 2013; Karmann & Maltriz, 2012). EMU membership also implied a greater degree of financial integration in Europe, encouraging investment to flow into Greece from across Europe (Tamakoshi & Hamori, 2013; Nelson, Belkin, & Mix, 2010), helping to fuel rapid economic growth between 2001 and 2007, averaging 4.3% per year (Kretsos & Vogiatzoglou, 2015; Nelson, Belkin, & Mix; 2010).

Abboushi (2011), Gibson, Hall and Tavlas (2010) and Degiannakis, Duffy, Filis and Livada (2015) have also argued that Greece's access to cheap debt, together with the implicit belief by Greek governments that European authorities would bail Greece out in future if the need ever arose, encouraged Greek governments to maintain intensely pro-cyclical fiscal policy, explaining why the debt burden increased even as the economy grew rapidly in the 2000s. Abboushi (2011) calculates that this translated into Greek government expenditure in excess of 50% of GDP for every year between 2001 and 2008. This pro-cyclical fiscal posture amplified Greek inflation in the period after Greece joined the EMU, driving up Greek prices and wages with dire knock-on effects for Greek competitiveness as detailed below (Strobel, 2005; Lapavitsas et al., 2010).

## 2.3. Capital Influx from Other EMU Members

The joining of the EMU was therefore a tremendously important moment in Greek economic history: It transformed the credibility of Greece as a debtor, allowing for easy access to cheap debt, it lowered interest rates in Greece and it attracted significant additional capital flows due to a heightened degree of financial integration with Europe, boosting growth and leading to a period of relative prosperity for Greece between 2001-2007 (Pappas, 2011).

But authors suggest that Greece lived dangerously in the good years, given that government continued to amass significant debts and deficits during these strong growth years (Dellas & Tavlas, 2013), and given that the country continued to post very high current account deficits as imports continued to grow larger than exports by ever-greater margins (Pappas, 2011; Milios & Sotiropoulos, 2010).

Pappas (2011) studied the determinants of strong capital flows into Greece in the early 2000s and found that the influx of capital was driven by increased financial integration with Europe, and positive market sentiment related to Greece's entry into the EMU; and not necessarily by a fundamental improvement in the competitiveness or attractiveness of the Greek economy. This is an interesting conclusion, given that there is an established literature that proposes that capital flows are a function of healthy macroeconomic indicators, such as stable and low inflation (Campos & Kinoshita, 2003), balanced government budgets (Calvo, Leiderman, & Reinhart, 1994; Campos & Kinoshita, 2003) and strong economic growth prospects (Gibson & Tsakalotos, 2001; Faisal, Arezki, & Funke, 2005).

Pappas' (2011) finding is supported by a number of other studies that suggest that Greece was experiencing rapid economic growth on the back of cheap credit and a significant capital influx, without any real improvements in productivity or competitiveness (Antzoulatos, 2011; Milios & Sotiropoulos, 2010; Arghyrou & Tsoukalas, 2010; Blanchard, 2007).

A number of scholar have argued that the significant influx of European capital, coupled with pro-cyclical expansionary fiscal policy, created a number of microeconomic distortions in Greece, such as heightened price and wage inflation and excessive private credit extension to households in Greece (Michaelides, Papageorgiou, & Vouldis, 2013; Papanikos, 2014; Malliaropulos, 2010). These distortions created real risks for Greece, the implications of which will be discussed in the following section.

## 2.4. Section Summary

- The EMU authorities did not adequately enforce the fiscal regulations of the SGP, allowing Greece and others to maintain large fiscal deficits.
- The EMU entry allowed Greece access to easy credit at significantly-reduced rates, enabling it to amass significant debt throughout the 2000s, even as its economy grew rapidly.
- Greece benefitted from significant capital inflows due to increased financial integration with Europe, yet did not improve its productivity or underlying competitiveness.

# 3. THE DETERIORATION OF GREEK COMPETITIVENESS

There is an interesting tension in the literature between scholars who explicitly identify the Greek crisis as a sovereign debt crisis (Yildiz & Yildirum, 2014; Polito & Wickens, 2014; Featherstone, 2011) and those who argue that the roots of the crisis were in the deterioration of Greek competitiveness in the 2000s and the resultant extreme current account deficits (see: Antzoulatos, 2011; Krugman, 2014; De Grauwe, 2011; Kouzis, 2011; Malliaropulos, 2010; Dellas & Tavlas, 2013; Balcerowicz, 2014). The scholars in the former group analyse the crisis through the prism of debt accumulation and an eventual collapse of confidence in the Greek state's ability to repay its debts; whilst the latter analyse the crisis through the prism of reduced competitiveness and unsustainable current account deficits. The core causes of Greece's deteriorating competitiveness (as proposed by the latter group) are detailed below.

## 3.1. The Impact of Euro Membership on Competitiveness

The argument goes that when Greece joined the EMU, it adopted a much more valuable currency (the Euro) than it had previously had (the Drachma). The weaker Drachma had for years helped to boost the competitiveness of Greek exports to Europe (Antzoulatos, 2011; Balcerowicz, 2014) and when it was phased out in favour of the Euro in 2001, Greek exporters had lost a major competitive edge and had to make up for it by becoming more efficient, more productive and more competitive (Dellas & Tavlas, 2013; Oltheten, Sougiannins, Travlos, & Zarkos, 2013).

Unfortunately, Greece had failed to respond to this challenge effectively (Doukas, 2013; Henning & Kessler, 2012; Malliaropulos, 2010) and this resulted in a significant trade imbalance with the rest of Europe, and especially with Germany, with Greece importing much more than it was exporting. Antzoulatos (2011), Krugman (2014), Ebner (2013) and others indicate that this resulted in significant current account deficits in Greece throughout the 2000s. These current account deficits were in turn facilitated by the massive influx of European capital (ensuring significant capital account surpluses) as outlined above, allowing for continued growth despite less competitiveness (Reddy, 2011; Antzoulatos, 2011).

Greece's difficulties with remaining competitive whilst using the Euro has been highlighted by several scholars who have proposed a dual-Euro regime whereby a more valuable 'hard Euro' is adopted for the core Euro countries in Northern Europe, whilst a less valuable 'soft Euro' is adopted for the struggling Southern European countries to assist them with competitiveness. This has been labelled the 'option of last resort' by these scholars if the current reforms are not able to sufficiently improve Greek competitiveness (Arghyrou & Tsoukalas, 2010; Stockhammer & Sotiropoulos, 2014).

## 3.2. The Impact of Wages and Regulations on Competitiveness

Malliaropulos (2010) estimates that Greece lost roughly 10% competitiveness between 2001 and 2010, where competitiveness is defined as relative unit labour costs; or more colloquially, as the cost of labour per unit of output as compared to major trade partners.

Oltheten, Sougiannins, Travlos and Zarkos (2013) finds slightly different results, suggesting that Greece lost anywhere between 9% and 27% of competitiveness on unit labour costs between 2001 and 2010, depending on how the calculations are done. The Bank of Greece (as cited by Malliaropulos, 2010) puts the deterioration of competitiveness for the same period at between 18% and 21%. There therefore appears to be consensus that Greek unit labour cost competitiveness did decline, despite different studies finding different magnitudes (Reddy, 2011; Zartaloudis, 2014).

Dullien and Fritsche (2009) and Dimoulas (2014) argue that rigidities in Greek labour regulation contributed to the problem. A high level of regulation meant that it was impossible for the price of Greek labour to be priced down, and that the price of labour in fact escalated significantly in the years after 2001, despite becoming less and less competitive. These rigidities included complicated collective bargaining structures than enforced national agreements on all firms (Kretsos, 2011), a very high degree of regulation of hiring and firing practices (Kouzis, 2011), highly regulated pay structures which ensured that many workers received 14-16 monthly salaries per year in some industries (Kretsos, 2011), high levels of regulation of temporary employment (Papanikos, 2014), high social security contributions for employers (Thiemann, 2013) and high severance packages, especially for white collar workers (Kretsos, 2011). Thiemann (2013) further indicates that over an 11 month period between 2011 and 2012 an OECD investigation found 555 different restrictive provisions in Greek labour regulations, which they claimed could lead to ‘market distortions’. Clearly, the regulatory burden in Greece had contributed to the deterioration of unit labour cost competitiveness.

The political science literature provides important insights into why these labour market rigidities were in place, arguing that Greek unions, and in particular Greek public sector unions, had vociferously opposed any labour market reforms for many years before the crisis (Kretsos & Vogiatzoglou, 2015). Kretsos (2011) points out that Greek unions had aggressively employed strikes in the past to oppose any measures aimed at increasing flexibility in the Greek labour market, as evidenced by the fact that 44% of all general strikes across all of Europe occurred in Greece in the period between 1980 and 2008. This is an enormous percentage, given that Greece only represents 2% of the European GDP. This again suggests that the internal political climate in Greece played an important part in setting the country up for crisis.

### 3.3. The Role of Destructive Institutions

The political science literature and public administration literature also details the impact of destructive institutions on Greece's competitiveness. Katsimi and Moutos (2010) detail for example how the well-established Greek tradition of clientelism, whereby governments seek and secure political support by providing particular benefits to certain interest groups, systematically eroded efficiency in Greece. This has been associated with destructive, anti-competitive oligopolistic regulations that protect the interests of a few entrenched firms in certain industries; or with regulations that limit the number of individuals in certain professions, effectively shutting out new entrants (Envagelopoulos, 2012).

Other destructive institutions include the open politicisation of unions and the civil service, undermining service delivery and efficiency in state institutions and giving unions significant political influence (Fouskas, 2013). The argument is that these institutions indirectly eroded competitiveness by creating an environment of reduced efficiency.

Interestingly, the discussion on the role of destructive institutions again reveals an ideological split in the political science literature, with leftist scholars (see Sakellaropoulos & Sotiris, 2014; Kretsos & Vogiatzoglou, 2015; Fouskas & Dimoulas, 2012) assigning blame to 'capitalist' institutions for eroding the productive base of the Greek economy. From the leftist perspective, Greece was unfairly subjected to 'equal-playing-field' competition with the rest of Europe when it joined the EMU, eroding local Greek industry in favour of cheaper exports from the rest of Europe. For these scholars, the EMU in itself is a destructive 'capitalist' institution which is at the heart of the crisis. More mainstream scholars (Envagelopoulos, 2012; Katsimi & Moutos, 2010; Fahrholz & Wojcik, 2012) advance institutional arguments more in line with the issues described in the previous paragraph. Again, the qualitative content analysis process has included studies from both perspectives to ensure a balanced outcome.

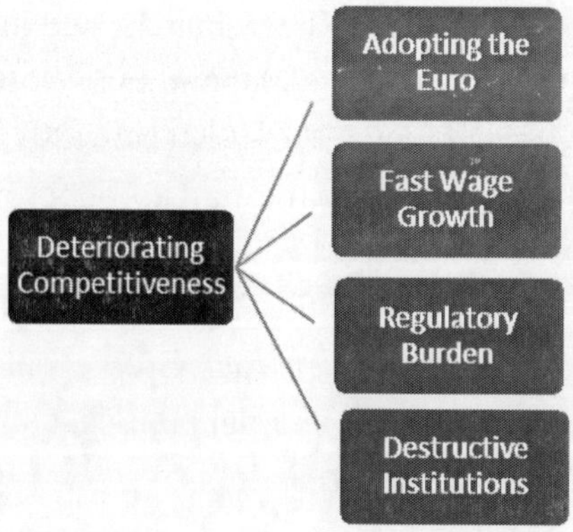


Figure 6. Factors contributing to deteriorating Greek competitiveness in the 2000s.

## 3.4. European Divergence

Antzoulatos (2011), Ebner (2013), Malliaropulos (2010) and Merler and Pisani-Ferry (2012) find that the influx of capital and credit into Greece in the years after 2001 fuelled rapid economic growth, higher employment and increased inflation, which also drove Greek wages upward. Nelson, Belkin and Mix (2010) find that Greek wages increased by 5% per year between 2001 and 2007, more than double the Eurozone average, and clearly undermining Greek competitiveness. The result is that increased Greek wages and lowered competitiveness made Greek exports less attractive, contributing to the current account deficit.

The literature on current account deficits in Europe in the period after 2001 includes significant discussion about the lack of 'convergence' of European economic performance after Eurozone integration. Balcerowicz (2014) explains that after 2001, it was expected that less developed economies such as Greece would be forced to become more competitive given that the 'easy' route to competitiveness (currency devaluation) had been removed by Euro membership. It was therefore expected that there would be internal renegotiations in Greece and other new Euro entrants whereby the countries would reorganise themselves to ensure international competitiveness – and in particular it was expected that this would include labour market deregulation to allow for wage deflation (Hampl, 2013). But instead, Greece and other peripheral economies were able to fuel growth and employment with the easy access to cheap credit that came with Euro membership (Arghyrou & Chortareas, 2008; Lapavitsas et al., 2010), averting the need for politically-unpopular renegotiations and competitive reforms during the 2000s. The literature suggests that this failure to improve competitiveness lead to a 'divergence' of economic performance amongst the Euro members (Balcerowicz, 2014; Henning & Keesler 2012; Dullien & Fritsche, 2009; Hampl, 2013). This meant that Greek growth and inflation was higher than in most other European countries after Greece secured EMU membership, whilst competitiveness declined and current account and fiscal deficits widened (Belke & Dreger, 2013). This led to a systematic imbalance in the Eurozone, where smaller and less competitive countries such as Greece were dependent on inflows from more competitive countries, such as Germany, to finance current account and fiscal deficits (Ca'Zorzi & Rubaszek, 2012).

The differences in economic performance between Germany and Greece in the period after 2001 is often used as the most dramatic example of Eurozone divergence (Dellas & Tavlas, 2013; Belke & Dreger, 2013; Dulien & Fritsche, 2009). Numerous studies cite a variation of the graph in Figure 7:

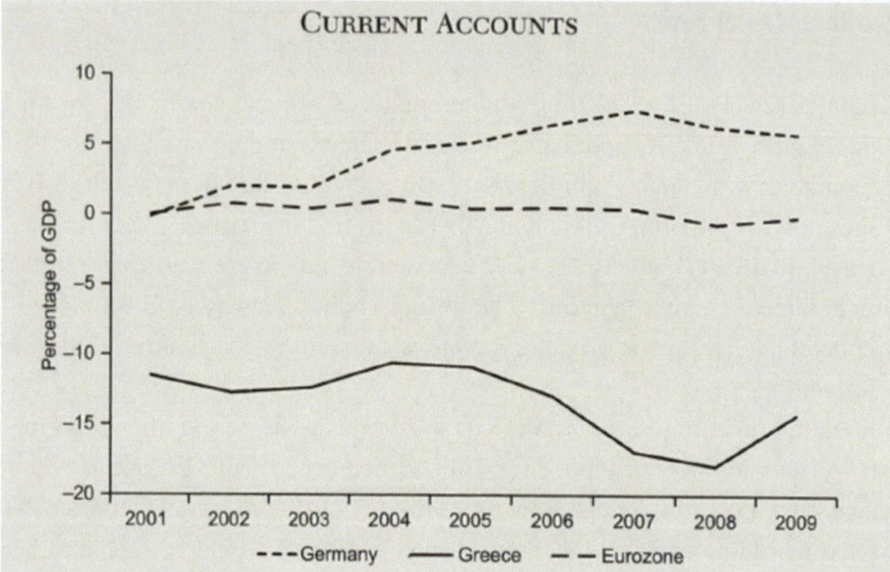


Source: Dellas and Tavlas (2013).

Figure 7. Current accounts (Germany, Eurozone, Greece) 2001-2009.

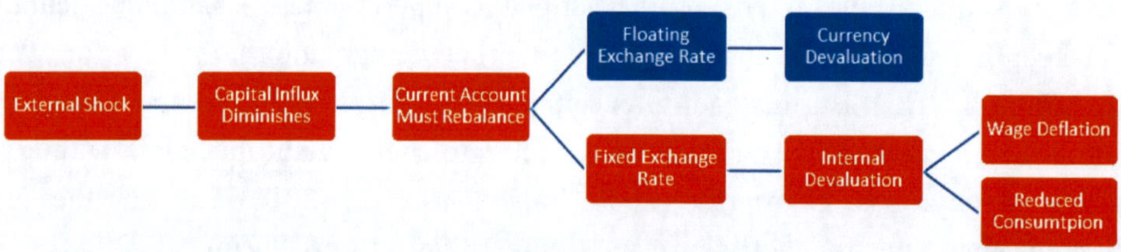


Figure 8. The impact of an external shock on the current account. Greece's experience is mapped in red.

There are some important conclusions to be drawn from this graph: Firstly, Greece maintained an enormous current account deficit in excess of 10% of GDP throughout the entire period after joining the EMU. This underlines how significant the capital inflows were during that time, given that the surplus on the capital account has to balance the deficit in the current account (Milios & Sotiropoulos, 2010). Secondly, it supports the thesis that countries like Germany benefitted from the Euro, given that it could outcompete less competitive countries using the same currency, thereby racking up significant current account surpluses (Krugman, 2014; Dellas and Tavlas, 2013; Belke & Dreger, 2013; Arghyrou & Tsoukalas, 2011). Thirdly, even though the Eurozone as a whole maintained a roughly balanced current account (exports roughly equalled imports across all countries), there are major differences between the Eurozone countries, with some maintaining current account surpluses and others maintaining current account deficits, owing mostly to differences in competitiveness (Antzoulatos, 2011). The graph therefore serves as further evidence of divergence in the Eurozone, and in this case between Germany and Greece (Dellas & Tavlas, 2013; Ca'Zorzi & Rubaszek, 2012).

But the question is, how does this divergence, and the underlying competitiveness problem, morph into a sovereign debt crisis? Antzoulatos (2011) argues that Greece's competitiveness problem forced government to fuel growth with expansionary fiscal policy that was financed by significant budget deficits. The option to indulge in politically-expedient, debt-financed expansionary policy was enabled by EMU membership, which temporarily allowed Greece to grow its economy with cheap credit and without having to address the fundamental problems of competitiveness it faced (Fouskas & Dimoulas, 2012). This was a politically-expedient option for Greek governments at the time, given that competitiveness reforms were generally unpopular in Greece, and were particularly-strongly opposed by labour unions in the 2000s (Kretsos, 2011).

The influx of capital was however highly dependent on external investors' willingness to continue pouring money into Greece, underlining just how vulnerable Greece had become to external shocks in the late 2000s. Krugman (2014) sheds more light on Greece's vulnerabilities towards the late 2000s. He argues that divergent economic performance coupled with EMU membership would have spelled disaster in the event of any external economic shock. Consider the basic balance of payments identity:

$$\text{Capital Account} + \text{Current Account} = 0$$

In short, net capital flows into country A (the capital account) must equal the negative of net exports of country A (the current account). In the case of Greece, the current account persistently indicated large deficits, and therefore had to be compensated for by significant capital inflows. The problem is that in the case of an external shock which affects capital inflows, the current account must necessarily adjust to become less negative, or even positive. Shambaugh (2004) indicates that under a floating exchange rate regime, this would usually translate into a currency devaluation which encourages increased exports to improve the current account. But in the case of Greece, which is a member of the EMU and which has no ability to influence the value of the Euro, the current account can only be improved by reducing consumption or by improving competitiveness through reducing labour costs. This is referred to as an 'internal devaluation' in the literature (Krugman, 2014; Blanchard, 2007). Gibson, Palivos and Tavlas (2014) find that internal devaluation is associated with very high societal costs.

The literature overwhelmingly indicates that the troika-enforced reform and austerity measures that have been implemented since 2010 as part of the various bailout agreements have been explicitly aimed at such an internal devaluation to improve Greek competitiveness (Theodossopoulos, 2013; Verney & Bosco, 2013; Fouskas & Dimoulas, 2012; Mitsopoulos & Pelagidis, 2014). Indeed, it would appear that the European authorities have attempted to enforce the reforms that it expected would occur after Greece joined the EMU in 2001 (Hampl, 2013).

One final point should be made in this section: Although the literature mostly argues that Greek current account deficits were large and potentially risky in the 2000s, there are nuanced differences between various authors on what exactly drove the current account deficits to their significant scope. The majority of studies appear to support the hypothesis that a deterioration of Greek competitiveness drove the current account deficits by lowering exports, by increasing imports and by necessitating expansionary government spending that was fuelled by external debt (Arghyrou & Tsoukalas, 2011; Blanchard, 2007; Fouskas & Dimoulas, 2012; Nelson, Belkin, & Mix, 2010; Kouretas & Vlamis, 2010; Malliaropulos, 2010; Antzoulatos, 2011; Dellas & Tavlas, 2013). Milios and Sotiropoulos (2010), Choupis (2011) and Doukas (2013) hold a different view though. They argue that the current account deficit primarily developed because of an increase in the capital account surplus that occurred because of EMU financial integration. They argue that the fault lies not with Greek competitiveness, but rather with the excessive speculative capital inflows from external investors who wished to invest in the fast-growing Greek economy. Studies from both perspectives have been included in the qualitative content analysis to ensure balanced results.

## 3.5. Section Summary

- Abandoning the Drachma and adopting the stronger Euro undermined Greek competitiveness by eliminating currency-devaluation as a competitiveness-enhancing tool.
- The debt-fuelled growth of the early 2000s increased inflation and wages in Greece without increases in productivity, lowering the relative competitiveness of Greek firms.
- The complex regulatory structure in Greece contributed to the deterioration of competitiveness.
- Lower relative competitiveness translated into large current account deficits, making Greece dependent on significant capital inflows.
- The combination of reduced competitiveness and EMU membership meant that the only way to improve the current account imbalance was through a painful process of internal devaluation.

# 4. The Unfolding of the Crisis

By 2007, Greece was primed for crisis. As discussed, a number of factors had aligned to make Greece highly sensitive to external shocks, and in particular to any shocks that may affect the credibility of Greek sovereign bonds. As reviewed in previous sections, the Greek government built up a significant stock of debt, and maintained significant fiscal deficits. Its ability to repay its debt was contingent on continued economic growth and the confidence of global financial markets. Greece also experienced a significant reduction in its competitiveness, leading to growing current account deficits that necessitated growing capital inflows to sustain the Greek economy. Again, stability and growth was highly dependent on the markets' willingness to continue investing in Greece.

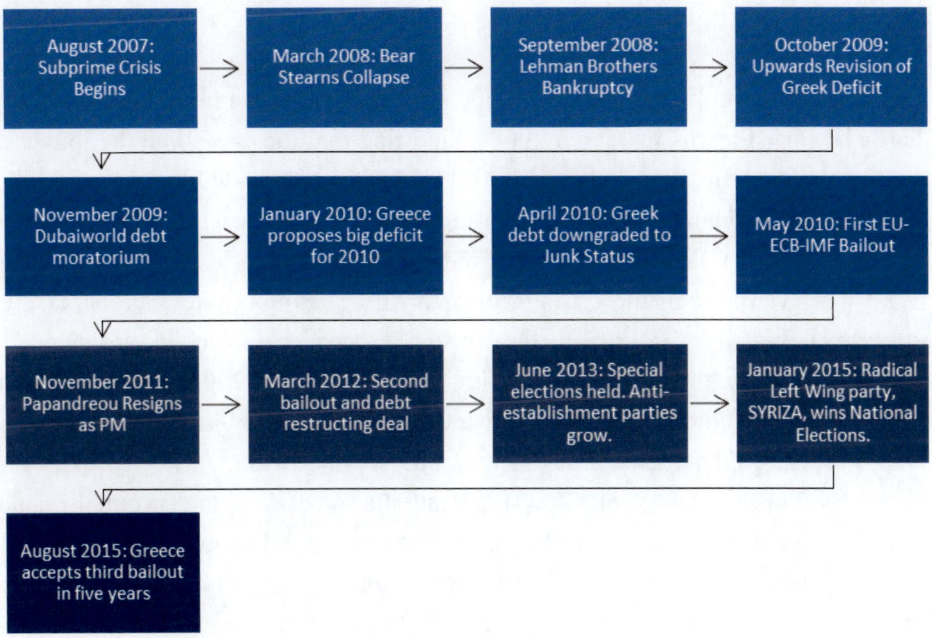


Figure 9. A brief timeline of the key events that triggered developments in the Greek crisis.

The United States subprime mortgage crisis that erupted in August 2007 (Petersen, Senosi, & Mukuddem-Petersen, 2012) thus occurred at a time of particular vulnerability for Greece as stated above (Kouretas & Vlamis, 2010). The surveyed literature thus generally charts the evolution of the Greek crisis by using the United States subprime mortgage crisis of 2007-2008 as the trigger point (Dellas & Tavlas, 2013; Lakakis & Kousis, 2013; Kokkoris, Olivares-Caminal, & Papadakis, 2010). The chart below provides an overview of the evolution of the crisis.

## 4.1. August 2007 – February 2008

Interestingly, the initial impact of the US financial crisis on Greece was relatively limited (Giordano, Pericoli, & Tommasino, 2013). The difference between Greek 10 year government bond yields and German 10 year government bond yields remained relatively stable throughout the end of 2007 and the early part of 2008, with Greek bond yields eclipsing German yields by 0.3%, or 30 basis points (Baltas, 2013; Dellas & Tavlas, 2013), as was the case for the period before the crisis. The crisis did however trigger a Eurozone-wide recession in 2008 (Ozturk & Sozdemir, 2015) and required significant additional government expenditures from Eurozone countries, including Greece, to respond to the recession (Reinhart & Rogoff, 2011; Tagkalakis, 2012).

## 4.2. March 2008 – August 2008

By March 2008, the financial crisis in the United States became more serious, with the collapse of Bear Stearns in March 2008 suggesting that the crisis may be longer and more painful than anticipated (Abboushi, 2011). The unprecedented degree of financial integration in global financial markets also meant that the increasing instability in the United States affected financial institutions and investors the world over (Baltas, 2013). This meant that even though the crisis originated in the United States, its increasingly-damaging effects would be felt across the world. European countries in particular were significantly affected, with the Eurozone going into recession in 2008 (Baltas, 2013) and with countries facing additional debt burdens due to governments' crisis recovery efforts (Ali, 2012; Furceri & Zdzienicka, 2012; Reinhart & Rogoff, 2011).

Howard, La Foucade and Scott (2009) indicate that recessions and external financial shocks almost always require significant, and expensive stabilisation policies. This left Greece in a precarious position, given that it came into the crisis with significant debt, was facing a recession and would likely have to further increase spending in order to overcome the challenges posed by the crisis (Pronobis, 2014). The result was that investors began to perceive Greek sovereign bonds as more risky vis-à-vis its more secure Eurozone counterparts, explaining why the spread of Greek bonds over German bonds grew moderately to 0.6% at this point in time (Abboushi, 2011).

## 4.3. September 2008 – December 2009

With the collapse of Lehman Brothers in September 2008, the financial crisis worsened significantly. This resulted in a further increase of the Greek sovereigns' spread over Germany's to 2.5% by the end of 2008 (Dellas & Tavlas, 2013). In the early stages of 2009, it appeared that the financial crisis began to recede, and so Greek spreads were gradually lowered to 1.2% by September 2009 (Baltas, 2013).

But towards the end of 2009, two major shocks significantly eroded confidence in the Greek government's ability to honour its obligations. Firstly, in October 2009 the newly-elected Greek government announced that the previous government had understated the projected fiscal deficit for 2009, revising it to an enormous 15.6% of GDP, up from an initial projection of 6% of GDP (Georganta, 2011). This again points to the significant public administration and political challenges Greece faced at the time (Featherstone, 2011). Secondly, in November 2009, DubaiWorld, a major investment holdings company owned and operated by the Emirate of Dubai, requested a debt repayment moratorium for 6 months. These two events together had exceptionally destructive implications for Greece. The DubaiWorld development caused a significant increase in risk aversion amongst international investors (Dellas & Tavlas, 2013; Giordano, Pericoli, & Tommasino, 2013; Arghyrou & Tsoukalas, 2011). At the same time the unexpected revelation that the Greek government had been understating its debt by significant margins undermined the credibility of the Greek state as a debtor, increasing the risk premium associated with Greek sovereign bonds and therefore dramatically increasing the Greek spreads to about 5% by the beginning of 2010 (Fouskas, 2013). The Greek debt restatement also raised questions about the competence of the Greek state (Featherstone, 2011).

Giordano, Pericoli and Tommasino (2013) raise an interesting point about the Greek situation at this point in time. They argue that Greece suffered from 'wake-up call' contagion after the DubaiWorld problem surfaced. This 'wake-up call contagion' occurs when an event motivates investors to reconsider the underlying fundamentals of other investments. Giordano, Pericoli and Tommasino (2013) suggest that the DubaiWorld problem was a 'wake-up call' for investors to begin re-evaluating the risks in Greece and elsewhere. The result was that investors became less attracted to Greek debt, driving up the yields on Greek sovereign bonds.

### 4.4. 2010-2011

Arghyrou and Tsoukalas (2011) suggest that the Greek crisis reached boiling point towards the end of 2009 when the Greek government proposed an enormous new deficit for 2010. The proposed deficit was a seminal moment. Various political science scholars have used it to illustrate the inability of Greece's political leadership to grasp the severity of the situation in 2009/2010, and the inability of Greece's political leaders to develop effective solutions to the crisis (Vasilopoulou & Halikiopoulo, 2013; Karyotis & Rudig, 2015; Fouskas, 2013).

According to Arghyrou and Tsoukalas, the 2010 deficit announcement became the first clear signal that Greece's continued Euro membership was in doubt. Consider the context: By this time, it was clear that the global financial markets were losing their confidence in Greece as spreads between Greek government bonds and German government bonds began to grow alarmingly. In the face of this challenging situation, the Greek government failed to take significant action to curb its deficit. The argument is that the enormous deficit of 2010 represented a continuation of the failed and unsustainable economic strategy of the 2000s at a time when reform was non-negotiable. The Greek government was, again, attempting to fuel growth with spending and debt without tackling the underlying competitiveness problems in the economy. In order to improve competitiveness to the point where it was able to service its growing debt burden, Greece would either have to undergo painful internal devaluation, or a currency devaluation (Krugman, 2014; De Grauwe, 2011). The 2010 budget was a seminal moment because it showed that the Greek government did not have the insight or political will to engage in pro-active internal devaluation (Sklias & Maris, 2013); and in so doing it had signalled a de facto preference for currency devaluation. Of course, currency devaluation would not be possible as a Euro member, signalling to the markets that the country was not fully committed to its Euro membership (Arghyrou & Tsoukalas, 2011).

And once the credibility of Greece's commitment to the EMU had been dented, the benefits of EMU membership were similarly undermined. Investors became wary of a Euro exit and a currency devaluation that would erode the value of their investments in Greek debt (Robbins, 2015). This caused a self-reinforcing negative spiral: increased risk premiums on Greek debt drove up Greek sovereign debt yields, further undermining the sustainability of the Greek situation, further increasing fears of a potential exit from the Euro, which again reinforced the move to increased risk premiums.

By early 2010, the spiral had taken hold and the Greek situation became untenable. The situation was further inflamed when both Standard and Poore's and Moody's downgraded Greece's sovereign debt to junk status in April 2010, causing the spread on 10-year Greek sovereign bonds to grow to almost 10%. This made it impossible for Greece to access financing from the global financial markets (Mink & De Haan, 2012; Buiter & Rahbari, 2012; Kouretas & Vlamis, 2010) and forced it to approach the European Union for financial assistance (Dellas & Tavlas, 2013).

The European authorities responded in May 2010 with a negotiated joint ECB-IMF-EU ('Troika') bailout package of €110 billion that was conditional on Greece increasing VAT and excise taxes, whilst putting in place a number of harsh austerity measures to cut public old age pensions, cut public sector wages and other social spending initiatives. The target was to reduce expenditure by 11% of 2010 GDP over three years (Sugawara, 2011). Schwartz (2010) and Mink and De Haan (2012) indicate that the European authorities had strong political and economic incentives to support a bailout, in contravention of Eurozone treaties that prohibit such bailouts, given that European banks held enormous amounts of Greek debt. Greece owed €75 billion to French banks, €45 billion to German banks, €15 billion to UK banks and €9.7 billion to Portuguese banks, amongst others. Allowing Greece to default would therefore likely trigger a European banking crisis, something which the Eurozone could hardly afford at the time (Lekakis & Kousis, 2013).

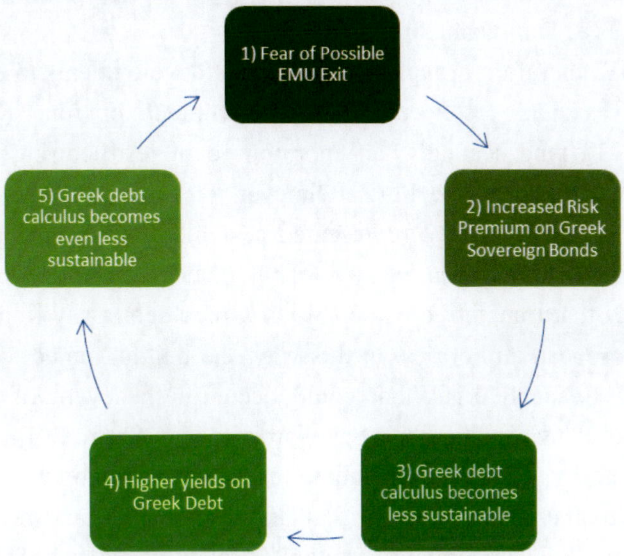


Figure 10. The spiral of collapsing confidence in Greek sovereign bonds.

The Troika bailout in May 2010 had averted a Greek default and potential exit from the Euro, but several scholars have argued that it did not go far enough to achieve the needed reforms in Greece (Pronobis, 2014; Ozturk & Sozdemir, 2015; Baltas, 2013; Martin & Waller, 2012). Arghyrou and Tsoukalas (2011) argue that the failure to achieve significant reform meant that the underlying need for devaluation was not sufficiently addressed, and therefore the threat of a potential Euro exit by Greece was not fully nullified by the first bailout. Greek sovereign bond yields therefore continued to climb throughout the rest of 2010 and 2011, making it impossible for Greece to access capital from the global financial markets (Dellas and Tavlas, 2013).

## 4.5. 2012-2015

By mid-2011, it became clear that Greece would need another bailout, and possibly a renegotiation of its debts, given that it had failed to stabilise its financial position and that it increasingly appeared that insolvency was inevitable (Fouskas & Dimoulas, 2012). The country was also experiencing serious political, social and economic upheaval as its government was attempting to resolve the crisis (Kretsos & Vogiatzoglou, 2015). It had entered a deep and sustained recession (Sklias, Roukanas, & Maris, 2012), a large anti-austerity protest movement had organised numerous national strikes that was causing havoc (Psimitis, 2011) and by November 2011 George Papandreou resigned as prime minister after reneging on a commitment to test proposed austerity measures in a national referendum (Fouskas & Dimouals, 2012).

The year of 2012 therefore brought two important developments to Greece: Firstly, a special election was held to elect a new government in June (Vasilopoulou & Halikiopoulou, 2013). And secondly, an enormous debt restructuring and bailout deal was negotiated in March/April of 2012 (Zettelmeyer, Trebesch, & Gulati, 2013).

The debt restructuring of 2012 represented a significant amount of debt relief for Greece, reducing total debt burden by 50% of GDP. It included a number of complex financial procedures that transferred ownership of Greek debt away from private holders and towards the European authorities. In this way, the bailout aimed to insulate Europe against a potential financial crisis that could occur in the event of a Greek bailout (Zettelmeyer, Trebesch, & Gulati, 2013; Sakellaropoulos & Sotiri, 2014). It also included a raft of new austerity measures, including a number of labour reforms aimed at improving competitiveness (Malakos, 2013; Petmesidou, 2013) and required significant write-downs of debts held by private creditors (Krajewska, 2014). This brought some temporary relief to Greece, but did not fundamentally alter the trajectory of the Greek situation given that large deficits remained and Greek spreads continued growing up to 35% by mid-2012, meaning that the country was still locked out of the global capital markets (Dellas & Tavlas, 2013).

The election in June 2012 also brought about significant political changes. It produced a strong drop-off in support for both the traditional centre-left party (PASOK) and the traditional centre-right party (ND), with both parties losing significant amounts of support to anti-establishment forces on the extremes. The extreme right wing anti-immigrant party, Golden Dawn and the far left, populist, anti-establishment party, SYRIZA, made significant inroads in the election. This forced a coalition between the traditional opponents of the centre - ND and PASOK (and a third minor partner – DIMAR) - to form a majority government (Vasilopoulou & Halikiopoulou, 2013). The election result was indicative of growing dissatisfaction with Greek leaders' compromises with European authorities, and a growing degree of Euroscepticism in the Greek electorate (Dobrescu & Durach, 2014). The growing opposition against the traditional governing parties appears to be rooted in a collapse of trust in these parties by the electorate and fierce opposition to measures aimed at internal devaluation (Vasilopoulou, Halikiopoulou, & Exadaktylos, 2014; Karyotis & Rudig, 2015).

Since then, the collapse of the established parties has continued, with SYRIZA winning the expedited 2015 elections, and the protest movement gaining additional momentum (Gibson, Palivos, & Tavlas, 2014). Greece's economic performance has also remained dismal. By 2013, unemployment had reached 25%, debt-to-GDP was hovering at 180% and the country was still experiencing negative economic growth, having never emerged from the recession that began in 2008 (Ozturk & Sozdemir, 2015).

The crisis continues to unravel at the time of writing, with the Greek government having accepted harsh austerity measures as part of a third bailout deal in five years on 14 August 2015. The new €85 billion deal includes a Greek commitment to introduce significant additional austerity measures (more cuts in pensions, a rise of the retirement age, cutting tax breaks for farmers), new taxes on a number of goods and services, privatisation of a number of state assets, further deregulation of the labour market, deregulation of a number of product markets and deregulation of a number of professions (The Guardian Newspaper, 2015). In so doing, it appears again that European authorities have attempted to force an internal devaluation in Greece to improve competitiveness and fiscal sustainability. Only time will tell if these measures will succeed in the face of enormous social and political opposition.

At this point it is unclear how the crisis will play out, but the literature has outlined a number of significant implications, including rising Euroscepticism and growing support in Greece for leaving the Eurozone (Dobrescu & Durach, 2014); continued political instability and a growing protest movement (Sklias & Maris, 2013; Malakos, 2013; Streeck, 2014); the reformation and scaling down of the Greek welfare state (Petmisidou, 2013) that will no doubt have enormous social consequences for the Greek people; the total renegotiation of the Greek labour dispensation (Kretsos & Vogiatzoglou, 2015); and immense economic pain that has no doubt lowered the quality of life of the Greek people (Ozturk & Sozdemir, 2015).

## 4.6. Section Summary

- The global financial crisis which originated in the United States subprime mortgage market is considered the starting point of the crisis.
- A number of key events eroded confidence in the Greek economy and the Greek state, acting as important trigger moments in the unfolding of the crisis. These events include: The beginning of the 2008 recession, the collapse of Lehman brothers, the Dubai World debt moratorium, the unexpected upward revision of Greek debt estimates in 2009, the announcement of an unexpectedly-large Greek budget deficit for 2010 and the resignation of George Papandreou in late 2011.

- The crisis reached boiling point when investors began to suspect a potential exit from the Euro by Greece.
- Implications of the crisis include social upheaval, such as the formation of the Greek protest movement and the scaling down of the social welfare state.
- Implications of the crisis include important political developments, such as the rise of Euroscepticism in Greece and the rise of extremist political parties such as SYRIZA and Golden Dawn.
- The crisis has had a negative impact on the quality of life of the Greek people.

## 5. METHODOLOGY

The literature review has clearly found a complicated set of interrelated factors ranging from politics, public administration, monetary economics, general economics and financial economics that caused the Greek crisis. A great deal of studies that deal with the different aspects of the crisis have been identified. The quantity, diversity and variety of methodologies employed is a particular strength of the literature on the Greek crisis, whilst the lack of integration of research outcomes, in particular between the different disciplines, remains a weakness (Malakos, 2013; Sklias & Maris, 2013; Gibson, Palivos, & Tavlas, 2014).

The literature review therefore supports the initial assessment that the knowledge on the Greek crisis remains fragmented, and that it could thus benefit from systematic analysis and integration to generate new insights (Shirazi, 2015) and to establish an effective summation of the knowledge on the crisis (Krippendorf, 1989).

As a first step, Figure 11 summarises the preliminary findings of the literature review.

As can be seen, a large number of factors have been identified from a number of academic disciplines, and an initial attempt at ordering of causality has produced a simplistic first-view of the causes as suggested by the literature. It is however clear that a much more systematic and rigorous analysis of the literature is required to develop a full understanding of the interrelationships between the various causes and indeed to comprehensively uncover all of the causes.

In order to construct a holistic conceptual model of the causes of the Greek crisis, as the title suggests, this study applied qualitative content analysis to deconstruct the literature into its constituent concepts, to determine relationships between the various concepts in order to answer the research questions.

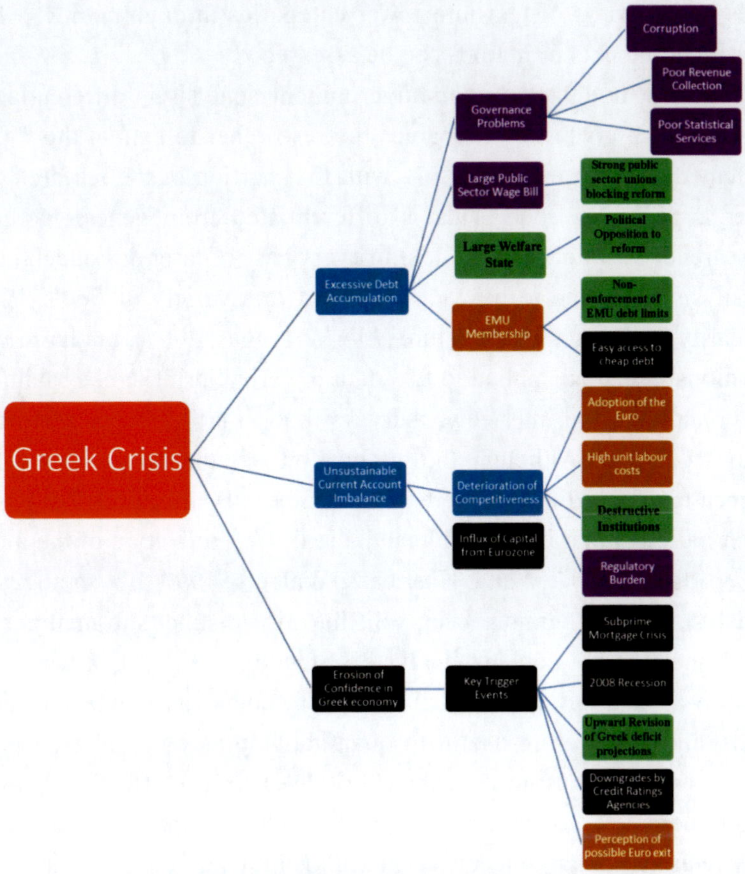


Figure 11. Summary of preliminary assessment of the drivers of the Greek crisis, and table explaining preliminarily-estimated dominant discipline for each concept.

## 5.1. Qualitative Content Analysis

Content analysis originated as a research technique in communication research in the early 20th century and was originally intended to provide a quantitative description of communication, and in particular communication in media (Berelson, 1952). Early applications were focused on mass media output in order to, for example, analyse how often certain topics were communicated on certain news outlets (Cho & Lee, 2014).

But over time content analysis evolved to be much more widely applied. Krippendorf (1989) defined it as the description of the content of communication, and suggested that it could be used to combine large pools of data into simplified conceptual maps. Since Krippendorf, the definitions of content analysis have shifted slightly. Hsieh and Shannon (2005) define content analysis as a research method that enables subjective interpretation of the content of text data through systematic classification and coding that helps to identify themes and patterns in texts. Stemler (2001) defined content analysis as a process that compresses many words of text into fewer categories through coding, whereby the presence of certain arguments or notions can be assessed.

It should be noted though that qualitative content analysis is differentiated from a general coding approach given that it enables the researcher to extract those portions of the research deemed relevant to the study – with that portion of the research then being classified under a particular code. This is differentiated from general coding, which requires the researcher to code the entire text in every case (Glaser & Laudel, 2013).

Content analysis has come to be widely applied to a variety of fields. It has found particular popularity in the nursing literature (Elo & Kyngas, 2007), but has a wide range of other applications. It can be applied to text data in verbal, print or electronic form; and the data can be obtained from interviews, surveys, books, articles or academic literature (Hsieh & Shannon, 2005). Although the application of content analysis to academic literature has been relatively limited, there are a number of studies that have piloted this approach, which indicates that it is feasible and a realistic application of the method (See Duriau, Reger, & Pfarrer, 2007; Wang, Haertel, & Walberg, 1990; Eby et al., 2005).

Content analysis has furthermore been split into two distinct sub-methods – namely qualitative and quantitative content analysis (Stemler, 2001). Quantitative content analysis is used in a relatively mechanical manner to count the number of mentions of particular words, and is therefore useful to quantitatively asses the presence of certain words in communication. It has however been criticised for not effectively assessing the nuance of more complex communication, and for not effectively establishing the relationship between particular concepts (Heikkilä & Ekman, 2003; Shapiro & Markoff, 1997).

Qualitative content analysis developed as an alternative to quantitative content analysis. Elo and Kyngas (2007) describe qualitative content analysis as a method to condense text into its conceptual meaning, often resulting in the creation of conceptual maps. Schreier (2012) describes it as a method to systematically describe the meaning of qualitative material. Heikkilä and Ekman (2003) indicates that qualitative content analysis is often utilised to develop an understanding about the 'what', 'why' and 'how' of a particular topic.

Qualitative content analysis is further divided into two subcategories: inductive qualitative content analysis and deductive qualitative content analysis (Elo & Kyngas, 2007). Cho and Lee (2014) and Elo and Kyngas (2007) suggest that inductive qualitative content analysis is appropriate when there exists fragmented knowledge about a particular topic, whilst deductive qualitative content analysis is more appropriate if a particular hypothesis is to be tested. The primary operational difference between the two methods is that the inductive approach assesses the text without pre-designed codes and allows the codes to emerge as research is conducted, whilst the deductive approach assesses the text with pre-designed codes given that particular hypotheses are being tested.

Although the literature for the most part refers to approaches without pre-designed codes as 'the inductive approach', some have called it 'emergent coding' (Stemler, 2001) or 'conventional qualitative content analysis' (Hsieh & Shannon, 2005).

Qualitative content analysis generally consists of three phases (Elo & Kyngas, 2007; Morse & Field, 1995). These steps are: Firstly, the preparation phase, where the appropriate units of analysis are identified. Secondly, the analysis phase, which includes coding and abstraction, aims to make sense of the content. Polit and Beck (2004) describe abstraction in this sense as a description of the research topic through generating codes. Codes can then be combined with other, similar codes, to produce themes, and the interrelationship of themes can help to start generating an understanding of the content. Dey (1993) suggests that the creation of codes rests on the researcher's insights, but that there are a number of methods (see the analysis section) to ensure validity of results. In order to better establish relationships between concepts, propositional coding (Stemler, 2001; Gläser & Laudel, 2013) can also be adopted to track how often certain concepts are linked in the content. The third phase of the process is presenting findings, which can either be done in tabular formats or through conceptual maps.

Other scholars have expanded on the three steps, such as Mayring (2000), who suggested that five steps are more appropriate: 1) develop the research question, 2) determine the themes and their subcodes, 3) revise the codes if necessary, 4) apply the codes to the text, and 5) interpret and present the results. Hsieh and Shannon (2005) have offered a similar 4-step process.

This study will adopt an *inductive* qualitative content analysis approach. It has been judged to be the best approach for the purposes of this study given that it will allow for the conceptual integration of the literature to produce a conceptual model (Krippendorf, 1989) of the causes of the Greek crisis that can incorporate textual input from multiple disciplines.

The inductive approach has been chosen since the knowledge on the Greek crisis remains fragmented, and since the study will be descriptive and will not set up hypotheses prior to the analysis. It should be noted that within the inductive field of qualitative content analysis, there is also a range of openness to generating codes (Glaser & Laudel, 2013), ranging from total openness (i.e., no prior consideration of possible codes), to somewhat more guided coding approaches where particular research questions stimulate thoughts on initial codes. This study will adopt a somewhat more guided approach given that the research is framed by research questions; but the process will remain open for the development of codes that do not necessarily pertain to the initial questions. This will allow for an inductive approach whereby codes are developed in an emergent manner (Stemler, 2001) as text is assessed, but where some prior thought is given to appropriate codes given that particular research questions have been formulated (Glaser & Laudel, 2013).

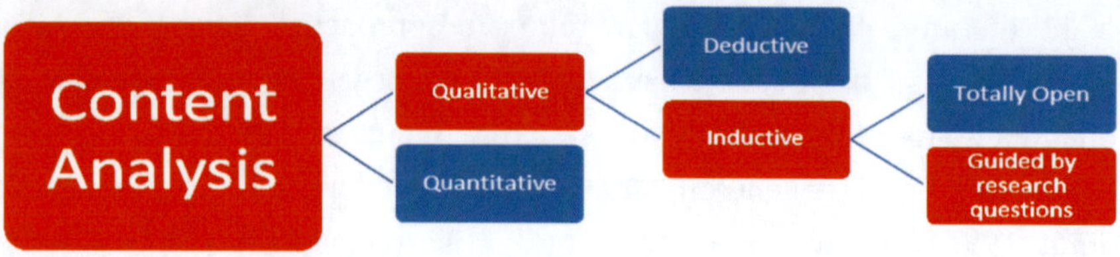


Figure 12. Summary of methodological options within the field of content analysis. This study will adopt the approach in red.

Content analysis has been chosen for this study given that there already exists a large field of diverse research on the Greek crisis; and that it was judged that the study could most successfully add value to the field by integrating different strands of research. Shirazi (2015) details how such integrative efforts can generate new insights and add value to the existing research.

The qualitative approach has been chosen given that the objective of the conceptual mapping exercise is to present a nuanced view of the causes of the crisis that goes beyond merely tabulating the repetition of certain words, suggesting that a purely quantitative approach is not ideal (Heikkilä & Ekman, 2003; Shapiro & Markoff, 1997). It should be noted that the study did still apply some quantitative measures (such as tabulation of codes and their relative percentages), but went further to produce a conceptual map of codes and their interrelationships (Cho & Lee, 2014).

Inductive qualitative content analysis has furthermore been chosen given that it is ideal for answering the kinds of 'what', 'how' and 'why' questions that have been identified in the research questions (Heikkilä & Ekman, 2003); and given that a particular hypothesis is not being tested as would be the case with deductive qualitative content analysis.

It should finally also be noted that a number of alternative research methods were considered. Possible alternatives were grounded theory (Strauss & Corbin, 1994), quantitative content analysis (Cho & Lee, 2014), systematic review (Needleman, 2002) or integrative review (Shirazi, 2015).

**Table 1. Summarising the motivations for research design elements**

| Design Element | Motivation |
|---|---|
| Content Analysis | Best option for integration and conceptual mapping |
| Qualitative | Best option for integrating nuanced communication |
| Inductive | Not testing particular hypotheses |
| Guided by Questions | Research was framed by particular research questions |

Grounded theory was judged to be too ambitious given that the aim of this study is purely descriptive, and not aimed at developing new theory. Both quantitative content analysis and systematic review appeared attractive given their abilities to produce effective summations of the literature, but neither effectively enabled the creation of a conceptual model, which is the primary aim of the study. Both were therefore judged not to be appropriate methodologies for this study. An integrative review using analytico-synthetic integration (Shirazi, 2015) appeared appealing given its ability to help synthesise content from diverse perspectives into a holistic whole, but given the novelty of the approach and the fact that the mechanics of the method are still being defined, qualitative content analysis emerged as the preferred option.

## CONCLUSION

The literature review has found numerous potential causes of the Greek crisis, with the preliminary investigation indicating that the causes are clustered around three main issues: the accumulation of excessive government debt, the collapse of confidence in the ability of the Greek state to repay its debts and the Greek state and unsustainable current account imbalances. These issues have been found to be highly interrelated, and to have highly interrelated sub-drivers.

The sub-drivers include a variety of factors from different disciplines. Political science contributes important elements such as the political opposition to reforms, union opposition to reforms and the failure of the EU to enforce the debt limits of the SGP. Public administration contributes important elements related to problems of governance in Greece, including corruption, weak revenue collection, a bloated public sector, a significant regulatory burden and poor statistical services. Monetary economics contributes the important implications of EMU membership, the adoption of the Euro and the fears around the possible exit from the Euro. Economics more generally contributes the deterioration of Greek competitiveness, Greece's high unit labour costs, Greece's excessive debt and excessive current account deficits. Financial economics contributes important elements concerning global financial markets' loss of confidence in Greek sovereign debt, including a number of important trigger events, the influx of capital into Greece after 2001, the effects of the 2008 subprime mortgage crisis and the impact of credit ratings agencies' downgrades.

It is clear that no single study or no single discipline currently effectively encapsulates all of these interrelated issues in a systematic manner, suggesting that this study adds significant value to the collective knowledge on the causes of the Greek crisis by integrating the existing knowledge into a descriptive conceptual model that tells the 'whole story.'

Qualitative content analysis has been identified as the ideal research methodology to enable the construction of such a conceptual model, given that the necessary research has already been conducted, but that cross-disciplinary conceptual integration (Krippendorf, 1989) has remained outstanding until now.

The literature review therefore confirms that there is available literature on the Greek crisis. (Question 1) The literature review has furthermore confirmed that all the other posed research questions about the Greek experience in the period before the crisis (Questions 2-7) are relevant and legitimate questions, given that those issues feature prominently in the literature; but do so without being effectively integrated.

*Chapter 3*

# RESEARCH METHODOLOGY

As has been discussed in the literature review chapter, this study will adopt an inductive qualitative content analysis approach (Cho & Lee, 2014; Mayring, 2000; Glaser & Laudel, 2013) to create a conceptual model of the causes of the Greek crisis. This will be discussed in greater detail along four subsections: (1) Research approach and strategy, (2) Research design, data collection methods and research instruments, (3) Sampling and (4) Data analysis methods.

## 3.1. RESEARCH APPROACH AND STRATEGY

Using inductive qualitative content analysis, the research process essentially assessed the existing academic texts to determine the dominant academic opinion – across multiple disciplines – on the causes of the Greek crisis. In this way, content from political science, economics, public administration, monetary economics and financial economics was distilled into its constituent concepts. The concepts were then integrated to produce a more comprehensive and cross-disciplinary explanatory model for the causes of the crisis than currently exists in the literature.

The practicalities of the research process have been mapped out in Figure 13 below. The research followed a typical inductive qualitative content analysis approach (Cho & Lee, 2014), with the added element of including source material from a variety of academic disciplines.

The *qualitative* approach was chosen given that the communication in academic texts was judged to be too nuanced to merely count the repetition of certain words, instead requiring a qualitative approach to allow for more subjective interpretation of the texts (Schreier, 2012; Heikkilä & Ekman, 2003). The research furthermore adopted an *inductive* content analysis approach given that the inductive approach is generally used for integration of fragmented knowledge (Elo & Kyngas, 2007; Cho & Lee, 2014), whilst the deductive approach is used to test specific hypotheses. The inductive approach was thus more appropriate in this situation.

It is also important to reiterate that the initial research assumption - that the terminology and research across the different fields were sufficiently-alike to enable integration with this methodology - was met, allowing for integration through qualitative content analysis as suggested by Krippendorf (1989). This conclusion was reached given that the key concepts in the different disciplines indicated clear interrelationships as will be shown in the analysis section.

Finally, it is also important to note that the qualitative variation of content analysis has been chosen specifically because it allows for the creation of multidimensional conceptual matrices (Glaser & Laudel, 2013) as explained below, whilst the quantitative approach was judged inappropriate given that it only allows for the counting of the prevalence of certain terms (Krippendorf, 1989; Erlandson, Harris, Skipper, & Allen, 1993; Shapiro & Markoff, 1997). As discussed in the literature review, content analysis as an overarching approach has also been judged as the best option for the purposes of this book. A number of alternatives were considered (systematic review, integrative review, grounded theory, quantitative content analysis), but content analysis was chosen given that qualitative content analysis provides the best approach for the integration of cross-disciplinary information into a single conceptual model (Stemler, 2001).

## 3.2. Research Design, Data Collection Methods and Research Instruments

The process began by assessing the whole of the academic literature relating to the Greek crisis, and producing the literature review. During this process, it was identified that the most prominent explanations for the causes of the Greek crisis comes from the fields of political science, public administration, economics, monetary economics and financial economics. The study will therefore attempt to integrate the findings from these five fields into a single conceptual model. It should be noted that some scholars (Sklias & Maris, 2013; Malakos, 2013) have already suggested that such integration is required given the relative compartmentalisation of the research on the Greek crisis.

The first step in the research process was therefore to do a preliminary scan of the literature, which resulted in the literature review. The second step involved selecting the studies for inclusion in the qualitative content analysis process. This required decisions to be made on two fronts: Firstly, how many studies to include; and secondly, which studies to include. This step is depicted by 'process A' in Figure 13.

The content analysis literature is not clear on how many texts are required or appropriate to ensure validity of results, given that studies take place in vastly different contexts (Krippendorf, 1989). For guidance on establishing an appropriate number of studies, three prominent studies that applied content analysis to academic literature were examined (See Duriau, Reger, & Pfarrer, 2007; Wang, Haertel, & Walberg, 1990; Eby et al., 2005). Duriau, Reger and Pfarrer (2007) included 98 studies. Wang, Haertel and Walberg (1990) included 150 studies, although a significant number of these were shorter research notes. Eby et al. (2005) however only included 90 studies. It was therefore decided that this particular book would include 100 studies to match the scale of other comparable content analyses. The process followed in selecting the 100 studies is rigorously explained in the sampling section below. A full list of the selected studies can be found in Appendix 1.

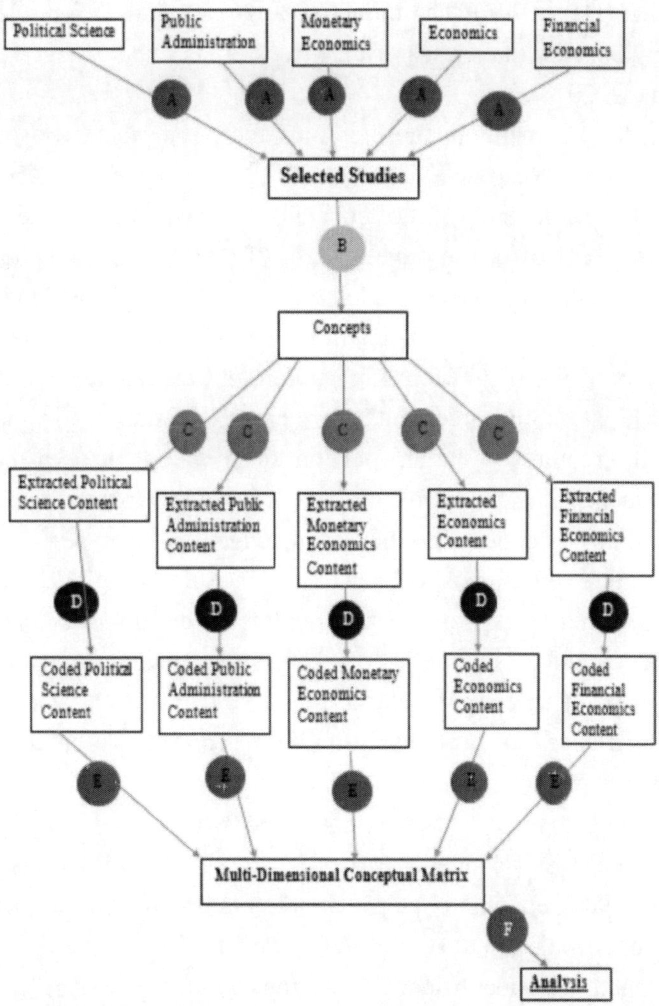


Figure 13. Flow chart of research methodology.

Once the studies had been selected, concepts were developed through which the meaning of the academic articles can be condensed into their constituent parts. This occurred during **'process B'** in Figure 13. The literature differs on how concepts should be developed. In the case of deductive qualitative content analysis, the concepts are developed prior to assessment of the literature by using existing theory (Elo & Kyngas, 2007). This is usually done when a particular hypothesis is to be tested, in which case the researcher simply applies the concepts relevant to the hypothesis. But for the purposes of this study, the inductive approach was followed. In the inductive case, concepts are developed as the text is examined. This allows for an emergent approach, where codes are developed based on what is encountered in the text, with a focus on finding recurring concepts (Shapiro & Markoff, 1997). This approach is preferable in the case where knowledge on the topic is fragmented (Stemler, 2001; Elo & Kyngas, 2007; Polit & Beck, 2004) and relies on the intuition and insight of the researcher to develop appropriate concepts (Dey, 1993). The inductive approach is therefore clearly preferable given that the knowledge on the causes of the Greek crisis remains fragmented (Sklias & Maris, 2013; Malakos, 2013).

There are also disagreements in the literature about the practical aspects of concept development in the inductive case. Mayring (2000) suggests that 20-50% of the texts should be assessed for the development of concepts, after which all the text (including the 20-50% which was assessed for the development of concepts) should be systematically divided into the constituent concepts. Schreier (2012) disagrees and suggests that assessing 10-20% of the literature is sufficient for the development of concepts. Scholars (Mayring, 2000; Schreier, 2012; Hsieh & Shannon, 2005; Cho & Lee, 2014; Glaser & Laudel, 2013) are however in agreement that increased variability in the texts that are analysed necessarily requires a larger portion of the texts to be analysed for the development of concepts. This study followed a conservative approach and assessed 50% of the texts to develop concepts. This has been judged to be necessary given that the cross-disciplinary nature of the texts to be analysed includes a high degree of variability. It obviously also required texts from each discipline to be included in the 50% that is used for concept development. Eventually, 38 concepts were identified and the full list of the concepts and their interpretations can be found in Appendix 2. This is a significant list, but it was judged necessary to expand the list of concepts to be able to explain the complex phenomenon being examined.

It is also important to note however that even though the research approach was inductive, the development of concepts was somewhat guided by the research questions that were posed at the outset. This is an acceptable method to provide some structure to the process of concept development (Glaser & Laudel, 2013).

Once concepts had been identified, the sections in all texts that refer to any of the concepts were extracted and sorted separately from the original text (Glaser & Laudel, 2013; Schreier, 2012; Mayring, 2000; Cho & Lee, 2014) as part of '**process C**'. A total of

1142 distinct extracts were identified and listed separately per article. Interestingly, this is the most significant difference between qualitative content analysis and traditional coding approaches – traditional coding simply codes every part of every text, whilst qualitative content analysis goes through step C in the flow chart where relevant portions of the text are extracted first (Glaser & Laudel, 2013).

And once sections had been extracted, concepts were applied to the extracted sections to condense those sections into their core meaning (Krippendorf, 1989; Heikkilä & Ekman, 2003). The study followed a propositional conceptual approach (Stemler, 2001), where concepts are explicitly applied in propositional or causal manner in order to capture the relationship between concepts across the literature. This occurred during **'process D'** and resulted in Appendix 3, which shows every piece of extracted content, and how it was condensed into a core set of propositional codes. Consider, as an example, the following extract from Baltas and Chair (2013):

> '*Greece joined the EU in 1981, ahead of Spain and Portugal, and getting access to generous European funds, whose use could hardly be described as prudent. Nonetheless, public indebtedness continued to soar and by 1996 it doubled once again, reaching 113% of GDP. This is due to the disproportionate social benefits, such as increased salaries and redundant appointments in the public sector, increased pensions, early retirements, public enterprises with large deficits etc., which created substantial budgets to be financed by continuous borrowing.*' (Baltas & Chair, 2013, p. 6) [*High debt*, caused by *poor governance*, a *large public sector* and a *generous welfare state*]

The quote in italics represents an extracted portion of their article that was judged to be relevant for this study, and the section in brackets is the propositional concepts that condenses the meaning of the extract into its central meaning. The underlined portions represent the concepts that were interpreted to be relevant to this extract. The 'high debt' concept refers to Baltas and Chair's reference to a high debt-to-GDP ratio. The 'poor governance' concept refers to Baltas and Chair's suggestion that European funds were not spent prudently. The 'large public sector' concept refers to the mention of increased salaries and redundant appointments in the public sector. And the 'generous welfare state' concept refers to the mentions of pensions, early retirement and disproportionate use of social benefits. The meaning here has been interpreted as 'Greece had high debt' as the primary concept, with 'poor governance', a 'large public sector' and a 'generous welfare state' being cited as reasons for the high debt.

This process was followed with each of the 1142 relevant extracts that were identified in the selected group of studies. Each extract was condensed using the simple propositional conceptual approach proposed by Stemler (2001): [*Primary concept,* caused by *concept X, concept Y,* etc.].

Finally, the information from each extracted section was summarised along three dimensions in a multidimensional conceptual matrix in Microsoft Excel in order to enable effective analysis (Glaser & Laudel, 2013). The three dimensions are: time dimension, material dimensions and causal dimensions of each extract (Kyngas & Vanhanen, 1999). This process of multidimensional sorting of the sections is denoted by '**process E**' in Figure 13, and resulted in the creation of a multidimensional conceptual matrix that was used as the primary tool of analysis. The spreadsheet is too large to attach as an appendix, but has been made available as a supporting document in soft copy.

By way of illustration, the extract from Baltas & Chair (2013) was presented as follows in the multidimensional conceptual matrix:

**Table 2. Example line from the multidimensional conceptual matrix**

| | Material Dimensions | | Time Dimension | Causal Dimensions | | |
|---|---|---|---|---|---|---|
| Primary Concept | Author(s) | Discipline | Year of Publication | Poor Governance | Generous Welfare State | Large Public Sector |
| High Debt | Baltas & Chair | Financial Economics | 2013 | Yes | Yes | Yes |

Of course, in the actual matrix, all 38 identified concepts are listed on the horizontal axis under causal dimensions. This primary concept registers a 'yes' with the three causal concepts listed above, and nothing with the other 35 codes under possible causal dimensions, given that none of the other concepts were identified in the extracted passage from Baltas and Chair (2013). This is in line with the propositional conceptual analysis as proposed by Stemler (2001) and others (Glaser & Laudel, 2013; Schreier, 2012). In this way, each cell under causal dimensions becomes a binary data point (yes or nothing) which either identifies it as having a causal relationship with the primary concept identified or not. This process was repeated for all 1142 lines of primary concepts that were identified in the extracts along 38 potential causal dimensions, essentially creating in excess of 43 000 binary data points on the multidimensional conceptual matrix that allow for interesting analyses to be conducted.

Once the matrix was completed, systematic analysis could be conducted as denoted by '**process F**' in Figure 13. The analysis process will be described in the data analysis section.

The step-wise '**A**' to '**F**' progression in Figure 13 as described above therefore represents this study's interpretation of Mayring's (2000) five steps of qualitative content analysis, or Hsieh and Shannon's (2005) four steps of qualitative content analysis, with particular focus being given to this study's cross-disciplinary approach in assessing the content of the texts.

The '**A**' to '**F**' progression in Figure 13 therefore also summarises the total research design, whilst data collection is represented by the '**A**' to '**E**' portion of the process given that the collection of data involves identifying the studies, identifying the concepts, extracting the appropriate content, applying the concepts to the extracted content and importing the propositional codes into the multidimensional conceptual matrix. The data only becomes usable for analysis once it reaches the point of a binary variable in the spreadsheet.

Finally, the multidimensional conceptual matrix in Microsoft Excel was used as the primary research instrument that enabled analysis of the collected data during '**process F**'.

## 3.3. SAMPLING

It was explained above that during '**process A**' in Figure 13, decisions had to be made regarding the ideal number of studies, and the nature of the studies to be included in the analysis. As discussed, by examining previous attempts at content analyses of academic literature (See Duriau, Reger, & Pfarrer, 2007; Wang, Haertel, & Walberg, 1990; Eby et al., 2005), it was established that 100 studies would be an appropriate number. This therefore leaves the question of which studies to include.

### 3.3.1. Inclusion Criteria

The content analysis literature suggests that inclusion criteria is an appropriate method to identify the ideal texts for analysis (Shreier, 2012; Mayring, 2000; Lee & Cho, 2014) and calls this an important part of the 'preparation phase' of the process (Hsieh & Shannon, 2005).

The content analysis literature however is not particularly prescriptive about how to develop inclusion criteria or what the ideal categories are for such criteria, largely leaving it up to the researcher to decide the appropriateness of inclusion criteria on a study-by-study basis (Glaser & Laudel, 2013). Previous studies using content analysis on academic literature (Duriau, Reger, & Pfarrer, 2007; Wang, Haertel, & Walberg, 1990; Eby et al., 2005) was thus again examined for guidance on how inclusion criteria are to be developed for such studies.

In each case, the authors developed inclusion criteria to narrow down the literature only to the most relevant studies. This is in line with the general application of inclusion criteria in other fields, which Wakefield (2015) indicates is widely used to narrow down samples of literature to only the most relevant content. The inclusion criteria for each of the studies above involved essentially three elements: 1) A defined period within which the texts had to be published, 2) Certain key words or key themes in the chosen texts and 3) Publication in an academic journal that was accessible through the mainstream academic databases. In each case the inclusion criteria were also clearly and explicitly stated. Randolph (2009) suggests that clarity and an explicit stating of the inclusion or exclusion criteria is critical, since it should allow anyone doing the same search on the same databases to come up with a similar list of literature.

This study has therefore aimed to follow the process piloted by Duriau, Reger and Pfarrer (2007), Wang, Haertel and Walberg (1990) and Eby et al., (2005), whereby inclusion criteria were used to narrow down the literature to only the most relevant studies. Wakefield (2015) also proposes a number of useful potential categories for generic inclusion criteria, including: The methodology employed in studies, the language of the study, the year of publication, studies that only include certain topics and the size of the study.

After assessing the previous content analyses of academic literature and Wakefield's (2015) suggestions, the following inclusion criteria were developed:

1) *Time Dimension:* Only studies published after 2003 were included. This decision was made given that Greece's joining of the EMU in 2001 had a significant impact on the country and played an important role in setting the scene for the Greek crisis (Fouskas & Dimoulas, 2012). Studies before 2003 were not likely to have incorporated the impact of EMU membership on Greece sufficiently.
2) *Accessibility:* Only studies that were freely accessible on the Graduate School of Business' academic databases were included. The databases are discussed in a later section. This decision was made given that there was no budget available to pay to access literature.
3) *Academic Journals Only:* Only studies that were published in academic journals were included. Database searches produced large numbers of articles that appeared in periodicals. These were not included, as the study set out to only include credible academic journal articles. This is in line with the approach proposed by Wakefield (2015) and Randolph (2009); and indeed in line with the approach followed by Duriau, Reger and Pfarrer (2007), Wang, Haertel and Walberg (1990) and Eby et al. (2005).
4) *Relevance:* Studies had to explicitly deal with the Greek economic crisis, or it at least needed to deal with Greece, as part of the broader European debt crisis, at some point in the study. This excluded a large number of studies that only dealt with the European debt crisis, but never addressed Greece explicitly. Importantly, Greece did not necessarily have to feature in the headline or the abstract, but at some point the article needed to explicitly discuss the economic difficulties in Greece.
5) *Length:* Given that this a qualitative content analysis, only studies that produced a sufficient number of relevant extracted sections were included; in other words, only studies that contributed enough relevant content. There was little guidance in the literature on the appropriate number of extracted sections to use as the minimum 'cut off' point for inclusion. Given that the average extracts per article

was 11.42, the minimum cut-off point was decided to be 5, or roughly half the average. In other words, only articles with 5 or more extracted sections were included in the study. It was judged that articles with fewer than 5 relevant paragraphs would not contribute sufficiently to the study.

6) *Language:* Given that no translation services are available, only studies that were published in English were used.

It should be noted that although specific methodologies were considered as possible inclusion criteria, it was not judged to be feasible in this case given the variety of disciplines that have been employed in the study of the Greek crisis, each employing vastly different approaches.

### 3.3.2. The Search Process

The search process began with a number of searches on the databases that are available to the University of Cape Town's Graduate School of Business students. Content on the Greek crisis was mostly found on Science Direct, Ebscohost and Econlit. Various search terms were used to gain access to as many articles as possible. Search terms included 'Greek', 'economic', 'crisis', 'governance', 'debt', 'financial crisis', 'Euro', 'European Monetary Union', 'politics', 'austerity' and 'internal devaluation', amongst others.

These searches produced large amounts of relevant articles. The reference lists of these articles were also used to source additional articles. Unfortunately, a number of the referenced articles were not available on the UCT databases, but some were available on Google Scholar.

This produced a total pool of over 200 articles. At this stage all six inclusion criteria were applied to limit the pool to only the most relevant literature (Randolph, 2009; Wakefield, 2015).

### 3.3.3. Cross-Disciplinary Complications

This study has followed the sampling approach piloted by other content analyses, but with the exception that it had to contend with the stated aim of building a cross-disciplinary conceptual model. The traditional sampling methods therefore had to be amended to ensure cross-disciplinary integration was possible (Krippendorf, 1989).

In order to ensure that sufficient content was extracted from each discipline, the sampling was subdivided into five groups – representing financial economics, economics, monetary economics, political science and public administration – with each group contributing 20 studies to the final pool of selected studies.

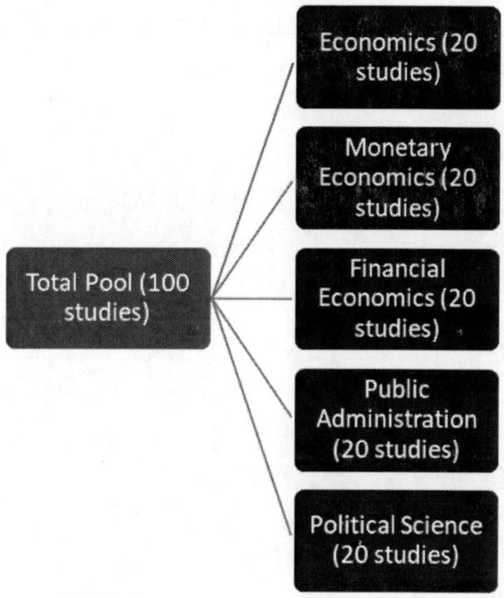


Figure 14. The sampling allocation per discipline.

The inclusion criteria and search process above was therefore applied to each discipline individually to reach the target of 20 studies per discipline and 100 in total. After all the inclusion criteria were applied, roughly 120 articles remained across the five disciplines. In selecting the final 100 studies, preference was given to those studies that contributed more extracts, and that therefore included more relevant content to the study.

## 3.4. Data Analysis Methods

Qualitative content analysis that utilises propositional coding and conceptual matrices is ideally suited to understanding the causal relationships between concepts in the texts (Gläser & Laudel, 2013). Indeed, this is the primary reason why qualitative content analysis was chosen as the methodological approach for this study.

In order to understand the interrelationships between the concepts, the multidimensional conceptual matrix can easily be manipulated to conduct the analysis. According to Gläser and Laudel (2013) and Cho and Lee (2014), this takes the form of intelligent and systematic sorting of the various columns.

In this case, the analysis process took the following steps:

1) The analysis began with the sorting of the matrix using the 'discipline' column. This allows for the grouping of each of the disciplines, and all of the lines of

concepts relating to them, separately. At this point, each discipline was assessed on its own before integration took place. This assessment included a count of all the primary concepts identified by that discipline. These primary concepts were then tabulated per discipline to indicate which issues are most prominently focused on in each discipline. This is line with Heikkilä and Ekman (2003), Shapiro and Markoff (1997) and Cho and Lee (2014) who all indicate that qualitative content analysis can still be utilised to present certain aspects of the findings in a quantitative manner. The most prevalent primary concepts for each discipline were then also be isolated by sorting by the 'concept' column within each discipline and tabulating the causal concepts for each of the most prevalent primary concepts. Causal relationships were then depicted in conceptual maps per discipline.

2) Further analysis took place by assessing the entire data set across all five disciplines. This required sorting by the 'concept' column. The most prevalent primary concepts were then tabulated for the entire 100 studies (and 1142 primary concepts) identified. Each primary concept was then isolated, and a secondary tabulation of causal concepts was made to determine the most prevalent concepts causing each primary concept. This allowed for integration of all the literature in a systematic manner in the form of a conceptual model.
3) The conceptual model was then utilised to answer the research questions.
4) Interesting other applications of the multidimensional conceptual matrix was tested to determine if there were other key differences in the literature, such as changing perceptions over time by sorting by year of publication. Additionally, each concept was investigated to determine which discipline contributed most towards each concept.

*Chapter 4*

# RESEARCH FINDINGS

This section discusses the findings and analysis of findings in a step-wise manner in line with the structure described above and depicted below:

The process therefore begins with an assessment of each discipline individually to determine the key causes of the crisis as identified by each of the disciplines.

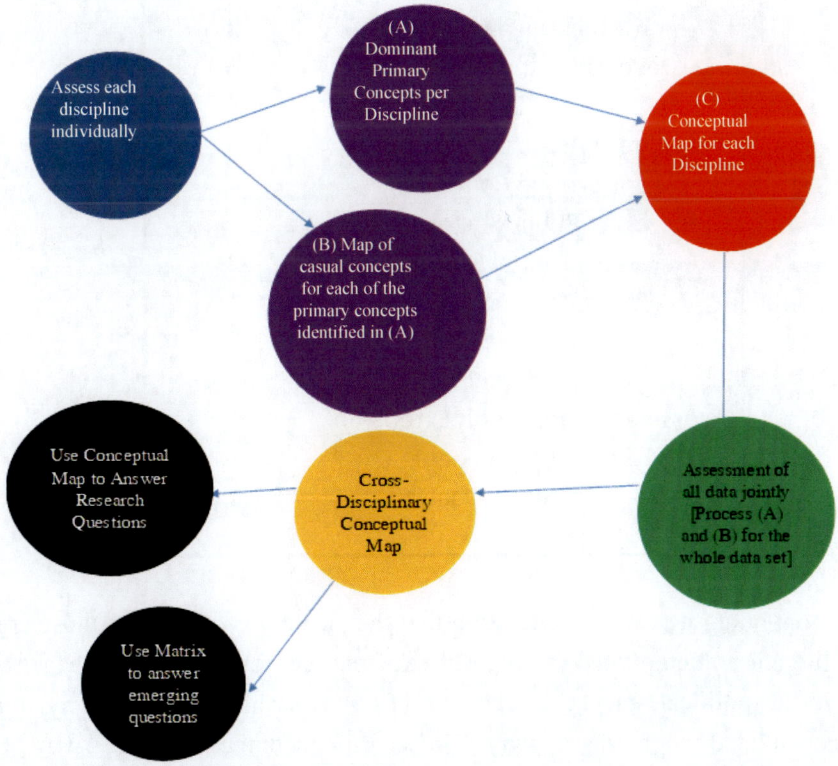


Figure 15. A depiction of the analysis process.

## 4.1. Political Science

Isolating the political science primary concepts and tabulating them produced the following results:

**Table 3. Political science primary concepts**

| Primary Concepts | Count |
|---|---|
| High Debt | 63 |
| Lack of Competitiveness | 40 |
| Political Opposition to Reform | 32 |
| Collapse of Confidence | 21 |
| Political Instability | 17 |
| Poor Governance | 13 |
| Failed Austerity | 12 |
| Corruption | 10 |
| Fear of EMU Exit | 9 |
| Large Welfare State | 8 |
| Internal Devaluation | 8 |
| Destructive Institutions | 6 |
| Lack of Trust | 5 |
| Current Account Deficits | 5 |
| Poor Revenue Collection | 4 |
| Large Public Sector | 4 |
| Large Informal Sector | 2 |
| Regulatory Burden | 1 |
| Military Spending | 1 |
| Low Productivity | 1 |
| Excessive Private Credit Extension | 1 |
| Access to cheap debt | 1 |
| Bank Undercapitalisation | 1 |
| Capital Influx | 1 |

Before continuing it is worth reiterating that the primary concepts are those concepts which the literature attempts to offer causal explanations for. As can be seen from the table below, the political science literature focuses overwhelmingly on why it is that Greece accumulated high debt, why Greece lost competitiveness, why Greece experienced internal political opposition to reform and why Greece experienced a loss of confidence in its sovereign bonds. This finding is in line with what was expected given the description in sections *1.1-1.3* and *3.3* of the literature review. Interestingly, and as shall be shown later, the dominant primary concepts do not differ greatly between the various disciplines. The causal concepts (i.e., what caused these problems to occur) is where the primary differences are.

**Table 4. High debt causal concepts (political science)**

| High Debt Causal Concepts | Count |
|---|---|
| Poor Governance | 20 |
| Corruption | 15 |
| Large Welfare State | 15 |
| Destructive Institutions | 12 |
| Large Public Sector | 10 |
| Financial Crisis | 9 |
| Political Opposition to Reform | 8 |
| Poor Revenue Collection | 7 |

The logical next step is therefore to explore the causal explanations offered by the political science literature for each of the primary concepts above. In order to do so, each primary concept within the political science discipline was isolated, and its causal factors tabulated to determine the most prominent causal concepts. These are outlined below:

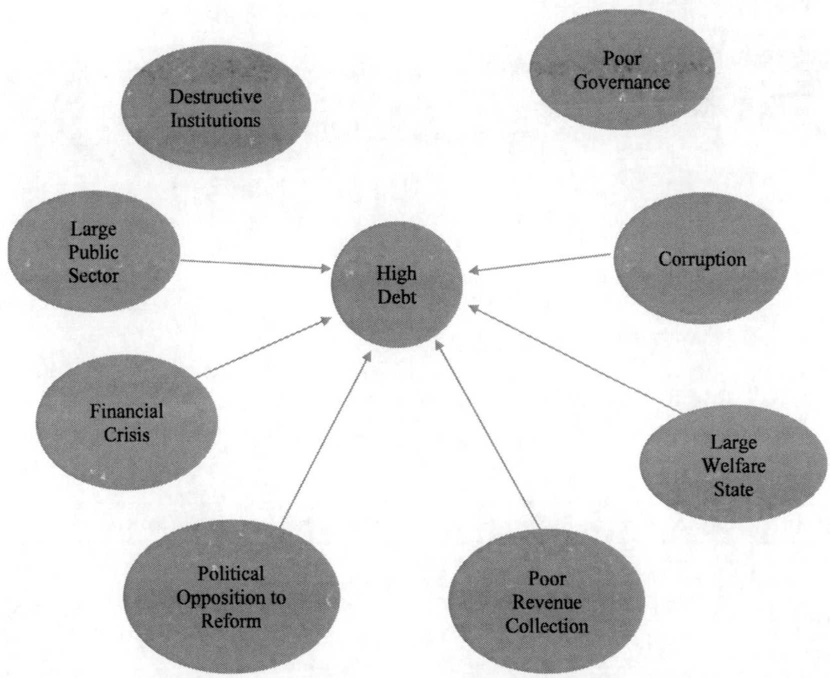


Figure 16. Why the Greek government has high debt, as explained by the political science literature.

The same approach was followed for the 'lack of competitiveness' concept below.

**Table 5. Lack of competitiveness causal concepts (political science)**

| Lack of Competitiveness Causal Concepts | Count |
|---|---|
| Regulatory Burden | 10 |
| Poor Governance | 9 |
| Destructive Institutions | 9 |
| EMU Membership | 8 |
| Large Public Sector | 7 |

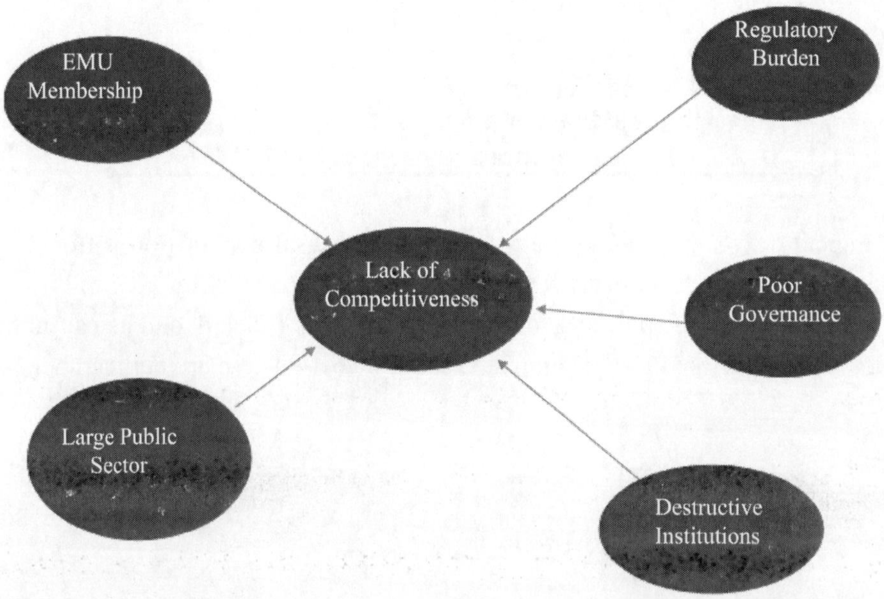


Figure 17. Why Greek firms became uncompetitive, according to the political science literature.

Similarly, the causal concepts for political opposition to reform were also investigated:

**Table 6. Political opposition to reform causal concepts (political science)**

| Political Opposition to Reform Causal Concepts | Count |
|---|---|
| Strong Public Sector Unions | 10 |
| Destructive Institutions | 8 |
| Internal Devaluation | 8 |
| Corruption | 7 |

A number of issues should be noted at this stage. Firstly, for each of the three examples above ('High Debt,' 'Lack of Competitiveness' and 'Political Opposition to Reform') only the most prominent causal concepts were included in the tables here and in the conceptual maps. The literature on content analysis is not prescriptive on what percentage of mentions a particular concept should reach before being included in the conceptual mapping, leaving it up to the discretion of the researcher. In these cases, only the top several causal effects were included, with the cut-off point being seven or more mentions in each case.

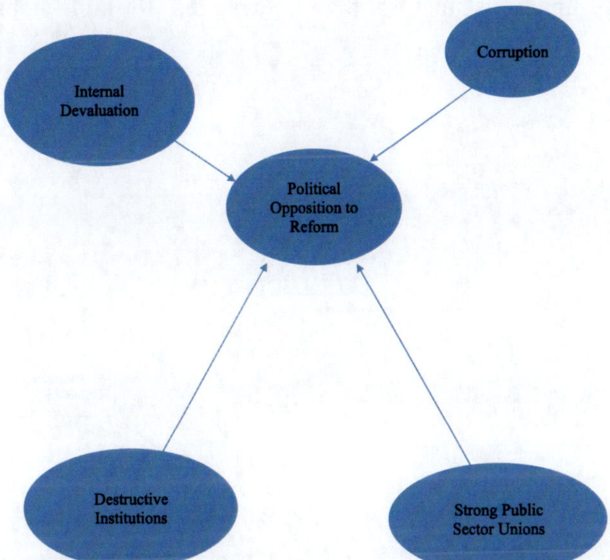


Figure 18. The reason why political opposition to reform occurred, according to the political science literature.

Secondly, the full findings and all tables (including all causal concepts for all the most significant primary concepts) can be found in Appendix 4 for each of the disciplines.

Thirdly, it should be noted that by completing this process for all variables, it became clear that there were various 'layers' of causation to be explored. Consider, for example, the concepts above. 'Political opposition to reform' was identified as a key driver of the Greek government's high debt accumulation over many years (call this causal layer 1). But then 'political opposition to reform' was also explored as a primary concept, with its causal concepts unpacked on the previous page (call this causal layer 2). Continuing with this process it was found that some of the causal concepts for 'political opposition to reform', such as corruption, had causal concepts as well, requiring yet another set of causal concepts to explain why corruption occurred so often (call this causal layer 3). As the analysis progressed, it became clear that true *root causes* of the crisis were to be found in the higher layers of causation; with the lower levels of causation showing cascading levels of symptoms that eventually lead to the trigger of the crisis.

Fourthly, and as a technical note, it may be observed that the number of causal concepts identified for particular primary concepts, exceed the number of times those primary concepts were identified. This is because each primary concept identified in the literature (i.e., each row in the excel spreadsheet) may have multiple causal dimensions along the various columns. 'High debt,' for example, was mentioned as a primary concept on 63 occasions in the political science literature, but the causal concepts mentioned in explaining why 'high debt' occurred tally to 96, given that a number of the extracts referred to numerous factors that contributed to high debt for the Greek government.

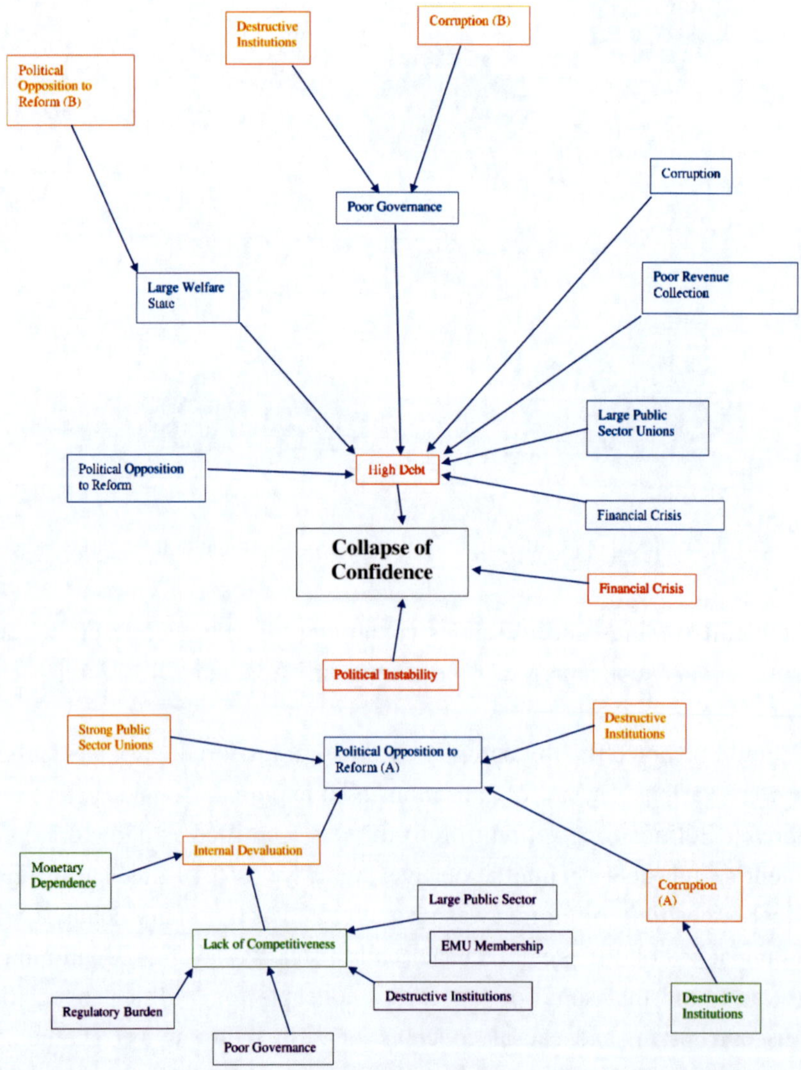


Figure 19. The causes of the Greek crisis – political science.

Finally, and as should be clear now, the analysis process is exceptionally arduous, given that each of the prominent primary concepts, for each of the disciplines, must be unpacked individually to construct the eventual conceptual map per discipline. For the sake of brevity, this process has been condensed in the sections below to only include the tabulation of primary concepts per discipline, and the eventual conceptual map per discipline. Again, all of the supporting evidence in the form tabulations indicating the most prominent causal concepts per primary concept per discipline can be found in Appendix 4. The full conceptual model for the causes of the Greek crisis, according to the political science literature, therefore follows on the next page. This represents 'step C' (for political science) in Figure 15.

As can be seen from Figure 19, the political science literature paints a picture of a complex set of interacting factors that eventually lead to a collapse of confidence in the ability of the Greek state to honour its debts. Causal layers have been given different colours. The first and most basic level is denoted in red. At this level of analysis, the political science literature suggests that the collapse of confidence in the Greek state was caused by the high level of debt it accumulated, the political instability in the country in the period after 2009 and the financial crisis that originated in the United States in 2007 which acted as a key 'trigger' moment.

The next layer of analysis is denoted in blue and aims to explain two key factors: Why did the Greek government accumulate so much debt and why did political instability occur. As can be seen a range of political and governance-related reasons are identified at this level of analysis, as one would have expected given that this is the political science literature.

The next layer of analysis is denoted in orange and begins to tackle some of the root causes behind the governance and political challenges, most notably the existence of a strong public sector union movement and a set of destructive political institutions, such as clientelism, institutionalised rent-seeking behaviour and anti-competitive regulations (Katsimi & Moutos, 2010).

The final two layers are denoted in green and purple and primarily show how the political science literature explains the occurrence of an internal devaluation in Greece.

It should be noted that, for the purposes of simplification, explanatory concepts were only indicated once per concept in the conceptual map. 'Corruption' has therefore only been explained as a result of 'destructive institutions' at point 'Corruption (A)' in Figure 19, but the same causal concept (destructive institutions) counts for 'Corruption (B)' as well. The same principle applies for all other concepts, as evidenced by the elaboration of 'Political Opposition to Reform (A)' and not 'Political Opposition to Reform (B)' in Figure 19 above.

The overarching conclusion to be drawn from Figure 19, and therefore from the political science literature in general, is that the root causes of the Greek crisis are destructive political institutions, large and powerful public sector unions, corruption and a set of subsequent governance and political issues. It can also be concluded that the political science literature places particular emphasis on these factors together creating an environment of excessive public sector debt accumulation, given that 'high debt' was the most prominent primary concept in the political science literature surveyed.

## 4.2. Public Administration

The primary concepts identified by the public administration literature are as follows:

**Table 7. Tabulation of public administration primary concepts**

| Primary Concept | Count |
|---|---|
| High Debt | 74 |
| Lack of Competitiveness | 50 |
| Collapse of Confidence | 40 |
| Poor Revenue Collection | 20 |
| Poor Governance | 10 |
| Failed Austerity Measures | 10 |
| Large Welfare State | 9 |
| Current Account Deficits | 7 |
| Access to Cheap Debt | 5 |
| Excessive Private Credit Extension | 5 |
| Large Public Sector | 4 |
| Corruption | 4 |
| Political Opposition to Reform | 3 |
| Regulatory Burden | 3 |
| Large Infromal Sector | 2 |
| Political Instability | 2 |
| Capital Influx | 2 |
| Trust | 1 |
| Poor Statistical Services | 1 |
| Non-enforcement of EU treaties | 1 |
| Internal Devaluation | 1 |
| Downgrades | 1 |
| EMU Membership | 1 |
| Bank Undercapitalisation | 1 |

As discussed earlier, this is quite similar to the political science literature, with the most important difference being the increased prominence given to certain governance issues like 'poor revenue collection' and 'poor governance.' The full public administration conceptual map follows in Figure 20.

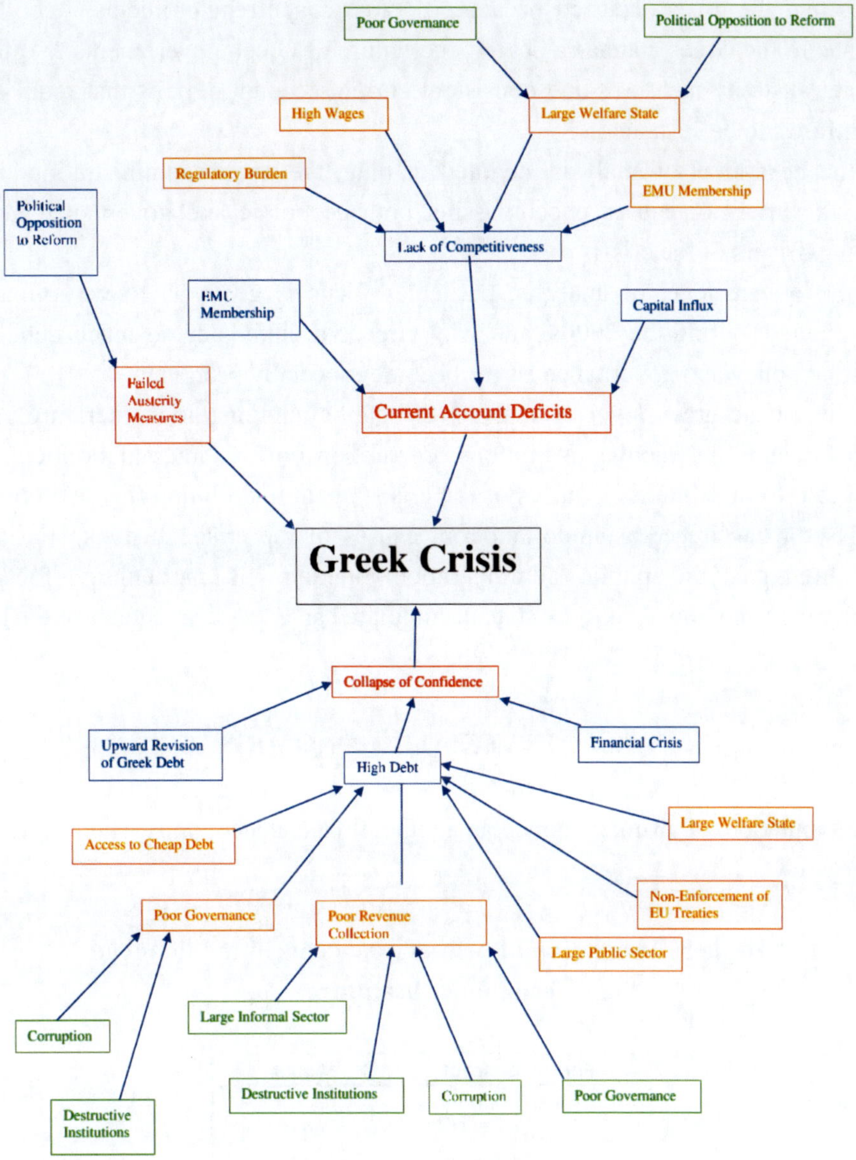


Figure 20. The causes of the Greek crisis – public administration.

The public administration literature is clearly somewhat similar to the political science literature, with the exception that it touches on some additional economic concepts such as the impact of current account deficits, competitiveness and the influx of European capital in the years after EMU membership. Additionally, it places greater emphasis on certain governance issues, such as poor revenue collection and EU-level governance with respect to the non-enforcement of EU-agreed upon debt and deficit limits.

The most basic analysis of the public administration literature, as denoted in red, indicates that the crisis occurred because of three concurrent problems: A collapse of confidence in the Greek state as a debtor, the failure of Greek governments to effectively implement austerity measures and consistent current account deficits that required large capital inflows to be sustained.

At the next level of analysis, denoted in blue, the public administration literature proposes a variety of causes encompassing both economic and governance factors as underlying drivers of the crisis.

At the orange level of analysis, particular focus is given as to why Greece lost competitiveness during the 2000s, and why Greece accumulated so much debt. At this level public policy and governance issues become especially prominent.

Finally, at the green level of analysis the public administration literature points to poor governance, destructive institutions, corruption and an internal political climate opposed to reform as the root causes of the crisis; again underlining the institutional and political setup in Greece as important root causes of the crisis. Just like the political science literature, the public administration literature is particularly focused on explaining why and how the Greek state accumulated an excessive amount of debt.

## 4.3. Financial Economics

The tabulation of primary concepts in the financial economics literature follows below:

**Table 8. Tabulation of primary concepts in the financial economics literature**

| Primary Concept | Count |
|---|---|
| Collapse of Confidence | 76 |
| High Debt | 32 |
| Access to Cheap Debt | 15 |
| Bank Undercapitalisation | 7 |
| Lack of Competitiveness | 6 |
| Poor Governance | 5 |
| Failed Austerity | 4 |
| Downgrades | 4 |
| Capital Influx | 3 |
| Political Instability | 2 |
| Fear of EMU Exit | 2 |
| Trust | 1 |
| Monetary Dependence | 1 |
| Internal Devaluation | 1 |

It is immediately apparent that the financial economics perspective is much more focused on the collapse of confidence in Greek sovereign bonds. The list of primary concepts is much shorter and much more concentrated, suggesting that financial economics is more focused on particular topics than the more wide-ranging approach taken by political science and public administration. Interestingly, and as one would expect, financial economics deals much more extensively with Greece's access to cheap debt in the 2000s, the health of Greek banks and the confidence in the Greek state as a debtor than political science and public administration.

The conceptual map for the financial economics literature follows in Figure 21.

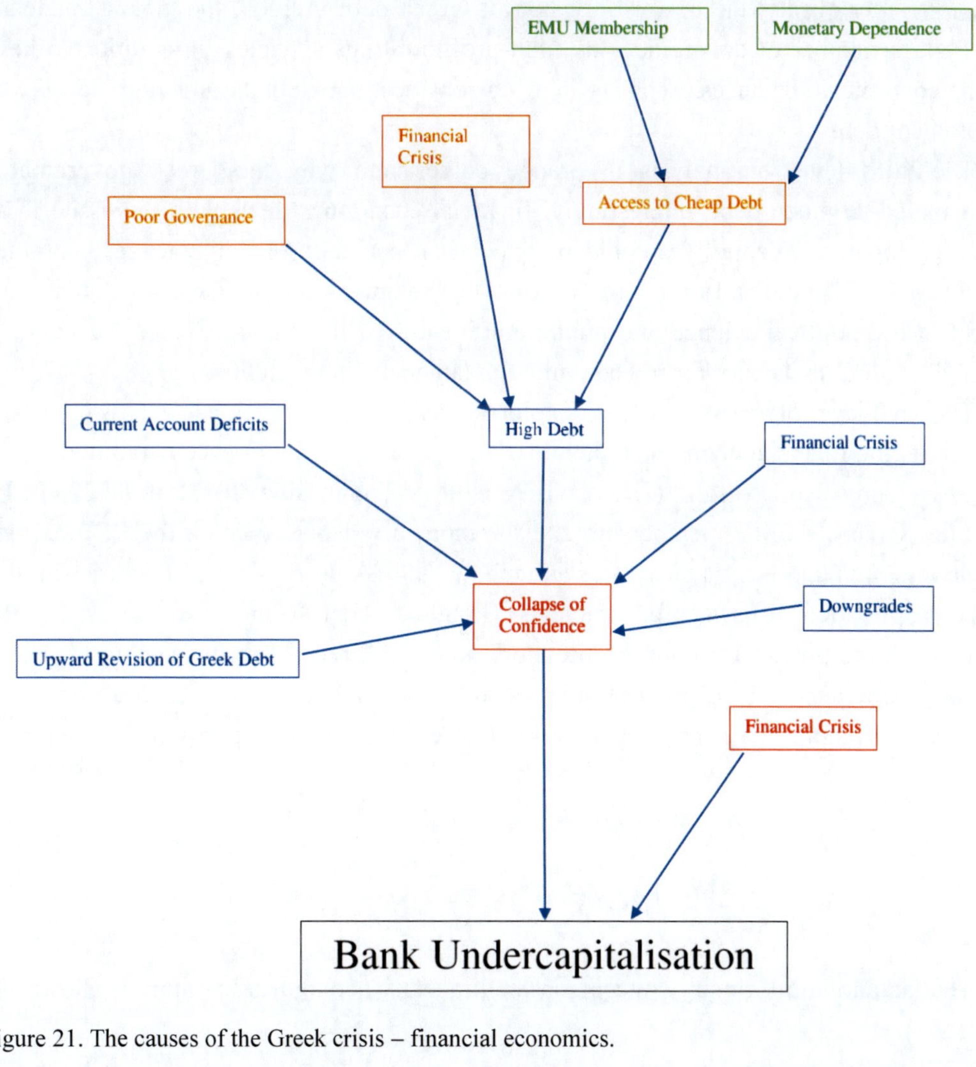


Figure 21. The causes of the Greek crisis – financial economics.

The first and most obvious observation about the financial economics conceptual map is that it is much simpler and smaller than politics science and public administration. This is a result of the fact that the financial economics literature is much more focused on a few key topics, such as when, how and why global financial markets lots confidence in Greek sovereign bonds, why financial markets were willing to give Greece so much debt before the crisis at such low rates and finally what the impact of the unravelling of the crisis was on Greek banks.

At the first level of analysis in red, the financial economics literature focuses on why Greek banks experienced balance sheet pressures before and during the crisis. It cites the collapse of confidence in Greek sovereign bonds (which Greek banks held in abundance) and the global financial crisis as the primary drivers.

At the second level of analysis in blue, the financial economics literature focuses extensively on why investors lost confidence in Greek sovereign bonds, identifying a number trigger events (the upward revision of Greek debt in 2009, the global financial crisis and a number of downgrades by high-profile ratings agencies) in addition to key macroeconomic imbalances, such as high current account deficits and high levels of government debt.

The third level of analysis in orange delves into why the Greek government accumulated so much debt. Interestingly, financial economics deals with this issue in a much-less nuanced manner (as could be expected) than the political science or public administration literatures. Instead, it focuses overwhelmingly on one factor that is largely absent in the political science and public administration literatures: Greece's access to cheap debt, despite its poor macroeconomic fundamentals in the 2000s.

The final level of analysis in green explores why it is that Greece had access to cheap debt, or as the financial economics literature would state it, why Greece benefitted from 'excessive spread suppression' (Giordano, Pericoli, & Tommasino, 2013) in the 2000s. It identifies Greece's EMU membership and the monetary dependence on the ECB as the key drivers of this, given that investors assumed equal risk profiles for all countries in the EMU, despite their differing 'fundamentals' (Pragidis, Aielli, Chionis, & Shizas, 2015). In this way, the financial economics literature points to Greece's mismanagement of the financial benefits of EMU membership as an important root cause of the crisis, in addition to a number of other trigger events that eroded confidence in Greek sovereign bonds.

## 4.4. Monetary Economics

The tabulation of primary concepts in the monetary economics literature is shown in Table 9.

**Table 9. Tabulation of primary concepts in the monetary economics literature**

| Primary Concept | Count |
|---|---|
| Collapse of Confidence | 47 |
| High Debt | 34 |
| Lack of Competitiveness | 32 |
| Access to Cheap Debt | 31 |
| Current Account Deficit | 11 |
| Internal Devaluation | 9 |
| Capital Influx | 8 |
| High Wages | 6 |
| Fears of Possible EMU Exit | 6 |
| Failed Austerity | 6 |
| Monetary Dependence | 5 |
| Excessive Private Credit Extension | 4 |
| Poor Governance | 3 |
| Bank Undercapitalisation | 3 |
| Regulatory Burden | 2 |
| Trust | 2 |
| Political Instability | 2 |
| Poor Revenue Collection | 1 |
| Political Opposition to Reform | 1 |
| Low Productivity | 1 |

Again, the dominant primary concepts are similar, but the causal concepts as illustrated below differ again, this time with a greater emphasis on EMU membership and monetary dependence's impact, especially on competitiveness.

The monetary economics conceptual map relays the causal explanation as theoretically outlined in *Section 3.3* and *Figure 8* in the literature review. A collapse of confidence (jointly caused by external shocks and internal problems) and the resultant need for internal devaluation, given Greece's monetary dependence on the European Central Bank and its inability to regain competitiveness through currency devaluation, triggered the crisis.

This is evidenced by the first level of analysis in red suggesting that the crisis was caused by a collapse of confidence in Greek sovereign debt and an internal devaluation.

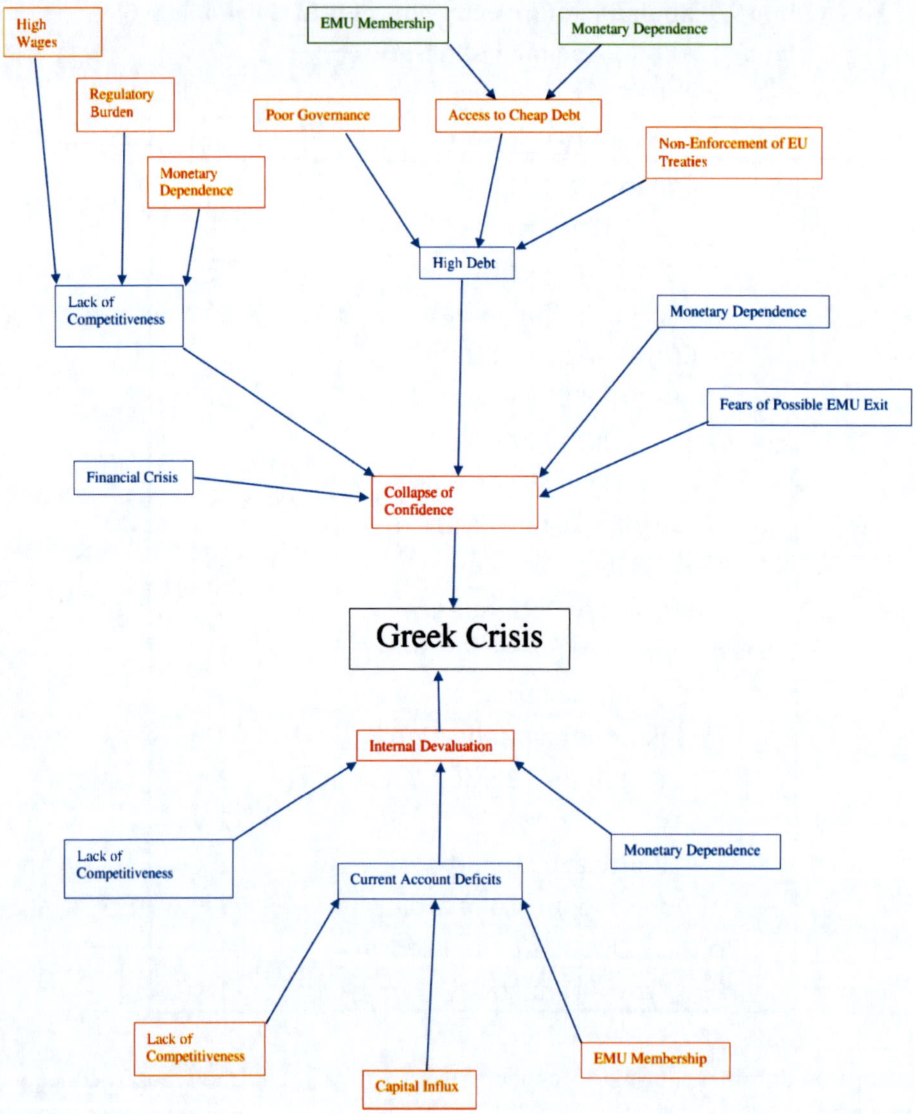


Figure 22. The causes of the Greek crisis – monetary economics.

The next layer of analysis in blue aims to explain why the collapse of confidence and internal devaluation took place. These causal factors are notably much more focused on Greece's monetary regime than the other disciplines, with 'monetary dependence' given Greece's EMU membership featuring prominently in both cases.

The orange layer of analysis explains why current account deficits occurred, why a lack of competitiveness occurred and why the Greek state accumulated so much debt. Again, Greece's EMU membership, and the role of adopting the Euro as currency, features prominently as causal factors in this layer.

Finally, the green layer of analysis explores how Greece was able to access so much debt at such cheap rates in the 2000s, and concludes, similarly to financial economics, that the access to cheap debt was driven by EMU membership which encouraged investors to consider all EMU countries as equally risk-free despite differing economic conditions in the EMU member countries (Gibson, Hall, & Tavlas, 2010).

The monetary economics literature therefore emphasises the effect of EMU membership and the resultant monetary dependence on European Central Bank in driving a lack of competitiveness in Greece, higher current account deficits, access to cheap debt and leading to an eventual forced internal devaluation given that Greece did not have the luxury of regaining competitiveness through currency devaluation.

## 4.5. Economics

The tabulation of primary concepts in the economics literature follows below.

The economics literature again involves similar primary concepts, with the exception that the high current account deficit is more prominent here than in the other disciplines.

The conceptual map for economics follows on the next page.

**Table 10. Tabulation of primary concepts in the economics literature**

| Primary Concept | Count |
|---|---|
| High Debt | 63 |
| Lack of Competitiveness | 49 |
| Collapse in Confidence | 45 |
| Current Account Deficit | 24 |
| Capital Influx | 9 |
| Internal Devaluation | 7 |
| Access to Cheap Debt | 6 |
| High Wages | 6 |
| Poor Revenue Collection | 6 |
| Excessive Private Credit Extension | 4 |
| Political Instability | 2 |
| Monetary Dependence | 2 |
| Pro-Cyclical Fiscal Policy | 2 |
| Regulatory Burden | 2 |
| Failed Austerity Measures | 2 |
| Trust | 2 |
| Fear of Possible EMU Exit | 1 |
| Poor Governance | 1 |
| Large Public Sector | 1 |
| Donwgrades | 1 |
| Bank Undercapitalisation | 1 |

The picture that emerges from the economics literature is quite clear: The crisis was as a result of a collapse of confidence in the Greek state as a debtor, and that collapse of confidence was caused by two sets of factors. Firstly, by the twin unsustainable fiscal and current account deficits (Antzoulatos, 2011; Pappas, 2011) and a number of 'trigger events' such the financial crisis, the downgrades and upward revision of Greek sovereign debt estimates that woke investors up to the dangers of Greece's unsustainable twin deficits (Giordano, Pericoli, & Tommasino, 2013).

This is evidenced by the first layer of analysis in red, which indicates that the collapse of confidence was caused by high government debt, high current account deficits and various trigger events like the upward revision of debt, the downgrades and the global financial crisis.

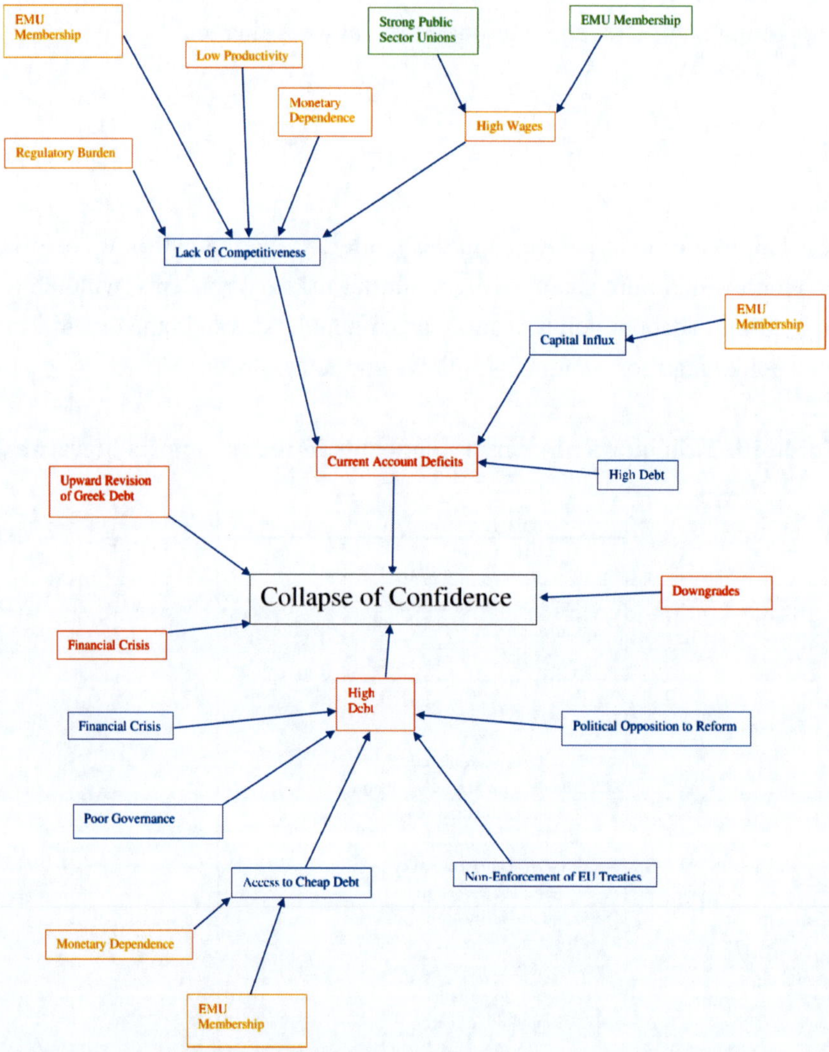


Figure 23. The causes of the Greek crisis – economics.

The second layer of analysis in blue explains why the twin deficits occurred. This layer focuses on the internal and external drivers of the twin deficits.

The orange layer of analysis unpacks this further, with particular focus on Greece's access to cheap debt, and the reduced levels of competitiveness in Greece in the 2000s. This was to be expected given *Section 3* of the literature review.

Finally, the green layer of analysis is unique to the economics literature and aims to explain why Greece experienced rapid wage inflation in the 2000s, pointing primarily to the role of strong public sector unions in demanding above—inflation wage hikes and EMU membership which indirectly increased wages by 'heating up' the economy and increasing inflation (Papanikos, 2014).

Having considered all of the disciplines individually, a number of key patterns have emerged, which informs the formation of the comprehensive conceptual map that encompasses all five of the disciplinary conceptual maps.

Firstly, the broad dominance of 'high debt', 'lack of competitiveness' and 'collapse of confidence' across all the disciplines is striking. Interestingly, one might argue, and in contrast to what has been said earlier, that the literature is already integrated given that all of the literatures refer to these concepts most often. But the key difference lies in the explanations for why these phenomena occurred; explaining why integration of the *causes* of the Greek crisis is indeed still required.

Secondly, the dominance of similar primary concepts across the different literatures quantitatively shows that the earlier assumption that disciplines would be similar-enough to integrate into one conceptual model, holds fast. Integration across the different disciplines can therefore take place to create a comprehensive conceptual model for the causes of the Greek crisis.

Thirdly, there seems to be a rough consensus that the crisis manifested itself as a collapse of confidence in the Greek state's ability to service its debt, with all other causal factors relating to the collapse of confidence or to higher levels of analysis.

## 4.6. Cross-Disciplinary Findings

Having established these preliminary conceptual maps, the analysis continued in order to map the overarching conceptual model including the entire data set. This used the same methods as prescribed by Gläser and Laudel (2013) and Cho and Lee (2014), namely the systematic sorting of columns and the relevant tabulations to determine the most prominent causal concepts for each of the primary concepts.

This process started by sorting the entire data set by concept, and tabulating all the primary concepts and the number of times they were mentioned. This results are shown in Table 11.

As was done for each of the disciplines, each of the primary concepts was then isolated, and their causal concepts tallied to determine the most prominent causal concepts for each of the primary concepts. As an example, the tabulation of causal concepts for 'High Debt' shown in Table 12. All other tabulations can be found in Appendix 4.

Using each of the tabulations of causal concepts for each of the primary concepts, the comprehensive interdisciplinary conceptual map was constructed. It is presented in Figure 24. Note that in order to save space, the heading was excluded from the page.

**Table 11. Tabulation of primary concepts for the entire data set**

| Primary Concept | Count |
|---|---|
| High Debt | 268 |
| Collapse of Confidence | 230 |
| Lack of Competitiveness | 166 |
| Access to Cheap Debt | 59 |
| Current Account Deficits | 47 |
| Political Opposition to Reform | 36 |
| Failed Austerity Measures | 34 |
| Poor Revenue Collection | 32 |
| Poor Governance | 31 |
| Internal Devaluation | 26 |
| Political Instability | 24 |
| Capital Influx | 23 |
| Fear of Possible EMU exit | 18 |
| Large Welfare State | 16 |
| Corruption | 14 |
| Excessive Private Credit Extension | 14 |
| Bank Undercapitalisation | 13 |
| High Wages | 12 |
| Trust | 11 |
| Regulatory Burden | 8 |
| Monetary Depenence | 8 |
| Large Public Sector | 8 |
| Downgrades | 6 |
| Destructive Institutions | 6 |
| Large Informal Sector | 4 |
| Pro-Cyclical Fiscal Policy | 2 |
| Low Productivity | 2 |
| Non-enforcement of EU treaties | 1 |
| Poor Statistical Services | 1 |
| Military Spending | 1 |
| EMU Membership | 1 |

**Table 12. Tabulation of causal concepts for 'High Debt' across the entire data set**

| High Debt Causal Concepts | Count |
|---|---|
| Poor Governance | 84 |
| Large Welfare State | 46 |
| Access to Cheap Debt | 45 |
| Non-Enforcement of EU Treaties | 38 |
| Poor Revenue Collection | 37 |
| Financial Crisis | 36 |
| Large Public Sector | 35 |
| Political Opposition to Reform | 29 |
| Corruption | 28 |
| Destructive Institutions | 22 |
| EMU Membership | 21 |
| Poor Statistical Services | 13 |
| Current Account Deficit | 12 |
| Lack of Competitiveness | 11 |
| Strong Public Sector Unions | 9 |
| Failed Austerity Measures | 7 |
| Regulatory Burden | 6 |
| Pro-Cyclical Fiscal Policy | 6 |
| Military Spending | 5 |
| Bank Undercapitalisation | 5 |
| Capital Influx | 5 |
| Ageing Population | 4 |
| Monetary Dependence | 3 |
| Large Informal Sector | 2 |
| Excessive Private Credit Extension | 2 |
| Capitalism | 1 |
| Upward Revision of Debt | 1 |

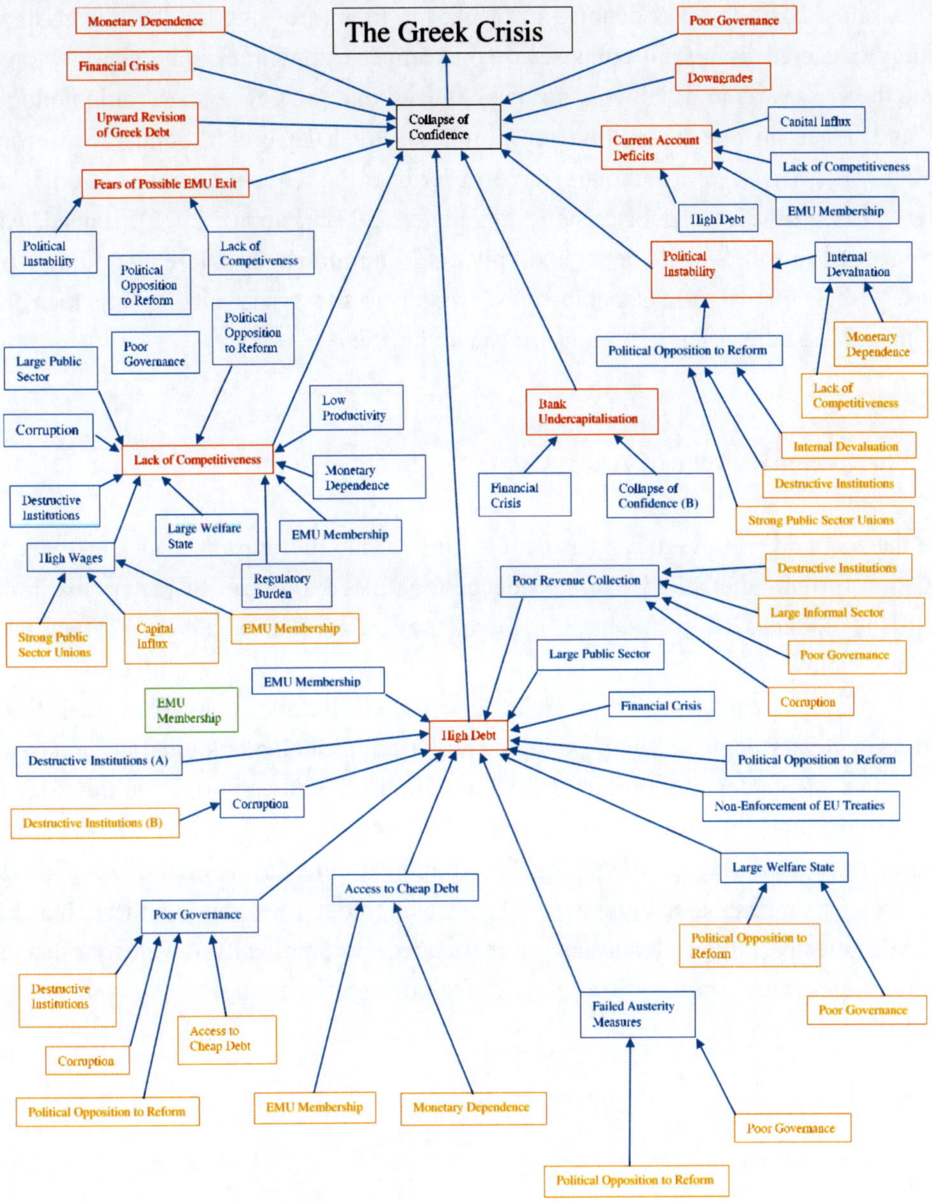


Figure 24. A cross-disciplinary conceptual model for the causes of the Greek crisis.

## 4.7. Analysis and Discussion

This section will conduct a step-wise analysis of the findings from Figure 24 above. As is obvious, the qualitative content analysis process has found a complex web of interrelated concepts that are identified as causal factors in the Greek crisis. The web may appear overly-complicated at first, but by distilling it into the layers of causality in a step-wise manner, the meaning becomes quite clear.

At its most basic level as denoted in black, the literature suggests that the crisis was ultimately triggered by a total collapse of confidence in the Greek state as a debtor. By the time the crisis was in full swing, no one believed that the Greek state could honour its debts, and hence no one was willing to purchase Greek sovereign bonds at affordable rates. This is why several scholars have described the Greek crisis as a crisis that manifested as a sovereign debt crisis (Antzoulatos, 2011; Pappas, 2011). Indeed, when Greece needed to roll over its debts it simply could not do so any more as no one would purchase Greek bonds at reasonable rates, triggering the crisis and forcing the Greek government to seek assistance from European authorities.

### 4.7.1. The Second Layer of Analysis

At the second level of analysis as denoted in red, the literature provides an extensive explanation for why the collapse of confidence took place. It offers 11 factors that jointly affected the collapse of confidence in Greek sovereign bonds. Those 11 factors are represented below:

Each of these causal concepts merit discussion. Below each conceptual link is explained in greater depth, with an example study finding such a link cited in each case.

Monetary dependence (through EMU membership and adoption of the Euro) is argued to have contributed to a collapse of confidence by monetary economists since it eliminated the possibility of devaluing the country's currency to make the high debt burden more manageable. Krugman (2014) for example shows how countries that have given up monetary independence have experienced systematically-lower confidence in their ability to service debts in difficult times than those who did not.

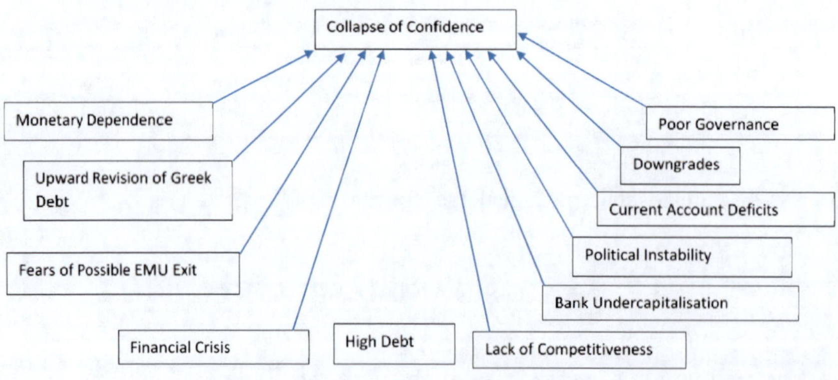


Figure 25. The causes of the collapse of confidence in Greek sovereign bonds.

The upward revision of Greek sovereign debt estimates in October 2009 by the newly-elected government of the time shocked financial markets and contributed to an overall collapse of confidence in the Greek state as a debtor. Gibson, Hall and Tavlas

(2010) for example details how spreads over German sovereign bonds increased dramatically in the aftermath of the upward revision of Greek debt estimates.

Fears of a possible EMU exit contributed to the collapse of confidence in Greek sovereign bonds given that an exit would have been followed by a massive currency devaluation and likely a significant default on Euro-denominated debt; and it would have excluded the possibility of a Eurozone bailout. Dellas and Tavlas (2013) for example explains clearly how the fear of possible exit drove up Greek spreads and undermined confidence in Greek sovereign bonds.

The financial crisis that originated in the United States is identified to be a key trigger moment that made investors more risk averse, and therefore encouraged a re-evaluation of the risks in the Greek situation, prompting a collapse of confidence in Greek sovereign bonds. Giordano, Pericoli and Tommasino (2013) outlines how this could be classified as a case of 'wake-up call' contagion, where the crisis woke investors up to the risks in Greece. The financial crisis also contributed to the problems in Greece by triggering a recession and necessitating increased government expenditure, but this impact is captured elsewhere on the conceptual map.

Excessive amounts of sovereign debt in excess of 100% of GDP has been found to be a key driver of the collapse of confidence in the Greek state's ability to meet its obligations. Investors simply realised that the Greek government had too much debt, and couldn't afford to service all of it anymore. This issue was comprehensively covered in a large number of studies (see Abboushi, 2011; Provopoulos, 2014; Reddy, 2011).

Lack of competitiveness contributed to the collapse of confidence by undermining Greece's ability to grow, and generate new revenues to repay its debts. Investors saw an uncompetitive Greece with a massive debt burden, and calculated that the country would not be able to grow fast enough to meet its debt obligations, resulting in a collapse of confidence in Greek sovereign debt. Reddy (2011) is an example study making this argument.

Bank undercapitalisation contributed to the collapse of confidence in Greek sovereign bonds, given that investors increasingly assumed that Greek banks would require state assistance, placing even more pressure on the Greek budget. As Greek banks came under pressure, investors were also concerned about the general functioning of the Greek financial system, contributing to the collapse in confidence. Eichler (2012) is one scholar who outlines this argument.

Political instability also contributed to the collapse of confidence, as investors feared that riots, strikes and political deadlock in Greece would prevent any meaningful corrective action or reform from taking place, further undermining confidence in Greek sovereign bonds. Kosmidou, Kousendris and Negakis (2015) for example quantitatively show how Greek spreads spiked at moments of intense political instability and uncertainty.

Significant and sustained current account deficits in excess of 10% of GDP eroded confidence in Greek sovereign debt, as it signalled the reliance of the Greek economy on an influx of capital to sustain consumption. This was not deemed to be sustainable, and together with high fiscal deficits, suggested that Greece was operating in an unsustainable manner. Provopoulos (2014) outlines the impact this had on confidence in Greece as part of a discussion on Greece unsustainable 'twin deficits' (fiscal and current account deficits).

Downgrades by credible credit ratings agencies proved to be important trigger moments in the collapse of confidence in Greek sovereign bonds. Zettelmeyer, Trebesch and Gulati (2013) show how spreads on Greek bonds increased dramatically in the days after each of the downgrades in the period between 2009-2012.

Poor governance finally also contributed to the collapse of confidence. Various scholars (see Ali, 2012; Kaplanoglou & Rapanos, 2013) have argued that the manifestly poor governance of successive Greek governments (from both sides of the ideological spectrum) had convinced investors that Greece did not have the leadership and governance capacity to lead itself out of the impasse it found itself in as the global financial crisis struck.

### 4.7.2. The Third Layer of Analysis

The third layer of analysis, denoted in blue in Figure 24, unpacks the causes behind some of the 11 factors that drove the collapse of confidence. This involves the unpacking of 6 of those concepts in greater detail. The third layer of analysis therefore, in effect, consists of 6 sub-models that can be analysed individually.

#### *4.7.2.1. What Caused High Debt Accumulation?*

The process begins with an analysis of why Greece accumulated so much debt.

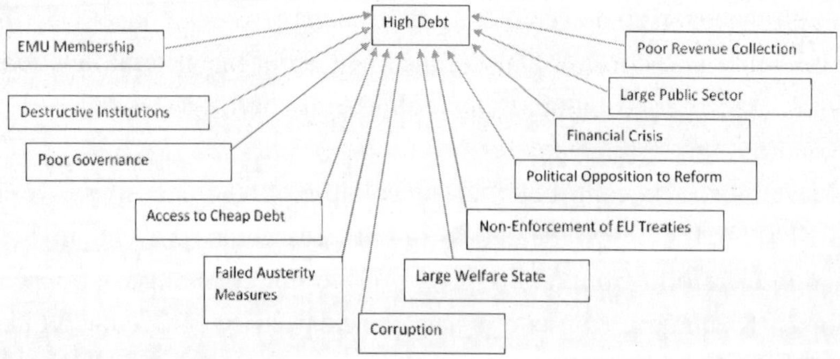


Figure 26. The causes of high debt accumulation for the Greek state.

The literature identifies 12 causal factors in explaining why the Greek state accumulated so much debt (Figure 26).

EMU Membership is identified as a key driver of the increased debt, given that investors were willing to purchase much larger amounts of sovereign debt from EMU members than from European non-EMU members, given the credibility provided by ceding monetary policy control to the (very credible) ECB. This allowed for excessive debt accumulation without investors paying too much attention to Greece's internal problems. Baltas and Chair (2013) make a strong argument along these lines.

Destructive institutions contributed to the accumulation of debt by encouraging high government spending in order to secure political support. This has been widely discussed in the literature as Greek clientilism or political rent-seeking (Sklias & Maris, 2013).

Poor governance contributed to high debt given that successive Greek government adopted overly-expansionary fiscal policies and failed to manage internal statistical services effectively; and failed to exercise effective budgetary management (Featherstone, 2011).

Corruption contributed to high debt by allowing money to 'leak' from the fiscus, causing significant losses for the Greek state and inflating the national debt. Fouskas (2013) is an example study making this argument.

Access to cheap debt is closely linked to the 'EMU membership' causal factor listed above. This concept suggests that high debt occurred because Greek governments could access debt easily and cheaply because of EMU financial integration, encouraging spending and deficits instead of frugality. Arghyrou and Tsoukalas (2010) suggests this is at the root of debt accumulation.

The failed attempts at austerity measures in the latter 2000s when the Greek government realised that it was coming under pressure was also identified as a driver of high debt. These measures needed to be implemented effectively and speedily in order to curb debt levels, but the Greek government failed to do so. Verney and Bosco (2013) is an example study in this regard.

The large welfare state, requiring significant government spending on social assistance programmes such as pensions clearly contributed to high debt levels by requiring enormous government expenditure, especially as the Greek population aged (see Matsaganis & Leventi, 2011).

The non-enforcement of EU treaties helped Greece to accumulate high debt, given that the treaties cap annual deficits at 3% of GDP and total debt to 60% of GDP. If these were enforced, Greece would have had no choice but to contain spending (Robbins, 2015).

Political opposition to reform contributed to debt accumulation by creating political incentives for high expenditure and maintaining the status quo. The internal political climate in Greece clearly made it difficult for Greek governments to tackle the fiscal challenge (Sklias & Maris, 2013).

The global financial crisis caused faster debt accumulation by forcing the economy into recession, increasing the relative size of existing debt in relation to GDP, and by necessitating increased government expenditure to overcome the challenges posed by the global financial crisis (Kouzis, 2011).

The significant size of the public sector, and in particular the public sector wage bill, drove up government expenditure and deficits, contributing to the accumulation of debt (Evangelopoulos, 2012).

Finally, poor revenue collection clearly contributed to high debt levels by lowering the Greek government's revenues and exacerbating deficits (Matsaganis & Leventi, 2011).

### *4.7.2.2. What Caused a Lack of Greek Competitiveness?*

The second major concept that is explained is Greece's lack of competitiveness in the 2000s. This outlined in Figure 27.

The literature identifies 11 prominent causes of Greece's lack of competitiveness, making this another very significant theme across all of the disciplines.

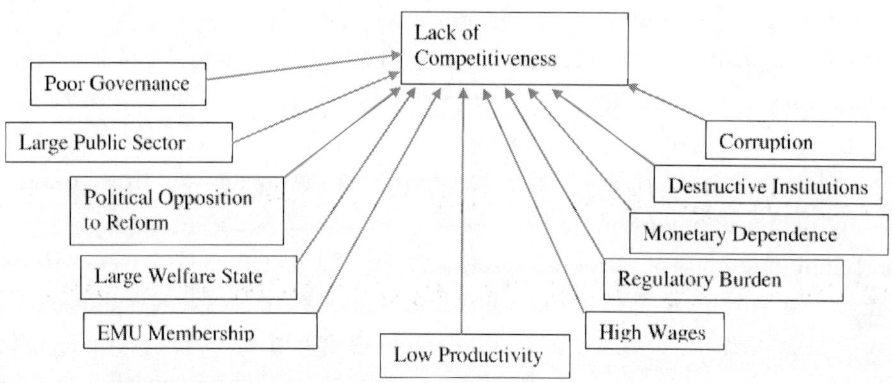


Figure 27. The causes for Greece's lack of competitiveness.

Poor governance is identified as causal factor as Greek governments introduced complex and burdensome regulations, weighing down the competitiveness of Greek firms. Additionally, Greek public policy appeared to fan the flames of rapid wage and price inflation in the 2000s, further undermining the competitiveness of Greek firms (Kretsos & Vogiatzoglou, 2015).

The large public sector in Greece, in particular the presence of Greek state-owned entities in certain industries, crowded out private investment. These state-owned entities often operate under the protection of state-sanctioned monopolies, which drive up prices, reduce efficiency and therefore negatively affects the competitiveness of the Greek economy (Oltheten, Sougiannins, Travlos, & Zarkos, 2013).

Political opposition to reform contributed to the lack of competitiveness, given that reforms aimed at increasing competitiveness and deregulation in certain areas was consistently blocked by powerful interest groups (Vasilopoulou & Halikiopoulou, 2013).

The large welfare state contributed to the lack of competitiveness by requiring significant social security contributions by employers, adding additional layers of expenses for employers (O'Donnel & Tinios, 2003).

EMU membership undermined the domestic competitiveness of Greek firms given that the EMU agreements allowed free flow of goods and services throughout the European economy, placing Greek firms in direct competition with more efficient competitors in 'core' countries like Germany, France and the Netherlands (Oltheten, Sougiannins, Travlos, & Zarkos, 2013).

Comparatively low productivity (vis-à-vis Greece's European competitors) and rapid wage inflation in the 2000s (expressed as 'high wages' in Figure 27) meant that Greek labour cost per unit of output lost became significantly less competitive during the 2000s. Malliaropulos (2010) estimates this eroded as much as 10% of Greek competitiveness.

The excessive regulatory burden in Greece has been extensively outlined by numerous scholars (Antzoulatos, 2011; Krajewska, 2014; Pappas, 2011). In short, Greece had enforced a complex set of regulations on its business sector that were costly and time-consuming to implement. Greek labour regulations, which were especially rigid, contributed especially significantly to eroding the competitiveness of Greek firms.

Monetary dependence eroded competitiveness by introducing the stronger Euro and phasing out the weaker Drachma, eliminating the competitive edge that Greek firms enjoyed by operating in a weaker currency (Arestis & Karakitsos, 2012).

Destructive institutions, such as oligopolistic regulations and other anti-competitive policies, negatively affected efficiency and competitiveness (Sklias & Maris, 2013).

Finally, corruption fostered crony-capitalist relationships between the Greek government and Greek firms, rewarding firms for relationships with government, as opposed to purely rewarding efficiency and delivery. This undermined competitiveness in the general economy (Fouskas, 2013).

#### *4.7.2.3. What Caused High Current Account Deficits?*

The literature provides a more focused explanation of current account deficits, primarily citing only four key causal concepts.

Firstly, the tremendous influx of European capital (especially German capital) into Greece during the 2000s is found to have facilitated the current account deficit. In other words, Greece was consuming more than it was earning, and the difference was made up by an influx of foreign savings (Leao & Palacio-Vera, 2011).

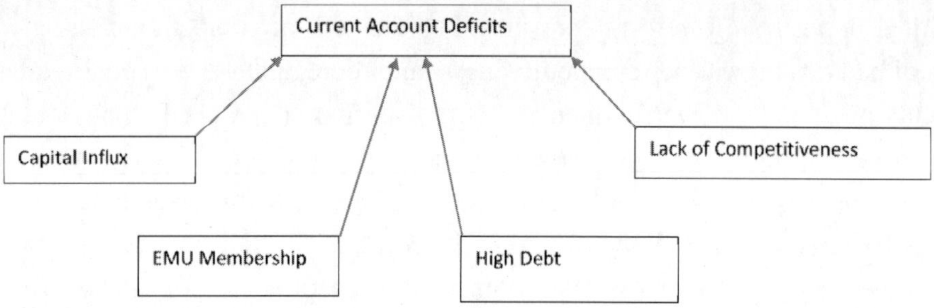


Figure 28. The causes of Greece's high current account deficits.

Secondly, EMU membership created an environment that resulted in current account deficits by easing the flow of capital between countries, and by eroding the competitiveness of Greek firms as explained in the previous section (Leao & Palacio-Vera, 2011).

Thirdly, a number of scholars make the case that the current account deficit was driven primarily by negative private sector saving in the form of high and sustained fiscal deficits (Provopoulos, 2014; Oltheten, Sougiannins, Travlos, & Zarkos, 2013).

Finally, and most prominently throughout the literature, it is argued that the eroding competitiveness of the Greek economy meant that imports became relatively more attractive and Greek exports became less attractive, causing imports to far exceed exports and resulting in a significant current account deficit (Belke & Dreger, 2014; Papanikos, 2014).

#### *4.7.2.4. What Caused the Fears of a Possible EMU Exit by Greece?*

As can be seen, the fears about Greece's possible exit from the EMU are primarily defined around three issues.

Firstly, the political instability during the height of the crisis (including strikes, political disagreements between the major parties and violent riots) raised fears that Greece's political situation was not stable enough to facilitate effective implementation of corrective measures, forcing an exit from the EMU, a significant currency devaluation and a likely debt restructuring (Vasilopoulou & Halikiopoulou, 2013).

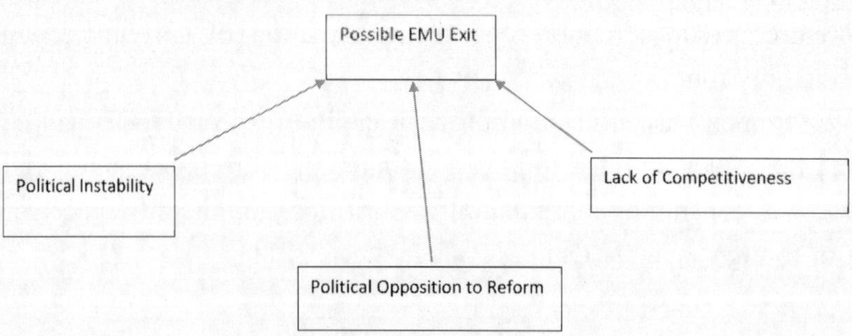


Figure 29. The causes of fears about Greece's possible exit from the EMU.

Secondly, political opposition to reform also ratcheted up fears. It should be noted in Appendix 2 that the difference between 'political opposition to reform' and 'political instability' is subtle, yet quite important. 'Political instability' refers to particular tangible events, such as protests and riots or political clashes in Parliament, whilst 'political opposition to reform' refers to the general political preference in Greece to defend the status quo and avoid austerity and competitiveness-enhancing reforms. Clearly the fear was that Greek political opposition to reform would, in the medium to long run, lead to the election of a government that would exit from the EMU before implementing harsh austerity and competitiveness reforms (Dobrescu & Durach, 2014).

Thirdly, it was feared that Greece's competitiveness deficit with the rest of Europe was so large, that it would require an impossibly-large internal devaluation to rectify. From this perspective, an exit from the EMU and a currency devaluation appeared more likely than staying in the EMU and enforcing a painful internal devaluation (Kasimati & Veraros, 2013).

*4.7.2.5. What Caused Political Instability in Greece?*

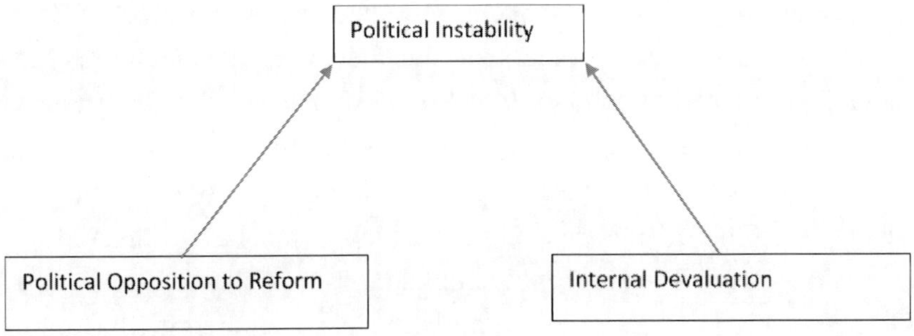


Figure 30. Causes of political instability in Greece.

Two factors were identified as key drivers of political instability.

Firstly, the underlying political opposition to reform throughout the country. This manifested itself in the belief that Greece and ordinary Greeks were being treated unfairly by the European authorities, and resulted in a massive protest movement throughout Greece (Karyotis & Rudig, 2015).

Secondly, the troika-enforced internal devaluation in Greece, which aims to lower wages, lower consumption and dramatically cut social welfare expenditure, has enormous implications for social welfare and quality of life of the Greek people. This has inflamed the political instability and protest movement in the country (Vasilopoulou, Halikiopoulou, & Exadaktylos, 2014).

*4.7.2.6. What Caused Bank Undercapitalisation in Greece?*

The literature also focuses its explanation of bank undercapitalisation around two key causal concepts – the global financial crisis and the collapse of confidence in Greek sovereign bonds.

The global financial crisis affected banks in Greece much like other banks around the world. It significantly devalued the assets on banks' books and compromised some expected cash flows. This placed pressure on Greek banks, causing some to become 'undercapitalised' (Tamakoshi & Hamori, 2014).

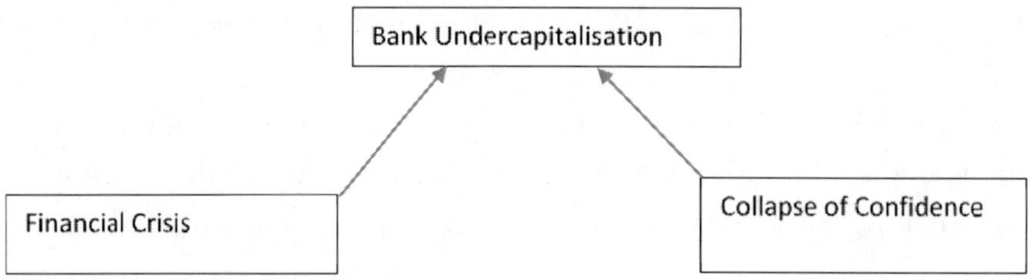


Figure 31. The causes of bank undercapitalisation in Greece.

The collapse of confidence in Greek sovereign bonds also affected Greek banks, given that they were significant holders of that debt. As the possibility of a Greek sovereign default on those bonds rose, Greek banks' balance sheets became more and more risky (Bhanot, Burns, Hunter, & Williams, 2014). This is why the bailout negotiations consistently aimed to insulate Greek and other European banks from Greek sovereign debt, given that a full-scale Greek default could have triggered a European banking crisis with potentially-catastrophic implications (Lekakis & Kousis, 2013).

It should be noted that 'collapse of confidence' has been identified as both an effect of ('Collapse of Confidence (A)' in figure 24) and cause of ('Collapse of Confidence (B)' in Figure 24) bank undercapitalisation. This suggests a mutually-reinforcing negative spiral between the collapse of confidence in Greek sovereign bonds and bank undercapitalisation.

## 4.7.3. The Fourth Layer of Analysis

Having investigated and discussed all of the causal factors identified at the blue level of analysis in Figure 24, we now turn to the next level of analysis, as denoted by the orange concepts in Figure 24.

This level of analysis delves deeper into some of the causal concepts that was discussed in the previous section. It essentially consists of nine substructures. Each is dealt with below.

### 4.7.3.1. What Caused Poor Governance in Greece?

The literature identifies four primary causal concepts behind poor governance in Greece.

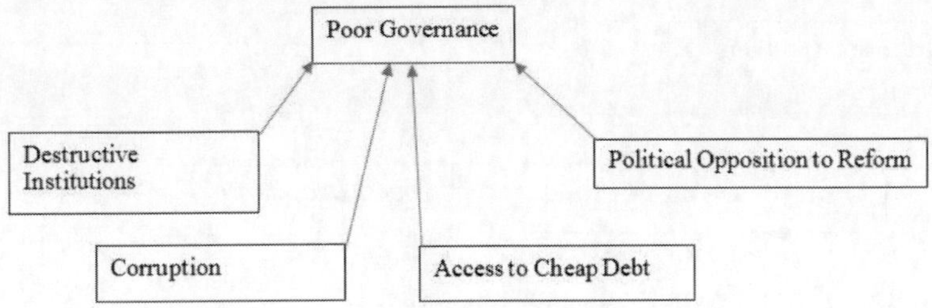


Figure 32. The causes of poor governance in Greece.

Firstly, it identifies destructive institutions as an important factor. These destructive institutions refer to the politicisation of the state apparatus, the politicisation of unions and the rent-seeking interactions between the Greek government and influential interest groups (Zartaloudis, 2014).

Secondly, corruption is identified as a key challenge. In this instance, the literature generally refers to poor financial management and 'fiscal leakage' causing weak implementation capacity, especially in Greek local governments (Dimoulas, 2014).

Thirdly, access to cheap debt is argued to have contributed to poor governance, given that it presented the Greek government with an easy way out of its challenges – it could simply continue spending and racking up deficits at relatively low cost and did not have to confront the governance and competitiveness issues brewing in the country (Arghyrou & Tsoukalas, 2010).

Finally, political opposition to reform continually impeded reform-minded political leaders. Indeed, a number of political leaders from both sides of the ideological divide attempted to address the imbalances in Greece, yet could not muster enough political support to implement effective corrective measures given the political opposition to reform throughout the country.

### 4.7.3.2. What Caused Poor Revenue Collection in Greece?

Again, the literature provides four primary causal factors for poor revenue collection in Greece.

Firstly, destructive institutions are yet again identified as a problem. In this case, it refers to the institutionalised and socially-acceptable practice of widespread tax evasion in Greece. Numerous scholars have indicated how it had become totally justified in Greece to use any and all means possible to pay as little tax as possible. Some have even attempted to develop historical explanations for this, citing the occupation of Greece by the Ottoman Turks between 1453 and 1821, when it was a symbol of national pride for Greeks not to pay taxes to the Ottoman rulers (Kaplanoglou & Rapanos, 2013).

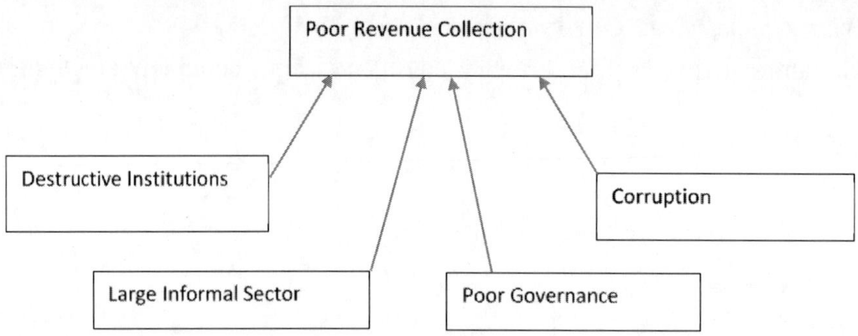


Figure 33. The causes of poor revenue collection in Greece.

Secondly, the large informal sector (the largest in Europe as a percentage of GDP), which is mostly unregulated, unobserved and untaxed, also made revenue collection particularly challenging (Yfantopoulos, 2013).

Thirdly, poor governance and in particular poor statistical services in government made revenue collection and revenue management more challenging for the Greek state (Katsimi & Moutos, 2010).

Finally, corruption played an important part. Some scholars have claimed that corrupt relationships existed between government officials and wealthy Greek interest groups, with government allowing those interest groups to avoid taxation in a corrupt manner (Fouskas, 2013).

#### *4.7.3.3. What Caused Such Strong Political Opposition to Reform?*

The literature has identified three primary causes for intense political opposition to reform.

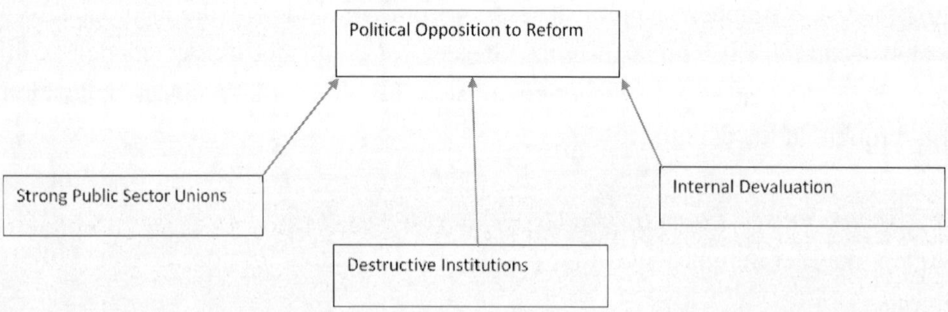


Figure 34. The causes of political opposition to reform in Greece.

Firstly, and by far most prominently, it identifies strong public sector unions as a key cause. The public sector unions in Greece are exceptionally well-organised, are very large, are militant and are well-positioned to disrupt government functioning. They are strongly opposed to austerity and internal devaluation, and have been consider the organisational 'tip of the spear' in managing nation-wide political opposition to reforms.

Numerous scholars have identified the particular strength of public sector unions in terms of numbers and organisation as a key driving force for effective political opposition to reform in Greece (O'Donnel & Tinios, 2003; Karyotis & Rudig, 2015; Theodossopoulos, 2013).

Secondly, destructive institutions are again found to have played a role. The long-established practice of clientelism in Greece, whereby Greek political parties gain support by offering particular benefits to sections of the population or certain interest groups, is judged to have played a role. Scholars argue that it had become the norm that strong interest groups could almost certainly expect to have their demands met by government. As such, these interest groups believed that painful reforms could and should be stopped, even if the economic calculus meant that the status quo was totally unsustainable (Sklias & Maris, 2013).

Thirdly, the enforced internal devaluation in Greece had come at an exceptional social cost, hardening opposition to reform in Greece, and as explained earlier, motivating political instability (Malakos, 2013).

*4.7.3.4. What Caused Greek Wages to Become so High in the 2000s?*

The literature identifies three key factors that drove high Greek wage inflation in the 2000s.

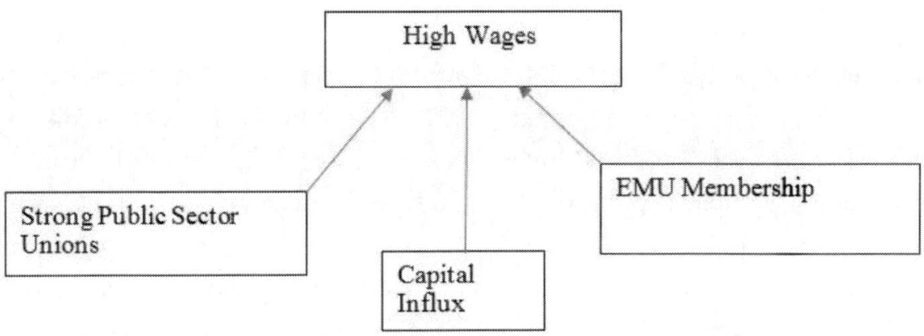


Figure 35. The causes of high wage inflation in Greece.

Firstly, strong public sector unions were able to demand wage increases far in excess of the inflation rate on a number of occasions during the 2000s. And given that Greek public sector jobs paid so well, the Greek private sector had to match or at least come close to these increases to remain attractive to talented employees. This resulted in overall rapid wage inflation throughout the Greek economy (Papanikos, 2014).

Secondly, the capital influx from the rest of Europe initially meant that Greece enjoyed rapid economic growth in the early 2000s, driving up general inflation and wage inflation (De Grauwe, 2011).

Thirdly, EMU membership raised wages rapidly after Greece joined the EMU given that workers received a real gain in the immediate aftermath of the phasing out of Drachma in favour of the Euro (Arghyrou, 2007).

*4.7.3.5. What Caused the Internal Devaluation in Greece?*

The two causes identified through the conceptual analysis must be jointly considered to make sense of. A lack of competitiveness in Greece has required corrective action, either in the form of currency devaluation or internal devaluation; but because of the monetary dependence implied by EMU membership, Greece has no choice but to enforce an internal devaluation (Belke & Dreger, 2014).

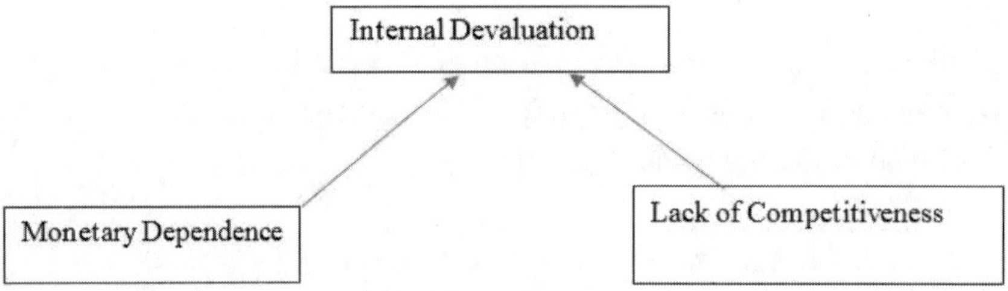


Figure 6. The causes of the internal devaluation in Greece.

*4.7.3.6. Why Did Greece have Access to Cheap Debt for so Long?*

Again, the two causes identified for Greece's access to cheap debt can best be understood jointly. When Greece joined the EMU, it gained enhanced credibility as a debtor, allowing it to access debt at lower rates. This was then sustained because of the credibility brought on by accepting the Euro and the European Central Bank's inflation-controlling monetary policy (Krajewska, 2014), protecting investors from the value of debts being deflated by expansive monetary policy. Of course, and quite interestingly, the very monetary dependence that initially acted as a blessing to lower the cost of Greek debt eventually became a curse when Greece came under pressure as it removed the option of currency devaluation as a possible crisis response mechanism (Krugman, 2014).

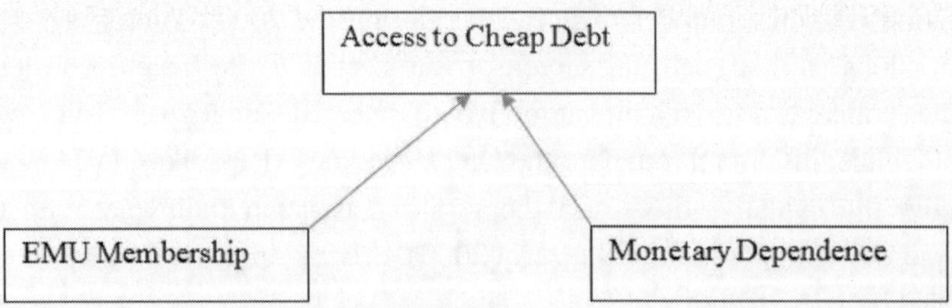


Figure 37. The causes of Greece's access to cheap debt.

*4.7.3.7. Why Did Initial Attempts at Austerity Fail in Greece?*

The initial attempts at austerity in Greece failed to make a significant impact of government debt and deficits, for two reasons.

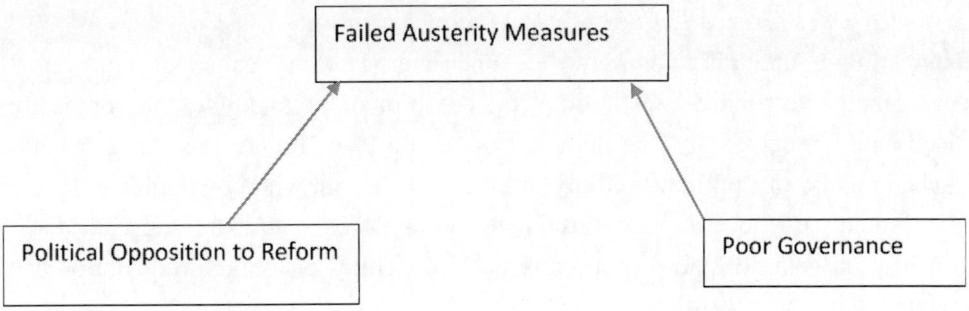


Figure 38. Causes of failed austerity measures in Greece.

Firstly, strong political opposition to reform meant that the austerity measures had little support and were in large part blocked in Parliament and elsewhere by opponents of the austerity measures (Evangelopoulos, 2012).

Secondly, even those measures that were accepted were not effectively implemented given the Greek government's poor governance and poor implementation capacity. Indeed, it became apparent that the austerity measures would struggle to be implemented given poor budgetary management throughout the state and its various entities (Provopoulos, 2014).

*4.7.3.8. Why Did Greece Develop a Large Welfare State?*

Two causal concepts have been identified to explain the formation and sustaining of the large Greek welfare state.

Firstly, and most importantly, the Greek people express clear support for a large welfare state and oppose reforms to make it smaller or less costly. The political gravity in Greece therefore supports the continued existence of a large welfare state in Greece (O'Donnel & Tinios, 2003).

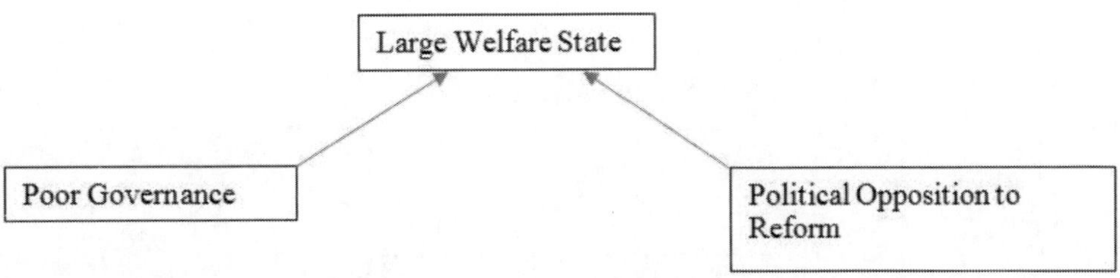


Figure 39. The causes of the large Greek welfare state.

Secondly, poor governance practices meant that the welfare state was constantly expanding, and became ever-more expensive due to the lack of efficiency and the costliness of the public service (Petmesidou, 2012).

*4.7.3.9. Why Does Greece Experience so Much Corruption?*

Interestingly, the literature identifies one overwhelming cause of corruption in Greece: destructive political institutions in the form of how politics has come to be practiced and perceived by the Greek electorate. It is found that there exists an entrenched culture of coalition-building through clientelism, whereby politicians promise certain elements of the electorate certain deliverables. The literature suggests that this kind of institutionalised quid-pro-quo approach to politics encourages corruption across the country (Dimoulas, 2014).

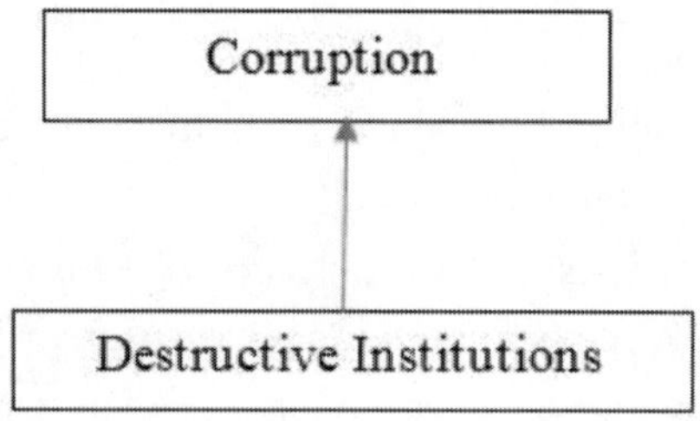


Figure 40. The cause of corruption in Greece.

### 4.7.4. The Fifth Layer of Analysis

The fifth layer of analysis, as depicted in **green** in Figure 24, contains only one conceptual relationship:

This layer merely explains the intense capital influx into Greece in the 2000s, showing that the influx was primarily caused by EMU membership which resulted in higher levels of financial integration with the rest of Europe, inviting capital to flow into Greece en masse (Palaiodimos & Tzavalis, 2015).

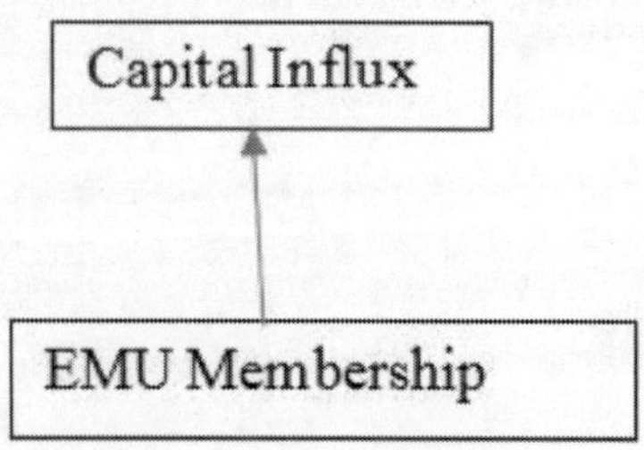


Figure 41. The cause of the Greek capital influx in the 2000s.

It should be noted that the fact that this is the only causal chain to reach a fifth layer of analysis is not particularly significant, and resulted coincidentally from the decision about where to unpack which concepts in the conceptual map.

Section 7 of the findings has therefore laid out the comprehensive interdisciplinary conceptual map, and has endeavoured to firstly explain each causal link substantively and secondly to provide references of example studies making such causal arguments in each case. As discussed before, each causal link is supported quantitatively by the tabulations emanating from the multidimensional conceptual matrix. The tabulations can be found in Appendix 4.

Having established the cross-disciplinary conceptual map, the study can now proceed to utilise the map to answer the research questions that were posed at the outset, noting one important caveat – Up until now, no formal analysis has been conducted to determine the dominant literature for each concept. The altered map on the next page includes this feature, this time with the different colours depicting the dominant literature for each concept. The colour key is as follows: Political science (red), public administration (blue), financial economics (green), monetary economics (purple) and *economics (orange).* Note once again that the figure caption has been excluded from the page to save space. The figure is captioned

A few methodological notes should be made at this point. Firstly, the dominant discipline for each concept was calculated by sorting the multidimensional conceptual matrix by the primary concept column, isolating each primary concept and tabulating the disciplines of each primary concept to calculate the number of times each discipline attempted to give a causal explanation for every primary concept. The results of these tabulations, and therefore the supporting evidence for the choice of dominant literature in each case above, can be found in Appendix 5.

But secondly, this process could not be conducted for all concepts since not all concepts featured as primary concepts, or only featured as primary concepts a few times. These included: 'EMU Membership,' 'Financial Crisis,' 'Strong Public Sector Unions,' 'Non-Enforcement of EU Treaties' and 'low productivity.' This is to be expected. These concepts were never themselves explained by the surveyed literature but were only used as causal concepts to explain other primary concepts. This therefore required an alternative approach to determine the dominant discipline for each of these five concepts.

The approach was as follows: In each case, the multidimensional conceptual matrix was sorted by the column that represented each concept. The rows that utilised the relevant causal concept were then isolated, and the disciplines for each row was tabulated to determine the dominant discipline in *using the concept in a causal manner*. The results of these tabulations can be found for each of these concepts in a separate section in Appendix 5.

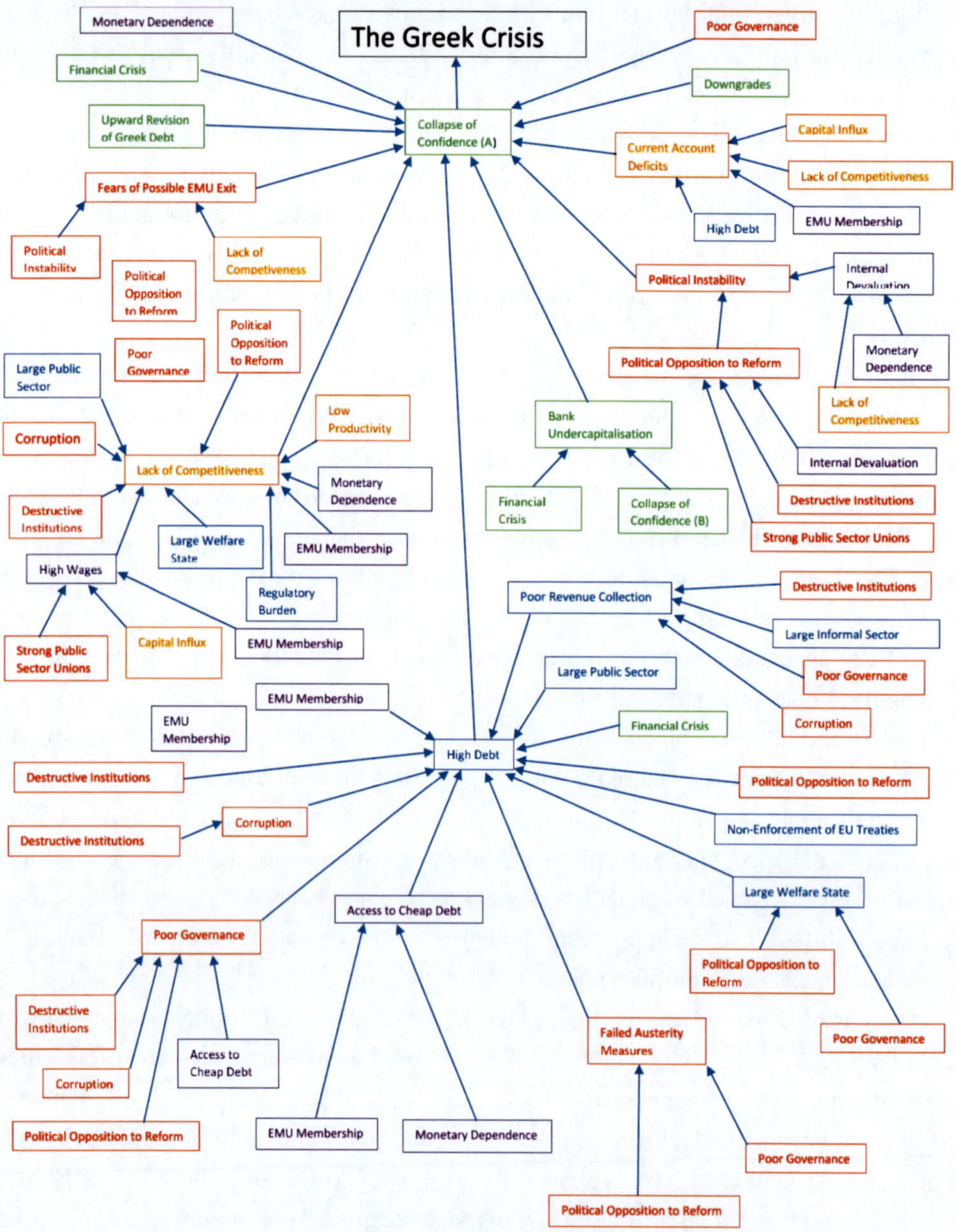


Figure 42. Dominant disciplines for the conceptual causes of the Greek crisis.

## 4.8. ANSWERING THE RESEARCH QUESTIONS

Even though the process from sections 1-7 above has indirectly answered the research questions, this section will provide explicit answers based on the final findings as represented in Figure 42.

### 4.8.1. Question 1 - Literature Review of the Greek Crisis

- What literature is available on the Greek crisis?
- What academic discipline does each study fall under?
- What literature pertaining to the Greek crisis will be helpful to this study, and what inclusion criteria should be utilised?

A plethora of literature was found on the available databases. These studies generally fell into one of five disciplines: Public Administration, Political Science, Economics, Monetary Economics and Financial Economics. One hundred of the most relevant studies have been included in this study, using the inclusion criteria as outlined in *Section 3.1 of the methodology* chapter. The final 100 studies selected for inclusion have been listed per discipline in Appendix 1.

### 4.8.2. Question 2 - Qualitative Content Analysis

- What are the dominant concepts identified in the qualitative content analysis process?
- What are the relationships between those concepts?
- What degree of conceptual overlap exists between the different disciplines?

**Table 13. The top 10 most prevalent primary concepts**

| Primary Concept | Count |
|---|---|
| High Debt | 268 |
| Collapse of Confidence | 230 |
| Lack of Competitiveness | 166 |
| Access to Cheap Debt | 59 |
| Current Account Deficits | 47 |
| Political Opposition to Reform | 36 |
| Failed Austerity Measures | 34 |
| Poor Revenue Collection | 32 |
| Poor Governance | 31 |
| Internal Devaluation | 26 |

The qualitative content analysis process yielded 38 prevalent concepts, which can be found in Appendix 2. Of these 38, it was found that the literature focused most prominently on trying to explain to following 'top 10' concepts:

A significant degree of conceptual overlap was found. The relationships between these concepts and the rest of the most relevant concepts out of the total pool of 38 have been mapped out in Figures 24 and 42.

### 4.8.3. Question 3 - Conceptual Model of the Causes of the Greek Crisis

- How can a conceptual model be constructed to summarise and integrate the content of the literature?

It was determined that a conceptual model could best be constructed by utilising qualitative content analysis and a multidimensional conceptual matrix to establish relationships between the various concepts identified in the literature. This process has ultimately resulted in the construction of Figures 24 and 42.

### 4.8.4. Question 4 - Greek Politics

- What role did public opinion play in the build-up to the crisis?
- What role did public opinions play during the crisis?
- Are there particular political institutions that contributed to the crisis?

Public opinion played a central role in the build-up to the crisis and during the crisis. In particular, the strong political opposition to reform in Greece was a central causal factor in the crisis. By examining the conceptual model in Figure 42, we can conclude that political opposition to reform played the following roles before and during the crisis (listed in no particular order):

1) Political opposition to reform contributed to the political instability in Greece since the crisis broke out in 2009. This political instability in turn played a crucial role in the collapse of confidence in the Greek state as a debtor.
2) The strength of the political opposition to reform created fears amongst investors that the Greek government may be forced to leave the EMU instead of implementing a harsh internal devaluation, in turn also helping to facilitate the collapse of confidence in the Greek state as a debtor.
3) Political opposition blocked reforms aimed at increasing competitiveness in Greece in the 2000s – such as deregulation of the labour market and reforms aimed at increasing competition in certain industries. This contributed to the deterioration of Greek competitiveness in the 2000s.
4) Political opposition also blocked various macro-economic and fiscal reforms attempted in the 2000s. These reforms may have been able to rescue Greece from its high debt-accumulation path. Political opposition to reform therefore

negatively affected governance, by incentivising poor governance aimed at short term political 'wins.'

5) Political preferences in Greece also created strong political incentives for higher spending and debt accumulation, and disincentives for reforms to cut spending, thereby contributing to an environment conducive to excessive government spending.
6) Political preferences also motivated successive Greek governments to maintain and expand the Greek welfare state, contributing to the state's debt burden.
7) Several attempts at austerity measures before the crisis were blocked because of strong political opposition to reform, scuppering potentially-crisis averting reforms.
8) The literature also details a number of political institutions that played a significant role in the crisis. The conceptual mapping process indicated that the destructive institutions often played a 'root cause' role in the crisis. The conceptual map indicates that destructive institutions had the following impacts:
9) A number of destructive institutions, such as oligopolistic regulations and job reservations were in place in part due to rent-seeking and clientelistic interactions between political parties and interest groups. This undermined the competitiveness of the Greek economy.
10) These same clientelistic institutions contributed to high debt, as political parties were incentivised to spend lavishly in government in an attempt to win the support of certain key constituencies.
11) Destructive political institutions also created an environment conducive to corruption, given the quid-pro-quo approach to politics.
12) The destructive political institutions motivated poor policy choices to benefit key interest groups, thereby contributing to the environment of poor governance.
13) Revenue collection was undermined by institutionalised tax avoidance, whereby many Greeks found it acceptable to engage in tax avoidance practices.
14) Political opposition to reform was also amplified by destructive political institutions, given that key interest groups believed they could have their demands met, even if those demands were not realistic in the economic conditions of the crisis period.

### 4.8.5. Question 5 - Greek Debt

- How much debt did Greece accumulate before the crisis?
- Why did the market provide Greece with so much debt for so long?
- Why did the Greek government accumulate so much debt?

The Greek government accumulated a large and unsustainable amount of debt, well in excess of 100% of GDP. The conceptual map provides the reasons as to why the market granted Greece access to cheap debt for so long under the 'access to cheap debt' concept. We can observe that two reasons are identified as the primary reasons:

Firstly, the Greek state became a much more credible debtor after joining the EMU in 2001. Investors appear to have considered all EMU members' sovereign equally-risk free in the period leading up to the crisis, implying that country specific risks were ignored and that an implicit belief existed that the Greek government would be bailed out if it ever did encounter fiscal difficulties.

Secondly, and closely related to the first point, this credibility was amplified by the fact that Greece had committed itself to the monetary policy of the European Central Bank and had thus given up monetary independence, meaning that investors could purchase Euro-denominated Greek debt without the risk of having the value of the bonds eroded by high inflation.

The conceptual map provides ample reasons for why Greece accumulated so much debt. In total, 12 reasons are provided. Briefly, those are:

1) Greece's EMU membership, given that it provided Greece with access to much more debt at cheap rates.
2) Destructive institutions that encourage political parties to spend heavily in government to secure political support.
3) Corruption, which resulted in fiscal losses and that thus amplified deficits.
4) Poor governance, which resulted in excessive spending and poor policy choices.
5) Access to an unprecedented amount of cheap debt, which incentivised increased expenditure instead of politically-unpopular, yet necessary, reforms.
6) Failed attempts at austerity, which did very little to stop excessive debt accumulation.
7) The large welfare state, which required enormous government spending to maintain.
8) The non-enforcement of EU treaties, which allowed Greece to freely maintain annual deficits far in excess of the SGP's 3% limit or to accumulate much more debt than the SGP's 60% debt to GDP limit.
9) Political opposition to reform, which blocked attempts at reducing expenditures and improving competitiveness in the 2000s.
10) The global financial crisis, which drove Greece into recession and which necessitated increased government spending, drove up Greek debt even faster than before 2007.
11) The large public sector, which employed a very large number of people at a significant premium. The public sector wage bill was government's single biggest budget line item.

12) Poor revenue collection, which meant that a large portion of taxes went uncollected, reducing the Greek government's revenues and inflating deficits.

### 4.8.6. Question 6 - Greece and the Global Financial Markets

- Why did the global financial markets lose faith in Greek sovereign bonds?
- What internal and external shocks affected market confidence in Greece?

The conceptual map in Figure 42 identifies the reasons as to why the global financial markets lost faith in Greek sovereign bonds under the 'collapse of confidence' concept. It identifies 11 causes for this:

1) The monetary dependence on the European Central Bank, which turned into a liability once the markets turned on Greece, given that it could not restore competitiveness by devaluing its currency.
2) The global financial crisis, which made investors more risk-averse and therefore more responsive to the country-specific risks in the Eurozone.
3) The upward revision of Greek debt estimates in November 2009, which undermined confidence in the Greek state.
4) The possibility of an EMU exit, given that it may have caused a significant Greek default.
5) The lack of competitiveness of the Greek economy, which suggested to investors that the Greek economy may struggle to grow fast enough to sustain its high debt levels.
6) The very high debt to GDP level, which became increasingly unsustainable in the Greek situation. The country simply had too much debt.
7) The uncercapitalisation of Greek banks, which raised the possibility of an expensive bank bailout and/or potential collapse of the Greek financial system.
8) Political instability, which threatened to make the country ungovernable to the extent that corrective actions could not be implemented in the wake of the crisis.
9) The unsustainable current account deficit, which suggested to investors that Greece was highly dependent on foreign capital to sustain itself.
10) The downgrades by credible ratings agencies, which alerted investors to the fact that Greek sovereign bonds became an increasingly-risky investment.
11) Poor governance, which raised doubts in the minds of investors about the ability of the Greek leadership to effectively lead the country out of its challenging position.

The key shocks feature within this list. The 'internal' shocks are: (1) The upward revision of Greek debt in November 2009, (2) The emerging risk of bank undercapitalisation and (3) The political instability that occurred with the evolution of the national anti-austerity protest movement. The 'external' shocks are: (1) The global financial crisis, which originated in the United States in 2007 and (2) The downgrades by credit ratings agencies. The other causal factors have not been judged as shocks as they have rather developed gradually over time.

### 4.8.7. Question 7 - Greece and the Eurozone

- Did Eurozone membership help or hinder Greece in the build-up to and during the crisis?

The conceptual map suggests that EMU membership played a very significant role in the crisis, identifying at least 6 key implications of EMU membership. Those are:

1) EMU membership contributed to a lack of competiveness by promoting the free flow of goods and services throughout the Eurozone, placing Greek firms under renewed competitive strain from external competitors.
2) EMU membership contributed to excessive wage inflation by providing workers with real gains in the transfer from the Drachma to the Euro.
3) EMU membership enabled a significant capital influx into Greece due to the heightened degree of financial integration with Europe, resulting in rapid economic growth but also in high wage and price inflation, further eroding competitiveness.
4) EMU membership contributed to Greece's high debts, by enabling Greece to gain more access to debt at reasonable rates.
5) EMU membership allowed Greece to access debt cheaply, with investors treating all EMU member countries' sovereign bonds similarly despite country-specific differences in the period before the crisis.
6) EMU membership helped to create an environment where large and sustained current account deficits was possible (for a period) by facilitating the flow of capital between European countries and by eroding Greek competitiveness.

It therefore appears that Eurozone membership provided Greece with significant savings on its sovereign debt and provided significant growth opportunities given the influx of capital into Greece in the years after EMU membership. These were positive factors, but were badly managed by the Greek government who continued to spend aggressively in a pro-cyclical manner during this period. EMU membership in itself was thus a boon to Greece in the 2000s; but Greece's bad management of the benefits of EMU membership set the scene for the crisis.

Finally when the global financial crisis occurred and the Greek crisis began, EMU membership was a definite hindrance as indicated by two important causal implications of monetary dependence: Firstly, EMU membership (expressed as monetary dependence in this case) contributed to the collapse of confidence in Greek sovereign bonds by eliminating the possibility of monetary flexibility to soften the blow of the various other issues affecting the country. And secondly, EMU membership forced an internal devaluation to address the country's internal competitiveness problems given that currency devaluation was not an option as an EMU member.

## 4.9. Research Criteria and Limitations

Good qualitative research needs to explicitly show validity, reliability, transferability, confirmability, authenticity and dependability (Weber, 1990). This section will therefore show how the analysis process and findings meets these criteria.

### 4.9.1. Validity

Leacock, Warrican and Rose (2009) and Baskarada (2014) describe validity as the existence of appropriate evidence to justify the outcome of the study. They furthermore differentiate between two types of validity, namely internal and external validity. Internal validity essentially requires the study to have sufficient proof for its findings (Erlandson, Harris, Skipper, & Allen, 1993). The study has produced extensive conceptual maps based on the outcomes of the qualitative content analysis process. Internal validity has been insured given that all conceptual relationships are supported by the quantitative data presented in appendices 4 and 5. Such quantitative support for conceptual relationships is sufficient in cases where the coding and analysis was conducted by one individual (Oleinik, Popova, Kirdina, & Shatalova, 2014). The only potential question around validity in this case is the choice of 'cut off point' for inclusion in the conceptual map. As discussed before, a number of concepts were not included in the eventual conceptual maps given that they did not feature very prominently. The literature is not prescriptive on how such a choice for inclusion is to be made (i.e., what level of prominence must be reached before inclusion can occur), and relies on the insights of the researcher to make the decision. There is thus no way to conclusively show validity of inclusion choices, with the exception that the inclusion rule (only the most prominent causal and primary concepts to be included) was applied consistently.

External validity requires triangulation of results through some external source of information on the same subject matter (Erlandson, Harris, Skipper, & Allen, 1993; Shapiro & Markoff, 1997). This is more challenging, given that there is little other work that similarly synthesises content from different perspectives on the Greek crisis. Cho and Lee (2014) and Baskarada (2014) proposes that expert interviews or academic sources can be useful sources of triangulation. The study therefore triangulated relationships in the conceptual map by citing an example study which found the same relationship for each conceptual relationship identified. This was outlined in Sections *7.1 to 7.4* above. It should be noted that although each relationship has been cited in the literature before, relationships have not as yet been presented as comprehensively and in such a cross-disciplinary manner before.

### 4.9.2. Reliability

Weber (1990) and Baskarada (2014) identifies reliability – essentially whether the results of the study can be trusted – as a key concern for qualitative content analysis. Baskarada (2014) and Oleinik, Popova, Kirdina and Shatalova (2014) elaborate that reliable studies would be reproduced if another academic performed the same analysis using the same data. Unfortunately, Weber (1990) and Cho and Lee (2014) suggest that the best way to ensure a high level of reliability in qualitative content analysis is to have the content analysis process be conducted concurrently and separately by at least two researchers, but preferably by even more researchers. In cases where two or more researchers developed and applied concepts separately and concurrently, the reliability of the content analysis process can be quantitatively confirmed with measures of correlation such as Krippendorf's $\alpha$ (Hayes & Krippendorf, 2007) or Scott's $\pi$ (Scott, 1955). Unfortunately, in this study concurrent content analysis by numerous researchers was not feasible. Weber (1990) and Baskarada (2014) suggest that developing thorough recording criteria for each concept is an alternative method to ensuring reliability in cases where concurrent content analysis is not an option. This approach was thus followed, and the recording criteria have been laid out in Appendix 2.

### 4.9.3. Confirmability

Confirmability concerns are very similar to concerns around the external validity of the study (Leacock, Warrican, & Rose, 2009). Shenton (2004) and Steinberg (2004) defines confirmability as the ability to prove that the research was not the outcome of the researcher's own predispositions. Confirmability in this case is therefore shown by citing example studies that find similar conceptual relationships for each of the conceptual relationships that was depicted on Figures 24 and 42. This represents both triangulation and proof that research outcomes are not the result of predispositions, given that the findings are supported by independent research. Houghton, Casey, Shaw and Murphy (2013) indicate that confirmability in qualitative research can be further strengthened by leaving an 'audit trail' of research activities. This has clearly also been done, given that all extracted content, all data in the form of the multidimensional conceptual matrix and all tabulations have been attached in Appendices 3 to 5.

### 4.9.4. Transferability

Transferability requires the researcher to provide sufficient detail about research methodology and the context of the research (Shenton, 2004). Sufficient detail in this case is judged as the amount of detail someone else would need to decide whether the findings of the study are applicable to other settings. Houghton, Casey, Shaw and Murphy (2013) and Shenton (2004) suggest that transferability is best ensured by providing extensive descriptions about the research context and methodology. Steinberg (2004) suggests that transferability requires the researcher to be precise and detailed about when and where the research outcomes do apply.

This study has ensured transferability in that detailed descriptions are provided of the context and the methodology utilised, in line with Shenton (2004) and Houghton, Casey, Shaw and Murphy's (2013) recommendations.

But the purpose of the study is not to create generally-applicable theory, but rather to provide a descriptive conceptual model of a single phenomenon. Transferability as Steinberg (2004) proposes is therefore not of paramount importance in this study. There are however some broad insights that may be developed from the conceptual model. These insights, and their transferability, will be discussed in the conclusion.

### 4.9.5. Dependability

Dependability refers to the appropriateness and trustworthiness of the research process (Cho & Lee, 2014). Houghton, Casey, Shaw and Murphy (2013), Cho and Lee (2014) and Lincoln and Guba (1985) all suggest that dependability can be improved by keeping an audit trail of all methodological actions and by presenting representative quotations for application of concepts. The audit trail has been presented in Appendices 3 to 5; and an example application of a concept to an extract has been included in the methodology section. Shenton (2004) suggests that it is very difficult to establish true dependability for qualitative content analysis, given the subjective nature of the research process. As a minimum, Shenton recommends that scholars should at least attempt to enable future scholars to repeat the study. It is judged that the methodological and analysis process has been explained in enough detail to enable such a future reproduction of the study.

### 4.9.6. Authenticity

Authenticity refers to the fair and honest expression of all differences of opinion in the research (Morrow, 2005; Shannon & Hambacher, 2014). This is particularly important when conducting qualitative research with a variety of data inputs. In the case of conducting interview-based research this would require doing interviews with people who may have differences of opinion on particular subject matter (Shenton, 2004). In the case of content analysis, authenticity requires text sources from multiple perspectives to be included if multiple perspective do indeed exist on the topic being researched (Cho & Lee, 2014). This study has endeavoured to ensure authenticity in two ways: Firstly, it has included studies from a variety of disciplines, each offering slightly different perspectives on the causes of the Greek crisis. Secondly, and in the cases where differences of opinion existed within disciplines, studies from all sides were included. This was particularly pertinent in the case of the political science literature, where there appears to be significant differences of opinion between leftist and more mainstream scholars.

### 4.9.7. Limitations

The limitations of the study must also be considered. Three important limitations have been self-imposed. Firstly, by adopting a purely qualitative content analytical approach, the study has been limited to the summation and integration existing knowledge.

Secondly, the crisis has been limited to the *causes* of the crisis. Indeed, as the crisis has unfolded a growing literature on the *effects* of the crisis, and in particular the social effects of the crisis, has emerged. The line between the literature on the *causes* of the crisis and the *effects* of the crisis is often a fine one; but in order to keep the complexity and variety of concepts in the study manageable, it was decided to limit the study to the causes of the crisis.

Thirdly, the particular methodological and analysis approach was exceptionally effective at extracting concepts and confirming the links between concepts in a systematic manner with quantitative support for findings (see the tabulations in Appendix 4). This was a particular strength of the process. The approach has a weakness though: It emphasises majority opinion and marginalises minority opinions (i.e., only the most frequently-mentioned causal relationships are depicted in Figures 24 and 42, with the less-frequent ones being discarded). Crucially, the study is therefore limited to constructing a conceptual map of the most *prevalently-identified* causes of the Greek crisis; and not necessarily of all identified causes of the Greek crisis, given that the minority opinions were not included. This is an important limitation to take into account when interpreting the findings. It should be noted that this did not undermine the cross-disciplinary nature of the study, given that each discipline was represented by an equal number of studies.

## 4.10. Emergent Questions

Finally, a number of questions other than the formally-posed research questions emerged as the analysis was conducted. Given the functionality of the multidimensional conceptual matrix, a number of other questions could be investigated.

Firstly, the matrix could be sorted by year to determine if there were significant differences of opinion between the various years within which the largest concentrations of studies occurred. Most studies were conducted in the aftermath of the crisis in the period 2010-2015. The multidimensional conceptual matrix was therefore sorted by year and the primary concepts for each year between 2010 and 2015 were tallied and tabulated. These tabulations can be seen in Appendix 6. The results indicate that the literature is strikingly consistent over the 6 year period and focuses predominantly, in each year, on why Greece accumulated high debt, why a collapse of confidence in Greek sovereign bonds took place and why and Greece lost international competitiveness. The literature's focus therefore did not shift over the six years as the crisis unfolded.

Secondly, the various disciplines' conceptual maps could be compared to see how the disciplines varied in their explanations of certain phenomena or in their use of causal concepts. One interesting consideration is to ask how the disciplines vary in their use of political issues as a key causal element in the crisis. The public administration literature and the political science literature that was surveyed clearly place the political context at the heart of the crisis, citing it as a major contributing factor to the accumulation of debt, the collapse of confidence in Greece, the lack of competitiveness in the country and the perpetuation of poor governance. Interestingly, monetary economics and financial economics places almost no emphasis on political factors, as can be seen in Figures 21 and 22. Finally, economics appears to balance the two perspectives by including some reference to political issues in the lack of competitiveness in Greece and the accumulation of high public debt.

Thirdly, the multidimensional conceptual matrix can be sorted by causal concept to determine what the dominant outcomes are that each causal concept are 'responsible for'. As an example, the multidimensional conceptual matrix was sorted by the 'high debt' causal concept. It emerged that high debt was used as a causal concept on 134 occasions.

These 134 rows in the matrix were then isolated and sorted by primary concept. The primary concepts were then tallied and tabulated, resulting in Table 14.

The table shows, overwhelmingly, that high debt was most often identified as a cause of the collapse of confidence in Greek sovereign bonds. The role of the 'high debt' concept in the study is therefore mostly associated with precipitating the collapse of confidence, and to a much lesser extent with contributing to current account deficits, given that some scholars have argued (Polito & Wickens, 2014; Dellas & Tavlas, 2013) that negative public sector saving contributed heavily towards the current account deficits in the 2000s.

This process could be repeated for all 38 causal concepts in the multidimensional conceptual matrix, but it was judged that the conceptual maps in Figures 24 and 42 already depict the most significant causal relationships.

**Table 14. The outcomes of high debt**

| High Debt (as causal concept) | Count |
|---|---|
| Collapse of Confidence | 102 |
| Current Account Deficit | 8 |
| Downgrades | 4 |
| Lack of Competitiveness | 4 |
| Internal Devaluation | 3 |
| Fears of Possible EMU Exit | 3 |
| Bank Undercapitalisation | 2 |
| Capital Influx | 2 |
| Failed Austerity | 2 |
| Political Instrability | 2 |
| Destructive Institutions | 1 |
| Political Opposition to Reform | 1 |

*Chapter 5*

# RESEARCH CONCLUSIONS

The introduction laid out how the literature on the Greek crisis was predominantly spread over five disciplines: political science, public administration, financial economics, economics and monetary economics. It was furthermore indicated that the research across the five disciplines gave unique and differing perspectives on the crisis.

These differing perspectives have been systematically laid out in Figures 19-23, showing each of the disciplines using a range of concepts to explain the development of the crisis. The figures show a degree of conceptual overlap, but also some significant differences.

The political science literature was found, as depicted in Figure 19, to assign political factors such as destructive political institutions and political opposition to reform as root causal factors in Greece's rapid debt accumulation and the collapse of confidence in the Greek state's ability to repay its debts.

The public administration literature, as depicted in Figure 20, finds that important governance issues contributed to the occurrence of the crisis. This included poor governance, poor revenue collection, corruption and a large and inefficient public sector that contributed to Greece's high debt and the collapse of confidence in the ability of the Greek state to repay its debts.

The financial economics literature, as depicted in Figure 21, finds a different set of causal factors, pointing to trigger events such as the global financial crisis, the downward revision of Greek debt and downgrades by credit ratings agencies as key moments in the collapse of confidence in the Greek state's ability to repay its debts. Financial economics also identifies the impact on these factors on bank capitalisation as a key driver of the crisis.

The monetary economics literature, as depicted in Figure 22, finds yet another set of causes for the Greek crisis, identifying the crucial role played by Greece's accession to the EMU and its resultant dependence on the monetary policy of the ECB in explaining how and why Greece was able to access so much debt so cheaply, why Greece became less competitive and why Greece was forced into a painful internal devaluation.

The economics literature, as depicted in Figure 23, emphasises the deterioration of competitiveness of the Greek economy, its drivers (high wages, low productivity, regulatory burdens and an influx of capital) and implications (high current account deficits and reliance on foreign investment) in driving the collapse of confidence in the Greek state's ability to repay its debts.

This study's primary contribution is to deepen the understanding of the Greek crisis by providing an integration of these five strands of research into a single, cross-disciplinary conceptual model as depicted in Figures 24 and 42. The cross-disciplinary conceptual model explains the interactions of all identified concepts in precipitating the Greek crisis. It adds value in numerous ways: Firstly, it is simple and easy to understand. It is an effective one-page summation of an enormous body of research across five disciplines that until now has been difficult to grasp in its entirety.

Secondly, it shows, for the first time, how concepts from the five fields *interacted* to cause the crisis. Indeed, the political developments in Greece did not happen in isolation and neither did the economic developments nor the governance challenges. But until now, the research has dealt with each of these factors in isolation. But as is clear from the conceptual map, these issues are intricately interconnected and any research on the Greek crisis must deal with these issues in a holistic manner to come to accurate conclusions; and crucially, to produce recommendations that are rooted in reality.

Thirdly, the model provides unique insights for policy makers to avoid such crises in future, and to assist in appropriate policy development. A range of concepts touch very clearly on public policy issues (governance, corruption, revenue collection, destructive institutions, and regulatory burdens) and can guide the creation of better policies in future. Particularly, policy makers in fixed exchange rate regimes who do not have the luxury of competitiveness-enhancing currency devaluation may be persuaded to proactively defend the competitiveness of their economies (through reducing regulatory burdens, providing appropriate state support and encouraging competition and efficiency) to protect themselves against the need for painful internal devaluations as discussed throughout.

Fourthly, the constructed conceptual model in Figures 24 and 42 provides a complex causal 'chain of events' through which the development of the Greek crisis can be understood, and which is not immediately apparent or sufficiently comprehensive when simply investigating the causes of the crisis within one particular discipline. This study tells the whole story, as opposed to the various pieces of the story each of the disciplines tell in isolation.

Finally, the interpretation of the 'whole story' as presented in Figures 24 and 41 provides valuable new insights. Those are as follows: Clearly, high levels of sovereign debt were central to this story. Although this was known before this study was conducted, the findings suggest that the collective understanding of the drivers of high sovereign debt in Greece must be updated: It is not just a matter of poor spending decisions and unfortunate external events (such as the global financial crisis); but rather the symptom of a very particular enabling environment. Poor spending decisions were prevalent, but the true root causes of the sovereign debt pile-up are the domestic political environment and the access to cheap debt that came with EMU membership after 2001. The political dimension in particular has until now been isolated to discussions in the political science literature and deserves more attention from researchers in the other fields. A generalizable finding here is therefore that analyses of sovereign debt in Greece and other countries must take a very wide range of factors into consideration, and not just simply measures such as debt-to-GDP or announced policies by government. Researchers must ask whether the political environment is enabling enough to allow for announced policies to be implemented (in the Greek case it was not enabling for austerity measures) and whether government has the practical capacity to implement its policies (Greece did not have the capacity to implement effective austerity).

Another important insight is that the crisis was in effect a crisis of confidence in Greece's ability to repay its debts. A large number of factors contributed to the crisis in Greece, but fundamentally, the erosion of confidence in the ability of the Greek state to repay its debts was the core cause of the crisis, as is depicted in Figures 24 and 42. All other concepts identified either directly or indirectly help to explain how and why confidence was lost. The implied key to resolving the crisis is therefore to regain the confidence of the global financial markets by demonstrating fiscal discipline, by showing effective political leadership and returning Greece to the path of international competitiveness. Another important lesson from the study that is critical in the immediate term, is the need for the current SYRIZA government to establish a clear, unambiguous and credible commitment to stay in the EMU. It has been shown that fears about a possible Greek exit from the EMU, or 'Grexit,' are an important driving force behind the reduced confidence in the Greek state as a debtor.

The assessment of findings was furthermore structured in a manner that allowed for the analysis to be layered, in order to reach root causes. This was an important benefit of the chosen methodology, given that until now causes in the literature have been discussed in a haphazard manner without explicit ordering of causality between the various issues at play. This study identified a number of root causes, but the most prevalent and widely dispersed across Figures 24 and 42 was the idea that destructive institutions in Greece were an important root cause of the crisis. This raises a serious concern: The very nature and fabric of Greek politics and Greek society has become riddled with destructive norms that produce suboptimal outcomes. Reforming such institutions (such as the practice of clientelism in Greek politics; or the widespread belief that tax evasion is acceptable) can only be exceptionally challenging given their rootedness in Greek society and history. This will require highly deliberate, intelligent and determined efforts by Greek leaders to challenge these institutions and enact reforms at the institutional level to ensure a more competitive Greece in future.

Perhaps the most fundamental insight that emerges from this study is therefore that far-reaching institutional reforms are necessary for Greece to become a more open, transparent and competitive society. And there is no doubt that such reforms will be enormously-difficult to implement. But the involvement of the 'Troika' in Greece, together with the current dire situation which forces Greece to confront its challenges head-on, may provide Greek leaders with a unique window of opportunity to enact the necessary drastic reforms which have been elusive until now.

In conclusion, it is judged that the study has effectively contributed to deepening the knowledge on the Greek crisis; and has successfully overcome the 'research silos' on the causes of the Greek crisis, offering unique new insights in the process.

## FUTURE RESEARCH DIRECTIONS

The following future research directions are possible given the research conducted in this study:

1) Given that an extensive study of the *causes* of the crisis has been completed using a novel application of the qualitative content analysis on the academic literature on the Greek crisis, a similar study can be conducted on the *implications* of the crisis. Special emphasis could be placed on linking particular implications with particular causes to understand what the full effects of the Greek crisis has been on the Greek economy and the quality of life of the Greek people.
2) Given that this study has presented the findings of the academic literature on the Greek crisis, it may be useful to conduct a similar content analysis of articles in selected publications from the financial press to determine the degree of overlap between the depiction of the crisis in the popular media and the academic literature.
3) This study has developed a cross-disciplinary conceptual model of the causes of the Greek crisis under some significant limitations: Only one individual was involved in the research, with no budget allocated to it. An additional study should be conducted where these limitations are relaxed to enable concurrent extraction of content and conceptual analysis by multiple scholars to improve validity of results. A budget allocation would also allow for a broader range of studies (some of which can only be accesses if paid for) to be accessed.
4) This study has provided a detailed perspective on the causes of the Greek crisis. Similar studies could be conducted on other major sovereign debt crises –

perhaps with a focus on other PIGS (Portugal, Ireland, Greece and Spain) countries – to compare the causes of the crises in the various European countries. Alternatively, further research could be conducted on sovereign debt crises in other parts of the world to determine how the Greek experience compares to others countries' experiences.

5) Given that this study has produced a conceptual model of the causes of the crisis based on qualitative analysis of the academic literature, quantitative researchers may now set out to find quantitative proof to generalise some of the relationships established in Figures 24 and 42 for the Greek case. Studies could focus on the predictive power of certain destructive political institutions in determining whether financial or sovereign debt crises occur in certain countries. Similarly, the predictive power of monetary dependence or deteriorating competitiveness could be tested as indicators of sovereign debt crises.

# Appendix 1. Studies Selected for Qualitative Content Analysis

| Monetary Economics | |
|---|---|
| **Author(s)** | **Title** |
| Arghyrou & Tsoukalas (2010) | The Option of Last Resort: A two-currency EMU |
| Gibson, Hall & Tavlas (2010) | The Greek Financial Crisis: Growing Imbalances and Sovereign Spreads |
| Arghyrou & Tsoukalas (2011) | The Greek Debt Crisis: Likely Causes, Mechanics and Outcomes |
| Dellas & Tavlas (2013) | The Gold Standard, the Euro and the Origins of the Greek Sovereign Debt Crisis |
| Balcerowicz (2014) | Euro Imbalances and Adjustment: A comparative Analysis |
| Krugman (2014) | Currency Regimes, Capital Flows and Crises |
| De Grauwe (2011) | A fragile Eurozone in search of better governance |
| Oltheten, Sougiannins, Travlos & Zarkos (2013) | Greece in the Eurozone: Lessons from a decade of experience |
| Eichengreen & Accominotti (2013) | The mother of all sudden stops: Capital Flows and Reversals in Europe 1919-1932 |
| Strobel (2005) | Leaving EMU: a real options perspective |
| Brittan, Tietmeyer, Bergsten, Eichengreen & Meltzer (2010) | The Euro: Will it still be around five years from now? |
| Hamilton & Olson (2014) | Was the Euro Good for Greece? |
| Arghyrou (2007) | The price effects of joining the Euro: Modelling the Greek Experience using non-linnear price-adjustment models |
| Mitsopoulos & Pelagidis (2014) | Why did forceful internal devaluation fail to kickstart export-led growth in Greece? |
| Arghyrou (2009) | Monetary policy before and after the Euro: Evidence from Greece |
| Arestis & Karakitsos (2012) | The US dimension of the Euro Zone Debt Crisis |
| Kasimati & Veraros (2013) | Should Greece adopt a dual-currency regime to resolve its economic crisis? |
| Creighton (2011) | Greece's Debt Crisis: The price of cheap loans |
| Stockhammer & Sotiropoulos (2014) | Rebalancing the Euro Area: The costs of internal devaluation |
| Karras (2011) | From Hero to Zero? The role of the Euro in the current crisis: Theory and some empirical evidence |

The selected studies are presented per discipline (20 per discipline):

## Appendix 1. (Continued)

| Economics | |
|---|---|
| **Author(s)** | **Title** |
| Antzoulatos (2011) | Greece in 2010: A crisis without Catharsis |
| Krajewska (2014) | Fiscal Policy in the Countries Most Affected by the Crisis: Portugal, Ireland, Greece and Spain |
| Belke & Dreger (2013) | Current Account Imbalances in the Euro Area: Does catching up explain the development? |
| Pappas (2011) | The Short-term determinants of capital flows in a small open economy: The case of Greece |
| Kouretas & Vlamis (2010) | The Greek Crisis: Causes and Implications |
| Lianou (2012) | Lessons from the Greek Tragey: Europe needs Economic Convergence |
| Malliaropulos (2010) | How much did competitiveness of the Greek economy decline since EMU entry? |
| Ozturk & Sozdemir (2015) | Effects of Global Financial Crisis on Greece Economy |
| Abboushi (2011) | Analysis and Outlook of the Greek Financial Crisis |
| Provopoulos (2014) | The Greek Economy and Banking System: Recent Developments and the way forward |
| Reddy (2011) | Greek Crisis and Its Impact on the World Economy |
| Michaelides, Papageorgiou & Tsionas (2014) | Is the Greek Crisis in the EMU contagious? |
| Leao & Palacio-Vera (2011) | Can Portugal Escape Stagnation without Opting out from the Eurozone? |
| Yildiz & Yildirum (2014) | An Empirical study on fiscal sustainability in the Eurozone |
| Papanikos (2014) | Greek Labor Market, the Euro and the Current Crisis |
| Thiemann (2013) | Is Greece at a turning point? |
| Koo (2011) | How to avoid a Eurozone Breakup |
| Degiannakis, Duffy, Filis & Livada (2015) | Business Cycle Synchronisation in EMU: Can fiscal policy bring member-countries closer? |
| Michaelides, Papageorgiou & Vouldis (2013) | Business Cycles and Economic Crisis in Greece (1960-2011): A long run equilibrium analysis in the Eurozone |
| Polito & Wickens (2014) | How the Euro Crisis Evolved and how to avoid another: EMU, fiscal policy and credit ratings |

| Political Science | |
|---|---|
| **Author(s)** | **Title** |
| Fouskas & Dimoulas (2012) | The Greek Workshop of Debt and the Failure of the European Project |
| Fouskas (2013) | Whatever happened to Greece? |
| O'Donnel & Tinions (2003) | The politics of pension reform in Greece -Lessons from Public Attitudes |
| Sklias & Maris (2013) | The political dimension of the Greek Financial Crisis |
| Kouzis (2011) | The impact of the crisis on labour relations and collective agreements in Greece |
| Choupis (2011) | The crisis in the Greek economy and its national implications |
| Streeck (2012) | The construction of a case for the Greek people to repay their debt |
| Envagelopoulos (2012) | Rent-seeking in the Greek economic drama |
| Sakellaropoulos & Sotiris (2014) | Postcards from the Future: The Greek Debt Crisis, the Struggle Against the IMF-EU Austerity Package and Open Questions for Left Strategy |
| Kretsos & Vogiatzoglou (2015) | Lost in the Ocean of Deregulation: The Greek Labour Movement in a time of Crisis |
| Verney & Bosco (2013) | Living Parallel Lives: Italy and Greece in an Age of Austerity |
| Vasilopoulou & Halikiopoulou (2013) | In the shadow of the Grexit: The Greek election of 17 June 2012 |
| Malakos (2013) | Greece Facing Herself: The Past and Present as Fate |
| Dobrescu & Durach (2014) | Euroscepticism: A sign of a Europe in distress |
| Karyotis & Rudig (2015) | Blame and Punishment: The Electoral politics of extreme austerity in Greece |
| Finger (2015) | What next in the Greek crisis |
| Vasilopoulou, Halikiopoulou & Exadaktylos (2014) | Greece in Crisis: Austerity, Populism and the Politics of Blame |
| Hembruff (2013) | Critical Review: The Politics of Sovereign Debt |
| Theodossopoulos (2013) | Infuriated with the infuriated |
| Kovras (2010) | The Parliamentary Election in Greece, October 2009 |

## Appendix 1. (Continued)

| Financial Economics | |
|---|---|
| Author(s) | Title |
| Kokkoris, Olivares-Caminal & Papadakis (2010) | The Greek Tragedy |
| Baltas & Chair (2013) | The Greek Financial Crisis and the Outlook of the Greek Economy |
| Georganta (2011) | Greek Fiscal and Financial Data: More than meets the eye |
| Zettelmeyer, Trebesch & Gulati (2013) | The Greek Debt Restructuring: An Autopsy |
| Eichler (2012) | The impact of banking and sovereign debt crisis risk in the Eurozone on the euro/US dollar exchange rate |
| Karmann & Maltritz (2012) | Sovereign Default Risk and Recovery Rates: What government bond markets expect for Greece |
| Giordano, Pericoli & Tommasino (2013) | Pure or Wake-up call Contagion? Another Look at the EMU Sovereign Debt Crisis |
| Tamakoshi & Hamori (2014) | Greek Sovereign Bond Index, Volatility and Structural Breaks |
| Georgoutsos & Migiakis (2013) | European Sovereign bond spreads: Financial integration and market conditions |
| Argitis & Nikolaidi (2014) | The financial fragility and the crisis of the Greek Government Sector |
| Bi & Traum (2012) | Estimating Sovereign Default Risk |
| Papandreou (2010) | A new Global Financial Architecture: Lessons from the Greek Crisis |
| Gomez-Puig, Sosvilla-Rivero & Ramos-Herrera (2014) | An update on EMU sovereign yield spread drivers in times of crisis: A panel data analysis |
| Pragidis, Aielli, Chionis & Shizas (2015) | Contagion effects during financial crisis: Evidence from the Greek Sovereign Bonds Market |
| Bratis, Laopodis & Kouretas (2015) | Creditor moral hazard during the EMU debt crisis |
| Gibson, Hall & Tavlas (2014) | Fundamentally Wrong: Market Pricing of Sovereigns and the Greek Financial Crisis |
| Bhanot, Burns, Hunter & Williams (2014) | News Spillovers from the Greek Debt Crisis: Impact on the Eurozone Financial Sector |
| Gomez-Puig & Sosvilla-Rivero (2015) | The causal relationship between debt and growth in EMU countries |
| Palaiodimos & Tzavalis (2015) | The EMU effects of asset market holdings and the recent financial crisis |
| Kosmidou, Kousendris & Negakis (2015) | The impact of EU/ECB/IMF bailout programs on the financial and real sectors of ASE during the Greek sovereign crisis |

| Public Administration | |
|---|---|
| **Author(s)** | **Title** |
| Featherstone (2011) | The Greek Sovereign Debt Crisis and EMU: A failing state in a skewed regime |
| Nelson, Belkin & Mix (2010) | Greece's Debt Crisis: Overview, Policy Responses and Implications |
| Schimmer & Kunisch (2011) | Greek Drama behind the scenes of EU integration |
| Matsaganis (2011) | The Welfare state and the crisis: The case of Greece |
| Ali (2012) | The impact of the sovereign debt crisis on the eurozone countries |
| Robbins (2015) | The Greek Debt Crisis: The need for 'Heroic' Economic Policy Reforms in the European Monetary Union |
| Matsaganis & Leventi (2011) | The distributional impact of the crisis in Greece |
| Kaplanoglou & Rapanos (2013) | Tax and Trust: The Fiscal Crisis in Greece |
| Martin & Waller (2012) | Sovereign Debt: A modern Day Greek Tragedy |
| Petmesidou (2013) | Is social protection in Greece at a Crossroads? |
| Kretsos (2011) | Grassroots Unionism in the context of economic crisis in Greece |
| Dimoulas (2014) | Exploring the impact of employment policy measures in the context of crisis: The case of Greece |
| Lapavitsas et al (2010) | Beggar Thyself and Thy Neighbour |
| Yfantopoulos (2013) | Dynamic Aspects of the Underground Economy in Greece |
| Milios & Sotiropoulos (2010) | Crisis of Greece or Crisis of the Euro? A view from the European 'periphery' |
| Christopoulou & Monastiriotis (2014) | Greek Public Sector Wage Premium Before the Crisis: Size, selection and relative valuation of characteristics |
| Zartaloudis (2014) | The impact of the fiscal crisis on Greek and Portuguese Welfare States: Retrenchment before the Catch-up? |
| Fahrholz & Wojcik (2012) | The Bail Out! Positive Political Economics of Greek-type Crises in the EMU |
| Zahariadis (2013) | Leading reform amidst transboundary crises: Lessons from Greece |
| Katsimi & Moutos (2010) | EMU and the Greek Crisis: The political economy perspective |

# APPENDIX 2. IDENTIFIED CONCEPTS AND RECORDING CRITERIA

As discussed in the methodology section, concepts were developed by reading 50% of the studies listed above (10 from each discipline) and identifying recurring concepts that were judged to be relevant to the study and relevant to the research questions. This process was open to the development of concepts in an emergent manner, but was also somewhat guided by the research questions posed in order to provide some direction. This is in line with the approach proposed by Glaser and Laudel (2013).

The concepts identified are listed below, with the core meaning of each concept described and recording criteria provided in each case. Thirty-eight (38) concepts were identified in total.

**Concept: 'High Debt'**

**Description:** Refers to any suggestion that the Greek government had accumulated a lot of debt, or that the Greek government was incurring large deficits.

**Recording Criteria:** For this concept to apply, the author had to explicitly refer to Greek *government* debt or deficits. The author furthermore had to state or imply that the total stock of debt or the deficit(s) for a single period or a number of periods were high.

**Concept: 'Downgrades'**

**Description:** Refers to any instances of Greek sovereign credit rating downgrades by any of the top three credit ratings agencies (Fitch, Moody's or Standard and Poor's).

**Recording Criteria:** For this concept to apply, the author had to state or imply that a downgrade by at least one of the 'big three' credit ratings agencies had impacted Greece in one way or another.

**Concept: 'Financial Crisis'**

**Description:** Refers to any implications that the global financial crisis had on Greece. The 'global financial crisis' here refers to the financial crisis of 2007-2008 that originated in the United States subprime mortgage market. This concept also covered any mentions of the recession triggered by the global financial crisis.

**Recording Criteria:** For this concept to apply, the author had to state or imply that the global financial crisis or the resultant 'great recession' had impact Greece in one way or another.

**Concept: 'Upward Revision of Debt'**

**Description:** Specifically refers to the upward revision of Greek sovereign debt estimates in late 2009 by the incoming Greek government of George Papandreou. The concept refers to the first upward revision in October 2009 and all additional upward adjustments in the weeks and months after that.

**Recording Criteria:** For this concept to apply, the author had to state or imply that the upward revision of Greek debt in October 2009, or the subsequent follow-up upward revisions, had affected Greece in some way.

**Concept: 'Collapse of Confidence'**

**Description:** Refers to any suggestion that investors became less confident in the ability of the Greek state to repay its debts. This includes explicit references to reduced confidence, but also implicit suggestions in reduced confidence. For example, any discussion of 'increased spreads' were interpreted as a de facto decrease in confidence in the Greek state's ability to repay its debts.

**Recording Criteria:** For this concept to apply, the author had to state or imply that reduced confidence in Greece's ability to repay its government debt had some effect on the country. Reduced confidence could either be explicitly stated by the author, or implied through a discussion of 'increased spreads' or 'more expensive debt'.

**Concept: 'Non-Enforcement of EU Treaties'**

**Description:** Refers to any suggestion that the breaching of EU treaty-enforced government debt or deficit limits played a role in the crisis. The Stability and Growth Pact is the most-referred to treaty that was aimed at containing debt, and that was not enforced.

**Recording Criteria:** For this concept to apply, the author had to refer to an EU treaty (most likely the SGP) that aimed to contain debt for EMU members. The author also had to state or imply that Greece had breached the limits of these treaties. Finally, the author also had to state or imply that nothing was done to enforce the treaties. Failure to mention any enforcement actions in the face of debt or deficits in excess of treaty thresholds was interpreted as an implication that nothing was done to enforce treaties.

**Concept: 'Political Opposition to Reform'**

**Description:** Refers to political opposition to any proposed measures to curb government spending, or to introduce reforms to make Greece more competitive. Opposition can take the form of electoral choice, expressions of political preferences by interest groups or by political parties in Greece's parliament.

**Recording Criteria:** For this concept to apply, the author had to refer to opposition that was loosely political in nature. In other words, either explicitly political such as electoral choices, but also implicitly political such as public expressions of opposition. 'Opposition' in this case does not include violent demonstrations or strikes, as those aspects are captured in another concept. The proposed reform that was being opposed had to specifically be aimed at curbing government expenditure or improving Greek competitiveness.

**Concept: 'EMU Membership'**

**Description:** Refers to any suggestion that European Monetary Union membership, or adopting the Euro, or abandoning the Drachma, had played any part in the crisis.

**Recording Criteria:** For the concept to apply, the author had to state or imply that EMU membership (or the implications of EMU membership) had affected Greece in one way or another.

**Concept: 'Large Welfare State'**

**Description:** Refers to Greece building and maintain a large welfare state. This includes any suggestions that Greece paid large amounts of pensions, had a large social safety net, or that a large portion of the national budget was spent on social assistance.

**Recording Criteria:** For the concept to apply, the author had to state or imply that Greece had a large welfare state or was spending significantly on social assistance or social welfare programs such as pensions; and that this large welfare state had an in pact on the country that was somehow relevant to the crisis.

**Concept: 'Internal Devaluation'**

**Description:** Refers to the need to deflate Greek consumption and wages to regain competitiveness; particularly because a currency devaluation was not possible given Greece's EMU membership.

**Recording Criteria:** For the concept to apply, the author had to state or imply that Greek wages and Greek consumption had to be forced lower to improve competitiveness. The term 'internal devaluation' did not necessarily need to be used; and EMU membership does not necessarily need to be mentioned, but the need for wage and price deflation to facilitate improved competitiveness must be stated or implied.

**Concept: 'Monetary Dependence'**

**Description:** Refers to the monetary policy implications of joining the EMU. Specifically, this refers to suggestions that Greece's monetary policy options were limited due to EMU membership by not being able to devalue its currency, print its own currency or decide its own monetary policy in general. This also includes dependence on the European Central Bank for monetary policy.

**Recording Criteria:** For the concept to apply, the author had to state or imply that Greece had lost monetary independence, or had to refer to some of the implications of losing monetary independence, such as loss of seigniorage revenues or loss of the ability to devalue its currency; and that this had implications which affected Greece.

**Concept: 'Failed Austerity'**

**Description:** Refers to the failed attempts at austerity measures by Greek governments in the period before 2009; and to the failure of the initial rounds of austerity measures as imposed by the 'Troika' to significantly reduce the Greek debt-to-GDP ratio. Also refers to the inability of reforms to increase competitiveness sufficiently.

**Recording Criteria:** For the concept to apply, the author has to state or imply that Greek governments failed to implement effective austerity measures in the period before or during the crisis. The failure could refer to either inability to reduce debt to GDP or competitiveness.

**Concept: 'Military Spending'**

**Description:** Refers to high levels of military spending by the Greek state in the period leading up to the crisis in 2009 and during the crisis. Can refer to specific deals to purchase military equipment or to a high military budget in general.

**Recording Criteria:** For the concept to apply, the author has to state or imply that Greece's military spending was too high, and specifically, that it contributed to government debt accumulation and high deficits.

**Concept: 'Ageing Population'**

**Description:** Refers to the fact that the average age in Greece has steadily been increasing in Greece in the last 25 years.

**Recording Criteria:** For the concept to apply, the author must state or imply that the increasing average age of Greek citizens has had an impact on Greek society or government that is relevant to the crisis.

**Concept: 'Lack of Trust'**

**Description:** Refers to the deterioration of trust of the Greek people in Greek governments in general before and during the crisis. Also refers to the deterioration of trust in Greek governments from external observers. 'Trust' here refers to a basic level of belief that government speaks the truth and will follow through on commitments.

**Recording Criteria:** For the concept to apply, the author must state or imply that the people of Greece, or external observers, had lost a degree of trust in the Greek government; and that this deterioration of trust had some part to play in the Greek crisis.

**Concept: 'Large Informal Sector'**

**Description:** Refers to the fact that Greece had a large informal sector which is not regulated, which does not record its business with government and which is not taxed.

**Recording Criteria:** For the concept to apply, the author has to state or imply that Greece had a large informal sector. This includes references to an 'untaxed sector' or 'black market' sector; the author furthermore has to imply that these large informal sector had some impact on Greece which was relevant to the crisis.

**Concept: 'Poor Statistical Services'**

**Description:** Refers to any failure, weakness or inaccuracy of the Greek state's internal statistical services.

**Recording Criteria:** For the concept to apply, the author had to state or imply that any problem with the Greek state's internal statistical services had played a part in the crisis.

**Concept: 'Fears of Possible EMU Exit'**

**Description:** Refers to fears that evolved in the wake of the crisis that Greece may leave the EMU. Also refers to any suggestion that Greece may face internal political pressure to leave the EMU; or that the Greek government was not fully committed to staying within the EMU.

**Recording Criteria:** For the concept to apply, the author had to state or imply that there existed a fear amongst external observers that Greece may leave the EMU; and that this fear of a possible exit may have played a role in the crisis.

**Concept: 'Political Instability'**

**Description:** Refers to political instability in two forms: Either, in the form of leadership changes in government and in major political parties (i.e., power changing hands constantly and therefore hampering continuity in the recovery effort); or in the form of the national anti-austerity protest movement, national strikes or general violent and disruptive unrest in the form of public gatherings.

**Recording Criteria:** For the concept to apply, the author had to state or imply that political instability occurred in either of the two forms explained above, and that this had an impact on Greece that was relevant before or during the crisis.

**Concept: 'Capitalism'**

**Description:** Refers broadly to free-market, capitalist economic policy which advances the efficient functioning of markets, the free flow of capital and maximisation of the profitability of capital in Greece.

**Recording Criteria:** For the concept to apply, the author had to state or imply that capitalism – either in the form of a specific policy or concept or as a broad institution or idea – had contributed to the crisis in one form or another.

**Concept: 'Access to Cheap Debt'**

**Description:** Refers to Greece's access to sovereign debt at reduced interest rates in the period after EMU membership in the 2000s. Includes outright references to 'cheap debt' and includes more nuanced referenced to 'excessively supressed sovereign spreads' and 'generally low sovereign spreads'. Importantly, this concept refers to debt that was cheaper than justified by Greece's macroeconomic fundamentals.

**Recording Criteria:** For the concept to apply, the author must state or imply that Greece had access to cheap debt after joining the EMU. The author must furthermore state or imply that debt must be cheaper than is justified by Greece's macroeconomic fundamentals and that this had a relevant impact on Greece in explaining the occurrence of the crisis.

**Concept: 'Poor Revenue Collection'**

**Description:** Refers to the Greek state's inability to collect a large portion of the taxes it should be collecting. Importantly, this does not refer to the various regulatory loopholes that allow certain sectors of the Greek economy not to pay significant taxes as that issue is covered by another concept. This refers specifically to a practical inability to collect the taxes due to the Greek state, despite the various regulatory loopholes in place.

**Recording Criteria:** For the concept to apply, the author must state or apply that the Greek state was unable to collect all of the taxes due to it, and that this caused some effect relevant to the development of the crisis.

**Concept: 'Pro-Cyclical Fiscal Policy'**

**Description:** Refers to the destructive implications of government fiscal policy on two occasions: Firstly, high government spending in an environment of high growth and high inflation before the crisis in the 2000s; and secondly, reduced government spending after the crisis struck and recession set as part of the 'Troika-imposed' austerity measures.

**Recording Criteria:** For the concept to apply, the author must state or imply that Greek fiscal policy was destructive by reinforcing either the overheating of the economy in the 2000s or by reinforcing the recession in the post-crisis period. The author also has to state or imply that this had some impact on Greece which was relevant to the crisis.

**Concept: 'Bank Undercapitalisation'**

**Description:** Refers to any suggestion that Greek banks did not hold enough assets – and in particular liquid assets – to cover the obligations arising from their liabilities in the period after the crisis.

**Recording Criteria:** For the concept to apply, the author must state or imply that banks were undercapitalised, or more colloquially that banks were under financial pressure. Furthermore, it must be stated or implied that this played a relevant role in the crisis.

**Concept: 'Capital Influx'**

**Description:** Refers to the large amount of foreign capital that flowed into Greece in the 2000s.

**Recording Criteria:** For the concept to apply, the author must state or imply that a large amount of foreign capital flowed into Greece in the form of various investments in the 2000s, and that this played some role in the crisis.

**Concept: 'Poor Governance'**

**Description:** Refers to any instances of ineffective, weak or poor public sector governance that resulted in suboptimal societal outcomes. Can refer to practical governance challenges, but also to poor government policy in general.

**Recording Criteria:** For the concept to apply, the author must state or imply that governance –either in some practical sense or in a broader policy sense – was ineffective; and that this contributed to the crisis. Crucially, this excludes pro-cyclical fiscal policy decisions, which have been captured by another concept.

**Concept: 'Large Public Sector'**

**Description:** Refers to the fact that Greece has built maintained a large public sector. May refer to it in terms of number of people employed, the total public sector wage bill, the public sector as percentage of total GDP or more generally in terms of the public sector's broad involvement in various sectors of the economy.

**Recording Criteria:** For the concept to apply, the author must state or imply that the public sector was large, or disproportionately big, and that this played a role in the crisis.

**Concept: 'Lack of Competitiveness'**

**Description:** Refers to the deterioration of Greek competitiveness in the 2000s, particularly referring here to international competitiveness vis-à-vis its European trading partners. The focus here is specifically on general cost competiveness.

**Recording Criteria:** For this concept to apply, the author must state or imply that private Greek firms became less cost competitive vis-à-vis their European counterparts in the 2000s; and that this had a relevant impact on Greece.

**Concept: 'Regulatory Burden'**

**Description:** Refers to two separate regulatory issues: Firstly, a complex set of loopholes which made revenue collection more difficult and allowed certain sectors of Greek society to avoid taxes. Secondly, and more prevalently in the literature, this refers to the complex set of labour, environmental and other regulations as enforced by the state that businesses and small businesses had to comply with.

**Recording Criteria:** For the concept to apply, the author must state or imply that there was a regulatory burden, and that it had some costs that were relevant to the crisis.

**Concept: 'Dubai World Default'**

**Description:** Refers to the Dubai World debt repayment moratorium of November 2009, whereby the entity (owned by the Emirate of Dubai) essentially was unable to repay its debts.

**Recording Criteria:** For the concept to apply the author must state or imply that the Dubai World debt repayment moratorium had an impact on Greece that was relevant to the crisis.

**Concept: 'Destructive Institutions'**

**Description:** Refers to a number of destructive institutions which undermined the effective functioning of the political system and the functioning of the market economy in Greece. Firstly, it refers to the destructive institutions in Greece's political culture, such as the overdue influence of large interest groups, the politicisation of the union movement, the politicisation of the state apparatus, clientilistic relationships between the state and individuals and interest groups and any other institutions that create an environment of political support in exchange for political favours. Secondly, it refers to destructive institutions in various industries such as job reservations, entrenched oligopolies and anti-competitive regulations which protect existing operators and diminish competition.

**Recording Criteria:** For the concept to apply, the author must state or imply that the destructive institutions as outlined above exert some cost on Greek society, and that these costs were relevant to the crisis.

**Concept: 'Current Account Deficits'**

**Description:** Refers to the large current account deficits that occurred in Greece throughout the 2000s.

**Recording Criteria:** For this concept to apply, the author must state or imply that Greece's current account deficits in the 2000s were large, that the size of the current account deficits were problematic and that the problems associated with such large current account deficits were relevant to the crisis.

**Concept: 'Low Productivity'**

**Description:** Refers to Greece's comparatively low private sector productivity as measured by output per unit of labour, and as compared to Greek firms' European competitors.

**Recording Criteria:** For the concept to apply, the author had to state or imply that Greece suffered from comparatively low productivity in the 2000s, and that this had negative effects for Greece that were relevant to the crisis.

**Concept: 'High Wages'**

**Description:** Refers to the high wages in Greece in the 2000s, expressed as wages per unit of output. In some instances discussion is also focused on high wage inflation (relative to the rest of Europe).

**Recording Criteria:** For the concept to apply, the author must state or imply that Greek wages were high, or were rapidly rising (in the form of high wage inflation), and that this had consequences that were relevant to the Greek crisis.

**Concept: 'Excessive Private Credit Extension'**

**Description:** Refers to the rapid pace of private credit extension in Greece in the 2000s to private Greek citizens.

**Recording Criteria:** For the concept to apply, the author must state or imply that private credit extension in Greece was high, and higher than in the period before Greece joined the EMU, and that this had effects on Greece that were relevant to the crisis.

**Concept: 'Strong Public Sector Unions'**

**Description:** Refers to the strength of public sector unions in terms of their numbers of members, their ability to extricate concessions from government, their influence in Greek public policy and public life and the political impact during election campaigns.

**Recording Criteria:** For the concept to apply, the author must state or imply that public sector unions in Greece were strong in the various ways expressed above, and that this relative strength of the Greek public sector unions as an interest group had implications for Greece that were relevant to the crisis.

**Concept: 'Corruption'**

**Description:** Refers to the prevalence of public sector corruption in Greece. This corruption may take the form of corrupt relationships between political leaders or state officials and certain interest groups, but also includes lower-level corrupt activities that involve inappropriate payments and relationships between Greek officials and Greek citizens.

**Recording Criteria:** For the concept to apply, the author must state or imply that corrupt activities as described above were prevalent in Greece and that their prevalence had impacts on Greece that were relevant to the crisis.

# Appendix 3. Extracted Content with Applied Concepts

Please note that this section has been excluded from the turnitin submission to not compromise the turniitin score, but has been included in this soft copy submission and in hard copy.

## The Greek Tragedy (Kokkoris, Olivares-Caminal & Papadakis, 2010)

1) 'Following the most recent restatement of Greek data by Eurostat, Greece reached a budget deficit of 13.6 per cent and a Debt/GDP ratio of 115 per cent in 2009. The profile of deficit reduction is more modest in the revised Stability and Growth Program (SGP) than it was in SGP published in February, reflecting the upward revision of estimated deficit and the downward revision to the growth projections. In the revised SGP, the Greek government is aiming for a budget deficit of 4.9 per cent of GDP in 2013 with an outstanding debt/GDP ratio of 149 per cent. The restatement of the data together with the effect that the global financial crisis had on the economy led the rating agencies to downgrade Greece to Ba1 (Moody's) with stable watch, BBþ (S&P) and BBB (Fitch) with negative watch.' [*Downgrades*, caused by *high debt*, *financial crisis* and *upward revision of debt*]

2) With a total nominal debt outstanding at h298.5 billion (as of December 2009), that is debt/GDP ratio at 115 per cent and above (way over the prudent 60 per cent to 90 per cent threshold), Greece is obliged to pay high interest rates compared to other countries. [*Collapse of Confidence*, caused by *high debt* and *non-enforcement of EU treaties*]

3) As an EMU member, there are two main constraints that the member countries are facing. First, loss of monetary independence (ability to print money). Second, no control of setting a benchmark interest rate that drives the cost of money on the domestic economy. These two issues are interlinked monetary policies, both of which have been delegated to the European Central Bank. The combination of higher interest rates and austerity measures to reduce budget deficits, and thus control sovereign debt, can be a 'toxic' one that raises many questions. [*Monetary dependence*, caused by *EMU membership*]

4) Given that Greece does not have control over its currency in order to buy its way out (by means of printing money, devaluating the currency and external inflation), and given that interest rates may soon increase, internal devaluation (adjustment of internal salaries and prices) is the only viable solution. [*Internal devaluation*, caused by *monetary dependence*]

5) The 'Dionysian' days of joy and excess where Greeks were still able to obtain what is commonly referred to in banking and financial circles as 'a free lunch' are over. Now politicians have to deal with angry voters feeling the pinch in their pockets while trying to get Greece out of this delicate situation. [*High debt*, caused by *political opposition to reform*]

6) Following the most recent restatement of Greek data by Eurostat, Greece reached a budget deficit of 13.6 per cent and a Debt/ GDP ratio of 115 per cent in 2009. The profile of deficit reduction is more modest in the revised Stability and Growth Program (SGP) than it was in SGP published in February, reflecting the upward revision of estimated deficit and the downward revision to the growth projections. [*High debt*, caused by *non-enforcement of EU treaties* and *upward revision of debt*]

## THE GREEK FINANCIAL CRISIS AND THE OUTLOOK FOR THE GREEK ECONOMY (BALTAS & CHAIR, 2013)

1) The sovereign debt crisis in the euro area and the real economy during the spring of 2010 has revealed that the monetary and fiscal policy framework of the European Monetary Union (EMU) is still incomplete. It quickly became obvious that the rules-based framework for fiscal policy created by the Excessive Deficit Procedure (EDP) and the Stability and Growth Pact (SGP) when the EURO was introduced was insufficient to prevent a debt crisis despite its emphasis on keeping public sector deficits low. [*High debt*, caused by *financial crisis* and *non-enforcement of EU treaties*]

2) Public debt was 126 per cent of GDP in 2009 and has now reached 170 per cent. Although Greek debt accounts for merely 1 per cent of global debt, the possibility of a sovereign default has endangered the survival of the euro and with it the world economy due to the interrelationship of the global financial system. [*Collapse of Confidence*, caused by *high debt*]

3) Greece joined the EU in 1981, ahead of Spain and Portugal, and getting access to generous European funds, whose use could hardly be described as prudent. Nonetheless, public indebtedness continued to soar and by 1996 it doubled once again, reaching 113% of GDP. This is due to the disproportionate social benefits, such as increased salaries and redundant appointments in the public sector, increased pensions, early retirements, public enterprises with large deficits etc., which created substantial budgets to be financed by continuous borrowing. [*High debt*, caused by *poor governance*, a *large public sector* and a *generous welfare state*]

4) The successive Greek governments were buying social peace and votes by the means of public spending and state borrowing. [*High debt*, caused by *poor governance*, *generous welfare state*, *political opposition to reform*]

5) Being in the Eurozone, the government could continue borrowing at lower rates of interest than would be the case if Greece were on its own. Hence, deficits and debt in Greece did not appear suddenly as an earthquake, but were accumulating over decades. Such bad policies were tolerated over a long time. [*High debt*, caused by *EMU membership* and *poor governance*] ALSO [Access to *cheap debt*, caused by *EMU membership*]

6) Excessive government borrowing took place in the next couple of decades and accelerated after January 2001, when Greek entry into the Euro allowed the government to borrow at practically zero spreads. [*High debt*, caused by *EMU membership* and *cheap debt*]

7) Due to the deterioration of its financial indicators, Greece was downgraded with respect to its borrowing credibility and the difficulty in securing funding at reasonable rates led the country to seek help from the International Monetary Fund, the European Union and the European Central Bank, known as the IMF-EU-ECB bail. [*Downgrades*, caused by *high debt* and *collapse of confidence*]

8) It seems that the horizontal tax policies have been proved unsuccessful, for in most cases considerable increases in the statutory tax lower, rather than increase, tax revenues. This is due to the deeper than anticipated recession and the continuing ineffectiveness of the tax collection system. [*High debt*, because of *poor revenue collection*]

9) Apart from the inexcusable behaviour of Greek politicians, the Greek economy is clearly in bad shape in terms of deficit in GDP and unemployment. [*High debt*, caused by *poor governance*]

## THE GREEK WORKSHOP OF DEBT AND THE FAILURE OF THE EUROPEAN PROJECT (FOUSKAS & DIMOULAS, 2012)

1) From this viewpoint, institutions do not work, tax-collecting mechanisms are nonchalant and the culprits have since 1974 been the two governing political parties, the populist PASOK of Andreas G. Papandreou in the 1980s and early 1990s, and the New Democracy (ND). Both of them failed to arrest the huge state bureaucracy blocking development, modernization and supply-side economics, hence the origins of the debt. Overall, patronage, clientelism, tax evasion and a huge public sector, that is to say domestic factors alone, are responsible for Greece's plight today. [*High debt*, caused by *poor governance*, *large public sector*, *corruption*, *poor revenue collection*]

2) The roots of the turmoil in Europe lie in the world crisis that commenced in 2007. Briefly put, the bankruptcy of Lehman Brothers in September 2008 led to a banking crisis, which ushered in a global recession. European economies were hit by collapsing exports and contracting credit. The worst was averted through state intervention, partly to support banks, partly to sustain aggregate demand. But state intervention led to the next and more severe stage of the crisis, that of public debt. And as the public debt crisis got deeper, it threatened to re-ignite the banking crisis. [*High debt*, caused by *financial crisis*] ALSO [*Collapse in confidence*, caused by *high debt* and *financial crisis*]

3) All peripheral countries, including Greece, were forced to join the Euro at high exchange rates, the ostensible purpose being to secure low inflation, that is, the traditional objective of Germany's central bank since the years of the Weimar Republic.13 The direct effect of this policy was to reduce the competitiveness of the periphery. Moreover, and as Germany was able to discipline its working class to accept low wages making, in turn, its economy even more internationally competitive thus boosting its trade surpluses, peripheral countries such as Greece began registering trade deficits. [*Lack of competitiveness*, caused by *EMU membership*] ALSO [*Current Account Deficits*, caused by *lack of competitiveness*]

4) This is why we consider that the two main parties that have ruled Greece since the fall of the colonels in summer 1974, PASOK and ND, should go. These parties are as much responsible for the plight of the country as global financial capital itself. Liberal and social democratic arguments about 'corruption', eradication of 'clientelism', 'populism', 'cronyism', 'nepotism' and so forth make sense only if placed in this class context. [*Poor Governance*, caused by *corruption*]

5) Statistics in Greece is a very sensitive issue. We should remember that the story of the Greek debt blew out of all proportion—and the downgrading of Greek sovereign bonds/debt began—when the PASOK government, once in office in October 2009, revealed that Greek GDP figures were fictional, whereas the deficit was double-digit,

almost three times higher than the previous forecast. [*Collapse of Confidence*, caused by the *upward revision of debt* and *poor statistical services*]

6) The current crisis is due to the nature of monetary union, the mode of integration of peripheral countries in the Euro-zone and the impact of the crisis of 2007–2009. [*Collapse in confidence*, caused by *EMU membership* and the *financial crisis*]

7) According to multiple announcements by the Ministry of Finance in September–October 2011, more than 6000 individuals owe more than 150,000 Euros each to the Inland Revenue. For the sake of comparison, the total amount these individuals owe to the tax authorities is in the region of 30 billion Euros, whereas the annual spending of the Greek state for wages is less than 23 billion Euros. No accident, therefore, that the public debt doubled from 2000 to 2009 (Table 3), and especially at the expense of the average Greek consumer. [*High debt*, caused by *poor revenue collection*]

8) By exaggerating both the threat coming from Turkey and Greece's and Cyprus's own vulnerability, the 'realists' of the Greek cabinets could bid for high-tech expensive military gear: in 2009 defence expenditure in Greece was over 3 per cent of GDP, as opposed to 2.4 per cent for France, 2.7 per cent for Britain, 2 per cent for Portugal, 1.4 per cent for Germany, 1.3 per cent for Spain and 4.7 per cent for the USA. At the beginning of the full-fledged crisis of 2010, Greece bought six warships from France at a cost of 2.5 billion Euros and six submarines from Germany at 5 billion Euros. [*High debt*, caused by *poor governance* and *military expenditure*] ALSO [*Military spending*, caused by *poor governance*]

9) From 1994 to 2009, the Greek economy lost almost 40 per cent of its competitiveness, and this despite the fact that GDP growth remained relatively good (Table 3); domestic and external borrowing increased (Table 6); and the ASE's price index was doing quite well. There is no doubt, therefore, that whereas the trade deficit is a substantial source of the overall Greek debt, numerous other factors, mainly of domestic origin, have to be factored into every calculation. Trade deficits are articulated in the current account, and especially in the structure of the unequal trade interaction between Greece and the European core, particularly Germany, Italy, France and the Netherlands. Some 70 per cent of Greek imports come from Europe, whereas some 55 per cent from EU member states. [*High debt*, caused by *current account deficits*] ALSO [*Current account deficit*, caused by *lack of competitiveness*]

## The Greek Sovereign Debt Crisis and EMU: A Failing State in a Skewed Regime (Featherstone, 2011)

1) The problems of co-ordination and control that arise from this setting are evident in the processes of budget management. As of 2009, the government budget was based on

some 14,000 separate 'budget lines' where each 'line' represents grouped items of expenditure within part of the public administration.3 The plethora of such lines obscures public spending on specific items and the management system lacks the capacity to track and assess the efficacy of such spending. Within this system, not only is there a lack of knowledge on which to assert effective accounting control – let alone to engage in policy evaluation in relation to changing government priorities – there is also much scope for clientelistic and corrupt practices as a results. Alongside relatively weak control of public expenditure have been the problems of raising tax revenue. Tax evasion amongst key sectors has been rife.4 The EU Commission estimated that uncollected tax revenue in 2006 amounted to 30 per cent (or 3.4 per cent of GDP) in 2006 (in.gr, 2009a). The system is vulnerable to corruption: international estimates of the incidence of irregular payments made place Greece in a worse position than any other EU-15 state and 86th out of 133 states internationally (World Economic Forum, 2009, p. 348). [*High debt*, caused by *poor governance* and *corruption*]

2) A second paradox of Greek governance has been the juxtaposition of liberal democratic formal structures alongside a political culture marked by clientelism, rent-seeking and corruption (Mitsopoulos and Pelagidis, 2006, 2010). The short-term, piecemeal political attitudes that stem from this culture severely constrain reform initiatives on politically sensitive issues such as the pension, health or labour market systems, as Simitis found when prime minister. [*High debt*, caused by *political opposition to reform* and *corruption*]

3) The Greek model of capitalism has been for a domestic market of anti-competitive regulation, barriers to entry, relatively cheap labour and stable product demand (Featherstone and Papadimitriou, 2008). The constituency for liberal market reforms has been limited and shallow. [*Lack of competitiveness*, caused by *burdensome regulatory environment*]

4) The problems of governance are evident in the 'weak state' scenario of public spending (Walsh, 1994). Successive governments have sustained high levels of public debt: indeed, it has fluctuated around the equivalent of 100 per cent of GDP since 1993. Much of this is related to the inelastic expenditures of the public sector wage bill where governments face strong union resistance to cutbacks and have themselves made major use of public sector jobs as pre-election favours to voters (in.gr, 2009b). In times of austerity, governments have found it politically more expedient to increase taxes (or sell off assets) rather than to reduce state spending. [*High debt*, caused by *big public sector, political opposition to reform, strong public sector unions*]

5) Against this backdrop of inherited weaknesses and falling credibility, the financial markets highlighted Greece as being in danger of default on its foreign borrowing. All three major credit rating agencies further downgraded Greece's status, with Fitch leading the way on 8 December 2009 and Standard Poor eventually judging Greek bonds on 27 April 2010 to have 'junk status'. As Greece faced a maturing of a sizeable portion of its

foreign debt on 19 May 2010, the sequence of downgrades greatly exacerbated its position. [*Collapse of Confidence*, caused by *high debt*, *downgrades*, *financial crisis* and *upward revision of the debt*.]

6) In any event, Greece's debt may be close to 150 per cent of GDP by 2013. To some in the markets, the Greek position – even after its 2010 bail-out – seemed untenable with a major risk of it having to default on its debts. Moreover, the actions of both Ecofin and the ECB were seen by some as having exacerbated Greece's predicament. [*Collapse of confidence*, caused by *high debt* and *poor governance*]

7) Maastricht had created a stress on rules of self-discipline, but had signally failed to supply much central competence to check and intervene in cases of 'moral hazard' concern. When the credit squeeze and economic recession spread, the Greek condition exposed the weakness of the EMU governance structure. [*High debt*, caused by *EMU membership* and *non-enforcement of EMU treaties*]

## Greece in 2010: A Tragedy Without (?) (Catharsis Antzoulatos, 2011)

1) That the situation in Greece was unsustainable. To begin with, the country's current account deficit was comparatively far higher. The big budget deficit, despite several years of fast growth, was a further indication of underlying structural imbalances. Among other potential repercussions, it could fuel destabilizing expectations in a period of turmoil. [*Collapse of confidence*, caused by *high debt* and *current account deficit*]

2) For one thing, the widening current account deficit since the mid 1980s, which accelerated sharply after Greece's accession to the EMU, is strong evidence of the de-industrialization of the country that took place over the past three decades. [*Current account deficit*, caused by *lack of competitiveness* and *EMU membership*]

3) For one thing, national saving was way too low, hovering around 10 percent since the late 1980s, and below 10 percent since 2005. Among the OECD members, only Poland had a lower gross national saving rate. In addition, a large proportion of investment was in infrastructure projects, necessary but not sufficient ingredients for sustainable growth, and construction. [*Current account deficit*, caused by *poor governance* and *political opposition to reform* and *excessive private credit growth*]

4) Even worse, Greece had a big budget deficit. More imbalances, fewer policy options, higher probability of destabilizing expectations and dynamics. One deficit is enough for a crisis, two are a recipe for catastrophe—as economic history teaches and logic suggests. [*Collapse of confidence*, caused by *high debt*, *poor governance* and *current account deficit*]

5) This section presents evidence consistent with the assessment that the budget deficit was a symptom of the pressure on the Greek government by the eroding competitiveness of the country. In addition, the conditions in the international financial markets and the prevailing economic orthodoxy eased this pressure yet, on the negative side, allowed for the imbalances to build up to unsustainable levels. [*High debt*, caused by *lack of competitiveness*, *easy access to cheap debt*, *EMU membership* and *current account deficit*]

6) It additionally implies that the current account deficit was a likely cause for the budget deficit. With all the caveats in mind when translating econometric evidence to causal relationships, it seems that an improvement in competitiveness and rising private credit, the latter supporting private demand, were easing the pressure on government spending. [*High debt*, caused by *current account deficit*, *EMU membership* and *easy access to private credit*]

7) Even if one disagrees with the message of the previous section, that the budget deficit is rather a symptom not a root cause of the Greek tragedy, he cannot but agree that the prescription for catharsis must have as a basic ingredient the restoration of the country's competitiveness and the attendant correction of the current account deficit. Yet, this is very difficult to achieve: The necessary adjustments are big, bigger than those envisaged in the stabilization program, while the necessary political and social consensus did not—as of the time this paper was written—exist. [*High debt*, caused by *current account deficit*, *lack of competitiveness* and *political opposition to reform*] ALSO [*Lack of competitiveness*, caused by *political opposition to reform* and *regulatory burden*]

8) With Greece having as currency the euro and trading mainly with her EUpartners, the required real depreciation is not likely to come from nominal depreciation—the euro is not expected to fall that much any time soon. The only alternative is price deflation. To this end, the production cost must decline through productivity increases, wage decreases, or both. [*Internal devaluation*, caused by *lack of competitiveness* and *EMU membership*]

9) History is not on the side of Greece in this Herculean effort. Since the mid-1980s, several administrations recognized the problem, yet they either failed to tackle it or chose to avoid the unpopular policy choices it presented. More recent administrations evidently chose to overlook the problem. Indicatively, the previous administration, March 2004 to October2009, did little to address it despite that it fully recognized the problem. In an interview in 2004, the then newly-elected prime minister is quoted as having said "Greece is a country that does not invest, does not produce, does not export. How can she survive in the tough world of globalization?" [*Lack of competitiveness*, caused by *poor governance*, *political opposition to reform* and *regulatory burden*]

10) As for the current administration, that was elected in October 2009, it inherited the very difficult situation described in the introduction, with the yawning twin deficits and the accumulated structural rigidities behind them, but judging from the results, did

not handle it efficiently. [*Collapse in confidence*, due to *poor governance* in the face of the *financial crisis*, *high debt* and *current account deficit*]

11) The procrastination in introducing the stabilization program and the lack of a clear strategy for growth are strong indications that it underestimated the severity of the twin deficits in a world where financial markets had become a lot less accommodative than before the onset of the global financial crisis in 2007. [*High debt*, caused by *poor governance*, *access to cheap debt* and *financial crisis*]

12) To summarize the main characteristics of the Greek tragedy unfolding in 2010, the persistently high and widening current account deficit was warning for an unavoidable crisis—long before the budget deficit. Yet, the country, instead of tackling the problem chose the easy option of addressing its symptoms: The government stepped in, becoming an ever larger employer, for the lack of reasonable opportunities in the private sector of the uncompetitive economy, and, additionally, becoming one of the most important customers of private enterprises. As a result, the budget deficit deteriorated. Even worse, it fostered a culture of dependence on the state and of entitlement, as well as corruption. [*High debt*, caused by *current account deficit*, *large public sector*, *lack of competitiveness*, *poor governance* and *corruption*]

13) The easy option was facilitated by rising private debt, which masked that the rising living standards were with borrowed money and hence on borrowed time, plus the permissive conditions in the international financial markets until 2007. The latter allowed the financing not only of the budget and the current account deficits—in essence market discipline did not work, but also of private spending by allowing Greek banks to tap international savings to make up for the inadequate national savings. [*High debt*, caused by *easy access to debt*, *excessive private credit extension*] ALSO [*Current account deficit*, caused by *excessive private credit extension*]

## Greece's Debt Crisis: Overview, Policy Responses, and Implications (Nelson, Belkin & Mix, 2010)

1) Over the past decade, Greece borrowed heavily in international capital markets to fund government budget and current account deficits. The reliance on financing from international capital markets left Greece highly vulnerable to shifts in investor confidence. Investors became jittery in October 2009, when the newly-elected Greek government revised the estimate of the government budget deficit for 2009 from 6.7% of GDP to 12.7% of GDP. There are now questions about whether Greece will be able to repay its maturing debt obligations and interest payments, totaling €54 billion ($73 billion), in 2010. [*Collapse of confidence*, caused by *upward revision of debt* and *high debt*]

2) The debt crisis has both domestic and international causes. Domestically, analysts point to high government spending, weak revenue collection, and structural rigidities in Greece's economy. Internationally, observers argue that Greece's access to capital at low interest rates after adopting the euro and weak enforcement of European Union (EU) rules concerning debt ceilings facilitated Greece's ability to accumulate high levels of external debt. [*High debt*, caused by *poor governance*, *poor revenue collection*, *regulatory burden*, easy access to *cheap debt*.]

3) Greece is currently facing a classic sovereign debt crisis. Greece accumulated high levels of debt during the decade before the crisis, when capital markets were highly liquid. As the crisis has unfolded, and capital markets have become more illiquid, Greece may no longer be able to rollover its maturing debt obligations. [*Collapse of confidence*, caused by *high debt*, *global financial crisis*, and *easy access to cheap debt*]

4) During the decade preceding the global financial crisis that started in fall 2008, Greece's government borrowed heavily from abroad to fund substantial government budget and current account deficits.7 Between 2001, when Greece adopted the euro as its currency, and 2008, Greece's reported budget deficits averaged 5% per year, compared to a Eurozone average of 2%, and current account deficits averaged 9% per year, compared to a Eurozone average of 1%.8 In 2009, the budget deficit was more than 12% of GDP. Many attribute the budget and current account deficits to the high spending of successive Greek governments, 9 among other causes discussed below. Both Greece's budget deficit and external debt level are well above those permitted by the rules governing the EU's Economic and Monetary Union (EMU). Specifically, the EU's Stability and Growth Pact calls for budget deficit ceilings of 3% of GDP and external debt ceilings of 60% of GDP. Greece is not alone, however, in exceeding these limits. [*High debt*, caused by *current account deficit*, *poor governance* and *non-compliance to EMU treaties*]

5) Although the outbreak of the global financial crisis in fall 2008 led to a liquidity crisis for many countries, including several Central and Eastern European countries, the Greek government initially weathered the crisis relatively well and had been able to continue accessing new funds from international markets. That said, the global recession resulting from the financial crisis put strain on many governments' budgets, including Greece's, as spending increased and tax revenues weakened. Since late 2009, however, investor confidence in the Greek government has been rattled. In October 2009, the new socialist government, led by Prime Minister George Papandreou, revised the estimate of the government budget deficit for 2009, nearly doubling the existing estimate of 6.7% of GDP to 12.7% of GDP. This was shortly followed by rating downgrades of Greek bonds by the three major credit rating agencies. In late November, questions about whether Dubai World, a state-controlled enterprise, would default on its debt raised additional concerns about the possibility of a cascade of sovereign defaults for governments under the strain of the financial crisis. [*Collapse of confidence*, caused by *upward revision of debt*, *downgrades* and the *Dubai World Default*]

6) Countries with large external debts, like Greece, were of particular concern for investors. Allegations that the Greek government falsified statistics and attempted to obscure the level of its debt through complex financial instruments have also contributed to a drop in investor confidence. Before the crisis, Greek 10-year bond yields were 10 to 40 basis points above German 10-year bonds. With the crisis, this spread increased to an all-time high of 400 basis points in January 2010 and is currently at 340 basis points.15 High bond spreads indicate declining investor confidence in the Greek economy. [*Collapse of confidence*, caused by *upward revision of debt* and *financial crisis*.]

7) During the past six years, the central government's expenditures increased by 87%, while revenues only grew by 31%, leading to budget deficits above the EU's agreed-upon 3% of GDP threshold. Observers identify a large and inefficient public administration in Greece, costly pension and healthcare systems, tax evasion, and a general "absence of the will to maintain fiscal discipline"20 as major contributors to Greece's debt. [*High debt*, caused by *poor governance*, *large public sector*, *political opposition to reform*, a *large welfare state* and *non-enforcement of the EMU treaties*]

8) According to the OECD, as of 2004, spending on public administration as a percentage of total public expenditure was higher than in any other OECD member, "with no evidence that the quantity or quality of the services are superior."22 Successive Greek governments have taken steps to modernize and consolidate the public administration. However, observers continue to cite over-staffing and poor productivity in the public sector as an impediment to improved economic performance. An aging Greek population—the percentage of Greeks aged over 64 is expected to rise from 19% in 2007 to 32% in 2060—could place additional burdens on public spending and what is widely considered one of Europe's most generous pension systems. Weak revenue collection has also contributed to Greece's budget deficits. Many economists identify tax evasion and Greece's unrecorded economy as key potential revenue streams through which the government could improve its fiscal position. [*High debt*, caused by *poor governance*, *large public sector*, *large welfare system* and *poor revenue collection*.]

9) Greek industry is suffering from declining international competitiveness. Economists cite high relative wages and low productivity as a primary factor. According to one study, wages in Greece have increased at a 5% annual rate since the country adopted the euro, about double the average rate in the Eurozone as a whole. Over the same period, Greek exports to its major trading partners grew at 3.8% per year, only half the rate of those countries' imports from other trading partners. Some observers argue that for Greece to boost its international competitiveness and reduce its current account deficit, it needs to increase its productivity, significantly cut wages, and increase savings. [*Lack of competitiveness*, caused by *regulatory burden*, *high wages* and *low productivity*]

10) Greece's adoption of the euro as its national currency in 2001 is seen by some as a contributing factor in Greece's buildup of debt. With the currency bloc anchored by economic heavyweights Germany and France, and a common monetary policy

conservatively managed by the European Central Bank (ECB), investors have tended to view the reliability of euro member countries with a heightened degree of confidence. The perceptions of stability conferred by euro membership allowed Greece, as well as other Eurozone members, to borrow at a more favorable interest rate than would likely have been the case outside the EU, making it easier to finance the state budget and service existing debt. The lack of enforcement of the Stability and Growth Pact is also seen as a contributing factor to Greece's high level of debt. In 1997, EU members adopted the Stability and Growth Pact, an agreement to enhance the surveillance and enforcement of the public finance rules set out in the 1992 Maastricht Treaty's "convergence criteria" for EMU. The rules call for budget deficits not to exceed 3% of GDP and debt not to exceed 60% of GDP. The Pact clarified and sped up the excessive deficit procedure to be applied to member states that surpassed the deficit limit. [*High debt*, caused by *EMU membership*, *access to cheap debt* and *non-enforcement of the EMU treaties*] ALSO [*Access to cheap debt*, caused by *EMU membership*]

11) As mentioned above, the Greek pension system, considered one of the most generous in Europe, has long been a target of advocates of Greek economic reform. The Papandreou government has pledged both to reform pension institutions and to crack down on social security contribution evasion. At least one government official has been reported as saying that measures will include raising the average retirement age from 61 to 63 (the statutory retirement age in Greece is 65) and calculating pensions on the basis of lifetime contributions as opposed to the last five years of earnings, as is now the case with some civil service pension schemes.35 Prime Minister Papandreou has announced a similar effort to tighten public regulation and strengthen accountability in what is widely considered an inefficient Greek health care system. [*High debt*, caused by *large welfare system*, *poor revenue collection* and *poor governance*]

## Greek Fiscal and Financial Data: More than Meets the Eye (Georganta, 2011)

1) After almost two decades of Excessive Deficit Procedures (EDP) missions to Greece led by Eurostat, as late as November 2010 Eurostat still expressed reservations on the quality of the data reported by Greece"s Statistical Institute for 2009, on issues such as Social Security Funds" accounting, the classification of some public entities or the recording of off-market swaps. [*Collapse of confidence*, caused by *poor statistical services*]

2) The basic problems are traced in the lack of independence of the Hellenic Statistics Authority and the structure of the Greek Statistical System. Of course, these problems are not unique in the statistics only, but are endemic in all spheres of the socio-

economic structure of Greece, with her governments traditionally exercising almost absolutely stifling control on any individual or business creative effort by having promoted clientelism to its extreme form. [*Poor governance*, caused by *poor statistical services* and *corruption*]

3) As we can in the recently published (April 2011) EDP [7] Consolidated Inventory of sources and methods (p.4), financial statements are NA/NU (not available/not used) for the year 2009. The question is how the deficit and debt numbers were compiled without balance sheets and without profit and loss accounts. In spite of this the deficit for the crucial year 2009 was announced as equal to 15.4% the biggest in Europe. [*High debt*, caused by *poor statistical services*]

4) In order to classify economic entities into the GG sector, which determines the deficit, statistical experts have to make sure that the criteria described in the above subsection 3.1 are satisfied. Given that these criteria form a whole system on which ELSTAT's judgment has to be founded before any official publication is made, ELSTAT and Eurostat should have stressed the need for carrying out relevant research and studies, which, notably, have never been carried out before. Instead of this, the chairman of ELSTAT together with Eurostat publish the deficit figures after having refused to listen to any different voices towards the right direction. It is well known that the announced of the deficit number for the year 2009 had a deleterious effect on Greece"s socioeconomic policies. [*Poor governance*, caused by *poor statistical services*] ALSO [*Collapse in confidence*, caused by *poor statistical services*]

## The Greek Debt Restructuring: An Autopsy (Zettelmeyer, Trebesch & Gulati, 2013)

1) The Greek debt crisis began in October 2009, when the newly elected government of George Papandreou revealed that the country had understated its debt and deficit figures for years. The projected budget deficit for 2009, in particular, was revised upwards from an estimated 7% to more than 12% (it eventually ended up at 15.6%). [*Collapse of confidence*, caused by *high debt* and *upward revision of the debt*]

2) This set the stage for months of further bad economic news, which eroded market confidence in Greece and its debt sustainability and resulted in a number of rating downgrades, first by Fitch, then by S&P and Moody's. As the situation continued to deteriorate, Greek sovereign bond yields continued to rise, until spreads over German bunds shot up from 300 to almost 900 basis points during April, effectively excluding Greece from access to bond markets. [*Collapse of confidence*, caused by *downgrades* and *slow EMU response*] ALSO [*Downgrades*, caused by *high debt* and upwards *revision of the debt.*]

3) Despite initial German resistance, a three-year rescue package was agreed on 2 May 2010. It amounted to €80 billion in EU loans and a further €30 billion of IMF credit, and was to be paid out in tranches until 2012, conditional on the implementation of a fiscal adjustment package of 11 percentage points of GDP over three years, and structural reforms meant to restore competitiveness and growth. [*Lack of competitiveness*, caused by *regulatory burden*] ALSO [*High debt*, caused by *lack of competitiveness* and *regulatory burden*]

4) Initially, markets rallied, spreads fell sharply. However, market scepticism soon returned, particularly after Moody's downgraded Greece in mid-June, citing substantial macroeconomic and implementation risks associated with the Eurozone/IMF support package (Global Credit Research, 2010). By July, spreads again began to exceed 800 basis points. [*Collapse in confidence*, caused by *downgrades* and *poor governance*]

5) Notwithstanding market scepticism, Greece's programme achieved significant fiscal consolidation during 2010 (about 5% of GDP). In light of a deepening recession and growing domestic opposition to the programme, however, fiscal adjustment became stuck in the first half of 2011, at a time when the overall and primary deficit were still in the order of 10 and 5 percentage points, respectively, sovereign debt stood at over 140% of GDP, and output was expected to continue to decline at a rate of 3–4% for the next two years. [*High debt*, caused by *political opposition to reform*]

6) Most worryingly, structural reforms that were supposed to restore growth in the medium term were delayed, and reform implementation was weak. An IMF review ending on 2 June 2011 and published in mid-July hence concluded that Greece's outlook 'does not allow the staff to deem debt to be sustainable with high probability', and all but ruled out a return to capital markets until the end of the programme period in mid-2013. [*Collapse in confidence*, caused by *slow EMU response* and *poor governance*]

7) The deepening recession in Greece and the difficulties of the EU and IMF to agree on a credible package of structural reforms with the Greek government lowered expectations of the growth path that Greece might realistically achieve and exacerbated worries about its debt servicing capacity. [*Collapse in confidence*, caused by *financial crisis*, *slow EMU response* and *high debt*]

## Greek Drama Behind the Scenes of European Integration (Schimmer and Kunisch, 2011)

1) For instance, by creating a monetary union without also creating a fiscal union—as most other currency zones in the world are set up—the EU lacks an effective mechanism to enforce its participation rules. So rather than even out economic differences between countries, the Euro has exacerbated them while also seducing economically weaker

countries into higher levels of debt. [*High debt*, caused by *access to cheap debt*, *EMU membership* and *non-enforcement of EMU treaties*]

2) This fundamental flaw in the EMU's design has produced a rather obscure scene. Ever since the outburst of the Euro crisis, the EU has threatened its highly leveraged countries with ending its support even though the EMU itself partly accounts for the reasons behind the deficits. While Greece, for example, may always have been an economically weaker member of the EMU, it was the cheap financing enabled by the laxly governed EMU that made it possible for the country to fall prey to such high levels of debt. [*High debt*, caused by *EMU membership*, *access to cheap debt* and *lack of competitiveness*] ALSO [*Collapse of confidence*, caused by *slow EMU response*]

3) But for now, we remain in medias res, with much drama still to unfold. As Europe's most indebted countries deal with their deficits, the world economy awaits every sovereign bond maturity date in the EU with a level of suspense only Sophocles could conjure. [*Collapse in confidence*, caused by *high debt*]

## Fiscal Policy in the Countries Most Affected by the Crisis: Portugal, Ireland, Greece and Spain (Krajewska 2014)

1) The immediate cause of the Greek crisis was the information that the Greek government passed false statistical data to Eurostat. It turned out that over a number of years Greece distorted its statistics in order to undervalue the actual debt. It should be recognized that for many years public spending (government expenditure) was high.[*Collapse of confidence*, caused by *upward revision of debt* and *high debt*.]

2) Spending was high mainly due to three items: 1. Large military expenditures - Greece ranks second (after the U.S.) in terms of defence spending per capita among the 27 members of NATO. The high share of budgetary expenditure on salaries of public sector employees. For example, the average expenditure for this purpose in the Euro area is about 10% of GDP, while in Greece the expenditure for this purpose ranged from 11% (2007) to 13.5% (2009). High budgetary expenditure on servicing public debt in Greece - about 5-6%, and even 7% of GDP in 2011, compared to the Euro area average of 3% of GDP. [*High debt*, caused by *poor governance*, *large public sector* and *military spending*]

3) High spending on public administration is not a new phenomenon in Greece. It dates back to the government of Andreas Papandreou, who while taking over power in 1974 handed out state jobs to previously persecuted members of the socialist party PASOK. This practice was continued by later prime ministers. As a result Greece, with its population of 11 million, employs 650,000 state officials. In the opinion of the European Union and the IMF this is about 150,000 too many. Moreover, the wages of officials grew rapidly. The average salary in the public sector, which not long before the

crisis had been €1,900, reached twice higher than the national average. In addition, every public employee was entitled to 14 payments per year (the additional two were for Christmas and Summer Holidays), a monthly allowance for each child, and allowances for work in harmful conditions (Kot 2013). It is not surprising that successive governments went further into debt. [*Large public sector*, caused by *political opposition to austerity reform*] ALSO [*High debt*, caused by *large public sector*, *large welfare state*, *corruption* and *high wages*]

4) The adoption of the euro by Greece in 2001 allowed the use of low-interest loans to finance increased public spending. This system collapsed after the disclosure of information about the flawed statistical data. In November 2009, the Fitch rating agency downgraded Greece's credit rating from A to A–, and this was followed by other agencies. Greek securities were downgraded to junk bond status, and the prices of Greek bonds tumbled with the risk of insolvency of the country. [*Access to cheap debt*, caused by *EMU membership*] ALSO [*High debt*, caused by *access to cheap debt*] ALSO [*Collapse of confidence*, caused by *High debt*, *downgrades* and *upward revision of debt*]

5) The situation was so dire that there was talk of excluding Greece from the euro zone (the so-call 'Grexit'). Luckily for Greece, the "Troika" decided to provide financial assistance in the amount of €240 billion in exchange for Greece taking measures to improve public finances. [*Collapse of confidence*, caused by *possibility of EMU exit*]

6) These measures included: pressure to lower public expenditures (decrease employment in public sector, freeze and/or reduce the salaries of civil servants, extend the retirement age and freeze pensions); privatization of some public entities, including the postal service, in order to obtain funds to repay the debt; and implementation of a more flexible labour market by, inter alia, extending the work time to increase productivity, permitting work on Sundays, and the deregulation of 14 professions; measures aimed at eliminating corruption; and improvement in tax collection and the tax system. [*Lack of competitiveness*, caused by *large public sector*, *regulatory burden*, *low productivity*, *high wages*, *corruption* and *poor revenue collection*]

7) The global financial crisis which began in 2007-2008 in the USA had a negative effect on the economy of the European Union, mainly in the Euro area. The falling budget revenues during the recession were coupled with an increase in public expenditure resulting from the implementation of anti-crisis programs, which led to an increase in the budget deficit and public debt. [*High debt*, caused by *financial crisis*]

8) The phenomenon of tax evasion is in Greece very widespread and has a long history. Greeks like to refer to the time when the country was under the rule of the Ottoman Empire, and the failure to pay taxes was considered an act of courage and patriotism. But also since gaining independence, avoiding taxes has been the result of, on one hand, a complicated tax system, and on the other hand inefficient tax administration, lack of any penalties for evasion of taxes, widespread corruption and a developed grey economy, supported by a large share of small and medium-sized enterprises and an

economic structure conducive to tax fraud (agriculture, tourism, services). [*Poor revenue collection*, caused by *poor governance*, *corruption*, *regulatory burden* and *large informal economy*] ALSO [*High debt*, caused by *poor revenue collection* and *poor governance*]

9) In 2007, the share of budget revenue from taxes in relation to GDP in the countries under study was the lowest among the EU-17 countries. Despite the restructuring actions taken in 2011, these countries have not improved their position; it has even deteriorated. This means that the burden of restructuring activities was borne by means of external assistance. [*High debt*, because of *poor revenue collection*]

## CURRENT ACCOUNT IMBALANCES IN THE EURO AREA: DOES CATCHING UP EXPLAIN THE DEVELOPMENT? (BELKE & DREGER, 2013)

1) Public finances have deteriorated, especially in deficit countries. Triggered by the subsequent downgrading of rating agencies, risk premia demanded by holders of public debt increased (Bernoth and Erdogan, 2010). The 10-year sovereign yield spread for bonds issued by surplus and deficit countries widened up to 250 base points. Costs of risk insurance rose from 3 to 10% for Greek government bonds over the course of 2010, as measured by credit default swaps. [*Collapse of confidence*, because of *high debt* and *downgrades*]

2) Before the introduction of the euro area investors had to fear exchange rate depreciations owing to a higher inflation expectation. The common monetary policy with a low inflation target for the entire area contributed to the decrease of risk for investments in these countries. Because of the elimination of exchange risk, investments are based on more solid grounds. [*Access to cheap debt*, because of *monetary dependence*] ALSO [*Monetary Dependence*, because of *EMU membership*]

3) In anticipation of similar inflation, not only short-term, but also long-term nominal interest rate spreads declined fast across countries. However, while there was a tendency towards inflation convergence before the introduction of the common currency, inflation differentials increased since then, see Busetti et al. (2007). This has implied real interest rate divergence. Because of the decrease in real interest rates particularly in southern countries, the marginal return on capital exceeded its costs. At the same time, countries like Germany and France lost comparative cost advantage and experienced huge capital outflows as a result of higher real interest rates. [*Access to cheap debt*, because of *monetary dependence*] ALSO [*Capital influx*, because of *EMU membership* and *monetary dependence*] ALSO [*Excessive private credit extension*, because of *Capital influx*]

4) Current account imbalances point also to shifts in competitiveness via changes in the real exchange rate (Arghyrou and Chortareas, 2008). According to standard models, real exchange rate appreciations redirect demand from domestic to foreign goods. Under a common currency, fluctuations in the real exchange rate correspond to changes in relative prices and unit labor costs. Hence, deficit countries may have become less competitive because domestic prices increased more than foreign prices. External deficits may reflect a lack of competitiveness and overheating problems owing to overly optimistic expectations or asset price booms. [*Current account deficit*, because of *lack of competitiveness* and *monetary dependence*]

5) A current account deficit implies an excess of investment over savings. It can be caused by a variety of factors, such as an investment boom owing to better growth perspectives or a lack of savings as a result of excessive public consumption. The deficit is financed by a surplus in saving of other countries, i.e., international capital inflows. Prolonged deficits lead to an accumulation of foreign debt. [*High debt*, caused by *current account deficit*] ALSO [*Current account deficit*, because of *Capital influx*]

6) In the debate on global imbalances, the euro area countries have not received much attention so far. While the current account is on balance for the entire area, divergences between individual member states have increased since the introduction of the common currency. [*Current account deficit*, caused by *EMU membership*, *monetary dependence* and *lack of competitiveness*]

7) Therefore, an asymmetric response of the euro area members is required to reduce the imbalances. This involves a depreciation of the real exchange rate in the deficit countries via a cut in their unit labor costs, either through higher productivity or lower nominal wages. [*Internal devaluation*, caused by *monetary dependence*, *low productivity*, *high wages* and *lack of competitiveness*]

8) Owing to higher risk premia in the aftermath of the financial crisis, real interest rates have increased in the southern periphery. The countries have lost their capital cost advantage and experienced substantial capital outflows (Mordonu, 2011). The shift towards a more labor-intensive production is relieved by declining unit labor costs. Because of the ongoing trend towards an aging society and increased pressure to finance social security, fiscal consolidation remains on the agenda for all member states. [*Collapse in confidence*, caused by *financial crisis*, *lack of competitiveness*] ALSO [*High debt*, because of *large social welfare net*]

## WHATEVER HAPPENED TO GREECE? (FOUSKAS, 2013)

1) The conventional view is that the huge scale of Greek debt arose from the practice of 'clientelism' by the two main parties—the winning of votes through the creation of public sector employment—accompanied by widespread tax evasion and low tax-

collection rates. [*High debt*, caused by *corruption*, *large public sector* and *poor revenue collection*]

2) With its bourgeois breakthrough, and so its industrial revolution, truncated by the 1922 Asia Minor disaster, the country could not develop a strong economic base able to compete with the advanced core of Europe. Greece became effectively a 'subaltern' or dependent state within the European and global economy, unable to develop economies of scale. Its current-account deficit and balance-of-payments problems become chronic, creating a debt problem which has accumulated over many decades. [*High debt*, caused by *current account deficit* and *lack of competitiveness*]

3) Venizelos gave every impoverished refugee a small plot of land to till, hoping that the peasant and his family would as a result stay away from socialist and communist influence. Although politically effective, this policy was economically disastrous. It compartmentalised the only sector of the economy with the potential to compete internationally, depriving Greece of any prospect of developing a robust, export-led agricultural sector through economies of scale and technological development. Once again the country's international competitiveness was damaged, in turn worsening its national debt. [*Lack of competitiveness*, caused by *poor governance*, *political opposition to reform*] ALSO [*High debt*, caused by *lack of competitiveness*]

4) It was at this time that the Greek ruling elites invented a new strategy to stave off mass political protest: the large-scale recruitment of civil servants. It was a strategy which continued unabated after the restoration of democracy in 1974: for both of the new parties which alternated in power after that date, the right-wing New Democracy party and PASOK (the Pan-Hellenic Socialist Movement), it proved a useful means of winning and retaining support among key constituencies of voters. [*Large public sector*, caused by *political opposition to reform*]

5) By the 1970s, the Greek economy's dependence on wider European and Atlantic economic structures, its continuing inability to develop industrial economies of scale and PASOK–ND's bipartisan strategy of employing ever increasing numbers in the civil service took their toll on growth. [*Lack of competitiveness*, caused by *large public sector*, *corruption* and *poor governance*]

6) Both parties, however, financed this programme, as well as pro-welfare reforms, wage expansion and other clientelistic practices, not through taxation—as was the case in Western Europe and Scandinavia —but through domestic and external borrowing. The result was the further expansion of Greek national debt: from 20 per cent of GDP in 1975 to 120 per cent in 2008, the year before the financial crash. [*High debt*, because of *political opposition to reform*, *large welfare state*, *high wages* and *corruption*]

7) Challenged by an increasingly powerful labour movement, the cycle of debt creation via domestic and external borrowing was initiated and reproduced by the ruling elites of PASOK and ND for political and electoral purposes. In every electoral cycle since 1974, the incumbent party had replenished the state machine with unskilled labour

in order to contain its political decline. [*High debt*, caused by *strong public sector unions*, *corruption*, *political opposition to reform*] ALSO [*Political opposition to reform*, caused by *strong public sector unions*]

8) Throughout the 1980s, pension benefits and tax breaks were periodically introduced and withdrawn, all with the aim of excluding communist forces from power and dividing the trade-union movement while securing the political reproduction of the two-party system. In this sense, the clientelist and corrupt practices of the ruling classes during and after the Cold War should be seen as political strategies employed by a bipartisan elite seeking to maintain its rule in the absence of economic modernisation and growth. [*Corruption*, caused by *political opposition to reform*] ALSO [*Large welfare state*, caused by *political opposition to reform*]

9) If Greek debt arose originally from the country's very particular form of political economy and geopolitics, it has been exacerbated by two other factors. The first is defence spending. By exaggerating the threat coming from Turkey and the vulnerability of both Greece itself and Cyprus, the Greek establishment has been able consistently to argue that Greece needs a large and expensive military. In 2009, defence expenditure was as high as 3.2 per cent of Greek GDP, as compared with 2.4 per cent in France, 2.7 per cent in Britain, 2 per cent in Portugal, 1.4 per cent in Germany and 1.3 per cent in Spain. [*High debt*, caused by *poor governance* and *military spending*]

10) Fed by periodic but controllable tensions in Cyprus and the Aegean, this ensures that both polities continue to consume weapon systems, military aircraft and other military supplies made in the US and other NATO countries. At the same time, they aim to keep Greece's geopolitical and security orbit in the eastern Mediterranean away from Russian and Chinese interests. Most of the purchases of military equipment have taken place through the issuance of Greek sovereign debt. [*High debt*, caused by *poor governance* and *military spending*]

11) The second factor contributing to Greek indebtedness is tax evasion. But it is not the tax evasion of the ordinary Greek wage earner or the petty-bourgeoisie, which—if it has occurred—has never been a major cause. In terms of sheer scale, the tax evasion which matters is that of what might be called Greece's 'comprador' oligarchy. [*High debt*, caused by *poor revenue collection* and *corruption*]

12) It is impossible to estimate the scale of the tax evasion practised by the superrich comprador-cum-financial class which engaged in this new economic activity, but it is clear that it has been enormous. As the recent scandal of the so-called 'Lagarde list' of tax evaders demonstrates, Greece's PASOK–ND ruling elites cooperated to protect wealthy individuals from having to pay their dues to the state. In 2010, Christine Lagarde, then French Finance Minister, gave her Greek counterpart a list of 2059 names of wealthy Greek individuals to investigate for possible tax evasion. [*Poor revenue collection*, caused by *corruption*]

13) Greek shipping capital, a prime international force in world seaborne trade with no substantial base in Greece, plays a critical part in this story. A large part of the Greek merchant fleet is listed in the shipping register under flags of convenience, so no substantial tax income can be raised by the Greek state. This loss of income became particularly significant in the 1990s and 2000s: the global share of the Greek merchant fleet— which was just 1 per cent in 1947 and 12 per cent in 1970—soared to 17.4 per cent in 2000. [*Poor revenue collection*, because of *corruption*, *poor governance* and *regulatory burden*]

14) The first—which has been chosen by both PASOK and ND since the first bailout in June 2011—is further pursuance of austerity on the basis of the IMF–EU– ECB troika programme. The aim is to create a primary budgetary surplus and prevent the country's fiscal default within the Eurozone. This is technically feasible, but socially it looks impossible: the fabric of Greek society simply cannot bear the strain. And politically, it is dangerous. [*Collapse of confidence*, caused by *political opposition to reform*]

## The Welfare State and the Crisis: The Case of Greece (Matsaganis, 2011)

1) Upon entry to the euro area, Greece enjoyed a period of fast growth (averaging 4% in 2000–08). However, behind the façade of prosperity based on strong consumer demand, boosted by cheap credit, lay a largely uncompetitive economy. [*Excessive private credit extension*, caused *EMU membership* and *Capital influx*]

2) Its many weaknesses, signified by chronic fiscal and external deficits, and a large public debt, were made plain in October 2009, when the incoming government announced that earlier fiscal data had been misreported. The general government deficit for 2008 was corrected from 5.0% to 7.7% (later revised to 9.4%) of GDP, while the estimate for 2009 was raised from 3.7% to a staggering 12.5% (later to 15.4%) of GDP. [*Collapse of confidence*, caused by *high debt*, *current account deficits* and *upward revision of debt*]

3) The public debt estimate for 2009 was also revised from 99.6% to 115.1% (later to 126.8%) of GDP. At the same time, the current account deficit reached 14.7% of GDP in 2008, reflecting the country's steady loss of competitiveness (Bank of Greece 2011). [*Current account deficits*, caused by *lack of competitiveness*]

4) The revised figures stunned public opinion at home and shocked markets abroad. Coming not long after the onset of the international financial crisis, and coinciding with sluggish growth worldwide, the Greek case assumed unanticipated dimensions. In this context the country's dependence on foreign borrowing, heavier than hitherto thought, proved fatal: markets reacted by increasing spreads (that is, interest rate differentials from

German government bonds), and by lowering credit ratings (Featherstone 2011). [*Collapse of confidence*, caused by *upward revision of debt*, *global financial crisis* and *downgrades*]

5) On 3 March 2010, the government announced a first package of austerity measures, aimed at fiscal consolidation. Although costing the government a great deal in terms of popularity, the announcement failed to placate the markets. In April, Standard & Poor downgraded the country's credit rating to below investment grade (i.e., junk status), while spreads on 10-year government bonds continued to rise sharply to 1,000 basis points (i.e., 10 percentage points), from 200 basis points in January. [*Collapse of confidence*, caused by *failed austerity measures* and *downgrades*]

6) The [second] rescue package did manage to impress international markets, but caused strong domestic reaction. Civil unrest reached a paroxysm on 5 May 2010, in the context of a huge and largely peaceful demonstration, when three workers lost their lives as extremists set fire to a high-street bank in Athens. The tragedy cast further doubt on the country's future, and lengthened the odds that the rescue package might prove effective1. [*Collapse of confidence*, caused by *political opposition to reform*]

7) The Greek crisis is a combination of external forces (endemic turbulence in financial markets) and domestic weaknesses (chronic fiscal and trade deficits). [*Crisis*, caused by *high debt*, *financial crisis* and *current account deficits*]

8) Contrary to the experience of other countries, the case of Greece actually seemed to support the thesis that the welfare state was virtually unreformable. While social spending soared (usually without visible improvements in outcomes), reforms failed one after another (or, as in many cases, failed to be formulated in the first place), and the whole edifice appeared to be unassailable. It is in this sense that the welfare state, seemingly incapable for reform, contributed in a far from trivial way to the fiscal crisis of the state. [*Large welfare state*, caused by *political opposition to reform* and *poor governance*] ALSO [*High debt*, caused by *large welfare state*]

9) Nowhere was this more evident as in the case of retirement pensions2, the largest item of social expenditure and the most highly contested policy area in Greek politics over the last few decades. Pensions form the backbone of Greece's system of social protection, providing households with as much as 24.1% of their disposable income on average (ElStat 2010). [*Large welfare state*, caused by *political opposition to reform*]

10) In an ageing world, pension expenditure as a proportion of national income will rise everywhere. In view of that, over the last two decades most European countries have taken measures to counter the fiscal effects of unfavourable demographics. By and large, such measures have defused the 'pensions' time bomb'. For instance, spending on pensions in the EU as a whole was recently estimated to rise gently to 12.3% of GDP in 2040 and 12.5% in 2060 (EC 2009). Nevertheless, nowhere was pension expenditure projected to rise as steeply as in Greece: to 21.4% of GDP in 2040 and 24.1% in 2060 (EC 2009). True, the optimal level of pension spending cannot be determined a priori - it

must reflect social and political preferences. However, it is hard to view such a burden on public finances as other than unsustainable. [*Large welfare state*, caused by *aging population*]

11) Before the current crisis, although Greek pensions were clearly inequitable as well as unsustainable, attempts at significant reform had ended in failure. A combination of fierce opposition on the part of labour unions and other professional associations, and lack of resolve on the part of the political class, led to paralysis. Particular episodes of aborted reforms, and of legislation passed only at the cost of nearly total capitulation to the demands of privileged groups, are extensively documented in a growing literature. [*Large welfare state*, caused by *political opposition to reform* and *strong public sector unions*]

12) In a certain way, the failure to reform Greek pensions can be formulated in terms of political economy, or even as a result of a failure of representation. The existing state of affairs jeopardized future prosperity and violated distributional justice, but generated winners as well as losers – and the former were powerful in society and politics. As important stakeholders were under-represented (e.g. the young, women, non-standard workers), while others were not represented at all (e.g. the proverbial future generations), the political system seemed incapable of producing a solution. [*Large welfare state*, caused by *political opposition to reform* and *strong public sector unions*]

## THE SHORT TERM DETERMINANTS OF CAPITAL FLOWS IN A SMALL, OPEN ECONOMY: THE CASE OF GREECE (PAPPAS, 2011)

1) With the focus of the paper being on capital flows, it is useful to provide some relative information concerning capital flows in Greek economy from the early 1980s onwards. During the decade of the 1980s the volume of capital flows remained quite stable between €2bn and €4bn.1 Its volume increased during the 1990s, reaching €9bn in 1998. After half of the first decade of the new millennium it increased substantially and reached €30bn during the last two years of the decade. However the volume of the net foreign direct investment (FDI) remained quite moderate for the whole period at around €1bn. The fact that FDI inflows were quite low compared with total inflows reveals that the Greek economy failed to attract foreign direct investments; the major part of inflows refer to loans mainly to the Greek public sector (central government, central bank, public companies). [*Capital inflows*, caused by *high debt*]

2) The Greek capital account remained permanently in surplus during these three decades as a necessity for financing the excessive and long-lasting deficits of the current account. The permanent external deficits reveal clearly the diachronic loss of

competitiveness of the Greek economy. [*Current account deficit*, caused by *lack of competitiveness* and *Capital influx*]

3) Especially after the entrance into the Euro zone and the adoption of a hard currency like the EURO the competitiveness deteriorated even further. [*Lack of competitiveness*, caused by *EMU membership* and *monetary dependence*]

4) The structural problems of the Greek economy and the external and internal deficits forced Greece during 2010 to take steps to avoid bankruptcy. Now the markets "demand" macroeconomic discipline from the Greek government; however whether this discipline was always a prerequisite for the external funding of the Greek deficits is debatable. [*High debt*, caused by *easy access to cheap debt*] ASLO [*Collapse of confidence*, caused by *lack of competitiveness*, *regulatory burden*, *high debt* and *current account deficits*]

5) Thus external factors, which are outside a given country's control often determine the behavior of capital flows. In this sense the argument of market discipline, which is supposed to be imposed by capital markets to domestic economies, is not confirmed. Currently financial markets "dictate" macroeconomic discipline and the reduction of deficits to Greece. [*Collapse of confidence*, caused by *high debt* and *current account deficits*]

6) According to our results, however, the markets and fund managers up to 2009 seem to have ignored Greek economic fundamentals attached to the high yields of the Greek government bonds. [*High debt*, caused by *access to cheap debt*]

## THE POLITICS OF PENSION REFORM: LESSONS FROM PUBLIC ATTITUDES IN GREECE (O'DONNEL AND TINIOS, 2003)

1) Political opposition to pension reform appears to be rooted in a general lack of public appreciation of the case for reform combined with the desire to protect interest group privileges. Public ignorance and insecurity breed attitudes not conducive to reform. [*Large welfare state*, caused by *political opposition to reform*]

2) There tend to be substantial gaps between the scale of reforms analysts argue are necessary and the package of reforms politicians implement. The discrepancy, at least in part, can be attributed to sceptical public opinion, which constrains the political feasibility of pension reform. [*Large welfare state*, caused by *political opposition to reform*]

3) This is done through the examination of survey data from Greece, where a pension reform agenda of rationalisation has been considered, intermittently, since the late 1950s but where progress with the implementation of such reform has been modest. This lack of political progress, despite the strong distributional and economic case that exists for

pension reform, makes Greece a particularly interesting source of evidence on the role played by public attitudes in the policy process. [*Large welfare state*, caused by *political opposition to reform* and *poor governance*]

4) From examination of Greek attitudinal data, it appears that political opposition to pension reform is rooted in a general lack of public appreciation of the case for reform combined with the desire to protect interest group privileges. [*Political opposition to reform*, caused by *strong public sector unions*]

5) Public attitudes do not simply act as a given constraint on the reform process but are a product of the structure of the pension system itself. This two-way, reinforcing relationship between public attitudes and system characteristics makes the reform process more difficult. [*Political opposition to reform*, caused by *poor governance*]

6) The public pension system in Greece is a product of the Mediterranean Welfare State (Ferrera, 1996). The system as a whole is fragmented, lacking a unitary philosophy and widely adhered to operational rules. As a result, it is rather opaque and tends to be used as an instrument of clientelism within a general environment of state corporatism (Featherstone and Tinios, 2002). [*Corruption*, caused by *large welfare state* and *poor governance*]

7) Spending on pensions is high (12.1 percent of GDP compared to the EU average of 10.5 percent) but is poorly targeted with respect to distributional justice. [*High debt*, caused by *large welfare state*]

8) Civil servants' (primary) pensions are paid directly from the government budget, without the intermediation of a fund. The system is under severe fiscal pressure. Ad hoc public subsidies to the system, financed from general government revenues, amount to 3 percent of GDP and are not sanctioned by any law. [*High debt*, caused by *large welfare state*]

9) By international standards, average replacement rates (pensions relative to previous earnings) are high but display tremendous variation: civil servants, 109 percent; public enterprise workers, 98 percent; professionals, 90 percent; private sector employees, 62 percent; self-employed, 54 percent (Mylonas and de la Maisonneuve, 1999, Table 3).3 There is a considerably less generous system for those entering the labour market after 1 January 1993. [*High debt*, caused by *large welfare state*]

10) In Greece, as in other countries that had extensive, mature PAYG earnings related pension systems at the time demographic and economic conditions turned against PAYG, the move to funding has not been a realistic option and the reform agenda has been restricted to retrenchment and targeting of the PAYG system. [*High debt*, caused by *large welfare state* and *ageing population*]

11) The core of the Greek reform programme has always been system consolidation. It was only in recent years that the response to an ageing population was added to a case that was already, arguably, very strong. [*Large welfare state*, caused by *ageing population*]

12) The coexistence of PAYG finance with a multitude of sector specific pension providers results in a bewildering mosaic of crosssubsidies, which obfuscates the notion of a binding budget constraint. Such an environment encourages a clientelistic game of distributing privileges to specific sectors of the population and provides little incentive to control expenditures. [*High debt*, caused by *large welfare state* and *poor governance*]

13) High contribution rates and the lack of actuarial relationships between contributions and benefits create strong incentives for evasion of pension contributions. For example, high pension minima ensure that 70 percent of pensioners belonging to the main scheme for private sector employees receive the minimum pension, irrespective of contributions paid. [*Corruption*, caused by *large welfare state* and *poor governance*]

14) A deficit financed PAYG pension scheme is not best placed to provide the flexible supply of investment funds required by a modern economy. In addition to the impact on the capital market, the pension system impinges on the labour market. High and variable pension contributions depress the average demand for labour and distort the allocation of labour across sectors (Börsch-Supan and Tinios, 2002). [*Lack of competitiveness*, caused by *poor governance*, *corruption* and *large welfare state*]

15) Greece, after Italy, is the EU country experiencing the fastest demographic deterioration. This, combined with a generous PAYG pension system, poses a major threat to meeting the Stability and Growth Pact (SGP) criteria of EMU (Bank of Greece, 2001). [*High debt*, caused by *large welfare state* and *ageing population*]

16) Further, the increased exposure of Greek markets to competition arising from the Single European Market and globalisation make it increasingly difficult to sustain the cross-subsidisation across and within industries built into the current pension system (Börsch-Supan and Tinios, 2002). [*Lack of competitiveness*, caused by *large welfare state* and *EMU membership*]

17) Political progress with the implementation of this rationalisation agenda has been modest in the face of, often fierce, public opposition. [*Large welfare state*, caused by *political opposition to reform*]

18) Attempts at consolidation started in the 1960s, but it was not until the mid-80s, when the role of pension deficits in driving overall public sector deficits became apparent, that the need for major organisational reform was perceived as urgent. Between 1990 and 1992, in the face of fierce opposition and following failed attempts by the previous government, there was some rationalisation of the pension system by a conservative government (New Democracy). [*High debt*, caused by *large welfare state*]

19) Again, there was strong public opposition, with the trade unions taking a lead role, and the Government subsequently withdrew these proposals, whilst reiterating its determination to proceed with reform within its term of office. [*Political opposition to reform*, caused by *strong public sector unions*]

20) The root cause of the slow progress with pension reform in Greece has been identified as the absence of trust and the prevailing climate of conflict (Featherstone and Tinios, 2002). [*Political opposition to reform*, caused by *lack of trust in government*]

21) Part of the motivation for pension reform, in Greece as elsewhere, is fiscal strain on the PAYG system of finance created by demographic and economic conditions. [*High debt*, caused by *large welfare state* and *ageing population*]

22) Pension reform is recognised to be politically difficult. This is often thought to derive from the dynamic nature of the problem – a well-informed electorate has little incentive to vote in reform and every incentive to pass on costs to, yet to be enfranchised, future generations. Politicians, with short time horizons, have little incentive to protect the interests of future generations. [*Large welfare state*, caused by *political opposition to reform*]

23) There is widespread and intense dissatisfaction with the current pension system. Despite this, pension reform has been consistently blocked by fierce demonstrations of public opposition. This apparent inconsistency appears to derive from limited knowledge of the parameters of the current pension arrangements, lack of appreciation of the consequences of fiscal pressures on the system, aversion to change generated by its inherent uncertainty and, not least, the influence of powerful minorities. [*Political opposition to reform*, caused by *lack of trust* and *strong public sector unions*]

24) This, together with the relative strength of the various interest groups and the general discontent with the pension system, lends support to the proposition that powerful minorities maintain the status quo. The strongest labour unions are in the public sector and lobbying is more easily organised by the unified professions than it is by the disjointed self-employed. [*Political opposition to reform*, caused by *strong public sector unions*]

## The Political Dimension of the Greek Financial Crisis (Sklias and Maris, 2013)

1) Namely, high public deficits, irrational public spending, foreign debt, lack of exports, minimum competition basis, default functioning of the labour market, are among the profound variables that resulted in the crisis. [*Collapse of confidence*, caused by *high debt*, *poor governance*, *monetary dependence* and *lack of competitiveness*]

2) Using Greece and its crisis as an illustrative example we will show that the political and institutional development level is a critical component and a root cause for the Greek crisis. This skewed model was developed the last 30 years together with other political phenomena among others like, the statism, corruption, rent-seeking behaviour, political instability, populism, the blockage of reforms and parliamentary instability.

[*Destructive institutions*, caused by *corruption*, *large public sector* and *political opposition to reform*]

3) We also support the view that what in the first instance appears to be bad public financial practices and policymaking, is in essence a lack of the wider model of governance. [*High debt*, caused by *poor governance*]

4) As it is observed from this paper, Greece is a real laggard in every indicator of governance within the European Union (EU). [*Poor governance*, cause by *destructive institutions*]

5) The Greek crisis made evident that the Maastricht criteria are inadequate, and the EU has not developed practices that can support and affirm the political and institutional development and way of governance within its member states. [*Poor governance*, caused by *non-enforcement of EU treaties*]

6) More specifically, for the Greek case, as Mitsopoulos and Pelagidis (2009b) state, it is the design of the Greek political system that has led to rent seeking actions and the blockage of reforms. [*Political opposition to reform*, caused by *destructive institutions*]

7) Greece experienced the rise of irresponsible populism, unrestrained patronage politics, and a powerful culture of ethnocentrism that worked against the country's full Europeanization. To the extent that Greek society had willingly accepted the terms of the contract offered to it by Papandreou, most of his successors in power felt no need to reverse them. [*High debt*, caused by *political opposition to reform*, *destructive institutions*, *corruption* and *large welfare state*]

8) Under these conditions the state and the public sector in the 1980s in Greece expanded enormously and even though one could argue that this expansion was necessitated in order to avoid job losses in non-competitive sectors, it cannot justify the overall assessment and performance of the public sector. [*Large public sector*, caused by *lack of competitiveness*]

9) Under these conditions over the next decade Europeanization and modernization have not been supported by the necessary institutions and the wider model of governance which was skewed and was negatively affected by many political phenomena like corruption and statism. [*Political opposition to reform*, caused by *corruption*, *large welfare state* and *large public sector*]

10) In fact, Europeanization and modernization in Greece during the 1990's consolidate and legitimate the clientelistic basis of the Greek polity. It is characteristic that almost all attempts for reforms the past 30 years failed. [*Political opposition to reform*, caused by *destructive institutions*, *corruption* and a *lack of trust*]

11) In Greece the fiscal adaptation during the last 30 years was disappointing. This not only related to the public deficits and public debts but to the size, extension, function and efficiency of the public sector. There are huge and unsustainable public debts and public deficits but as it is known, Greece is not the only country within the Eurozone with these results. Instead, in the last three years 11 European countries failed to maintain their

public deficits below 60% (Figure 2). [*High debt*, caused by *large public sector*, *large welfare state* and *non-enforcement of EU treaties*]

12) The answer lies on the lack of political and institutional convergence. This element is the most important cause that prevents the economic convergence and the non-implementation of the main targets of the economic policy via fiscal adaptation, liberalization of capital movements, convergence of inflation and interest rates and stabilization of exchange rates as they are described in the Maastricht Treaty. [*Political opposition to reform*, caused by *destructive institutions*]

13) For example, as we argue below the maintenance and expansion of statism not only made the state unable to overcome the severe fiscal problems but also makes no sense the so-called 'creative accounting' which is also characteristic of political and institutional underdevelopment. [*High debt*, caused by *large welfare state* and *large public sector*]

14) The EMU from its early beginning was not based on each country's real ability to participate but on political calculations. Political and economic priorities have considerably overcome economic and fiscal principles in the formation and function of the EMU. Thus, the Eurozone failed to create the political, economic and institutional environment in which a country like Greece could increase its competitiveness. [*Lack of competitiveness*, caused by *EMU membership* and *destructive institutions*]

15) The decreasing competitiveness of the Greek economy was appearing in the current account deficits of the last decade clearly which in 2007 was 14.1% of GDP. Since 1995 the labour productivity in Greece was almost always lower than in the other European countries with the exception of Portugal. [*Current account deficits*, caused by *lack of competitiveness*] ALSO [*Lack of competitiveness*, caused by *high wages* and *low productivity*]

16) However, this is only one side of the problem because in Greece like in other peripheral countries well organized labour unions exist that not only affect the flexibility of the real wages but also the institutional reforms, with negative result on the overall competitiveness of the country (Lapavitsas et al., 2010). In this regard, as De Grauwe (2011) argues from 1999 to 2008, Greece and other peripheral European countries lost their competitiveness because their relative unit labour cost increased considerably. [*Lack of competitiveness*, caused by *large public sector unions* and *political opposition to reform*] ALSO [*Political opposition to reform* caused by *strong PS unions*]

17) Moreover, it is not strange that strong state monopolies prevail in Greece, which negatively affect productivity and competitiveness. For example, even now in the areas of electricity, telecommunication, water supply, postal services, railways and natural gas the state remains the main manager. [*Lack of competitiveness*, caused by *large public sector*]

18) Under these circumstances the productivity and competitiveness of Greece is not only a matter of prices which are affected by many factors but also a matter of the political, institutional underdevelopment and ineffectiveness of governance the last 30

years, under which the rate of investments remained very low. [*Lack of competitiveness*, caused by *poor governance* and *destructive institutions*]

19) The Greeks, in contrast to the other European countries, had made the state the main engine of economic growth and political and institutional development since 1980s. Thus, they failed not only to develop their skills and to produce manufactory products but also to remain competitive within the Eurozone. [*Lack of competitiveness*, caused by *large public sector*]

20) Even today, Greece's rank on the ease of doing business did not change from 2009 as it remains the 100th country in the world below Yemen, Vietnam, Guatemala and Jordan (World Bank, 2012). What is the most important cause for this observation? Why do Greek businesses not invest within their country as the other European businesses do? In a theoretical study Mo (2001) describes how corruption affects both political stability economic growth. Thus, one part of the answer can be found on the skewed governance model, the skewed state role and the model of political, economic and institutional development in Greece (Kaufmann et al., 2005). [*Lack of competitiveness*, *destructive institutions* and *poor governance*]

21) During this period of economic underdevelopment in relation to the other European countries, the state expanded enormously; take for example the law 1368/83, for the socialization of public enterprises and the nationalization of many public organizations, creating two major consequences. [*High debt*, caused by *large public sector* and *destructive institutions*]

22) Almost all the attempts for reforms, like for example the reform of the labour markets in 2000, failed because the governance hypothesis in Greece is inadequate. This 'institutional mess' (Tsebelis, 1995) was the main reason why the possibilities of political and economic reforms have been limited during the last 30 years in Greece. [*Political opposition to reform*, caused by *destructive institutions* and *poor governance*]

23) Secondly, the capacity for effective governance in Greece is limited. For example, Greece and Italy were the last European countries since 1996 in government effectiveness (Figure 6), which reflects perceptions of the quality of public services, the quality of civil service and the degree of its independence from political pressures, the quality of policy formulation and implementation, and the credibility of the government's commitment to such policies. [*Lack of competitiveness*, caused by *poor governance*, *destructive institutions*, *political opposition to reform* and *corruption*]

24) According to Mitsopoulos and Pelagidis (2009a) the creation and existence of powerful and well-connected organized interest groups is a result of the high administrative burden and poor governance. [*Political opposition to reform*, caused by *strong public sector unions*]

25) Populism has also been addressed as one of the main characteristics of the Greek national system. This may have been one of the root causes for mismanagement (De Grauwe, 2010; Tsakalotos, 1998). In this framework, modernizing the Greek economy

was very much connected with the function of a political system which was not ready to deal with a series of subsequent challenges. [*Poor governance*, caused by *political opposition to reform* and *destructive institutions*]

26) Thus, as Kazakos (2010) argues, the over grown development of the state, the political centralization and the cliental networks negatively affected the performance of the institutions and corruption. [*Destructive institutions*, caused by *large public sector* and *corruption*]

27) As Graycar and Villa (2011, p. 437) believe, corruption's main consequence is 'a loss of governance capacity, and this is a greater and more prevalent loss than a monetary loss'. In this regard, Koutsoukis and Sklias (2005) state that, among others, the most important factors that contributed to the phenomenon of corruption in Greece are a political system that favours clientelism, a complex legal framework that provides a scope for manoeuvres, as well as a political culture which provides space for such pathogenic behaviour. [*Poor governance*, caused by *corruption*] ALSO [*Corruption*, caused by *destructive institutions*]

28) The Greek crisis has important political elements and in this way the crisis will remain. As this paper has analysed, the economic factors have contributed to the crisis but they are not the root causes, which can be found only within the political and institutional model of development and the mode of governance. [*Collapse of confidence*, caused by *destructive institutions* and *poor governance*]

## THE OPTION OF LAST RESORT: A TWO-CURRENCY EMU (ARGHYROU AND TSOUKALAS, 2010)

1) The present turmoil in the Greek sovereign bonds market, as well as the increasing pressure on Spanish and Portuguese bonds, is not coincidental but symptomatic of a fundamental truth. This is that the eurozone is not an optimum currency area. [*Collapse of confidence*, caused by *EMU membership* and *monetary dependence*]

2) A significant body of academic research shows that since euro's introduction in 1999 the EMU periphery countries not only did not achieve real convergence towards the union's core countries but, on the contrary, have diverged further. [*Lack of competitiveness*, caused by *monetary dependence*] ALSO [*Monetary dependence*, caused by *EMU membership*]

3) Euro-participation provided periphery countries with a false sense of financial security preventing them from pursuing unpopular yet necessary fiscal and structural reforms. [*Access to cheap credit*, caused by *EMU membership*] ALSO [*Poor governance*, caused by *access to cheap credit*]

4) This caused substantial competitiveness losses leading to unsustainable public and external debts. One can write pages to analyse the latter's implications but the main point is simple. Debts provide the lender claims to future consumption the honouring of which implies either higher production or reduction of future consumption on behalf of the borrower. [*High debt*, caused by *lack of competitiveness*] ALSO [*Current account deficits*, caused by *lack of competitiveness*]

5) The increasingly loud market signal we receive in recent months is that the intra-EMU economic divergence has been allowed to reach such an extent as to render the servicing of existing debts from both sources quoted above increasingly unrealistic. To ignore this signal and blame the crisis on speculative attacks is to delude ourselves. What we observe is markets responding to unfavourable economic fundamentals rendering the euro's continued existence increasingly unsustainable [*Collapse of confidence*, caused by *lack of competitiveness*, *monetary dependence* and *high debt*]

6) But the enormity of the imbalances at the periphery economies makes the reforms' extensive and rapid implementation imperative to affect market expectations. This element of urgency and thoroughness raises doubts about the capacity of the periphery societies to bear the temporary yet substantial fall in living standards accompanying the necessary reforms. [*Internal devaluation*, caused by *lack of competitiveness* and *monetary dependence*]

7) Upon its introduction, the ECB will devalue the weak euro by a percentage enough to restore the competitiveness losses periphery countries have suffered over the last decade against their main trading partners, the core-EMU countries. This will give the periphery a competitiveness boost while it introduces extensive structural reforms. [*Lack of competitiveness*, caused by *monetary dependence*]

8) A major benefit of the proposed plan is its enhanced ability to provide an effective commitment device for EMU members to undergo reforms and fiscal consolidation as opposed to the existing evidently weak, non-enforceable sanctions' mechanism of the Stability and Growth Pact. [*High debt*, caused by *non-enforcement of EU treaties*]

## THE IMPACT OF THE SOVEREIGN DEBT CRISIS ON THE EUROZONE COUNTRIES (ALI, 2012)

1) Differently put, the current eurozone crisis is a public debt crisis. Table 1 shows that all PIIGS countries, France and Germany have exceeded the budgetary limit of 3% deficit in 2009-2010. The eurozone average exceeded 6%. [*Collapse of confidence*, caused by *high debt*] ALSO [*High debt*, caused by *non-enforcement of EU treaties*]

2) The Greek public finances recovery plan is still awaited and a mounting fear of a contagion phenomenon within the eurozone is felt day after day. Analysts still doubt the

ability of Greece to reorganize its accounts and timely meet its financial obligations (debt and interests pay-off) and subsequently revive its economy. Then, Greece called for help from its European partners and the IMF which agreed to lend it 110 billion euros over three years. In return, Greece should install, under the tight supervision of its creditors, a drastic budgetary scheme. [*Collapse of confidence*, caused by *high debt* and *slow EMU response*]

3) It jointly resulted from the world economic crisis and some country-specific factors; high indebtedness (142.8% of GDP in 2010, see Table 2) and a large budget deficit. [*Collapse of confidence*, caused by *financial crisis* and *high debt*]

4) … declaration on its public debt and budget deficit. The system could not stop the Greek government to fool Brussels again in 2009 by declaring a budget deficit between 6% and 7% not the real 15.4% deficit (see Table 2). [*High debt*, caused by *non-enforcement of EU treaties*]

5) At the same time, the stability pact which forces governments to remain within deficit limits and to respect indebtedness thresholds came in handy. In order to respond primarily to budget deficit explosions, the Maastricht Treaty set up a procedure targeting excessive deficits. Accordingly, public debt should not exceed a 60% limit and the annual public deficit is set at 3% of GDP. Within these limits, each country was able to conserve its economic and budget policies. Some analysts even assume that the protection of the euro has favoured lax economic and budget policies for some governments at the expense of the whole Eurozone. [*High debt*, caused by *non-enforcement of EU treaties* and *poor governance*]

6) Greece witnesses social problems. In front of these difficulties, the stability pact rules are no longer respected. [*Non-enforcement of EU treaties*, caused by *political opposition to reform* and *poor governance*]

7) The Greek experience has shown that neglecting difficulties may generate a circle of risk premium increases and a decrease in investors' trust. However, there is a more worrying second raison which is at the origin of financial market instability; a large number of European banking systems are undercapitalized. [*Collapse of confidence*, caused by *poor governance* and *bank undercapitalisation*]

8) The European Union must take advantage of the Greek crisis in order to repair the structural defects of the economic and monetary union issued from the Maastricht Treaty by installing an economic European government. Not only does the creation of such institution allow avoiding the debt crisis, but also it gives the EU a budget policy instrument which allows it to conduct coherent up-to-date politics. [*High debt*, caused by *non-enforcement of EU treaties* and *destructive institutions*]

9) The ECB and European governments failed to find the appropriate combination between monetary and budget policies as the EU does not have centralized decisions on economic policy able to fix and coordinate budget policies across European states. [*Lack of competitiveness*, caused by *EMU membership* and *monetary dependence*]

## The Impact of the Crisis on Labour Relations and Collective Agreements in Greece (Kouzis, 2011)

1) The labour market measures recently adopted in the context of the crisis affecting Greece are both a continuation of changes implemented since the early 1990s and a deepening of their logic. They consist of a whole array of measures to deregulate labour law and are being implemented as part of a reform agenda aimed at increasing flexibility, on the pretext of improving the competitiveness of the Greek economy by reducing labour costs. [*Lack of competitiveness*, caused by *regulatory burden*]

2) The economic crisis resulted, at the end of 2009, in unprecedented levels of public deficit and public debt (130 per cent of GNP). This led the government to sign the memorandum on the support for the Greek economy with the "troika" of the European Union (EU), the European Central Bank (ECB) and the International Monetary Fund (IMF). [*High debt*, caused by *financial crisis*]

3) Within this framework, the European Commission kept Greece under constant pressure to bring in measures promoting wage reductions and increased labour flexibility. Second, the role of the ECB has been decisive in the establishment of a wage austerity policy imposed on the eurozone countries by the Stabilization Pact and accompanied by tight control of developments around the three criteria for the operating conditions of monetary union. [*Lack of competitiveness*, caused by *regulatory burden*]

4) Nonetheless, in terms of competitiveness, the Greek economy is in bottom place within the EU-15, alongside Portugal, and Greece's unemployment is the second highest, after that of Spain. [*Current account deficit*, caused by *lack of competitiveness*]

5) At the same time, according to estimates by the relevant services of the Labour Ministry, there were almost 800,000 undeclared workers, the majority of whom (70 per cent) were of Greek nationality and the rest were immigrants, mostly undocumented. [*Large informal economy*, caused by *regulatory burden*]

6) When it came to breaches of labour law, a very widespread phenomenon, Greece topped the table within the eurozone. That is why, well before the crisis, the phrase "medieval labour conditions" was already widely used. [*Large informal economy*, caused by *regulatory burden*]

7) According to estimates, only 28 per cent of wage earners are unionized. The majority of these (55 per cent) work in the public sector, where union density ranges from 60 to 90 per cent. [*Lack of competitiveness*, caused by *strong public sector unions*]

8) The first measures, in the midst of the crisis, apply to the public sector, with a large number of interventions targeting the pay of civil servants and public enterprise workers, coupled with major staff reduction measures and plans for privatizations on an unprecedented scale. [*High debt*, caused by *large public sector*]

9) The changes to the collective agreement system, right in the middle of the crisis, have been well coordinated with the whole set of measures designed to achieve a strong, brutal reduction of wage costs. [*Internal devaluation*, caused by *lack of competitiveness*]

10) The new Greek labour market landscape that is being mapped out for the future is characterized by the devaluing of work and the erosion of earned income (already by 15–25 per cent, just over the past 15 months). These developments are linked to the dizzying increase in precarity and unemployment which, on official figures, has risen from 9 per cent to 16.5 per cent in the space of two years. That would mean 820,000 unemployed, but highly credible estimates suggest that the real unemployment rate is more like 20 per cent and will certainly rise even higher by the end of 2012. [*Internal devaluation*, caused by *lack of competitiveness*] ALSO [*Political opposition to reform*, caused by *Internal devaluation*]

## The Impact of Banking and Sovereign Debt Crisis Risk in the Eurozone on the Euro/US Dollar Exchange Rate (Eichler, 2012)

1) The costs of bank rescue programs and the associated rise in (implicit) government debt as well as record-high fiscal deficits produced by the crisis feed speculations about possible sovereign debt defaults in the EMU, particularly of the most vulnerable EMU member countries Greece, Ireland, Italy, Portugal and Spain. [*Collapse of confidence*, caused by *high debt* and *financial crisis*]

2) In May 2010, the Greek government was de facto illiquid and had to be bailed out by the EU/IMF rescue package. [*Collapse of confidence*, caused by *high debt*]

3) The austerity program of the Greek government did not lead to the desired results and it is proving difficult to get the Greek public debt back to a sustainable level. [*High debt*, caused by *failed austerity measures*]

4) In November 2011, market participants also began to worry about the sustainability of the Italian government finances and yield spreads of Italian government bonds (as well as Greek, Portuguese and Spanish government bonds) over the (allegedly risk-free) German government bonds are rallying. Even the ultimate event of withdrawals from the eurozone is now discussed by policymakers and the risk of such withdrawals is perceived by financial markets (Eichler, 2011). [*Collapse of confidence*, caused by *possible EMU exit*]

5) One of the most important consequences of the financial crisis for the eurozone is the rapid increase in banking and sovereign debt crisis risk in the EMU. [*Bank undercapitalisation*, caused by the *financial crisis*] ALSO [*High debt*, caused by the *financial crisis*]

6) The results indicate that higher sovereign debt crisis risk in vulnerable EMU countries leads to a significant depreciation of the euro against the US dollar (for two out of four specifications), whereas sovereign debt crisis risk in stable EMU countries plays no significant role. [*Collapse of confidence*, caused by *high debt*]

7) Moreover, capital withdrawals of investors are more likely triggered by higher sovereign default risk of the vulnerable EMU countries, which are more likely to default according to the financial market figures used. [*Collapse of confidence*, caused by *lack of competitiveness* and *high debt*]

8) The results of Tables 1 and 2 may also be used to study the sensitivity of the euro/US dollar exchange rate to changes in banking crisis risk versus changes in sovereign debt crisis risk. For the vulnerable EMU countries both financial crisis risks have quite a similar impact on the exchange rate. [*Collapse of confidence*, caused by *bank undercapitalisation* and *high debt*]

9) Moreover, I found that rising default risk of individual eurozone banks leads to a depreciation of the euro against the US dollar. [*Collapse of confidence*, caused by *bank undercapitalisation*]

## THE GREEK FINANCIAL CRISIS: GROWING IMBALANCES AND SOVEREIGN SPREADS GIBSON, (HALL & TAVLAS, 2010)

1) The entry of Greece into the euro area in 2001 provided that country's economy with a huge dividend in terms of sharply-reduced interest rates. The nominal interest rate on 10-year Greek government bonds declined from about 20 per cent in 1994, the time that the then-government announced a goal of bringing Greece into the euro area in 2001, to less than 31/2 per cent in early 2005. [*Access to cheap debt*, caused by *EMU membership*]

2) We argue that during the period 2001-2009 the Greek economy was marked by growing, unsustainable fiscal and external imbalances. We posit that the sharp reduction in interest-rate spreads that occurred during much of this period did not adequately reflect these imbalances. Our empirical results provide some evidence for this view. [*Access to cheap debt*, caused by *EMU membership*]

3) Among the benefits conferred by the euro on its members are the following. (1) For countries with histories of high inflation, such as Greece, it lowers inflation expectations and, therefore, interest rates. [*Monetary dependence*, caused by *EMU membership*]

4) (2) It eliminates exchange-rate fluctuations and the possibility of competitive devaluations among participating countries, thereby reducing risk premia and nominal interest rates. [*Access to cheap debt*, caused by *EMU membership*]

5) The lengthening of horizons and the reduction in interest rates stimulate private investment and risk-taking, fostering economic growth. The reductions in nominal interest rates under (1) and (2) lower the costs of servicing public-sector debt, facilitating fiscal adjustment and freeing resources for other uses. [*Access to cheap debt*, caused by *EMU membership*]

6) From 2001 through 2008, real GDP rose by an average of 3.9 per cent per year – the second-highest growth rate (after Ireland) in the euro area – underpinned by household spending for consumption, housing investment, and business investment. [*Excessive private credit extension*, caused by *Capital influx*]

7) Although entry into the euro area contributed to a period of prolonged and robust growth, and low (by Greece's historical standards) inflation, two deep-seated problems remained unaddressed; the country continued to run large fiscal imbalances and the country's competitiveness – already a problem upon euro area entry – continued to deteriorate. [*Collapse of confidence*, caused by *high debt* and *lack of competitiveness*]

8) Figure 2 reports data on fiscal deficits and government expenditure and revenue as percentages GDP, beginning with 2001. As indicated in the figure, fiscal policy was pro-cyclical throughout the period 2001 through 2009, with deficits consistently exceeding the Stability and Growth Pact's limit of 3 per cent of GDP by wide margins.4 Expansionary fiscal policy was mainly expenditure-driven, leading to a rise in the share of government spending (to over 50 per cent of GDP in 2009, from about 45 per cent in 2001). [*High debt*, caused by *non-enforcement of EU treaties*, *poor governance* and *pro-cyclical fiscal policy*]

9) Wage increases, adjusted for productivity changes, also exceeded the average increases in the rest of the euro area. With both prices and wages growing at relatively high rates, competitiveness declined (Figure 4). [*Lack of competitiveness*, caused by *high wages* and *low productivity*]

10) In the period 2001 through 2009, competitiveness, as measured by consumer prices, declined by around twenty per cent; as measured by unit labour costs, competitiveness declined by about 25 per cent. With relatively high real growth rates and declining competitiveness, the current-account deficit, which had already topped 7 per cent of GDP in 2001, rose to about 14.5 per cent of GDP in both 2007 and 2008 (Figure 5). [*Current account deficits*, caused by *lack of competitiveness*]

11) First, it lost the ability to set its own monetary policy. Second, it lost the ability to change the nominal exchange rate of its own currency. To compensate for the loss of these tools, the country needed to have the following: (i) relatively-low fiscal imbalances, so that fiscal policy could be used counter-cyclically in case of a country-specific shock, and (ii) flexible labour and product markets so that the country could be competitive without having to rely on changes in the exchange rate of a domestic currency to achieve and/or maintain competitiveness. [*Internal devaluation*, caused by *monetary dependence*

and *lack of competitiveness*] ALSO [*Lack of competitiveness*, caused by *monetary dependence*]

12) As mentioned above, however, competitiveness declined substantially during 2001-2009, despite the already large current-account deficits at the time of entry into the union. Moreover, instead of providing the role of an automatic stabilizer, the pro-cyclical stance of fiscal policy acted as a major source of shocks.5 Nevertheless, the low levels of interest-rate spreads during 2001-08 suggest that financial markets paid little attention to the unsustainability of the fiscal and external imbalances during that period. [*Access to cheap debt*, caused by *EMU membership*]

13) With the collapse (and sale) of Bear Stearns in March 2008, spreads widened to about 60 basis points, where they remained until the collapse of Lehman Brothers in September. The latter event brought spreads up to around 250 basis points during the first few months of 2009, but they gradually came back down to about 120 basis points in August and September of 2009. [*Collapse of confidence*, caused by *financial crisis*]

14) Then came a double shock in the autumn of 2009. Two developments combined to disrupt the relative tranquility of Greek financial markets. First, in October the newly-elected Greek government announced that the 2009 fiscal deficit would be 12.7 per cent of GDP, more than double the previous government's projection of 6.0 per cent.7 In turn, the 12.7 per cent figure would undergo further upward revisions, bringing it up to 15.4 per cent of GDP. [*Collapse of confidence*, caused by *upward revision of debt*]

15) Second, in November 2009 Dubai World, the conglomerate owned by the government of the Gulf emirate, asked creditors for a six-month debt moratorium. That news rattled financial markets around the world and led to a sharp increase in risk aversion. [*Collapse of confidence*, caused by *Dubai World Default*]

16) In light of the rapid worsening of the fiscal situation in Greece, financial markets and rating agencies turned their attention to the sustainability of Greece's fiscal and external imbalances. The previously-held notion that membership of the euro area would provide an impenetrable barrier against risk was shaken. [*Collapse of confidence*, caused by *high debt* and *current account deficits*]

17) Entry into the euro area provided Greece with the opportunity to benefit from the credibility of the monetary policy of the European Central Bank and the resulting environment of relatively-low inflation rates and low nominal interest rates. In turn, the low interest rates reduced the cost of servicing the public-sector debt, facilitating fiscal adjustment and freeing resources for other uses. [*Access to cheap debt*, caused by *EMU membership* and *monetary dependence*]

18) Instead of taking advantage of this environment to adjust the economy, during the period 2001-2009 successive Greek governments ran fiscal deficits that averaged over 6 per cent of GDP and they increased the share of government spending in the economy. [*High debt*, caused by *poor governance* and *pro-cyclical fiscal policy*]

# The Greek Debt Crisis: The Need for 'Heroic' Economic Policy Reforms in the European Monetary Union (Robbins, 2015)

1) Greece is in the midst of a devastating economic and financial crisis that the European Union has been trying ardently to resolve since the default of Lehman Brothers in 2008. [*Collapse of confidence*, caused by *financial crisis*]

2) At the heart of the EMU's economic problems are gaps in its structure and issues that were ignored or not fully considered when the EMU took effect in 1999. The principal requirement that Member States wanting to join the EMU had to meet was a budget deficit of 3 percent per year or less. [*High debt*, caused by *non-enforcement of EU treaties*] ALSO [*Lack of competitiveness*, caused by *EMU membership*]

3) Greece experienced one of the largest drops in deficit, as between 1992 and the time it was approved for the EMU in 2000, it had decreased its deficit by 10 percent.8 The shocking 10 percent figure can be attributed to intense short-term deficit reduction strategies by Greece in an effort to meet the 3 percent target (as well as to dishonest bookkeeping by Greece, which will be discussed later) [*High debt*, caused by *statistical misrepresentation*]

4) The market's reaction to the prospect of countries joining the EMU was the lowering of interest rates, thus making short-term borrowing strategies possible. [*Access to cheap debt*, caused by *EMU membership*]

5) Greece executed policies (supplemented by dishonest bookkeeping) to meet fiscal responsibility by 2000, but Greece did not have a sustainable fiscal responsibility plan after that point. [*High debt*, caused by *poor governance* and *bad stats*]

6) And while Greece had not adequately prepared for the years following the beginning of the EMU, the EMU itself did not have adequate means to enforce the deficit requirements it had imposed on all Member States. In 1999, the Stability and Growth Pact (SGP) came into effect. [*High debt*, caused by *non-enforcement of EU treaties*]

7) Unfortunately, in the years since Krugman wrote those words, the European Union has forced Greece, Spain, and other EMU countries to raise taxes and cut spending as the economy slumps—austerity measures that have been widely ineffective. [*Ineffective austerity measures*, caused by *counter-cyclical fiscal policy*]

8) For the purposes of this Note, assume the "sin" to which Krugman refers is an excess of debt in violation of the SGP. While the Greek crisis was caused in large part by the imprudent borrowing and spending of the government. [*High debt*, caused by *poor governance* and *non-enforcement of EU treaties*]

9) Regardless, both Spain and Greece are currently facing severe austerity measures demanded by the European Union. This is what Krugman refers to as "Europe's Big

Delusion: it's the belief that Europe's crisis was essentially caused by fiscal irresponsibility. [*Crisis*, caused by *lack of competitiveness*]

10) However, once the EMU came into effect, the principal economic regulatory mechanism, the SGP, failed to harmonize national economies the way the drafters of that legislation had hoped it would, as discussed below. As a result, economic harmonization failed in many respects while the ECB's monetary union continued to operate. [*Lack of competitiveness*, caused by *non-enforcement of EU treaties*]

11) Indeed, after the start of the EMU, the GIPSI countries (Greece, Italy, Portugal, Spain, Ireland) began borrowing large sums and applying them to manufacturing, thereby driving wages up and causing unit labor costs to increase. As a result, "[m]anufacturing in Europe's south became uncompetitive, which in turn meant that the countries that were attracting huge money inflows began running correspondingly huge trade deficits." [*Lack of competitiveness*, caused by *high wages* and *access to cheap debt*] ALSO [*Current account deficits*, caused by *lack of competitiveness*]

## THE GREEK DEBT CRISIS: LIKELY CAUSES, MECHANICS AND OUTCOMES (ARGHYROU AND TSOUKALAS, 2011)

1) Second, a shift in market expectations pricing a possible exit of Greece from the EMU, mainly due to the lack of commitment of Greek authorities to undertake unpopular structural reforms. [*Collapse of confidence*, caused by *possible exit from EMU*] ALSO [*Possible EMU exit*, caused by *poor governance* and *political opposition to reform*]

2) Its starting point can be traced at the onset of the USA sub-prime crisis in the summer of 2007 (see Figure 1). Starting from a value of 25 basis points (b.p.), the spread of the 10-year Greek government bond yield against the German bund entered a moderately ascending path reaching 65 b.p. in August 2008. A second, much more intense, phase followed between September 2008 and March 2009. This marked the peak of the global credit crunch crisis, by the end of which the Greek spread had reached 285 b.p. [*Collapse of confidence*, caused by *financial crisis*]

3) First, the run-up to a snap election called for 4 October 2009. This produced a landslide government change. Second, the new government's announcement in mid-October 2009 of a substantial overshooting in the previous government's projection for the value of Greece's 2009 budget deficit, from 6 to 12.7 per cent of GDP. Third, the submission by the new government to the European Commission, in midNovember 2010, of Greece's proposed public budget for 2010. [*Collapse of confidence*, caused by *upward revision of Greek debt*]

4) Negotiations among EMU member states in the first quarter of 2010 regarding actions to contain the crisis revealed a clear split. A number of countries, most

prominently Germany, opposed a Greek bailout, whereas others, including France, appeared more favourable. Eventually, on 25 March 2010, EU leaders agreed on a compromise, involving a mechanism of bilateral loans to Greece from other EU members, as well as IMF loans at rates lower than the market rate. [*Collapse of confidence*, caused by *slow EMU response*]

5) The announced plan involved a total sum of approximately 45 billion euros, with two-thirds coming from bilateral EU loans and one-third from the IMF. The plan's announcement failed to calm markets, which put Greek bonds under further intense pressure. Finally, and following another upward revision of the 2009 Greek budget deficit to 13.6 per cent of GDP, on 23 April 2010 Greek authorities formally requested the activation of the EU/IMF rescue mechanism. [*Failed austerity*, caused by *poor governance* and *upward revision of debt*]

6) This story's basic premise, i.e., unsustainable fiscal policy, is clearly present in the case of Greece. Also, since EMU accession in 2001, the country has experienced consistently higher inflation than the EMU average, resulting in substantial deviation from PPP, pronounced competitiveness losses and record current account deficits (see Arghyrou and Chortareas, 2008). [*Collapse of confidence*, caused by *high debt* and *lack of competitiveness*] ALSO [*Current account deficits*, caused by *Capital influx* and *lack of competitiveness*]

7) A possible interpretation of events surrounding the Greek crisis is then as follows: in the wake of the global credit crunch in late 2008/early 2009, Greek fundamentals were correctly judged by markets to have deteriorated enough to be inconsistent with long-run euro participation. To convey this message to Greek authorities, markets sold a substantial, yet still not critical, volume of Greek bonds, prompting the government to take corrective action. At that stage, Greek commitment to the EMU was not questioned and the authorities operated under the flat loss function (i.e., L1). [*Access to cheap debt*, caused by *EMU membership*] ALSO [*Collapse of confidence*, caused by *lack of competitiveness* and *financial crisis*]

8) The Greek government, however, perhaps with an eye to the forthcoming election, failed to recognise the message and no corrective action was taken. [*Failed austerity measures*, caused by *political opposition to reform*] ALSO [*Collapse of confidence*, caused by *failed austerity* and *political opposition to reform*]

9) Following the election of October 2009, the markets gave the new government a window of opportunity to signal its policy intentions. But like its predecessor, the new government did not interpret correctly the markets' signals. During a few crucial initial weeks in office, it appeared divided over its priorities and sent mixed signals regarding its policy intentions by charging (wrongly) the markets with putting Greek bonds under unjustified speculative pressure. [*Collapse of confidence*, caused by *possible EMU exit* and *poor governance*]

10) This proved to be a pivotal point, as markets interpreted the revealed unwillingness, or inability, of two successive Greek governments from both sides of the political spectrum to address unsustainable fundamentals as new information regarding the arithmetic of Greece's loss function. In response, for the first time in the crisis, they started questioning Greece's commitment to the euro. [*Fear of Possible EMU exit*, caused by *political opposition to reform*, *lack of competitiveness* and *poor governance*]

11) Therefore, the proposed budget submitted to the EU in mid-November 2010 was a game changer; it shifted the balance of expectations from credible to non-credible commitment, putting Greece from the flat to the steep loss function (L 2). This explains the steep increase in Greek bond spreads observed in mid-November/December 2009 in the absence of further negative news on fundamentals. [*Collapse of confidence*, caused by *possible EMU exit*]

12) In the markets' eyes, this restricts the already questionable government's ability to pursue reforms and reinforces the perceived temptation for Greece to leave the euro. This causes further negative shifts in expectations, further widening of spreads and an increasing cost of public debt which, in a circular process, causes further deterioration in expectations. [*Collapse of confidence*, caused by *deficit of trust*, *fear of possible EMU exit* and *high debt*]

13) If the analysis above is correct, what we have observed in November 2009 was the mutation of a challenging crisis of deteriorating fundamentals into a full-blown crisis of confidence in the Greek monetary regime. [*Fear of EMU exit*, caused by *lack of competitiveness* and *Collapse of confidence*]

14) The failure of the announced EU/IMF rescue plan to relieve the pressure on Greek spreads. It failed to do so because the Greek spread was not only driven by an increasing risk of default (to be fully explained below) but also increasingly strong expectations that Greece cannot bear, or is not willing to bear, the cost of reforms necessary to stay in the euro. [*Failed austerity*, caused by *fears of possible EMU exit*]

15) Investors assess Greek bonds as a stake into a risky project, namely the restructuring of a relatively low-income, undercompetitive and highly indebted economy, with two possible scenarios. First, an optimistic one, in which Greece would promote competitiveness-boosting reforms. In that case, starting from a low-income base, Greece would become a fast-growing economy whose bond prices would appreciate generating large gains for investors who took the bet. Second a pessimistic one, in which Greece would not promote reforms. In that case, Greek bond prices would depreciate and possibly involve losses for investors. [*Collapse of confidence*, caused by *lack of competitiveness*, *political opposition to reform* and *poor governance*]

16) In an undistorted environment, like the one prevailing before Greece's accession to the EMU, markets would price Greek bonds by assessing the probability of reform, i.e., future expected Greek fundamentals. In that case, Greek bonds would be priced at their fair value. We now introduce Greece's 2001 EMU accession into the analysis and

draw the analogy with Krugman's model. With Greece becoming a member of the single currency, considerably European (largely German) funds flow into the country. Markets perceived that the rest of the EMU countries had a vested interest in Greek reforms and Greece's continued participation in the EMU. This sentiment was further reinforced by Germany's long-term political commitment to the European integration project. Therefore, Greek accession was perceived to convey an implicit bailout guarantee to holders of Greek bonds, with Germany in the role of the guarantor played by the government in Krugman's model. [*Access to cheap debt*, caused by *EMU membership*]

17) Events then moved as follows: in the absence of an effective EU-sponsored mechanism of fiscal monitoring and imposed reform, Greek governments over 2001–09 did not implement sound economic policies, thus allowing further deterioration of fundamentals. [*High debt*, caused by *poor governance* and *non-enforcement of EU treaties*] ALSO [*Lack of competitiveness*, caused by *political opposition to reform*]

18) Due to the lack of reforms, EMU accession caused net costs rather than net benefits in a number of areas (see Arghyrou, 2006, 2009). As a result, starting in the summer of 2007, lower than anticipated returns on the Greek project gradually reduced the prices of Greek bonds, with losses accelerating significantly in the wake of the global credit crunch in 2009:Q1. [*Collapse of confidence*, caused by *lack of competitiveness*, *poor governance* and *financial crisis*]

19) At that point, with the Greek bond market coming under intense pressure, investors in the Greek project looked to Greece's main guarantor, Germany, to back the Greek economy. Germany, however, refused to do so: it initially responded with a policy officially described as 'constructive ambiguity' and then, to the markets' great surprise, in February/March 2010, made it clear that it was not prepared to help Greece unconditionally. The German stance was interpreted by markets as withdrawal of the fiscal guarantee for Greece. [*Collapse of confidence*, caused by *slow EMU response* and *fears of possible EMU exit*]

20) We conclude that the crisis and its escalating nature are the result of (i) steadily deteriorating macroeconomic fundamentals over the period 2001–09 to levels inconsistent with long-term EMU participation, and (ii) a double shift in markets' expectations, from a regime of credible commitment to future EMU participation under an implicit EMU/German guarantee of Greek fiscal liabilities, to a regime of non-credible EMU commitment without fiscal guarantees, respectively taking place in November 2009 and February/March 2010. Following this shift, resorting to the EU/IMF mechanism of emergency financing on 23 April 2010 was the only option available for Greece to avert an imminent EMU exit. [*Crisis*, caused by *lack of competitiveness*, *fear of EMU exit* and *slow EMU response*]

21) Either Greece will introduce the reforms necessary to address the initial source of the crisis, i.e., deteriorating fundamentals, in which case and, assuming a favourable external environment, her economy will gradually regain the markets' confidence and the

country will stay in the EMU, or Greece will not promote any reforms, in which case she will have no option than to leave the euro. [*Collapse of confidence*, caused by *lack of competitiveness*, *regulatory burden* and *political opposition to reform*]

## THE GREEK CRISIS: CAUSES AND IMPLICATIONS (KOURETAS AND VLAMIS, 2010)

1) The financial crisis that unfolded in mid-2008 led to a dramatic increase of public debt in many advanced economies. During the recent months, we have seen the transformation of the 2007 US subprime mortgage loan market crisis into a sovereign debt crisis in the eurozone.1 This overwhelming increase in the public debt has been to some extent the outcome of the effort by the governments to reduce the private debt that was accumulated during the years preceding the recent financial turmoil (Paul De Grauwe 2010a). [*High debt*, caused by the *financial crisis*]

2) The overall picture from these accounts is that private debt increased more than public over the whole period. This is exactly what we have observed since the peak of the crisis in October 2008 with governments being forced to bail out problematic banks, taking over a major share of the debts of failing financial institutions. [*High debt*, caused by *bank undercapitalisation*]

3) Some of these factors are endogenous; have to do with the structure of the Greek economy itself, the prolonged macroeconomic imbalances that the Greek economy faces and the credibility problem of macroeconomic policy [*Collapse of confidence*, caused by *high debt*, *current account deficits* and *lack of trust in the Greek government*]

4) There is no doubt that running consistently widening public deficits in conjunction with declining external competitiveness played a decisive role on the deteriorating fiscal stance of the Greek economy. The EU statistics agency, Eurostat, has recently revised upward the Greek budget deficit for 2009 and this has risen to 15.4% of GDP. Increased public expenditure in recent years led to dramatic increase in borrowing requirements and high levels of accumulated public debt. The level of Central Government Debt as of 31.12.2009 amounts to € 298.5 billion. [*High debt*, caused by *lack of competitiveness*] ALSO [*Erosion of trust*, caused by *upward revision of Greek Debt*]

5) We clearly observe that the debt/GDP ratio was constant until 1979 and at very low levels, about 25%. The inauguration of the socialist government led by the late Andreas Papandreou highlights the new era in the Greek fiscal stance as the structural break in the series indicates. The socialist government implemented an economic policy programme that was mainly based on inducing the income of the average Greek household through extensive borrowing from the markets. [*High debt*, caused by *large public sector* and *large welfare state*]

6) This process was also fuelled by the incoming capital flows from the EU in the form of agricultural subsidies and from the financing of infrastructure within the broader framework of the convergence and cohesion policies of the EU. [*Capital influx*, caused by *EMU membership*]

7) The lack of the necessary fiscal consolidation during the past ten years, when Greece was experiencing high growth rates, in relation to the continuous false reporting of fiscal data (in mid-October 2009, the newly elected government announced the budget deficit for 2009 was estimated to be 12.7% of GDP while the previous government was arguing in September 2009 that deficit would not be higher than 6.5% of GDP) have undermined the Greece's government credibility. [*High debt*, caused by *poor statistical services* and *pro-cyclical fiscal policy*] ALSO [*Erosion of trust*, caused by *poor statics* and *upward revision of debt*]

8) On top of that, the decline in competitiveness since EMU entry (Dimitris Malliaropoulos 2010) led to a persistent deficit in the current account. Increased "twin deficits" together with the lack of structural reforms in home regarding labour market flexibility, social security and market competition, obliged Greece to issue new bonds at short maturity periods and at higher interest rates compared to the "anchor" of the EMU, that is Germany. [*Lack of competitiveness*, caused by *EMU entry*, *regulatory burden* and *large welfare state*]

9) More specifically, in the spring-summer of 2008, the spread of the 10-year Greek government bond yield against the German bund ranged from 25-65 basis points. Then following the credit crunch, the Greek spread reached 285 basis points in March 2009. There was then a decline the Greek spread reaching 121 basis points in August 2009. [*Collapse of confidence*, caused by *financial crisis*]

10) As of this writing, it stands a bit higher than 900 basis points following the fears for a domino effect in the eurozone and the worries regarding the Greek government's ability and willingness to fully implement the austerity programme. [*Collapse of confidence*, caused by *poor governance* and *political opposition to reform*]

11) The Eurozone governments failed to give a clear signal indicating their readiness to support Greece, while the Greek fiscal crisis was escalating. Legal scepticism and questions like "are bailouts illegal?" were raised, mostly by Germany, for an issue which was partly political. [*Collapse of confidence*, caused by *slow EMU response* and *fears of possible EMU exit*]

12) Because of these disagreements among EU countries, markets assumed that the implicit guarantee on Greek debt by other EU countries has been withdrawn. While Eurozone policy makers were debating whether bailouts are illegal, at the same time there were some ambiguities about ECB's collateral eligibility criteria that is the ECB's policy to accept or refuse the downgraded (see Figure 5) Greek government bonds as collateral in liquidity provision presented. These ambiguities created problems for financial

institutions holding Greek government bonds. [*Collapse of confidence*, caused by *slow EMU response*]

13) Lastly, Greece and Greece's major trading partners in the Balkan peninsula were also hit by the 2007 global crisis - originating from the US sub-prime loan market crisis - but with a time lag (Prodromos Vlamis and Evaggelos Karousos 2010). Nevertheless, recession may have hit Greece somewhat less badly than other countries because a relatively small manufacturing sector and of the large share of the shadow economy which is estimated to be 25%-30% of GDP. [*High debt*, caused by *large informal economy* and *financial crisis*]

## THE GOLD STANDARD, THE EURO AND THE ORIGINS OF THE GREEK SOVEREIGN DEBT CRISIS (DELLAS AND TAVLAS, 2013)

1) The elimination of nominal exchange-rate fluctuations among the former currencies of members of the eurozone was expected to reduce exchange rate uncertainty and risk premia, lowering the costs of servicing the public sector debt, facilitating fiscal adjustment, and freeing resources for other uses. [*Access to cheap debt*, caused by *EMU membership*]

2) And that is precisely what happened—at least for a whüe. In the years immediately prior to and immediately after Greece's entry into the eurozone, nominal and real interest rates came down sharply, contributing to high real growth rates. From 2001 through 2008, real GDP rose by an average rate of 3.9 percent per year—^the secondhighest growtli rate (after tliat of Ireland) in the eurozone. [*Capital influx*, caused by *EMU membership*]

3) During the latter period, the absolute levels of nominal interest rates on the 10-year Greek instrument fluctuated in a range of 3.5-4.5 percent, compared with a range of 5.0-6.5 percent in the year prior to eurozone entry. [*Access to cheap debt*, caused by *EMU membership*]

4) Although entry to the eurozone contributed to a period of low interest rates and rapid real growth, deep-seated problems in the Greek economy remained unaddressed, reflecting a procyclical fiscal pohcy; as a result, the country continued to run large fiscal and external deficits. [*High debt*, caused by *pro-cyclical fiscal policy* and *poor governance*]

5) First, fiscal deficits consistently exceeded the Stability and Growth Pact's limit of 3 percent of GDP during the entire period, rising to 9.8 percent of GDP in 2008 and 15.6 percent of GDP in 2009.^ Second, flie widening of the deficits was mainly expenditure-driven; between 2005 and 2009 the share of government spending in GDP rose by 9 percentage points (to 54 percent), with the bnlk of the rise occurring between 2006 and

2009, a period that featured a government run by a conservative party. Third, beginning in 2007, the deficits underpinned an unsustainable increase in the government debt-to-GDP ratio, culminating in the crisis that erupted in late 2009. [*High debt*, caused by *non-enforcement of EU treaties*, *poor governance*, *large public sector* and *destructive institutions*]

6) The large and widening fiscald eficits contributed to growing current account deficits. There are two main series on the Greek current account. [*Current account deficit*, caused by *high debt*]

7) In the case of Greece, the widening of the current account deficit was caused entirely by the behavior of the public sector;^ net public saving (relative to GDP) feU from around minus four percent in 2001, to minus 15 percent of GDP in 2009. [*Current account deficit*, caused by *high debt*]

8) The global financial crisis that empted in August 2007, foUowing flie coUapse of flie U.S. subprime morigage market, initiaUy had little impact on Greek financial markets. Spreads on the 10-year instmment, which were in a range of 20-30 basis points during January-July of 2007, remained in flie vicinity of 30 basis points for the remainder of 2007 and the first few monflis of 2008 (Figure 1). With the coUapse (and sale) of Bear Steams in March 2008, spreads widened to about 60 basis points, where they remained until the collapse of Lehman Brothers in September of 2008. The latter event brought spreads up to around 250 basis points during tlie first few months of 2009, but they graduaUy came back down to about 120 basis points in August and September of 2009. [*Collapse of confidence*, caused by *financial crisis*]

9) Then came a double shock in the autumn of 2009. Two developments combined to disrupt the relative tranquility of Greek financial markets. First, in October the newly elected Greek government announced that the 2009 fiscal deficit would be 12.7 percent of GDP, more than double the previous government's projection of 6.0 percent. In tum, the 12.7 percent figure would undergo further upward revisions, so that the outcome was a deficit of 15.6 percent of GDP. Second, in November 2009 DubaiWorld, the conglomerate owned by the government of the Gulf emirate, asked creditors for a six-month debt moratorium. That news rattled financial markets around the world and led to a sharp increase in risk aversion. [*Collapse of confidence*, caused by *upward revision of Greek debt* and *Dubai World default*]

10) By early 2012, the Greek-Gennan spread had widened to about 4,000 basis points and it became clear diat Greece's rising debt burden was no longer sustainable. In March 2012, the Greek government agreed to a new €130 billion adjustment program widi the official lenders, and die countiy restructured its sovereign debt. [*Collapse of confidence*, caused by *high debt*]

11) To summarize the above discussion, Greece entered the eurozone with a current account deficit of about 10 percent of GDP (depending on the current account series used); the current account deficit widened sharply in the following years, leading to the

crisis that erupted in late 2009. The major factor underpinning Greece's large and growing current-account deficits was the decline in net public saving. [*Current account deficit*, caused by *EMU entry* and *high debt*]

12) As mentioned, the effective functioning of the gold standard required a liigh degree of wage-price fiexibiUty so that adjustment to extemal imbalances could take place. To bring about the necessary changes in wages and prices, money and credit flowed from countries experiencing extemal deficits to countries running extemal surpluses. [*Lack of competitiveness*, caused by *influx of capital* and *regulatory burden*]

13) The case of Greece under both the gold standard and the euro illustrates the importance of the adjustment mechanism. As noted, Greece tried to participate in the gold standard but was unsuccessful because it could not abide by its fiscal reqnirements. Gonsequenfly, it was not able to benefit from the gold standard adjustment mechanism, which would have contained the extemal deficits. In contrast, under the euro, Greece was able, upon entry, to borrow at near-core interest rates and at the same time, in the absence of an adjustment mechanism, remain a member without undertaking fiscal adjustment. [*High debt*, cause by *easy access to cheap debt*] ALSO [*Cheap debt*, caused by *EMU membership*] [*Current account deficit*, caused by *lack of competitiveness*, *Capital influx*, *regulatory burden* and *EMU membership*]

14) As shown in the table, M3 growth and credit growth were considerably higher in Greece, a country wifli an external deficit during the period in question, flian tliey were in Germany, a country with an external suiplus, or the eurozone as a whole, wliich had, essentially, balanced external accounts during that time. What is particularly striking is the much faster credit growth to the private sector (16.7 percent) in Greece than in Gennany (2.7 percent). In other words, money and credit flowed in the opposite direction of that needed to bring about external adjustment. [*Excessive private credit extension*, caused by *EMU entry* and *Capital influx*]

15) First, while the stock of government debt rose by €147.8 biUion from 2001 through 2009, domestic holdings of that debt declined by €22.1 biUion. Foreign holdings of Creek government debt rose by €169.9 biUion, accounting for more than the overaU increase in debt. Consequently, the share of Greek sovereign debt held by Greek residents fell from 56.6 percent to 21.3 percent while the share held by nonresidents rose from 43.4 percent to 78.7 percent. [*Capital influx*, caused by *high debt*]

16) Consequenfly, credit to flie private sector surged, especiaUy from 2001 until 2008; credit growth to the private sector accounted for flie bulk of the large expansion of total credit during 2001 to 2009 (Table 2). [*Private credit extension*, caused by *Capital influx*]

17) What underpinned the foregoing phenomenon was flie perception by inteniational investors that Greek sovereign debt carried litfle risk of default. The decrease in spreads on these financial instmments to about 30 basis points in the mid-2000s (Figure 1) suggests fliat markets indeed held such a perception. These perceptions,

however, seem to have been unreasonable in the face of historical evidence linking the probability of default to the size of public debt relative to CDP. [*Access to cheap debt*, caused by *EMU entry*]

18) The only way flie low risk premia can be justified is by assuming that investors expected that the core of the eurozone would have no choice but to bail out Creece in the event of a financial/fiscalc risis. The expectation of a bailout lowered the default risk and provided an incentive to issue increasing amounts of debt. [*Access to cheap debt*, caused by *EMU membership*]

19) The above process did not operate in the eurozone because investors did not draw a distinction between the sovereign debt of die core countries and the sovereign debt of the peripheral countries, such as Greece. Gonsequendy, there was no mechanism to adjust money and credit growth, and Greece was able to mn large current account and fiscal deficits without taking remedial policy measures. [*Lack of competitiveness*, caused by *excessive private credit extension*, *capital influx* and *access to cheap debt*]

20) At the same time, low interest rates greased the wheels of fiscal expansion by sending the message that there was no price to be paid for the buildup of sovereign debt. Hence, while external imbalances were essentially selfcorrecting under the gold standard, they were self-perpetuating in the eurozone due to the perception of an absence of credit risk. [*High debt*, caused by *poor governance*, *access to cheap debt* and *capital influx*]

## The Distributional Impact of the Crisis in Greece (Matsaganis & Leventi, 2011)

1) From the beginning of 2010 Greece has been in the throes of a severe financial and economic crisis – without doubt, the worst in living memory. After a decade of fast growth, the underlying weakness of the Greek economy was made evident in October 2009, when the incoming government announced that earlier fiscal data had been misreported. The fiscal deficit and public debt estimates for 2009 were radically revised1. Financial markets reacted by increasing spreads on Greek bonds and by lowering credit ratings (Meghir et al., 2010, Featherstone 2011). [*Collapse of confidence*, caused by the *upward revision of Greek debt* and *high debt*] ALSO [*Downgrades*, caused by *collapse of confidence* and *upward revision of Greek debt*]

2) When these failed to placate the markets, in May 2010 the government negotiated an unprecedented €110 billion rescue package with the EU, the ECB and the IMF. [*High debt*, caused by *failed austerity measures*]

3) Under the terms of the austerity measures, public sector pay and pension benefits were cut. Nominal reductions were compounded by rising inflation, caused by VAT hikes as well as rising oil prices internationally and product market rigidities domestically.

[*High debt*, caused by *large public sector*, *large welfare state*, *regulatory burden* and *poor revenue collection*]

4) In the context of tax reform, the government changed the schedule of personal income tax, raised the top rate and announced a clampdown on tax evasion. The measures took place when the Greek economy was already in recession, and made it deeper still. [*High debt*, caused by *poor revenue collection*]

5) Specifically, the austerity measures of spring 2010 were a combination of increases in indirect taxes, introduction of new direct taxes, personal income tax reform, cuts in public sector pay and in pensions. Later in the year, the fiscal squeeze affected other social benefits and public services. [*High debt*, caused by *poor revenue collection*, *large public sector* and *large welfare state*]

6) Until recently, wages and salaries in Greece (in the public as well as in the private sector) were paid in 14 monthly instalments. In 2010, the 13th and 14th salaries paid to civil servants and public utilities employees were abolished. In their place, flatrate vacation allowances totalling €1,000 a year were introduced for public sector workers earning less than €3,000 per month. Moreover, special allowances paid to civil servants2 were reduced by 20%. Public utilities employees, whose special allowances other than family allowances are part of base pay, had the latter cut by 10%. [*High debt*, caused by *large public sector*]

7) Personal income tax was restructured in April 2010. The new schedule is rather more progressive (with 9 tax bands instead of 5), and provides for a personal tax allowance of €12,000 per year and a higher top rate of 45% (for annual incomes over €100,000). Moreover, the tax base was extended to include unemployment benefits, large family benefits and non contributory disability benefits, when taxable income exceeds €30,000 a year. Various tax allowances and credits were also revised. Also, personal incomes over €100,000 in 2009 were made subject to a one-off emergency tax at 1%, while a similar (and much resented) tax was retrospectively levied on firms who had registered large profits in 2009. [*High debt*, caused by *poor revenue collection*]

8) Funding cuts, in some cases aggravated by a significant drop in social insurance organisations' income from contributions, undermined the regular payment of social benefits. In one instance (OEK rent benefit for private sector employees, the main housing benefit in Greece), payment of benefit was entirely suspended for 2010. In another instance (pensioners social solidarity supplement ΕΚΑΣ), the effort to weed out ineligible claimants intensified, with the inevitable result that some eligible recipients had their benefit suspended. [*High debt*, caused by *large welfare state*]

9) Finally, changes in labour law allowed collective agreements at industry- and firmlevel to set lower wages than those agreed under the National General Collective Wage Agreement, while entry wages below the statutory minimum were introduced for workers aged below 21. [*Lack of competitiveness*, caused by *regulatory burden*]

## The Crisis in the Greek Economy and Its National Implications (Choupis, 2011)

1) Despite the advent of "disaster capitalism" as a new model of "development," [1] the financial crisis that started in the United States morphed into a global menace that has impacted small economies the hardest. It exposed weak nations to the whims of a class of capitalists who thrive on manipulation of financial transactions that, in the final analysis, do not reflect actual wealth as measured by productivity, resources, and services. [*Crisis*, caused by *capitalism* and *financial crisis*]

2) In previous instances, too, bankers without borders and institutions without nations (they prefer the title "transnational") had also volunteered or were invited to "assist" Greece in overcoming its problems, most of which were externally caused in the first place. [*Lack of competitiveness*, caused by *capitalism*]

3) Can anybody seriously argue that today's Greek financial crisis is not directly related to the US collapse of 2008? [*High debt*, caused by *financial crisis*]

4) Extrapolating from similar situations in Chile, Argentina, and Japan, the global economic wizards are fervently erecting a firewall to contain the Greek crisis, and they offer antiquated solutions: reduce public expenditures, cut social services and education costs, privatize public corporations, and shift the burden of "financial reform" from the superrich to the salary- earners. This approach ignores Greek history, social values, and priorities. [*Failed austerity*, caused by *political opposition to reform*]

5) In fairness to the approach taken by the current Greek administration, not all causes of the current misery can be attributed to foreign factors. Let us be frank about it: Greek politicians of all political parties have been averse to serious thinking, long- range planning, or trying to understand the nexus of finance capital and geopolitics. [*High debt*, caused by *poor governance* and *destructive institutions*]

6) Greece did not have the luxury of addressing its crisis at the national level. Only a few years earlier, Greek leaders had forfeited the sovereign right of currency autonomy in vain hopes that they could outsmart the Europeans into financing their lifestyle. [*Internal devaluation*, caused by *monetary dependence*]

7) They did not pursue that road without help from the world's top "experts" in market manipulation: Goldman Sachs [5]. In sophisticated schemes on how to cook the books and "Europeanize" the Greek economy, Goldman Sachs baptized a phony cocktail of derivatives as "assets" to make the Greeks seem wealthier than they really were so that they could be admitted to the eurozone as an "advanced" economy. [*High debt*, caused by *corruption*, *poor governance* and *poor stats*]

8) Small economies like Greece absorbed the fallacy that the ratio of national debt to gross domestic product (GDP) and, by extension, to the family budget did not matter. The example they often used was Japan, whose disparity of debt to GDP was 200 percent. But

Japan was hardly a good example. That country still had currency autonomy and all of its debt was internally financed. [*High debt*, caused by *access to cheap debt*] ALSO [*Internal devaluation*, caused by *monetary dependence*]

9) For starters, Greek economic planners, with links to the major firms in New York, copied policies that hardly fit the Greek environment. They received the stamp of approval from US and European financiers [10]. Ironically, the core of the Greek financial meltdown coincides with the advent to power of a socialist leader, Costas Simitis, who turned into a fanatical advocate of free markets. [*Crisis*, caused by *capitalism*]

## THE CONSTRUCTION OF A MORAL DUTY FOR THE GREEK PEOPLE TO REPAY THEIR DEBT (STREECK, 2012)

1) The reason why Greek citizens are supposed to be responsible for the debt incurred by their governments and their central bank is that their country is, allegedly, a democracy. 'No taxation without representation' is reinterpreted to mean: 'With representation, full liability'. Greek citizens are made liable regardless of whether they have voted for the governments that have indebted them, or whether they have voted at all or whether they have ever benefited from the debt. Such is the magic of representative democracy. [*High debt*, caused by *poor governance* and *destructive institutions*]

2) Remarkably, selecting the Greekcitizens who are to be made to pay for 'Greece's' collective debt is left to a government run by the very same parties that have piled up the debt in the first place. [*High debt*, caused by *destructive institutions*, *corruption* and *large public sector*]

3) Did Greek politicians and central bankers fully inform their fellow citizens on the risks associated with the cheap credit they started taking up in their name upon entry into the Monetary Union? [*Poor governance*, caused by *access to cheap debt*]

4) Furthermore, under international law, sovereign countries can unilaterally cancel their debt or apply a 'haircut' to their creditors at their discretion. The ability to default at will is an essential element of national sovereignty, and of course providers of credit to governments know this. Behind it is the principle that countries are obligated first to their citizens and only then to other countries or to international organizations and the 'financial markets'. [*Internal devaluation*, caused by *monetary dependence*]

5) The 'clientelism' of the two main Greek political parties in the last two decades of the twentieth century was to an important extent funded by European regional and structural development funds. [*Corruption*, caused by *destructive institutions*.]

6) Admission to the Monetary Union had the welcome side effect that it enabled Mediterranean countries to borrow money in international financial markets at roughly

western European rates, replacing transfers fromnational treasuries with credit frominternationalbanks. [*Poor governance*, caused by *access to cheap debt*]

7) The European Union was acutely aware of the need to give Greece and the other Mediterranean countries access to cheap credit in lieu of fiscal transfers. As Monetary Union started, the Commission—in the person of the Commissioner in charge of financial services, Mario Monti—ruled that public debt from member states could indistinctly be used by banks as collateral for loan transactions (Gabor and Ban, 2012). It enabled Greece in particular to indebt itself at a previously unknown pace, without its interest payments skyrocketing (Figure 15). [*Access to cheap debt*, caused by *EMU membership*]

8) The need for Greece to take up credit resulted not least from its truly by zantine tax regime. The media like to point to widespread tax evasion among the working and middle classes, which fits in with the rhetoric holding them morally responsible for paying off the national debt on behalf of Greece as a whole. [*High debt*, caused by *poor revenue collection* and *corruption*]

9) It is remarkable, however, that the European Union never tried to make Greece rescind the constitutional tax privileges of the Orthodox Church6 or of Greek ship-owners. [*High debt*, caused by *regulatory burden*]

10) Tax competition is deeply written into the fabric of the Single Market and the European Union generally; it is considered economically healthy especially for the higher taxation countries in the North and West whose tax regimes are in this way put under pressure. [*Lack of competitiveness*, caused by *monetary dependence* and *EMU membership*] ALSO [*Poor revenue collection*, caused by *lack of competitiveness*]

11) In order for Greece to formally meet the criteria of admission to EMU, it had to engage in creative accounting, for which it needed the assistance of that bank-of-all-banks, Goldman Sachs. It is now known that Goldman made an extraordinary profit on that operation [9] It is not yet known enough, however, that the president of the Greek central bank at this time was one Lukas Papademos, who a few years later advanced to the position of vice president of the ECB, and from there to that of the prime minister of Greece, appointed by international capital markets to secure the repayment of Greek's debt to its creditors. [*High debt*, caused by *poor governance* and *poor stats*] ALSO [*Lack of trust*, caused by *poor stats*]

12) Another aspect of the Greek tragedy is the fact that rampant capital flight from Greece remained and remains entirely unchecked at both the national and the European level. Newspapers have again and again written about the vast amounts of Greek money that are flowing into the real estate markets of cities such as London,10 Paris and Berlin, greatly benefiting local owners of luxury houses and apartments. This is another result of the lifting of capital controls in the 1990s and thereafter, which was part and parcel of the Internal Market and, in particular, Monetary Union. [*Lack of competitiveness*, caused by *capitalism*]

## TAX AND TRUST: THE FISCAL CRISIS IN GREECE (KAPLANOGLOU AND RAPANOS, 2013)

1) This paper aims to highlight a number of shortcomings in the design and enforcement of the tax system in Greece, which have played a key role in the exacerbation of fiscal deficits that led to the current sovereign debt crisis. More precisely, we argue that these shortcomings resulting in low tax revenue are related to the structure of the Greek economy and to the failures of formal institutions (such as the poor functioning of the tax administration and lax tax enforcement). [*High debt*, caused by *poor revenue collection*] ALSO [*Poor revenue collection*, caused by *destructive institutions*, *poor governance* and *poor stats*]

2) Such failures are rooted in and at the same time reinforce failures of informal institutions, namely low levels of trust in institutions and perceived fairness of the tax system. [*Poor revenue collection*, caused by *trust deficit* and *destructive institutions*]

3) There is little doubt that the destabilising effects of the global financial crisis and some inherent weaknesses that were being built up in the euro area since the introduction of the common currency speeded up and accentuated the outbreak of the Greek fiscal crisis. [*High debt*, caused by *financial crisis* and *lack of competitiveness*]

4) Moreover, certain features of the Greek economic and sociopolitical reality played a crucial role in making Greece the weak link of the eurozone. [*Lack of competitiveness*, caused by *political opposition to reform* and *destructive institutions*]

5) More precisely, the sudden outbreak of the severe fiscal crisis in Greece has been the result not only of inappropriate fiscal policies, but also of poor domestic fiscal governance and weak fiscal institutions. The combination of these factors allowed for large public deficits over a long period of time, and the accumulation of a huge public debt that went out of control because of the global financial crisis (Kaplanoglou & Rapanos 2011). [*Collapse of confidence*, caused by *high debt*, *poor governance*, *destructive institutions*] ALSO [*High debt*, caused by *poor governance*, *poor stats*, *destructive institutions* and *financial crisis*]

6) The reasons for choosing the tax system are rather obvious. Failures in its performance were feeding into growing public deficits for a long period of time. [*High debt*, caused by *poor revenue collection*]

7) As indicated by Kaplanoglou and Rapanos (2011), revenue targets were being missed by a large margin throughout the decade preceding the outbreak of the crisis. Furthermore, the structure of the tax system and the improvement of its overall performance have been issues of hot debate among the Greek political parties, and figure prominently in the reports assessing the compliance of the Greek authorities with the fiscal programme supplementing the support package for Greece (IMF 2011). [*Lack of competitiveness*, caused by *poor revenue collection*]

8) In this paper, we will attempt to evaluate the Greek tax system and point out the particular features that make it not only inefficient in yielding adequate revenues to the state, but also a source of social injustice and a symptom of the lack of trust in the state–citizen relationship. [*Poor revenue collection*, caused by *poor governance*, *poor stats*, *destructive institutions* and *deficit of trust*]

9) The third section attempts to explain the above empirical findings in terms of the longstanding failures of formal institutions. Despite the fact that evidence is sparse and fragmentary, all available indicators point to the fact that the low and unfairly distributed tax yield is primarily due to the poor functioning of the tax administration, lax tax enforcement, inefficiency of tax collection and the lack of effective dispute resolution mechanisms. Such failures result in high tax evasion and a thriving underground economy. [*Poor revenue collection*, caused by *poor governance*, *poor stats*, *destructive institutions* and *deficit of trust*]

10) The first one is that in the real world citizens of democratic political jurisdictions perceive a connection between the taxes they pay and the government services provided to them. In this context, citizens could 'voluntarily' pay their taxes if they trust their government to deliver the services it has promised. The second issue is that, even if a citizen trusts her government, the citizen's behaviour will still be influenced by how she perceives other taxpayers to behave. [*Poor revenue collection*, caused by *lack of trust* and *destructive institutions*]

11) In the fourth section, therefore, we will attempt to draw a link between failures of formal and informal institutions. Within this framework, we argue that low tax revenues are linked with the low tax morale of Greek taxpayers and poor tax compliance behaviour, which are themselves a symptom of low levels of perceived fairness and of the lack of trust of citizens in their government and their fellow citizens. [*Poor revenue collection*, caused by *destructive institutions* and *lack of trust*]

12) Comparing Greece with the narrower and relatively more homogeneous group of eurozone countries, we observe that Greece and Portugal have the lowest direct/indirect tax revenue ratio of around 0.64 (depicted on the right axis of Figure 1), while for the same period Greece has by far the lowest direct tax/GDP ratio of around 8.3 per cent, compared with a eurozone average of 11.7 per cent. [*High debt*, caused by *poor revenue collection*]

13) Nevertheless, there is rampant evidence that low tax revenue yields in Greece are mainly the result of failures of the formal institutions in place, namely poor functioning of the tax administration, lax tax enforcement, inefficiency of tax collection mechanisms and ineffective dispute resolution mechanisms. A clear manifestation of such failures is the size of the shadow economy. [*Poor revenue collection*, caused by *poor governance*, *poor stats*, *corruption* and *large informal sector*]

14) Taking the example of VAT once more, according to a recent European Commission report (European Commission 2011b), the low VAT collection rate is mostly due to fraud and evasion. [*Poor revenue collection*, caused by *corruption*]

15) There is little doubt that the structure of the Greek economy aggravates the problem of tax evasion. The income of the self-employed, who presumably can more easily under-report their income, is a far larger fraction of GDP compared with the eurozone average (24 per cent as opposed to 12.5 per cent of GDP respectively, for the period 2005–09; OECD 2011a). Furthermore, Greece displays the highest proportion of the non-financial business economy workforce being employed in very small businesses across the EU-27. [*Poor revenue collection*, caused by *large informal sector*]

16) A meaningful comparison of the efficiency of the Greek tax administration with those of other OECD countries is severely constrained by the lack of data for Greece. [*Poor governance*, caused by *poor stats*]

17) The failures of formal institutions haunting the Greek tax system have had immense repercussions at the macro-public finance level. Over the ten-year period preceding the recent fiscal crisis, fiscal targets set by Greek governments were constantly missed by a large margin. There is a widely held view that in many EU countries, including Greece, politically motivated systematic optimism concerning economic growth was a key factor behind such deviations (Jonung & Larch 2006; IMF 2006). [*High debt*, caused by *poor revenue collection* and *poor governance*]

18) Based on the findings of this rather new branch of research, there are several noneconomic factors and drivers behind taxpayer compliance behaviour. Two categories of such factors that, in our view, play an important role, particularly in Greece, are: 1. Personal and social norms. 2. Trust, both in the government or state institutions and in other taxpayers. [*Poor revenue collection*, caused by *destructive institutions*]

## SOVEREIGN DEFAULT RISK AND RECOVERY RATES: WHAT GOVERNMENT BOND MARKETS EXPECT FOR GREECE (KARMANN AND MALTRITZ, 2012)

1) Until the beginning of the world financial crisis in 2007 sovereign defaults were seen as a problem related to poor and developing countries. However, during the recent world financial crisis (quasi) defaults of well-developed member states of the EU (Hungary, Latvia) and even the European Monetary Union (EMU) (Greece) also occurred. [*Collapse of confidence*, caused by *financial crisis*]

2) The estimated overall default probability not ably increases as early as the autumn of 2008,when severe strikes and riots against structural and economic reforms, which the Greek government was planning at that time,occurred.13 These events created doubts

about whether the Greek government would be willing and able to enforce the necessary reforms. [*Collapse of confidence*, caused by *poor governance* and *political opposition to reform*]

3) Since we are considering the overall default probability, its increase means that market participants already anticipated the likelihood that Greece would not serve its debt within the next 11 years. However, in the spring of 2009, the spreads lowered because the situation in Greece calmed down. Even during the relatively tranquil time in the autumn of 2009, the estimated overall default probabilities were about 30%. [*Collapse of confidence*, caused by *high debt*]

4) Towards the end of 2009 the spreads and, hence, the estimated default probabilities start to rise again, in advance of the upcoming crisis. Thereby, our estimated probabilities led downgrades of ratings assigned to Greece by the major rating agencies [14]. Starting at a temporary low of below 30% in October 2009, the estimated default risk begins to increase. The rating agencies reacted no earlier than December 8, when Fitch downgraded Greece from A– to BBB+. S&P followed on December 16 with an equivalent change. On the dates of the serating changes, the overall default risk is estimated to be above 70% and 80%, respectively. At the end of the year the default probability is about 70%, and in late January 2010, the probability is close to 90%. [*Collapse of confidence*, caused by *high debt* and *downgrades*]

5) We find that the major part of increased risk results from an increase in short-term risk, rising more significantly than overall risk during times of turmoil. This means, market participations seem to expect a crisis to occur sooner rather than later. [*Collapse of confidence*, caused by *political opposition to reform*]

## Sovereign Debt: A Modern Day Greek Tragedy (Martin and Waller, 2012)

1) While this is a constant concern with individual households, it is almost unimaginable that highly developed economies with democratic governments would default on their debt. Yet that is the harsh reality we face as Portugal, Ireland, Italy, Greece, and Spain—the so-called PUGS countries—struggle to get their debt under control. [*Collapse of confidence*, caused by *high debt*]

2) Consequently, in 1997, the Stability and Growth Pact was signed. This pact added two criteria for prospective members of the EMU. First, they were required to keep the ratio of their deficits as a fraction of GDP to 3 percent or less. Second, they were required to keep the ratio of their gross government debt to GDP at or below 60 percent. The idea was that the Stability and Growth Pact would impose economic discipline on governments of prospective members. This goal had varying degrees of success, as

shown in Figures 4 and 5. Countries had to meet a total of five economic criteria to join the EMU. Unfortunately, all of these criteria were to be met only before a country joined the EMU—once a country joined, the requirements of fiscal discipline vanished. [*High debt*, caused by *political opposition to reform* and *non-enforcement of EU treaties*]

3) What about Greece? As Figure 5B shows, Greece was moving in the wrong direction. Its debt-to-GDP ratio increased from 73 percent in 1990 to 103 percent in 2000. But the euphoria of creating a single currency to compete with the U.S. dollar led to the decision to allow Greece entry into the euro zone. Upon joining the EMU, the inflation rate in Greece converged to that of the rest of Europe, which is not surprising in a currency union. Somewhat more surprising is that the interest rate on long-term Greek debt converged to the rate paid by Germany and France. The same scenario held true for the debt of Spain, Italy, Ireland, and Portugal. [*Access to cheap debt*, caused by *EMU entry*]

4) Thus, financial markets came to view the sovereign debt of euro zone members as being perfect substitutes despite the absence of a fiscal union and the dramatically different fiscal positions of euro members. If the probability of default was the same for each country, then the convergence of inflation rates would justify equivalent interest rates on long-term debt. But given the disparity in fiscal positions, the probability of default was not the same for all countries, and interest rates should have reflected this. [*Access to cheap debt*, caused by *EMU membership*]

5) The fiscal situation in several euro zone countries has deteriorated significantly since 2008. Figures 6 and 7 show deficit-to-GDP and debt-to-GDP ratios for selected countries. In the summer of 2009, a new Greek government took power. At the time, Greece was believed to have a deficit-to-GDP ratio of just under 4 percent, while its debt-to-GDP ratio was about 125 percent. After inspecting the tax and spending data, the new government realized that the statistics were flawed: The deficit-to-GDP ratio was not just under 4 percent but rather just under 16 percent! Although everyone suspected the Greeks were misleading the markets with their fiscal numbers, no one thought it was this severe. [*High debt*, caused by *poor governance*, *poor stats* and *upward revision of debt*]

6) The fiscal shocks hitting these two small countries awakened the financial markets to the risk of default on sovereign debt. No longer did financial markets view the debt of European countries as perfect substitutes for one another. Markets began incorporating default risk into the interest rates charged to various governments to roll over their debt (Figure 8). Between January 2008 and January 2012, the spreads between Greek and German debt increased about 3,300 basis points, while the spread between Irish and German debt jumped to about 550 basis points (peaking at 1,164 basis points in July 2011). [*Collapse of confidence*, caused by *financial crisis* and *high debt*]

7) In response to increasing interest rates, the Greek and Irish governments began discussing or implementing unpopular austerity measures at home to get their fiscal houses in order. Through a combination of tax increases and reduced spending, Greece's

deficit-to-GDP ratio fell from 16 percent in 2009 to a projected 8 percent for 2011; Ireland's fell from a peak 31 percent in 2010 to 10 percent in 2011. Although this sounds like good news from the markets' point of view, the severity of the measures also suggested that voters in Greece or Ireland might revolt and decide to default rather than bear the costs of austerity. Alas, there is no magic elixir to deal with the burden of debt accumulated over decades. [*High debt*, caused by *failed austerity* and *political opposition to reform*] ALSO [*Internal devaluation*, caused by *high debt*]

8) Greek banks hold about 20 percent of Greek sovereign debt (€60 billion), and a Greek default would dramatically weaken the balance sheets of these banks. Thus, markets stopped rolling over the debt of these banks because of fears they would no longer be able to honor their obligations. This, in turn, meant that Greek banks could not roll over funding of Greek government debt. EU leaders, recognizing the gravity of the situation, decided in May 2010 to provide €500 billion in financing to the member countries facing difficulties rolling over their debt. The biggest contributors to the fund were Germany (€120 billion) and France (€90 billion). [*High debt*, caused by *bank undercapitalisation* and *financial crisis*]

## Rent-Seeking in the Greek Economic Drama (Evangelopoulos, 2012)

1) The austerity measures of the Greek socialist government of George Papandreou (2009–11) did not succeed because his government, which had replaced the conservative government of Kostas Karamanlis (2004–2007, 2007–2009), did not rein in the inefficient Greek public sector. In essence, the Papandreou government's austerity measures were neither far reaching nor comprehensive enough to deal successfully with Greece's dire fiscal situation. [*Failed austerity*, caused by *poor governance*, *large public sector* and *political opposition to reform*]

2) Andreas Papandreou set in motion Greece's fiscal excesses in the post–World War II era. He escalated both the fiscal deficit and the public debt enormously while brutally socializing factories, shipyards, refineries, and utilities as well as expanding the public sector tremendously. In 1981, he took over a public debt amounting to 29.7 percent of GDP; in 1990, when he lost the elections, the debt amounted to 80.7 percent of GDP. Yet even this high percentage seriously understated the public debt because it did not include the unpaid state collateral awarded to numerous state companies, public corporations, and public utilities. This ruinous public debt ultimately caused the first modern Greek fiscal crisis in 1993. [*High debt*, caused by *large public sector*, *large welfare state* and *destructive institutions*]

3) From the beginning of his term in office as a young, fresh Greek prime minister, Kostas Karamanlis led the country on a course of state gigantism that absorbed like a sponge all the revenues accumulated from five years of successful privatizations. Total public expenditure increased dramatically, seemingly without political or economic limit. As under Andreas Papandreou's control, the vast Greek public sector in Kostas Karamanlis's hands became a tool for his reelection and the consolidation of his political position. [*High debt*, caused by *large public sector*, *corruption* and *destructive institutions*]

4) A fourth irony, which amounted to Kostas Karamanlis's fatal mistake, was that before the elections of October 2009 he announced a freeze on the salaries of public-sector employees. Faced with the state of emergency in Greece's public finances, Karamanlis spoke the truth in the eleventh hour. But opposition came from the very people who had been hired, explicitly or implicitly, in the public sector. His followers—his political "army," his political "clients," to use the terminology of rent-seeking theory—did not follow him. [*Failed austerity*, caused by *political opposition to reform*, *corruption* and *destructive institutions*]

5) Viewed from the perspective of the political economy of rent seeking (Tullock 1967, 2005; Krueger 1974), modern Greece possesses all the characteristics of a deeply rent-seeking society (Mitsopoulos and Pelagidis 2009, 2011). In this type of society, politicians work as brokers in a system of political clientelism. They expand the public sector, exchanging jobs for votes. [*Large public sector*, caused by *poor governance*, *political opposition to reform* and *destructive institutions*]

6) They also push the private sector into bed with the public sector, assigning to the former secure profits, privileges, and finally explicit and legally established rents—with bribes and corruption forming the dark side of the modern Greek economy. [*Lack of competitiveness*, caused by *corruption* and *destructive institutions*]

7) On the basis of this trade-off between political and economic rents, farmers are enriched through subsidies, and workers' unions negotiate collective agreements that fix wages much higher than can be justified on productive grounds. [*Lack of competitiveness*, caused by *high wages*, *destructive institutions* and *corruption*]

8) In short, rent-seeking behavior is chronic in modern Greek society, resulting in the emergence of a generally inefficient institutional economic framework that is financed through a dramatically expanding public deficit and public debt and supported by a strong continental currency, the euro. [*Destructive institutions*, caused by *large state*, *corruption* and *monetary dependence*]

9) The names of Greek rulers change from "Karamanlis" to "Papandreou" and back again,1 and the nominal political direction changes between conservatism and socialism, but the size of the state remains stably excessive as well as anomalous, and fiscal conditions worsen at an accelerating rate. [*Large state*, caused by *poor governance* and *destructive institutions*]

# PURE OR WAKE-UP CALL CONTAGION? ANOTHER LOOK AT THE EMU SOVEREIGN DEBT CRISIS (GIORDANO, PERICOLI AND TOMMASINO, 2013)

1) At the beginning of 2009, ten years after the launch of the euro, many commentators viewed the single currency as a major success. In the run- up to the euro's introduction, interest rates had rapidly converged towards the low levels of the most creditworthy member states: in the period 1992–1998, the average spread of long- term government bond yields with respect to the German one had declined from about 200 to 24 basis points. From 1999 onwards spreads continued to narrow, and at the end of 2007 they were negligible (16 basis points on average). [*High debt*, caused by *access to cheap debt*] ALSO [*Cheap debt*, caused by *EMU membership*]

2) Due to the financial turmoil triggered by the Lehman Brothers bankruptcy, some tensions started to surface in September 2008, but at the end of that year the average yield spread in the euro area was still about 100 basis points. Strains on government securities markets became worrisome only towards the end of 2009 (Figure 1). The focus of concern was Greece. After a series of upward deficit revisions, the last of which was equal to nearly 3 percentage points of GDP in October 2009, the Greek government estimated the deficit at 12.7% of GDP in 2009, up from 7.7% in 2008. [*Collapse of confidence*, caused by *high debt*, *upward revision of debt* and *financial crisis*]

3) One lesson of the EMU crisis is that even countries with low levels of public debt and deficits can suffer a sudden deterioration of their fiscal position, for example as an effect of financial sector bailouts (which may transform private liabilities into public debt). This risk was considered obvious for emerging markets at least since the Asian crisis of the late 1990s, but it was not taken into account by the EMU rules and – as we show here – by investors. [*High debt*, caused by *financial crisis*]

4) However, this impact differed across borrowers. In particular, investors penalized governments with weaker fiscal and macroeconomic fundamentals more heavily. [*Collapse of confidence*, caused by *high debt*]

5) The analyses presented in this paper suggest that investors partially ignored macroeconomic indicators when pricing sovereign bonds before October 2009. [*Access to cheap debt*, caused by *EMU membership*]

6) At that date they started to discriminate among sovereigns based on the quality of their fundamentals. In particular, countries with worse fiscal conditions and external positions recorded much higher spread levels. In the terminology adopted in this paper, the sharp increase in spreads observed for some countries after the start of the Greek crisis was the result of a wake- upcall rather than pure contagion: the Greek crisis increased investors' sensitivity to the fundamentals of the other euro- area countries. [*Collapse of confidence*, caused by *lack of competitiveness* and *high debt*]

7) More broadly, it would help settle the debate about the relative merits of market- based as against rules- based fiscal and macroeconomic discipline, which is as old as the very idea of EMU. [*Easy access to cheap debt*, caused by *capitalism*]

## POSTCARDS FROM THE FUTURE: THE GREEK DEBT CRISIS, THE STRUGGLE AGAINST THE IMF-EU AUSTERITY PACKAGE AND OPEN QUESTIONS FOR LEFT STRATEGY (SAKELLAROPOULOS AND SOTIRIS, 2014)

1) The revelation of high levels of public debt, the downgrading by international grading agencies, the widespread assumption that a Greek default is highly probable and the consequent extreme rise in the cost of borrowing have led to draconian packages of austerity measures, a prolonged recession, a sharp decline in living standards and the imposition of a regime of limited economic sovereignty under the terms of supervision by the EU – IMF – ECB 'troika. [*Collapse of confidence*, caused by *downgrades*, *high debt* and *failed austerity*]

2) Deviant public borrowing and spending, constantly rising salaries undermining the competitiveness of Greek economy, and an unsustainable consumption mode. [*Lack of competitiveness*, caused by *high debt* and *high salaries*]

3) The broadening of the consumption base, mainly through access to cheaper credit, was necessary to keep high rates of growth, a tendency observed in most OECD countries. [*Excessive private credit extension*, caused by *EMU membership*]

4) Missing from this picture are other important aspects of the Greek Debt crisis As far as the Greek debt burden is concerned what is missing from the dominant discourse is that capital in Greece has enjoyed one the most lax tax regimes in Europe. Taxation on business earnings is one of the lowest; indirect taxes aimed mainly against households are the most important source of tax revenue; tax exemptions of all kinds are extremely widespread (for example scandalous exemptions of the Shipping Industry in what concerns VAT in business transactions4). [*Poor revenue collection*, caused by *destructive institutions*, *capitalism* and *corruption*]

5) At the same time, before the crisis there was conscious tolerance of on the part of the Greek government as a means to build class alliances, especially with small capitalists and the petty bourgeois strata. It is also important to note that deficits also reflected the pressure on Greek governments to accommodate big business both national and international: overpriced public works, extremely high cost of medical supplies and of course high military spending– a large part of it openly politically motivated with the

Greek government buying US fighter planes, French frigates and German inoperable submarines amidst a recession. [*High debt*, caused by *capitalism*, *corruption*, *military spending* and *poor governance*]

6) It is also worth noting that the recession of the Greek economy, and consequent debt burden, is not a simple local manifestation of the global capitalist crisis. It also reflected a deeper crisis of the whole 'developmental paradigm' of Greek capitalism that was based upon low labor cost, the exploitation of immigrant labor, the use of European funds and increased household consumption fueled by debt. [*Internal devaluation*, caused by *high debt*, *financial crisis*, *capitalism* and *excessive private credit extension*]

7) In the discussion of the Greek crisis, the whole question of the Eurozone and the consequences of Greece joining the European Monetary Union (EMU) had been left outside the discussion for a long time. Yet this is exactly the problem: The introduction of a common currency without a common authority and mechanisms of redistribution was intensifying regional imbalances, hurting workers in both core and periphery countries, yet benefiting the capital of the core European countries. [*Lack of competitiveness*, caused by *EMU entry*]

8) The introduction of the euro as a common currency accentuated the problems caused by the differences in competitiveness and productivity in European economies. [*Lack of competitiveness*, caused by *EMU membership*]

9) The Euro practically meant currency devaluation for higher productivity and competitive export countries and a currency overvaluation for lower productivity import countries, making even more obvious the differences in productivity and competitiveness. [*Lack of competitiveness*, caused by *EMU entry* and *low productivity*]

10) As even Paul Krugman acknowledges, [7] it was predictable that at some point the establishment of a single currency by countries with entirely different levels of productivity would bring to light a host of contradictions. These contradictions have to do with the different structural characteristics of each country, the uneven rates of capital accumulation, the unequal contributions to international competitiveness. [*Lack of competitiveness*, caused by *monetary dependence* and *regulatory burden* and *EMU membership*]

11) All these led not only to differentiations in the rates of inflation and a spiraling of public debt but also, and above all, to differences in international specialization of the national productive systems [8]. [*High debt*, caused by *lack of competitiveness*]

12) Current account deficits in the European South contrasted with the surpluses in Germany point to this structural imbalance in competitiveness [9]. It is also worth noting that the structural imbalances of the Eurozone were also instrumental in creating aspects of the debt crisis for countries such as Greece. Current account deficits and a decline in private savings led to an accumulation of external debt. [*High debt*, caused by *current account deficits*]

13) Consequently, the structural imbalances of the Eurozone have forced countries such as Greece towards a policy of internal devaluation, in the sense of a sharp reduction of wage costs, in order for the economy to have a new lower starting equilibrium. [*Internal devaluation*, caused by *lack of competitiveness* and *monetary dependence*]

14) The problem is that although processes of internal devaluation can be extremely violent socially, at the same time they are either unsuccessful in bringing forward the desire crises in competitiveness (amongst to the reasons because they tend to put too much stress on labor costs) or they must take too long. [*Political opposition to reform*, caused by *internal devaluation*]

15) Measures that until recently were aspects of 'wishful thinking' for the forces of capital have been rapidly introduced in a 'shock and awe' tactic of consecutive legislative coups. Moreover, the whole mechanism of EU-ECB-IMF 'supervision,' in reality something close to economic and financial occupation, led to successive waves of measures. Sharp reductions in both public and private sector wages, along with abolishing existing legislation on collective bargaining, led to a 25.2% reduction in real terms of average wages [15] [*Lack of competitiveness*, caused by *high wages*, *regulatory burden* and *large public sector*]

16) The reform of the pension system will lead to dramatic increases in pension age limits and decreases in pensions and, more importantly, to the change from a redistributive system based on the solidarity of generations (current workers' contributions pay for pensioners) to a system where pensions will be determined by the level of contributions introduced during the whole work-life. [*High debt*, caused by *large welfare system*]

17) The mass rallies and assemblies at city squares all over Greece in May-July 2011 exemplified the looming crisis of hegemony. This movement was based on the collective experiences of struggle in the past years, such as the December 2008 youth explosion, the massive strikes in 2010–2011, the movement of civil disobedience to increased toll prices, and the heroic struggle of the people of Keratea, a small town in the greater Attica region, which fought with riot police for months, successfully opposing plans for an environmentally disastrous landfill in their vicinity. [*Political opposition to reform*, caused by *internal devaluation* and *capitalism*]

18) The fact that the Greek government used extreme forms of police brutality in order to suppress the movement provides further evidence of the absence of legitimization and of the deepening hegemonic crisis. [*Political opposition to reform*, caused by *poor governance*]

# LOST IN THE OCEAN OF DEREGULATION: THE GREEK LABOUR MOVEMENT IN A TIME OF CRISIS (KRETSOS AND VOGIATZOGLOU, 2015)

1) This assistance was based on the condition that the Greek government would put in place one of the most radical structural adjustment programs ever implemented in Europe. In this context, the peculiar position of Greece on the global map of marketization is related to both economic and political reasons and an exceedingly fast-moving play of reforms and restructuring imposed by the international lenders and Greek authorities. [*Lack of competitiveness*, caused by *regulatory burden* and *large PS unions*]

2) The sovereign debt crisis has become a powerful lever of the growing precariousness of employment and the increasing fragility of protective regulations at work. This development is partly related to the incapacity of mainstream trade unions to mobilize rank-and-file members to resist the ongoing deterioration in workplace conditions and the systemic erosion of workers' power. [*Political opposition to reform*, caused by *internal devaluation* and *strong PS unions*]

3) After identifying the strong points of the latter's contributions, as well as the problems and challenges they are facing, we conclude that a diversified and innovative approach is required on the part of the labour movement in order to simultaneously address and exploit all sources of workers' power. The emergence of radical unionism in large urban areas is a fortunate development, but cannot be transplanted as a recipe for success in itself. [*Failed austerity measures*, caused by *political opposition to reform*]

4) At the time of writing, Greece's economic performance remains devastating. According to the data of the national statistical authorities (ELSTAT), the public debt stood at 175.7% at the close of 2013, despite the fact that the majority of memorandum commitments were met on time. [*High debt*, caused by *internal devaluation* and *poor governance*]

5) A drop in the GDP growth rate of more than 25% since 2008 has seriously dented the productive capacity of the Greek economy (OECD, 2014). Real incomes have declined and the population facing the risk of poverty has risen dramatically (INE-GSEE, 2013). According to the OECD (2014), total household income in Greece dropped by one third between 2007 and 2012. This drop in income is the largest in the OECD and four times as large as that recorded in the average Eurozone country. [*Lack of productivity*, caused by *internal devaluation*]

6) Furthermore, the social impact of fiscal consolidation has been aggravated by the lack of a general safety net, as well as low social spending and a traditionally weak welfare state (Petmesidou, 2013). Indeed, according to the OECD (2013), the Greek social protection system has been characterized by the fragmentation of benefits with limited targeting and benefits are largely restricted to those covered by the social security

system. It thus excludes young people and the long-term unemployed, as well as low-income households. [*High debt*, caused by *large welfare state* and *poor governance*]

7) Greek unions are politicized; the GSEE and ADEDY are pluralist in political terms, with their main fractions being affiliated or politically close to the main parties in the country. Currently, both the GSEE and ADEDY are controlled by a majority formed around the social-democratic PASKE fraction. In recent years (also preceding the crisis), the main lines of activity of both confederations have been centred on collective bargaining, on the one hand, and calling general strikes, on the other. [*Regulatory burden*, caused by *destructive institutions* and *strong PS unions*]

8) With regard to collective bargaining, and according to Zambarloukou (2006), Greece stands as an exemplar case of "state corporatism" following a long period of direct state interventionism that stigmatized collective bargaining structures and trade unions functioning. Furthermore, historical and political conditions promoted a peculiar interconnection between first-class union leaderships and strong bourgeois political parties based on a post-dictatorship social democratic consensus and an "exchange of gifts," the price of which has been an increasingly precarious workforce (Ioannou, 2000; Kretsos, 2011). [*Lack of competitiveness*, caused by *regulatory burden*, *corruption* and *poor governance*]

9) When it comes to general strikes, Greece represents an ideal study case because mainstream trade union resistance to structural labour market reforms has been largely restricted to frequent general strike activity. Not surprisingly, Greek trade unions are famous for being active in this field. According to Kelly and Hamman (2010), 38 out of 98, or 44%, of all the general strikes across Europe between 1980 and 2008 took place in Greece. [*Lack of competitiveness*, caused by *regulatory burden* and *political opposition to reform*]

## Living Parallel Lives: Italy and Greece in an Age of Austerity (Verney and Bosco, 2013)

1) Both in Greece in 2012 and in Italy in 2013, it took two elections to form a government. The election results sent shock waves through Europe and beyond, suggesting that Southern Europe might be drifting towards ungovernability. Following the Greek parliamentary election in May 2012, a country with a strong tradition of one-party majority governments could not even form a coalition. On this occasion, the only likely alliance had been so delegitimized by the dizzying drop in the vote of the two former major parties that it had become politically infeasible. [*Collapse of confidence*, caused by *political opposition to reform*]

2) The Greek and Italian elections of 2012–13 mark a second phase in the history of 'crisis elections' in Southern Europe. An earlier volume, Elections in Hard Times: Southern Europe, 2010–11, charted the electoral impact of the early years of the economic crisis across the region (Bosco & Verney 2013). It revealed a picture of declining participation, systematic incumbent punishment, frequently without a concomitant rise in support for the official opposition, and the rise of challenger parties (Bosco & Verney 2012). [*Political instability*, caused by *collapse of confidence*, *lack of trust*]

3) The implication was one of growing delegitimation of existing party systems in a context in which the crisis, by confining the policy options available to political leaders, was leading to a developing 'democracy without choices' [*Lack of trust*, caused by *Internal devaluation* and *poor governance*]

4) While the international economic crisis had already been well underway at the time of the previous Greek national election in October 2009, the extent of its consequences for the country was not yet apparent to the electorate. It was only in the immediate aftermath of that electoral contest that the new Greek government had revealed the true state of public finances, triggering the eurozone crisis. [*Collapse of confidence*, caused by *upward revision of Greek debt*]

5) These 'earthquake elections' provide the central focus of this volume. The common defining characteristic in both countries was the significant rise in protest voting. Therefore, besides articles examining the parliamentary elections themselves, this volume includes articles on two protest parties that achieved their first parliamentary breakthrough: the Five Star Movement (Movimento Cinque Stelle) in Italy and Golden Dawn (Xrysh) in Greece. [*Political instability*, caused by *political opposition to reform*] ALSO [*Failed austerity*, caused by *political instability*]

6) A second point concerns performance. On all four indicators shown in Tables 1 and 2, it is clear that both countries were badly hit by the crisis but Greece was hit much worse. In 2008, both countries entered recession but in 2010 Italy temporarily returned to positive growth while the same year saw the acceleration of Greece's uninterrupted economic decline. [*High debt*, caused by *financial crisis*]

7) For both countries, the collapse of Lehman Brothers in September 2008 resulted in rapidly rising borrowing costs. As panic spread through the international financial system, a major consequence for the eurozone members, previously able to borrow at roughly similar interest rates, was a reassessment of their creditworthiness on the basis of their individual public finance performance. As a result, the cost of executing the national budget and servicing the national debt, both already seriously high, began to spiral in both Italy and Greece. [*Collapse of confidence*, caused by *financial crisis* and *high debt*]

8) As shown in Tables 1 and 2, between 2007 and2012, the last year before the parliamentary election, the Italian national debt jumped by more than 20 per cent of GDP. In the case of Greece, between 2007 and 2011 (again the last year before the

parliamentary election) the rise was over 60 per cent of GDP. For both countries, the budget deficit peaked in 2009, in Italy reaching almost double and in Greece over five times the eurozone criterion of three per cent of GDP. [*High debt*, caused by *financial crisis*, *poor governance* and *failed austerity*]

9) However, from April 2010, when its sovereign credit rating was downgraded to junk status, Greece was excluded from the international money markets. The following month, the Greek government signed an agreement for a e110 billion loan from the EU and International Monetary Fund (IMF), accompanied by a Memorandum of Understanding laying out a detailed programme of fiscal consolidation and structural reform. [*Collapse of confidence*, caused by *downgrades*]

10) ´ypa ´rxoyn), promising there was no need for austerity. The first bailout was supported only by the governing PASOK and the small radical right party, Popular Orthodox Rally (LAOS), and vehemently opposed by the official opposition party, ND. It passed through parliament amid violent demonstrations, including a bank firebombing in which three people died. From Spring 2010, Greece faced a strong wave of anti-austerity protest, including repeated general and sectoral strikes and sometimes violent demonstrations, a 'Can't pay, won't pay' movement on public transport and toll roads, and yoghurt-throwing attacks on governing party MPs (Psimitis 2011; Vournelis & Sutton 2012). [*Political instability*, caused by *political opposition to reform*]

11) Meanwhile, from Spring 2011 the Greek government became a focus of strong international criticism for not meeting its Memorandum targets. In May and June 2011, as the government prepared a Medium Term Programme with e28 billion of austerity measures, an 'Indignant Citizens' protest camp was established in front of parliament, exercising pressure on MPs not to vote for the package. Fears that the bill, fought by the entire opposition, would not pass through parliament, led to a proposal for a grand coalition. [*Failed austerity*, caused by *political opposition to reform*] ALSO [*High debt*, caused by *political opposition to reform*]

12) Three days later, Papandreou unexpectedly announced he was going to ask the President to call a referendum on the second bailout rather than attempting to pass it through parliament. The proposal aimed to provide legitimacy not just for the new bailout, but also more generally for the government strategy of resorting to international loans and implementing their accompanying conditions. In the process, it was clearly hoped also to restabilise a government then on the verge of collapse. The referendum announcement caused consternation in the EU, where referenda had essentially been eschewed since the repeated European Treaty ratification debacles of the 1990s and 2000s. [*Collapse of confidence*, caused by *political instability*]

13) The clear disapprobation of European leaders expressed at Cannes exacerbated rising domestic discontent, providing the final blow to government legitimacy in both countries. In an interesting example of external–internal linkage, the intervention by the leaders of the EU's Franco-German axis was followed by the immediate loss of

parliamentary support by both the Greek and Italian prime ministers. [*Trust deficit*, caused by *Internal devaluation* and *failed austerity*]

## LESSONS FROM THE GREEK TRAGEDY: EUROPE NEEDS ECONOMIC CONVERGENCE (LIANOU, 2012)

1) The need for economic governance has two aspects: firstly, it is a political choice for the confrontation of the economic problem, and secondly, it is an economic demand for the effective use of economic assets (through coherence policies). Today, the fiscal policy comes under common rules enacted by the Treaty of the EU and the Stability and Growth Pact, which promote the fiscal discipline of the member states and a system of mutual observance so that the public deficit to the GDP does not exceed the limit of 3%. [*High debt*, caused by *political opposition to reform* and *non-enforcement of EU treaties*]

2) The Lisbon Treaty is not enough for integrated economic governance in the EU, as it did not reinforce the political union of Europe. Although it contributed to changes in the economic governance of the Eurozone, these changes were weak and inadequate, as they actually stepped back from the policies that the rejected European Constitution would have implemented. Fiscal policy remains under the authority of the member states. [*Lack of competitiveness*, caused by *poor governance* and *non-enforcement of EU treaties*]

3) The long duration of the crisis illustrates that the common currency and the European Central Bank are not adequate to support the common market and European financial integration. As the Greek fiscal problem has indicated, without a common economic and financial policy, the cohesion of the common currency and even of EU itself faces a great and unpredictable risk. [*High debt*, caused by *access to cheap debt* and *poor governance*]

4) In the case of the Greek fiscal problem, an ad hoc mechanism of support was created with a loan of 110 billion euros, including 30 billion euros from the IMF and 80 euros from the Eurozone. However, an ad hoc mobilization is not adequate. A unified centre of economic policy is needed and with it, an associated progress towards economic and political integration is essential. [*Failed austerity measures*, caused by *lack of competitiveness*]

5) The states would not easily leave their fiscal policy in a supranational level. It is a sensitive political section for national governments. Nevertheless, they should try. A coordination of fiscal policy is necessary, because it will favor the societies, reduce the economic gap, and improve the asymmetry between member states. The EU must act in order to stop objections. It must be understood that the nation state does not die, but it is reformed. [*High debt*, caused by *political opposition to reform*]

## IS SOCIAL PROTECTION IN GREECE AT A CROSSROADS? (PETMESIDOU, 2013)

1) Much of the debate on South European (SE) welfare states over the last decade focused on their imbalances and, particularly, on their pension bias crowding out resources for support to families at earlier stages of the life cycle, undeveloped social safety nets, high labour market segmentation, and great inequalities in social insurance coverage. [*Large welfare state*, caused by *poor governance* and *political opposition to reform*]

2) The first part of the paper critically discusses the deadlocks and crisis effects of a social welfare model (for a long-time prevailing in Greece) that combined rent-seeking statist practices with a 'male bread winner/familialist regime'. [*High debt*, caused by *large welfare state*]

3) Greece is facing the worst economic crisis since World War II. The sovereign debt crunch that emerged in 2009 (excessively high public deficit and debt levels disclosed after the revision of the budget gap) undermined the credibility of the country and led to escalating borrowing costs, bringing the economy near bankruptcy. [*Collapse of confidence*, caused by *high debt* and *upward revision of debt*]

4) However, in the two years following the 'rescue deal', the economy remained stuck into deep recession (GDP contracted by about 22% from 2008 to 2012 and is estimated to further plunge by nearly 5% in 2013), unemployment soared (reaching 26.8% in May 2013, the highest rate in the EU3), while social unrest escalated. [*Failed austerity*, caused by *lack of competitiveness* and *political opposition to reform*]

5) The alarmingly deepening crisis brought into relief that many of the assumptions embraced into the initial bailout plan for Greece's debt sustainability were problematic. A revision of the rescue programme in July 2011 (encompassing a 21% write-down on the face value of the bonds held by private bondholders) was soon considered by the international lenders not sufficient for stabilising the debt dynamics. A third iteration of the plan was agreed in late October 2011 for a fresh loan of 130bn Euros, in parallel with a 50% debt restructuring for private bondholders, with strict conditionalities exacting swinging budgetary cuts, labour market deregulation, drastic public employment reduction and other structural reforms. [*Lack of competitiveness*, caused by *high debt*, *regulatory burden* and *large public sector*]

6) Strikingly, a few months after the 'haircut' operation, and as soon as a shaky government coalition was formed, after two successive national elections (in May and June 2012), forecasts of a ballooning, unsustainable debt triggered a new round of programme revision. [*Collapse of confidence*, caused by *political instability*]

7) Deeper cuts to pensions, salaries and other expenses and further deregulation accompanied the fourth bailout iteration (of late November 2012) amidst persistent

uncertainty though as to the viability of the plan. [*High debt*, *large welfare state* and *regulatory burden*]

8) Rising social spending prior to the crisis is considered among the factors contributing to it, as though the welfare state in Greece had grown to its limits (Matsaganis 2011). Indeed social spending rapidly increased over the last three decades, and surely profligate borrowing by successive governments (combined with EU funding flowing into the country) significantly boosted expenses. [*High debt*, caused by *large welfare state*, *access to cheap debt* and *Capital influx*]

9) Closely linked to this is the very low level of state revenues in Greece (37% of GDP in 2008, compared to EU-15 average of 44%) and the highly regressive fiscal policy pursued, given extensive reliance on indirect taxes and the persistently huge tax evasion particularly from the well-off groups [5]. [*High debt*, caused by *poor revenue collection*, *corruption* and *large informal sector*]

10) Instead a configuration of rent-seeking statist-clientelistic structures and practices dominated socio-political integration for a long-time, making access by households, individuals and businesses to 'political credentials' a central means for the appropriation of resources and fostering a perception of social problems in individualist/familist terms. [*Poor governance*, caused by *corruption* and *destructive institutions*]

11) Second, enactment of social rights and social programmes (e.g., implementation of a national health system) occurred in a much shorter time period compared to North-West Europe, a condition accounting for weak consolidation of new institutions. Soon fiscal constraints became highly pressing, particularly under the project of Greece's joining the European Monetary Union and the subsequent fiscal discipline requirements of the Stability Pact. Expansionary trends slowed down and an urgent need for welfare state retrenchment emerged, even though the welfare state hardly reached a level of maturity compared to North-West Europe. [*High debt*, caused by *large welfare state*]

12) More than any other SE country, Greece developed a highly fragmented and polarised system with wide imbalances among the 130 social insurance funds in existence until recently. In the early 1980s, a social-democratic element was introduced with the establishment of a National Health System (NHS), indicating a path shift that, however, remained incomplete (private health expenditure kept growing and multiple health funds with inequalities in coverage continued to operate). [*Large welfare state*, caused by *poor governance*]

13) At the onset of the crisis, extreme fragmentation and polarisation in social insurance, swelling administrative costs and accumulated incentives for early retirement, in combination with rapid demographic ageing and negative economic growth hiked pension expenditure to over 13% of GDP (expected to nearly double by 2050). [*Large welfare state*, caused by *poor governance*, *corruption* and *ageing population*]

14) Social services are poorly developed and informal care within the family is key for meeting needs (Petmesidou 2006b). Growing demand for care due to changes in

demography, family patterns and gender roles has progressively been met by female migrant labour (either as co-residing or day-care minders, Guillén and Petmesidou 2008: 75). An informal privatisation pattern thus emerged where the family still plays. [*Large welfare state*, caused by *ageing population*]

15) Largely, under the bailout agreement, the main policy options embrace drastic falls in wages and salaries,6 significant hikes in indirect taxes7 and special levies8 that hit disproportionally low and middle-income earners; and considerable cuts in current and future pension entitlements, and social assistance benefits (a weak, anyway, element of income maintenance). [*Lack of competitiveness*, caused by *high wages*, *poor revenue collection* and *large welfare state*]

16) Under the pressure of achieving budget compliance in the upcoming years, the tax reform agenda opened once more in late 2012. New legislation further extended the tax base to factor in low-income groups, and abolished tax breaks and allowances (hurting particularly low- to middle-income families with children). These are regressive measures severely squeezing Greece's already austerity-hit lower and middle class. Harsh cuts in public health expenditure are prominent on the reform agenda too. [*High debt*, caused by *poor revenue collection* and *large welfare state*]

## In the Shadow of the Grexit: The Greek Election of 17 June 2012 (Vasilopoulou & Halikiopoulou, 2013)

1) May 2012 shook the main pillars of the Greek political system, resulting in the breakdown of the two-party domination of the political scene. The two main parties that had been ruling Greece in single-party governments during the previous 40 years, ND (N 1 á Dhmokratía—New Democracy) and PASOK (Panellhnio Sosialistikó Kínhma—Panhellenic Socialist Movement), attracted a combined vote of approximately 30 percent, translating into a record low number of parliamentary seats for these parties, which prevented either of them from forming a majority government in accordance with Greek parliamentary tradition. [*Political instability*, caused by *political opposition to reform*]

2) Anti-bailout, anti-establishment and populist forces made substantial gains. One of the main winners was SYRIZA (Synaspismo ´6 th6 Pizospastikh ´6 Aristera ´6—Coalition of the Radical Left), which quadrupled its 2009 results and succeeded in becoming these condelectoral force in Greek politics. Golden Dawn (Xrysh´ Aygh´), an extreme right-wing anti-immigrant political party, gained parliamentary representation for the first time, receiving approximately seven per cent of the votes cast. [*Possible EMU exit*, caused by *political opposition to reform*]

3) The election results confirmed many of the trends of the previous round, including electoral volatility, the fragmentation of the party system and the decline of PASOK, the

lack of a popular mandate to form a strong majority government and the rise of anti-establishment political forces. [*Political instability*, caused by *political opposition to reform*]

4) Greek political culture is characterised by the 'polarisation of political conflict and rhetoric'. These deep internal divisions are both historical—the product of the country's civil war legacy—and sociopolitical. They are the result of Greece's electoral system, a form of reinforced proportional representation that favours the ability of the winner to achieve an absolute majority through the granting of bonus seats, and the adversarial nature of its politics. [*Destructive institutions*, caused by *lack of trust*]

5) This system operates within a framework of consolidated mass clientelism that transcends left–right divisions—which Mouzelis and Pagoulatos (2002) term 'partitocratic' democracy. Featherstone (2005) has characterised Greece as a société bloquée, i.e., a society where systemic weaknesses, including historically embedded clientelism, rent-seeking behaviour, the near absence of policy communities and think-tanks, and a regime of 'disjointed corporatism', create problems of governability, impeding any reform attempts. [*Lack of competitiveness*, caused by *poor governance*, *corruption*, *destructive institutions* and *political opposition to reform*]

6) Large-scale and deeply embedded corruption entails a lack of accountability as essentially separate agents govern the entire system. These rent-seeking groups have vested interests in curtailing competition, increasing bureaucracy and hindering transparency in order to maximise their gains (Mitsopoulos & Pelagidis 2011). [*Corruption*, caused by *destructive institutions*]

7) The Greek sovereign debt crisis occurred against this backdrop of embedded clientelism and corruption. In a period of global recession, Greece found itself in the middle of a fiscal crisis of unprecedented character. Unable to refinance its high public debt and manage its worsening deficit, the country plunged into deeper recession, threatening to destabilise the whole euro area. [*High debt*, caused by *corruption*, *poor governance* and *financial crisis*]

8) The rescue package, amounting to e110 billion, led to the adoption of a number of highly controversial reforms, stringent austerity measures and a wave of trade union protests and strikes. [*Political opposition to reform*, caused by *internal devaluation*]

9) During this period, credit-rating agencies downgraded Greece's rating, warning of the possibility of the country's default. In an EU summit held on 26–27 October 2011, Greece's European partners agreed a 50 per cent bond debt 'haircut', known as Private Sector Involvement (PSI), in return for additional austerity measures.2 On 31 October, the then Prime Minister, George Papandreou, announced a controversial plan to hold a referendum over the bilateral loan agreement between Greece and its lenders (To Vima 2011). [*Collapse of confidence*, caused by *downgrades* and *political opposition to reform*]

10) The electoral results of 6 May 2012 further shook the main pillars of the Greek political system, engendering the breakdown of the two-party domination of the political scene. PASOK and ND jointly gained a mere 32 per cent of the vote. This translated into 41 and 108 parliamentary seats, respectively, which did not allow either party to form a majority government. Anti-bailout, anti-establishment and populist forces made substantial gains. [*Fears of EMU exit*, caused by *political opposition to reform*]

11) It is in this context that the campaign for the June elections took place: major domestic problems, including rising costs, low levels of consumption, a great dip in investment, fears over deepening recession, concerns over tax collection, immigration and welfare provision, as well as increasing external pressures for reform. [*Poor governance*, caused by *poor revenue collection*, *large welfare state* and *political opposition to reform*]

12) The inability of any party to form a majority government after 6 May, and the absence of cooperation which made a coalition government impossible, exposed Greece to further pressures from abroad. With default and euro exit a possibility, the economic crisis was becoming manifest as a political crisis as well, with fundamental consequences for both Greece and the EU. [*Collapse of confidence*, caused by *possible EMU exit* and *political instability*]

13) The uncertainty that followed the May election sent mixed signals abroad regarding the country's ability to implement the stipulations of the bailout agreements, maintained the various scenarios about Greece leaving the eurozone and/or the EU and had a negative effect on European financial markets. [*Collapse of confidence*, caused by *possible EMU exit* and *political instability*]

14) The main question was instead whether reform should take place within or outside the euro framework. By extension, the electoral result was a priori understood as either a vote to remain in the eurozone or a vote for anti-Memorandum parties for whom eurozone membership was not necessarily a priority and who could risk a potential exit. [*Fears of possible EMU exit*, caused by *political instability*]

15) This led to increasing polarisation between the pro-and anti-bailout forces (translated as pro- and anti- euroforces) into two main camps, i.e., the ND and SYRIZA camps, demands for strategic voting to keep the other forces out of government, and the packaging of all economic measures including austerity and public-sector and salary cuts in terms of a pro- or anti-euro choice. [*Political instability*, caused by *political opposition to reform*]

16) A number of Greek parties within the anti-bailout camp continued to press for a potential renegotiation. SYRIZA was the most prominent party and main contender for government. The party's campaign was characterised by inconsistency, ambiguity, radicalism and anti-establishment rhetoric. On the one hand, SYRIZA demanded the renegotiation of the terms and conditions of the Second Memorandum (or its full cancellation), while on the other it professed to be in favour of Greece remaining in the

eurozone—although not at any cost. [*Collapse of confidence*, caused by *possible EMU exit* and *political instability*]

17) From the right-wing camp, both ANEL and Golden Dawn were firmly anti-bailout. Both parties emphasised the issues of external intervention, national sovereignty and corruption, linking the bailout issue with nationalism through a populist rhetoric. ANEL's leader, Panos Kammenos, for example, professed 18 June as the day the Greek people 'will free our motherland from the loan sharks who have enslaved the nation; we will unite to free the country together' (To Vima 2012b). ANEL expressed its support for a full cancellation of the second Memorandum of Understanding. Golden Dawn leader Nikos Michaloliakos, in the party's pre-electoral televised spot (Golden Dawn 2012), emphasised the need for 'national independence' and 'national cleansing', drawing on the corruption issue. [*Political instability*, caused by *political opposition to reform* and *corruption*]

18) The election results marked the increasing polarisation of Greek society. The two main issues that dominated the election were the debates over the second Memorandum of Understanding (53 percent of those polled) and Greece's place in the eurozone (47 per cent of those polled) (Metron Analysis 2012b). [*Fears of possible EMU exit*, caused by *political instability*]

## How Much Did Competitiveness of the Greek Economy Decline Since EMU Entry? (Malliaropulos, 2010)

1) It is a common view among economists and analysts that competitiveness of the Greek economy has deteriorated significantly since EMU entry due to high wage and price inflation and the inability of Greece to devalue its currency after joining the euro. Estimates of this deterioration between 2000 and 2009, however, vary widely. [*Lack of competitiveness*, caused by *EMU entry*, *high wages* and *monetary dependence*]

2) Based on relative unit labor costs, they range between 9% (IMF) and 27% (Bank of Greece, see Table 1). Based on relative prices, competitiveness of the Greek economy seems to have deteriorated since 2000 by between 18% (ECB, Bank of Greece) and 21% (IMF). [*Lack of competitiveness*, caused by *high wages* and *low productivity*]

3) As a result, along with the painful process of fiscal consolidation, Greece faces the need for a substantial "internal devaluation", i.e., an outright decline in wages and prices in order to restore competitiveness and rebalance its economy towards external demand. [*Internal devaluation*, caused by *monetary dependence* and *lack of competitiveness*]

4) Because such a process of deflation will most likely deepen the recession and lead to a further increase of the debt-to-GDP ratio – as a result of the "snowball" effect --, markets doubt that Greece will be able to eventually stabilize its debt without some kind

of restructuring or even an outright default and exit from the euro area. [*Collapse of confidence*, caused by *fears of possible EMU exit* and *political opposition to reform*]

5) Our results suggest that competitiveness of the Greek economy has declined by 10% since 2000, both in terms of relative prices and in terms of relative unit labor costs, considerably less than most common REER indices suggest. [*Lack of competitiveness*, caused by *EMU entry*]

6) We find that most of the deterioration in competitiveness took place in the agricultural and the industrial sector. Interestingly, price competitiveness of the service sector (which makes up nearly 80% for the private sector in terms of gross value added) has not been affected, whereas wage competitiveness has deteriorated by about 5% since 2000. [*Lack of competitiveness*, caused by *high wages*]

7) Fourth, agriculture, which is one of the most protected sectors of the Greek economy, has witnessed the sharpest loss in competitiveness since 2000, because EU subsidies have acted as a disincentive to increase productivity in the sector. Policymakers ought to focus on policies which improve innovation and productivity in the sector rather than policies which guarantee prices or incomes. [*Lack of competitiveness*, caused by *regulatory burden*, *low productivity* and *destructive institutions*]

8) Fifth, over the past decade, Greek industries seem to have raised domestic prices excessively relative to the increase in wage costs, both in absolute terms as well as relative to trading partners. This has led to increased import substitution (i.e., increased imports at the cost of domestic production), as domestic producers became less competitive relative to foreign producers, and contributed to a worsening of the trade deficit. Economic policy must address this issue via structural reforms in product markets which weaken the pricing power of oligopolies and enhance price competitiveness. [*Current account deficit*, caused by *lack of competitiveness*]

9) Wage inflation over the past decade was a characteristic of all EMU periphery countries. This was mainly due to the decline in interest rates in the run-up to EMU and the resulting boost in consumption but also due to the natural need of these economies to catch up with the European North (the so-called "Balasa-Samuelson" effect). In fact, nominal wages in Greece have increased faster than productivity (as opposed to real wages, which increased by a total of 4% above productivity since 20002). [*Private credit extension*, caused by *EMU entry*]

10) The current discussion focuses on internal devaluation as one of the most important means of regaining lost competitiveness of the Greek economy. Estimates of common competitiveness indices suggest that the magnitude of such an internal devaluation is large, with prices and wages declining by as much as 20-30% in order for Greece to regain its loss in competitiveness since EMU entry. [*Internal devaluation*, caused by *lack of competitiveness* and *monetary dependence*]

11) This, in turn increases market uncertainty as to whether the Greek economy will be able to return to economic growth without restructuring its debt or even defaulting and abandoning the euro area. [*Collapse of confidence*, caused by *high debt* and *possibility of EMU exit*]

## GREEK SOVEREIGN BOND INDEX, VOLATILITY, AND STRUCTURAL BREAKS (TAMAKOSHI AND HAMORI, 2014)

1) The sudden large shocks to the Greek sovereign bond markets during the recent European debt crisis stunned the market participants. This is primarily because there is convention of treating government bonds as risk-free based on a sovereign entity's ability to either raise taxes, cut spending, print money or some combination of the three. [*Collapse of confidence*, cause by *high debt* and *monetary dependence*]

2) Since the introduction of the Euro and until the onset of the recent financial crises, many investors believed Euro-zone government bonds behave as if they were free of country-specific risks (e.g., Oliveira et al. 2012). [*Access to cheap debt*, caused by *EMU membership*]

3) Second, a striking increase in volatility disrupts the smooth functioning of the financial system, because financial institutions holding substantial amounts of sovereign bonds may suffer from potential impairment losses. Indeed, this was observed for major European banks during the debt crisis period. [*Bank undercapitalisation*, caused by *financial crisis* and *collapse of confidence*]

4) The detection of this break date through this procedure is interesting, because there is apparently no consensus in academic studies on when the European sovereign debt crisis commenced. For instance, Kasimati (2011) regarded November 17, 2009, when the Bank of Greece cautioned about the possibility of funding reduction from the European Central Bank, as the start of the crisis. In contrast, Tamakoshi (2011) chose December 16, 2009, when Standard & Poor's cut Greece's credit rating from A1− to BBB+, declaring a negative outlook on national solvency. [*Collapse of confidence*, caused by *financial crisis* and *downgrades*]

5) Our findings suggest that structural breaks in the mean and variance of the Greek bond return series occurred much later than these dates. In fact, in April 2010, the Greek sovereign debt was downgraded to junk bond status, resulting in heightened concerns across the eurozone and the agreement of a €110 billion bailout loan for Greece on May 2, 2010. [*Collapse of confidence*, caused by *downgrades*]

## GREECE FACING HERSELF: THE PAST AND PRESENT AS FATE (MALAKOS, 2013)

1) Today we are in dire straights, living through an acute crisis. We have reached a limit, we cannot go on being as we have been. In such a kind of crisis, reflection—and distance—becomes even more difficult but more necessary than ever. We are in a state of emergency and our predicament looks as bleak as ever, but it is now that we need to find the courage to take a step back and reflect on ourselves, because if we do not find this courage, we are bound, once more to externalize, to look for the roots of the crisis anywhere else except ourselves. [*Crisis*, caused by *destructive institutions* and *Political instability*]

2) The aim of this paper is to turn the lens inwards and try to substantiate three interdependent claims, namely, that having been obsessed with themselves, modern Greeks have not learned to think critically about themselves and the others, have not found ways to communicate meaningfully with each other and develop practices of communicative action, and have remained to a large extent unreconstructed, not being able to reform themselves. [*Political instability*, caused by *destructive institutions* and *lack of trust*]

3) Secondly, we have never deposed the ego from its sovereignty in the sense of deposing a king, we have never entered a 'being-for-the other'. Both at a personal level and at a collective level we have not developed the conception of not only being responsible to the other, but also being responsible for the other, every concrete other we come to face. [*Political opposition to reform*, caused by *destructive institutions*]

4) Thirdly, we have not developed a public personality capable of communicative action, engaging in a critically reflective way with traditional life forms, with preinterpreted, taken for granted, non-reflective ways of conduct, as well as with modern subsystems of instrumental rationality, which are undermining processes of communicative rationality and the pursuit of internal common goods. [*Failed austerity*, caused by *political instability*]

5) But having a positive right, for example, the constitutional right to form a political community, does not solve the problem of what kind of polis we want to be part of, what kind of goods this polis will pursue and by what kind of means. [*Poor governance*, caused by *destructive institutions*]

6) We have not grown accustomed 'to living with dissent in the realm of questions that admit of truth', [7] we do not know how to listen to the claims of others. The other seems to be an abstract, undifferentiated, generic other, a foreigner, rather than a concrete other, an autre rather than an Autrui. [*Political instability*, caused by *political opposition to reform*]

7) Amidst a nihilistic amoral indifference, that has blotted any creative impulse and scorned any showing of true character, it is not totally incomprehensible how a good percentage of Greek citizens now yearn for a 'Golden Dawn', albeit Nazi. [*Political instability*, caused by *political opposition to reform*]

8) We have opted for 'a strategy of hibernation, whose obvious weakness lies in its defensive character' [12]. The important and puzzling question about the rise of 'Golden Dawn' is not why an extreme right-wing party has risen to being the third party polling about 12 per cent and in such a country which, besides its cultural malaise described above, experiences also a severe economic crisis. [*Political opposition to reform*, caused by *destructive institutions* and *poor governance*]

9) The force of the better argument was gravely devalued. Universities, old and new, became the antechambers for recruiting political personnel, not only among students but also among teachers. In order to become a member of the academic staff you needed party connections, and after one was 'elected', with few notable exceptions, he or she was en route to becoming an MP, or some kind of political consultant. [*Corruption*, caused by *destructive institutions*]

10) Even very important, well-known Greek intellectuals from abroad like Cornelius Castoriadis were, literally, not allowed to give a talk because they were considered reformist, never mind read. What happened in Greek education in the last 35 years barely falls short of a crime. [*Political opposition to reform*, caused by *destructive institutions*]

## Grassroots Unionism in the Context of Economic Crisis in Greece (Kretsos, 2011)

1) It has been consistently argued by the IMF, the OECD and the European World Bank that the Greek labour market had to be radically reformed in order to overcome its institutional rigidities. Such pressures were evident long before the crisis and the subjection of Greece to economic control by the EU-IMF in April 2010. For example a number of practices were scrutinized by the IMF when the competitiveness of the country remained low, 1 namely the majority of Greeks receiving a pension before they are 65 years old and many workers receive 14 or even 16 monthly salaries per year. [*Lack of competitiveness*, caused by *regulatory burden*, *high wages* and *large welfare state*]

2) Within this approach, the employment protection in Greece has been considered a major obstacle to structural change and the liberalization of domestic markets, while the persistent and powerful opposition of labour and social movements were seen as restricting the state's ability to implement structural changes in the economy. [*Lack of competitiveness*, caused by *political opposition to reform* and *regulatory burden*]

3) According to studies prior to the upsurge of economic crisis in 2009, Greece had one of the strictest employment protection legislation (EPL) amongst the OECD countries [2] Typical examples include legislation relating to temporary employment, high severance payments especially for white collar workers, high social security employer contributions in comparison to many OECD countries and other EU member-states, implicit permanent job status for the vast majority of public servants, as well as various constraints on employers' hiring and firing policy [3]. At the same time every worker was covered by the national collective agreement signed by the upper level trade unions and the employer associations. [*Lack of competitiveness*, caused by *regulatory burden*, *large welfare state* and *strong PS unions*]

4) BOPU is one of the most militant trade union in the country characterized by a tradition of a left-wing leadership accompanied with a strong presence of rank-and-file left-wing activists. The story of BOPU demonstrates how grassroots union members and activists with experience in other social movements can break through and lead unions in the direction of future renewal in the current context of economic crisis and labour market deregulation. [*Political opposition to reform*, caused by *strong PS unions*]

5) Elements of the Greek labour movement indicate an enduring tradition of bargaining militancy, organizational unity and cohesion in comparison to other countries [5] Indicative of this development is the fact that 38 out of 98 or 44% of all the general strikes across Europe between 1980 and 2008 took place in Greece. [*Lack of competitiveness*, caused by *political opposition to reform* and *regulatory burden*]

6) Despite this, the dynamics of anti-union and de-regulatory change in Greece have become much stronger with the 2009–10 economic crisis. The Greek government agreed in May 2010 to a rescue plan for the economy ensuring an EU/IMF bailout package. The measures proclaimed by the initial and consequent bailout agreements stipulated among others wage cuts, pay freezes, massive dismissals in the public sector, restructuring of public enterprises, lower minimum wages for young workers and increase in retirement age. [*Lack of competitiveness*, caused by *high wages*, *large public sector*, *regulatory burden* and *large welfare state*] ALSO [*Regulatory burden*, caused by *political opposition to reform*]

7) In December 2010, the Greek government introduced further dramatic labour market reforms by forcing the decentralization of collective bargaining and abolishing any restriction in the number of dismissals at company level. [*Lack of competitiveness*, caused by *regulatory burden*]

8) There are four reasons to believe that industrial and social unrest will continue. The first three are associated with recent interrelated political and economic developments, while the fourth one is relevant to the historically strong roots of militancy in Greece. First, the upsurge in massive riots in December 2008 was inspired not only by the anger of youth for the fatal incidence of police brutality in the city centre of Athens. Long lasting riots were also related to the fact that it is the norm for young workers in

Greece, as in other European countries, to follow fractured transitions between education and work with periods interspersed by unemployment, poverty and low-paid employment. [*Political instability*, caused by *political opposition to reform*, *strong PS unions*, *poor governance* and *Internal devaluation*]

9) Secondly, various demonstrations have taken place in Athens and other Greek cities in 2010, as an immediate response to the implementation of austerity measures. The adoption of austerity measures combined with a sharp increase in unemployment and a decrease in GDP has in turn extended the anger and pessimism of the population across the country. Such negative feelings have been documented in existing surveys. [*Failed austerity measures*, caused by *political opposition to reform*]

10) BOPU incorporates broader issues of capitalist struggle and social justice in a functional and compatible way with the existing collective bargaining machinery and the existing regulatory framework. This amalgam of creating conflict with the employer strategies on the one hand and functioning with the collective bargaining machinery on the other shows that in the case of BOPU an effective articulation of workplace radical activists is possible. [*Regulatory burden*, caused by *strong PS unions*]

11) In any case, BOPU seems to be able to address the situation of labour market deregulation to a considerable extent; and to provide a new promise and hope to its members in contrast to the stereotype of the disengaged and passive worker in the services sector and other research findings which suggest that militancy does not significantly affect many employment terms and conditions. [*Lack of competitiveness*, caused by *political opposition to reform*]

## EXPLORING THE IMPACT OF EMPLOYMENT POLICY MEASURES IN THE CONTEXT OF CRISIS: THE CASE OF GREECE (DIMOULAS, 2014)

1) The destructive financial crisis that began in 2008 revealed the vulnerability of the Greek welfare and employment regime. In Greece, the development of public infrastructure and services had been made possible to an important extent via loans. This particular route to economic growth increased sovereign debt while encouraging household consumption, not least among lower- and middle-income groups. [*Collapse of confidence*, caused by *high debt* and *financial crisis*]

2) Under stiff financial pressures from the International Monetary Fund (IMF) and the European Central Bank (ECB), two elements of the so-called "troika", [1] the Greek authorities were officially obliged to undertake, as offsets for the provision of financial assistance, strict austerity measures in order to avoid default. [*Collapse of confidence*, caused by *high debt*]

3) After 1949, Greece saw the integration of western European-style state institutions with its traditional culture of clientelism and favouritism. In this context, the modern Greek social and political regime has been shaped around a mix of capitalist rationality and, what here is defined as, the eastern Mediterranean culture of clientelism and inter-permeable relationships between state services and the private (mainly family, small- and medium-sized enterprises) economy (Fouskas and Dimoulas, 2013). [*Poor governance*, caused by *corruption* and *destructive institutions*]

4) Since 1981, when it joined the European Union (EU), Greece has been an important beneficiary of EU Structural Funds. In the context of European economic unification, state loans and public debt soared and, until 2009, middle-class consumerism continued to grow at a rapid rate. [*Excessive private credit extension*, caused by *Capital influx*]

5) According to the mainstream literature, the Greek welfare regime is described as dual and unequal. On the one hand, it grants generous protection to the "insiders" by providing them with safe and well-paid employment and social security coverage, supported by family ties-cum-clientelism. [*Corruption*, caused by *destructive institutions* and *poor governance*]

6) In the dualist-regime argument, the pension system provides very generous pensions to those retired from public-service employment and certain other professions (including lawyers, doctors, judges, military personnel, police personnel, higher-level civil servants, dockworkers), while the pensions paid to farmers and labourers are very low and most retired private-sector workers receive the minimum national pension. [*Corruption*, caused by *large welfare state*]

7) Active labour market measures have supported clientelism, financially assisting certain segments of society, according to Dimoulas and Michalopoulou (2008). Usually, the beneficiaries of active employment policies in Greece are not the most vulnerable and disadvantaged unemployed persons but the "elites," those with established network contacts with political party leaders (Dimoulas and Michalopoulou, 2008). These labour market measures function indirectly as a method offering financial support to only part of the unemployed population, allowing politicians to manage the social problem of high unemployment in the context of traditional political networks by selecting the beneficiaries, thus valorizing extended clientelistic practices. [*Regulatory burden*, caused by *destructive institutions* and *political opposition to reform*]

8) Before the crisis, most unemployed persons with no social and unemployment allowances were able to live relatively comfortably owing to the prevalence of shadow economy activities, access to family assistance, high rates of home ownership, affordable public utilities, and universal social services (health, education) all of which collapsed with the financial crisis. [*High debt*, caused by *large welfare state* and *financial crisis*]

9) As stated, with the onset of the Greek government debt crisis, the troika obliged the Greek authorities to undertake strict austerity measures in order to avoid default.

These measures focused on the rapid reduction of salaries in the public sector, which were also transmitted to the private sector causing a severe reduction in the purchasing power of most Greeks (see Table 1). Furthermore, in agreement with the troika, a freeze was applied to new recruitment in the public services. As a result, the clientelist networks lost significant ground. [*High debt*, caused by *large public sector* and *corruption*]

10) The most substantial measures undertaken by the three successive Greek governments under the strict supervision of the troika were those that intended to increase the availability of work by reducing the cost of hiring and firing. These measures included: [*Lack of competitiveness*, caused by *regulatory burden*]

11) The debt burden compels the Greek State to direct high levels of expenditure to the amortization of debt. This prevents Greece from borrowing in the global financial markets, which has led to major reductions in public expenditure directed at social benefits, health, education and welfare provisions (Fouskas and Dimoulas, 2013). Moreover, the recent period has witnessed a rise in out-of pocket costs for health and social services [*High debt*, caused by *large welfare state* and *large public sector*]

12) The most serious austerity measures introduced under the strict supervision of the troik are late to the measures to reduce the cost of hiring and firing. Further welfare and labour market measures have focused on tightening restrictions on access to social security provisions, introducing stricter requirements for eligibility to benefits while decreasing both the duration and level of payments [*Lack of competitiveness*, caused by *large welfare state* and *regulatory burden*]

13) The public subsidization of employers' social security contributions ranges from 25 per cent to 100 per cent for each employee for a period of two to four years, depending on the employee target group [4]. The main criteria for this subsidy are that the firm has a maximum of 30 employees. To comply with this measure, employers are obliged to retain their workforce for an additional nine months. [*Lack of competitiveness*, caused by *large welfare state* and *regulatory burden*]

14) The "Great Recession" that emanated from the United States in mid-2007 caused an unconceivable and enduring financial crisis in Greece. Before the crisis, the European and global financial system provided the Greek economy with cheap and abundant monies which the national elites used to increase public and private consumption. [*High debt*, caused by *access to cheap debt* and *financial crisis*]

15) This particular financial mechanism permitted the social security and employment agencies to manage the constant coexistence of demographic pressures, low participation in official employment and high unemployment rates for nearly two decades (1993–2009). This was achieved without major public dissatisfaction by providing generous pensions to early retirees and affordable (although in highly inflated prices) goods and services to the middle classes. [*High debt*, caused by *access to cheap credit*, *large welfare state* and *ageing population*]

16) With the ready provision of international money, the social protection regime in Greece delayed the necessary adjustments required to confront the challenges caused by globalization and European Monetary Union. [*Lack of competitiveness*, caused by *EMU entry*, *access to cheap debt*, *large social welfare state* and *political opposition to reform*]

## BEGGAR THYSELF BEGGAR THY NEIGHBOUR (LAPAVITSAS ET AL., 2010)

1) The sovereign debt crisis that broke out in Greece at the end of 2009 is fundamentally due to the precarious integration of peripheral countries in the eurozone. Its immediate causes, however, lie with the crisis of 2007–2009. [*Collapse of confidence*, caused by *monetary dependence* and *financial crisis*]

2) State provision of liquidity and capital in 2008–2009 rescued the banks, while state expenditure prevented a worsening of the recession. The result in the eurozone was a sovereign debt crisis, exacerbated by the structural weaknesses of monetary union. [*High debt*, caused by *bank undercapitalisation* and *financial crisis*]

3) The institutional mechanisms surrounding the euro have been an integral part of the crisis. To be more specific, European monetary union is supported by a host of treaties and multilateral agreements, including the Maastricht Treaty, the Growth and Stability Pact and the Lisbon Strategy. It is also supported by the European Central Bank (ECB), in charge of monetary policy across the eurozone. The combination of these institutions has produced a mix of monetary, fiscal and labour market policies with powerful social implications. [*High debt*, caused by *access to cheap debt*, *EMU membership* and *non-enforcement of EMU treaties*]

4) A single monetary policy has been applied across the eurozone. The ECB has targeted inflation and focused exclusively on the domestic value of money. To attain this target the ECB has taken cognisance of conditions primarily in core countries rather than assigning equal weight to all. [*Lack of competitiveness*, caused by *monetary dependence* and *EMU membership*]

5) Fiscal policy has been placed under the tight constraints of the Stability Pact, though considerable residual sovereignty has remained with member states. In practice, fiscal rules have been applied with some laxity in core countries and elsewhere. Peripheral countries have attempted to disguise budget deficits in a variety of ways. Nonetheless, fiscal stringency has prevailed during this period. [*High debt*, caused by *non-enforcement of EU treaties* and *poor stats*]

6) Given these constraints, national competitiveness within the eurozone has depended on the conditions of work and the performance of labour markets, and in this regard EU policy has been unambiguous. The European Employment Strategy has

encouraged greater flexibility of employment as well as more part-time and temporary work. There has been considerable pressure on pay and conditions, a race to the bottom across the eurozone. The actual application of this policy across the eurozone has varied considerably, depending on welfare systems, trade union organization, and social and political history. [*Lack of competitiveness*, caused by *EMU entry*, *regulatory burden*, *high wages* and *low productivity*]

7) German competitiveness has thus risen further within the eurozone. The result has been a structural current account surplus for Germany, mirrored by current account deficits for peripheral countries. [*Current account deficit*, caused by *lack of competitiveness*]

8) Peripheral countries have thus lost competitiveness as the nominal compensation of German workers has remained practically stagnant throughout the period. [*Lack of competitiveness*, caused by *high wages* and *monetary dependence*]

9) Greece and Portugal sustained high levels of consumption, while Ireland and Spain had investment booms that involved real estate speculation. Across the periphery, household debt rose as interest rates fell. The financial system expanded its weight and presence across the economy. But in 2009–2010 it became apparent that these strategies were incapable of producing long-term results. [*Private credit extension*, caused by *EMU entry* and *Capital influx*]

10) Accelerated public borrowing in 2009 was induced by the crisis, and hence by the earlier speculations of the financial system. In this respect, the Greek state was typical of several others, including the USA and the UK. [*High debt*, caused by *financial crisis*]

11) Speculators focused on Greek public debt on account of the country's large and entrenched current account deficit as well as because of the small size of the market in Greek public bonds. Credibility was also lost by the Greek government because of systematic fiddling of national statistics to reduce the size of budget deficits. But the broader significance of the Greek crisis was not due to the inherent importance of the country. Rather, Greece represented potentially the start of speculative attacks on other peripherals—and even on countries beyond the eurozone, such as the UK—that faced expanding public debt. [*Collapse of confidence*, caused by *current account deficit*, *high debt*, *upward revision of Greek debt* and *poor stats*]

12) The Greek crisis, therefore, is symptomatic of a wider malaise. It is notable that the institutions of the eurozone, above all the central bank, have performed badly in this context. For the ECB private banks were obviously 'too big to fail' in 2007–2009, meriting extraordinary provision of liquidity. But there was no similar sensitivity toward peripheral countries that found themselves in dire straits. It made little difference that the problems of public debt were largely caused by the crisis as well as by the very actions of the ECB in providing banks with liquidity. [*Collapse of confidence*, caused by *slow EMU*, *poor governance*, *high debt* and *undercapitalised banks*]

13) The first alternative is to adopt austerity by cutting wages, reducing public spending and raising taxes, in the hope of reducing public borrowing requirements. Austerity would have to be accompanied by bridging loans, or guarantees by core countries to bring down commercial borrowing rates. [*High debt*, caused by *large public sector* and *poor revenue collection*]

14) It is likely that there would also be 'structural reform', including further labour market flexibility, tougher pension conditions, privatization of remaining public enterprises, privatization of education and so on. The aim of such liberalization would presumably be to raise the productivity of labour, thus improving competitiveness. [*Lack of competitiveness*, caused by *regulatory burden*, *large welfare state*, *large public sector* and *high wages*]

15) Yet, despite apparent legal constraints, it is not beyond the EU to find ways of advancing bridging loans, at the same time enforcing austerity through political pressure. Thus, the real problem with this option is not the institutional machinery of the eurozone. It is, rather, that the policy is likely to lead to aggravated recession in peripheral countries making it even more difficult to meet public borrowing targets. Poverty, inequality and social division will increase substantially. Even worse, it is unlikely that there will be long-term increases in productivity through a strategy of liberalization. Productivity increases require investment and new technologies, neither of which will be provided spontaneously by liberalized markets. [*Failed austerity*, caused by *political opposition to reform* and *lack of competitiveness*]

16) The third alternative is to exit from the eurozone. Even here, however, there are choices. There is 'conservative exit', which is increasingly discussed in the Anglo-Saxon press, and would aim at devaluation. Some of the pressure of adjustment would be passed onto the international sphere, and exports would revive. But there would also be losses for those servicing debt abroad, including banks. [*Collapse of confidence*, caused by *possible EMU exit*]

17) For both Greece and Portugal saving as a percentage of GDP became negative in the second half of the 2000s. Thus, high and rising consumption has been supported by rising household debt. [*Excessive private credit extension*, caused by *EMU entry*]

18) However, in peripheral countries things have been different. Unit labour costs have increased significantly as nominal labour costs have risen faster than productivity, with Greece in the lead. In short, peripheral countries have been losing competitiveness relative to Germany in the internal eurozone market. Care is obviously necessary in interpreting this picture. Greece, Portugal and Spain have run substantial balance of trade deficits. [*Lack of competitiveness*, caused by *high wages*, *low productivity* and *monetary dependence*]

19) The public sector of peripheral countries, and above all Greece, has been at the epicentre of the current turmoil. The reasons for this, however, are only partially related to the intrinsic weaknesses of the public sector in peripheral countries. The current crisis

is due to the nature of monetary union, the mode of integration of peripheral countries in the eurozone and the impact of the crisis of 2007–2009. Public sector debt has become a focus for the tensions that have emanated from these sources for reasons discussed below. [*High debt*, caused by *poor governance*, *financial crisis* and *access to cheap debt*]

20) The Greeks have led the way with persistent manipulation of national statistics throughout the 2000s as well as barely legal deals with Goldman Sachs that presented public borrowing as a derivative transaction. Public–private transactions have also been widely deployed in the periphery to postpone expenditure into the future, typically at a loss to the public. [*Collapse of confidence*, caused by *poor stats* and *upward revision of debt*]

## From Hero to Zero? The Role of the Euro in the Current Crisis: Theory and Some Evidence (Karras, 2011)

1) In the early stages of the global financial crisis of 2007 through 2009, the consensus was that membership in the euro area was a highly effective way of shielding a European economy, especially a small open one, from the most damaging consequences of the crisis. Conversely, an independent currency was thought to expose an economy to dangers that were, at least partly, avoidable. [*Access to cheap debt*, caused by *EMU membership*]

2) The classic example became Greece and the argument was that euro membership was the surest way to lead to a destabilizing trap of reduced competitiveness and high debt. The argument progressed so far that the entire euro architecture was thought to be unstable or undesirable (Brittan 2010; Economist 2010a). [*Lack of competitiveness*, caused by *EMU membership*] ALSO [High debt, caused by EMU membership]

3) The first group consists of just one country, Greece, which experienced by far the greatest decrease in average inflation (more than 6.5 percent), and thus the largest inflation benefit, since the creation of the euro. [*Access to cheap debt*, caused by *EMU membership*]

4) Euro membership has been typically accompanied by either a reduction in inflation (the inflation benefit of monetary integration) or no appreciable change. [*Access to cheap debt*, caused by *EMU membership*]

5) Consistent with the theoretical predictions, the empirical evidence shows a strong, negative relationship between cyclical synchronizations and volatilities. [*Collapse of confidence*, caused by *lack of competitiveness*]

## EUROSCEPTICISM: A SIGN OF A EUROPE IN DISTRESS (DOBRESCU AND DURACH, 2014)

1) The great disappointment, the gloom mood of the citizens from Greece, Cyprus, Spain, Portugal and, surprisingly, France, in contrast with the self-confident attitude of Germans and the mild enthusiasm of Eastern European countries suggest that the EU did not emerge stronger as a whole. Multiple divergences have already started to occur between the rich and the poor member states, between competitive regions and regions that lag behind, between debtors and creditors, between the North and the South and, we dare to anticipate, between the West and the East. [*Possible EMU exit*, caused by *political instability* and *internal devaluation*]

2) Due to high interest in this topic and its frequent occurrence in recent debates, Euroscepticism is explicitly or implicitly considered a product of the crisis, a result of Europe's recent difficult moments. This stance encourages a secondary, yet very important perception: there is deep pain, an illness which needs to be treated, cured and overcome once the crisis is over. From this perspective, Euroscepticism borrows some of the traits of the pervasive approach to crisis at European level: something that shouldn't have travelled to Europe (the dominant European perception at the outbreak of the crisis), but, once installed, would be of short duration and would finally be overcome. [*Fears of EMU exit*, caused by *internal devaluation*]

3) However, since 2008, it has become increasingly evident that this is a much more complex phenomenon, 'amassing' not just the excess and mistakes in the financial and banking system, but also the results of economic trends (for instance, delocalization or excessive interest in services over manufacturing) and costly delays in the Union's construction. To become truly efficient, the strategies for overcoming the crisis must address all of these causes. [*High debt*, caused by *financial crisis* and *poor governance*]

4) With the notable exception of Greece, all the other Southern states dominate the pessimistic group: Greece, Cyprus, Portugal, France, Italy, and, in addition: Hungary, the UK and Czech Republic. [*Political opposition to reform*, caused by *internal devaluation*]

5) Positive evolutions can also be seen in perceptions of the economic situation at national level ('good'+5 percentage points, 'bad'-4), and to a greater extent at European level (+7, 'bad'-7). While more Europeans perceive the situation of their national economy as 'good' compared with spring 2013, the gap between the different Member States has widened: 83 percentage points now separate Sweden, where 85% of respondents think that the economic situation in their country is good, and Greece, where just 2% of the population share this view [*Political opposition to reform*, caused by *internal devaluation*]

6) The feeling that "the worst is still to come" is the majority view in 16 Member States, led by Cyprus (87%), Greece (71%), Portugal (67%), France (66%) and Slovenia

(65%). Overall, a relative majority of European citizens consider that the European Union is going "in the right direction" to emerge from the crisis and face the new world challenges (43%), and this proportion has registered a slight increase since spring 2013 (+1). [*Fears of possible EMU exit*, caused by *political opposition to reform*]

7) Economic hardships caused a serious drop in the levels of trust in countries such as Spain, Greece, Portugal, Cyprus (which has the lowest levels of trust in the present) or Italy. The aforementioned countries dropped from trust levels around (or above) the average in 2009 to less de 25% in 2013. What is more puzzling is that Germany and France, the founders of the EU, experience themselves a crisis of support for the EU (with only 29% and 28% of respondents trusting the EU), albeit for different reasons. [*Trust*, caused by *internal devaluation*]

8) In terms of public perceptions on the national and European economy, there are serious gaps between member states. Germans, for example, are increasingly more satisfied with the state of the national economy (82% good in 2013) (Figure 4). Germany is also the only member state in which the economic situation was perceived as improving in the 5 years of crisis. Other content citizens can be found in the UK (38%), Poland (35%), Hungary (22%). Once again, the South falls far behind these results and also behind the EU average of 31%. It is the case of Greece (2%), Portugal (3%), Spain (4%), Cyprus (3%). [*Political opposition to reform*, caused by *internal devaluation*]

## European Sovereign Bond Spreads: Financial Integration and Market Conditions (Georgoutsos and Migiakis, 2013)

1) In this regard, until recently, several empirical works have, to a great extent, attributed the initially, after the monetary unification, enhanced interactions among euro-area sovereign bond yields to the monetary unification (see among others Baele et al., (2004), ECB (2005) and Commission of the European Communities (2007)). However, during the global financial crisis and the euro-area debt crisis, European sovereign bond spreads experienced a sharp widening and reached a level comparable to the ones existing in the pre-unification period. [*Access to cheap debt*, caused by *EMU entry*]

2) In recognition of the above developments, we have attempted to estimate the mean reversion properties of the EMU sovereign spreads vis-á-vis the Bund. We compare the results from conventional unit-root tests to those derived from the application of two popular nonlinear modelling techniques, i.e., Markov switching and STAR models. The results are in favour of the presence of different regimes which have been identified according to the volatility of the spreads. [*Collapse of confidence*, caused by *fears of EMU exit*]

3) The policy implication of our results is that the case of integration of the EMU sovereign bonds market was never strong in the sense that we were unable to derive a fast mean reversion which must be a prerequisite of an integrated market. [*Lack of competitiveness*, caused by *EMU entry*]

4) The only deviation from this result appears from the STAR models which clearly indicate a faster adjustment for high-debt EMU countries over the recent turbulent period. [*Collapse of confidence*, caused by *high debt*]

5) Also, the faster adjustment of the spreads of the high-debt countries indicates that there was an overreaction of the markets at the time of the outbreak of the crisis which, as other studies have shown, might be due to the importance of expectations not founded on actual financial or structural instabilities. [*Collapse of confidence*, caused by *high debt* and *financial crisis*]

## EURO IMBALANCES AND ADJUSTMENT: A COMPARATIVE ANALYSIS (BALCEROWICZ, 2014)

1) In addition, one must isolate and analyze the specificities of the eurozone—for example, why differences in risk premiums between such different countries as Greece and Germany were so small until recently, and why fiscal constraints in the member countries of the eurozone have proven so weak. [*Access to cheap debt*, caused by *EMU membership*]

2) Third, there is a lot of verbiage in the debate on the necessary solutions to the euro's problems, exemplified by such popular, but unclear, expressions as "fiscal union" or "political union." That rhetoric, used by the proponents of the further centralistic integration in the eurozone, reflects, I think, wishful thinking and an unreflective belief that a monetary union necessarily requires a political union. [*High debt*, caused by *poor governance*]

3) The problems that appeared in the PIIGS were (1) the financial booms that resulted in large imbalances and declining price competitiveness of the affected economies, and (2) the accumulations of microeconomic distortions, which together with chronically stressed public finance, have acted as a break on economic growth. [*Lack of competitiveness*, caused by *Capital influx*, *high debt* and *regulatory burden*]

4) Let me start with the boom-bust episodes. A sustained accelerated spending fuelled by credit and foreign capital inflows produced booms that tended to go bust. There is no bust without a previous boom. [*Excessive private credit extension*, caused by *Capital influx*]

5) Among the PUGS, Greece, Ireland, and Spain developed intensive booms that were largely financed by foreign portfolio and debt capital, mostly coming from more advanced eurozone economies (Ebner 2013). In addition, Greece accumulated massive microeconomic distortions. [*Capital influx*, caused by *EMU membership*]

6) The fiscal-to-financial crisis is dramatically exemplified by Greece. It typically starts with a sustained budgetary overspending that spills over to the financial sector, as financial institutions are big buyers of government bonds. Moreover, domestic financial firms often own a disproportionally large part of their country's sovereign debt— witness the problems of the Greek banks. This "home bias" has been due to official regulations such as the Basle risk-weighted capital requirements and to the informal links between the government and the banks. It is, of course, especially strong when the banks are stated-owned (Gonzales-Garcia and Grigoli 2013). [*Bank undercapitalisation*, caused by *high debt*]

7) The fundamental question that goes beyond Greece and the eurozone is: What are the root causes of the tendency of modern political systems to systematically overspend, which results in fiscal- to-financial crises or in chronically ill public finances that act as a brake on economic growth? This hugely important issue belongs to public choice and cannot be discussed here at greater length. [*High debt*, caused by *political opposition to reform*, *poor governance* and *destructive institutions*]

8) I can only point to the interaction of the destructive political competition (i.e., competing for votes with spending promises) and the weak, if any, fiscal constraints [1]. The solutions consist, therefore, in making political competition fiscally more responsible and strengthening the fiscal constraints on governments. [*High debt*, caused by *political opposition to reform* and *non-enforcement of EU treaties*]

9) However, in order to introduce and maintain them, a strong participation of civil society is again required. This is especially important in the larger EU countries, as they are less susceptible than the smaller ones to European pressures; indeed, they are largely behind them. The European rhetoric should not mask the realpolitik in the EU. The story of emasculating of the Stability and Growth Pact by Germany and France in 2005 is a case in point. [*High debt*, caused by *non-enforcement of EU treaties*]

10) There is little doubt that fiscal-to-financial crises have political roots. [*Collapse of confidence*, caused by *poor governance* and *political instability*]

11) There is one feature I have already mentioned, and which deserves special attention in this respect, namely, the extreme suppression of credit spreads among eurozone members with very different fundamentals. Until 2008, the narrow interest-rate spreads had been widely welcomed as a sign of success of the eurozone being a "true" monetary union. Only a few economists regarded this extreme suppression of the spreads as a reason to worry. [*Access to cheap debt*, caused by *EMU membership*]

12) In the case of Greece, it was mostly the government drat benefited from the narrowing of interest-rate spreads. Governments differ in their fiscal behavior depending on their socio-political system. However, one may safely assume that in the modem world governments tend to spend any windfall gains, unless there are sufficiently strong institutional or socio-political constraints [5]. Such constraints did exist in many Western countries in the 19th century due to a belief in balanced budgets and the strong position of fiscally conservative voters among the electorate. This belief has been severely weakened by macroeconomic statism (Keynesianism) and the related changes in the composition of the electorate. [*High debt*, caused by *access to cheap debt*, *poor governance* and *destructive institutions*]

13) The first one clearly constitutes a feature of the euro design and practice—namely, the modus operandi of the ECB. Buiter and Siebert (2005) were to my knowledge the first to point it out. As Harold James (2013) notes, "When the EC Committee of Central Bank Governors began to draft the ECB statue, it took the principle of invisibility and centralization of monetary policy as given. But this was not really justified either historically or in terms of economic fundamentals." George Soros (2011) is more specific: [*Monetary dependence*, caused by *EMU membership*]

14) Both nominal and real interest rates were suppressed in the future problem countries in the eurozone, thus fueling the demand for credit. Until 2008 the PIIGS displayed persistently higher inflation than the core members of the eurozone (ECB 2012). This resulted from the boom and the various distortions in the PIIGS that hampered the single market and the tendency for the prices of tradeables to be equalized across the members of the currency union. [*High wages*, caused by the *Capital influx*]

15) There is no space here for such a comprehensive comparison. However, even a glimpse at the available literature strongly suggests that the credit spreads in the eurozone were extremely suppressed. First, "between 2004 and 2007 when European sovereign bond spreads were nearly eliminated, the average spreads between Aaa and Bbb state bonds . . . were in the range of 58 to 46 basis point [*Access to cheap debt*, caused by *monetary dependence*]

16) These tendencies were strengthened by the ECB's easy monetary policy, international and domestic regulations that encouraged risky behavior of lenders and borrowers in the financial markets, and neglect of the agreed fiscal constraints by eurozone governments. As a result, the eurozone during the first 10 years of its existence did not have a mechanism for smoothly dealing with the emerging fiscal, financial, and structural problems. Rather, it had a mechanism for accumulating them and postponing their resolution. This is clearly visible when one compares the eurozone with the gold standard (see Dellas and Tavlas 2013). [*High debt*, caused by *access to cheap debt* and *non-enforcement of EU treaties*]

# Effects of Global Financial Crisis on Greece Economy (Ozturk and Sozdemir. 2015)

1) In 2007, the financial crisis that started in the US quickly gained a global dimension by influencing many developed and developing countries. The effects of the crisis were particularly more profound and destructive in some countries. Greece is also among these countries. In fact, it will be more accurate to describe the situation in Greece as triggered by the crisis not directly resulted from the crisis as deterioration in the economy and financial structure of the Greece had started long before the crisis. So, it can be argued that the situation became more apparent with the crisis. [*Collapse of confidence*, caused by the *financial crisis*]

2) The interesting point with regard to the problems faced in this process for European Union countries is the infirmity in the financial policies. When the problem is considered in terms of Greece another dimension with regard to instability, insufficiency and unreliability of political institutions can be seen besides weak public financial policy and ineffective financial policies. [*High debt*, caused by *political opposition to reform*, *poor governance* and *destructive institutions*]

3) It is possible to say that the current situation of Greece is a possible result of wrong policies applied in the last 25 – 30 years. This process is closely related with financial extravagancy and insufficiency of Greece government, unfair and infertile taxation system, unsustainable retirement, low competitive power, populist practices of political parties and organizational and political problems in EU and Euro Zone. [*High debt*, caused by *poor governance*, *poor revenue collection*, *large welfare state* and *political opposition to reform*]

4) However, although the passage to Euro, at first, had such positive effects as development, high inflation and credibility of economy policies, it was seen that it brought about some negative causes as well (Kouretas, 2012). Remarkable increases in public spending, together with wrong political choices, caused serious problems in competitive power of country and big financial instability. [*Lack of competitiveness*, caused by *EMU entry*]

5) For many years, Greece managed to contract debts with low interest rates by playing on basic economic indicators thanks to accountancy support provided by Goldman Sachs (Wagner & Machnowski, 2010). When the process before the crisis is taken into consideration, it is seen that the rate of Greece debts to its GDP is one of the highest in Europe. [*High debt*, caused by *access to cheap debt*]

6) The international competition power of the country significantly eroded. In addition to all these, probably the most attention grabbing elements which ignited the wick of the crisis are the government's approach and statements that increased the uncertainties and raised worries about the low reliability of financial statistics and the real

extend of financial problems and their possible financial results. It can be said that European Union Countries were late to read the indicators and failed to support Greece as the crisis escalated in the country. [*Collapse of confidence*, caused by *lack of competitiveness*, *poor governance*, *upward revision of debt* and *poor stats*]

7) Greece has experienced in recent years is decrease in tax revenues of the government. Tax revenues have perpetually been lower than expectations. When budget income and outcome of Greece and EU are compared, budget income in Greece is seen to be lower than the average of EU27 and EU17 and budget deficit is seen to be high (Graphic 3). It is argued that there are serious levels of tax evasions due to inadequacy of pressures and deterrent measures created by the high wage costs and heavy social security load. It is argued that the insufficiency of measures also increases malpractices (Meghir, Vayanos & Vettas, 2010). [*Poor revenue collection*, caused by *large welfare state*, *corruption* and *poor governance*]

8) This increased to 10.2 % during 2000s (Graphic 4). However, the state could not effectively use the financial resources coming from foreign debts to increase the production capacity and nor could it realize the structural reforms to increase competitive power. An important portion of foreign debt is used for import directed at consumption. [*Current account deficits*, caused by *lack of competitiveness*]

9) The erosion in competitiveness as well as chronic weakness of Greek economy explains the structure of current deficit and why the export performance is lower than the other European countries (Sklias, & Galatsidas, 2010). Greece imports more than it exports; in other words, it consumes more than it produces. The state provides some of its financing with foreign debt. The current account balance, which was in the rate of –7% of GDP in 2001 with the effect of decline in competitiveness, realized as the level of –15% of GDP in 2008. [*Current account deficit*, caused by *lack of competitiveness*]

10) When compared to previous periods, although the inflation rates were low in Greece between 2001 and 2009, they were at relatively high levels according to the EU criteria. In Greece, both prices and high increases in wages in comparison with the Euro zone have reduced the competitiveness of the country (Provopoulos, 2010). [*Lack of competitiveness*, caused by *high wages* and *low productivity*]

11) Fruitlessly and unconsciously waste of money due to practices causing economic and social degeneracy such as bribery, corruption and partisan behavior lie behind the high-level budget deficits, rapidly rising public debt, deficiency in investment spending and current account imbalance (Williams, 2010). [*High debt*, caused by *destructive institutions* and *corruption*]

12) In addition, in this negative process, two important developments that would shake the markets occurred in Greece in the end of 2009. The Greek Government coming to power in November 2009 revised the budget deficit of 2009 projected as 6.7% of GDP and brought down it to 12.7%. In April 2010, Statistical Office of the European Communities (Eurostat, 2013) declared that this rate would realize higher than 13.6%

(Nelson, Belkin & Mix, 2011). Then, this figure increased to 15.4% by following an upward course. [*Collapse of confidence*, caused by *upward revision of debt*]

13) Furthermore, Greece made a six-month loan postponement request from the Dubai World owned by the Government of Gulf Emirate in November 2009. This news made a serious shock in the financial markets and, in the light of the fact that the financial statement in Greece rapidly deteriorated, distracted the attention of financial markets and rating agencies to the sustainability of Greece's financial and external imbalance. [*Collapse of confidence*, caused by *Dubai World Collapse*]

14) International rating agencies' continuous credit rating downgrades of Greece discredited the investors. On the other hand, the measures taken by the Greek Government both provoked the reaction of the people and were unable to regain the trust of markets. After recognizing the seriousness of the incident and the size of the problem, the Government was forced to implement a plan to save the Greek economy by the EU and IMF. At the end of this process, in March 25th 2010, the Greek Government reached an agreement with IMF, European Central Bank (ECB) and European Commission on a 3-year and 110 billion euros plan, 80 billion funded by the EU and 30 billion by IMF (2013).

## DYNAMIC ASPECTS OF THE UNDERGROUND ECONOMY IN GREECE (YFANTOPOULOS, 2013)

1) The recent economic crisis is characterized with increasing unemployment, "moonlighting" and undeclared work, chronic poverty, fiscal imbalances; sluggish economic growth and a growing underground economy. [*Poor revenue collection*, caused by *large informal sector*]

2) Statistical estimates reveal that the down trend of the official economic and social growth can be "counter-balanced" by an uptrend in unofficial, informal or irregular economic activity. Williams and Renooy [1] find that the magnitude of this type of activity varies significantly among European Countries, and given its exclusion from the national accounts, international comparisons are seriously affected by the scale and importance of the underground sector In particular the European Council [2] declares that the underground economy is a threat to democracy, development end the rule of law, because: "it deprives state budgets of substantial amount of tax revenue, distorts competition in regular markets, flouts citizens' socio-economic rights, slows down economic progress, abuses public welfare systems and propagates lawlessness". [*Lack of competitiveness*, caused by *large informal sector*]

3) In the crisis-stricken economies of PIGS (Portugal, Italy Greece and Spain) large underground economies exist. While, according to Figure 1, Greece has the largest

underground economy estimated at 29.9% of the GDP, the rest of the PIGS present an average of around 25% which implies that one quarter of the economic activity is under-reported. According to OECD [3], Greece in particular experiences an overall increasing trend of underground economy overtime. [*Corruption*, caused by *large informal sector* and *destructive institutions*]

4) In 2004 Eurostat established an audit commission to assess the validity of the "Greek statistics". Eurostat officials expressed their reservation on "the reliability of Greek deficit and debt statistics" and argued that the Greek Government was sending "falsified" statistics during the whole decade of 2000's. [*Poor stats*, caused by *large informal sector*]

5) One important dimension of the Greek Statistics is the magnitude of the underground or hidden economy which is neither reported nor investigated at depth. Several estimates indicate that Greece is the country with the highest underground economy among the Euro zone States. [*Poor revenue*, caused by *large informal economy*]

6) The results of our analysis is indicate that the size and trends of shadow economy in a country is a difficult task. Shadow economic activities are developing all the time and they are continuously adjusting to changes in taxation, regulation, economic growth and political enforcement. [*Large informal economy*, caused by *poor governance*, *poor revenue collection*, *regulatory burden* and *destructive institutions*]

7) A recent study conducted by the Global Financial Integrity indicated that the Greek economy has lost over the period 2003–2011 around US$ 261 billion due to crime, corruption and tax evasion. Over the same period, Greece has experienced US$ 509 billion in illicit inflows and outflows of money which constitute a massive amount for the size of the Greek economy. Mr. Baker, head economist of the Global Financial Integrity, argues that the flows of illicit money "fuel the underground economy –including crime and corruption, lead to a deterioration of economic governance and cannot be taxed ...until world leaders address this system, illicit money will continue to flow freely". Figure 6 presents the annual estimates of illicit money flows in Greece. [*Poor revenue collection*, caused by *corruption* and *large informal economy*]

## CURRENCY REGIMES, CAPITAL FLOWS AND CRISES (KRUGMAN, 2014)

1) What I want to talk about instead is a question that some of us have been asking with growing frequency over the last couple of years: Are Greek-type crises likely or even possible for countries that, unlike Greece and other European debtors, retain their own currencies, borrow in those currencies, and let their exchange rates float? What I will argue is that the answer is "no"—in fact, no on two levels. First, countries that retain their

own currencies are less vulnerable to sudden losses of confidence than members of a monetary union—a point effectively made by Paul DeGrauwe (2011). [*Collapse of confidence*, caused by *monetary dependence* and *high debt*]

2) Beyond that, however, even if a sudden loss of confidence does take place, countries that have their own currencies and borrow in those currencies are simply not vulnerable to the kind of crisis so widely envisaged. [*Collapse of confidence*, caused by *monetary dependence*]

3) There is indeed a strong relationship between debt and borrowing costs—but only for countries on the euro, with little sign of any such relationship for advanced nations that have retained their own currencies. [*Collapse of confidence*, caused by *high debt* and *monetary dependence*]

4) First, evidence of the importance of the lender of last resort issue comes from the dramatic effect on spreads every time the ECB has signaled increased willingness to take on at least some of that role. Figure 3 shows Italian and Spanish spreads against German 10-year bonds—useful indicators of the overall state of the euro crisis—since 2010. You can clearly see the two episodes of widespread speculation against peripheral nations, indeed near panic, in late 2011 and again in the summer of 2012. You can also see the dramatic reduction in spreads following ECBaction. [*Collapse of confidence*, caused by *monetary dependence*]

5) What might cause this divergence? A natural answer, again, is to suggest that times of stress were times when investors feared liquidity crises due to the absence of euro lenders of last resort, and that Denmark benefited even though it was pegged to the euro because, unlike euro nations, it retained a central bank able to print money if necessary. [*Collapse of confidence*, caused by *monetary dependence*]

6) In the years since the Greek implosion brought sovereign debt to the center of economic policy discourse, debt crises have occurred exclusively in euro area nations or nations with large euro debts (about which more later), and the behavior of interest rates within Europe is consistent with the notion that euro nations are peculiarly vulnerable to self-fulfilling speculative attacks because they lack central banks able to perform the lender of last resort function. [*Collapse of confidence*, caused by *monetary dependence*]

7) On the other hand, every country that ran cumulative external deficits of more than 50 percent of GDP—Estonia, Slovakia, Spain, Malta, Cyprus, and Greece—did experience a crisis of confidence. In fact, we could almost dismiss debt as a factor if it weren't for Italy, which didn't run large external deficits but experienced a crisis nonetheless. [*Collapse of confidence*, caused by *high debt* and *current account deficits*]

8) In short, under current conditions the much-feared loss of confidence by foreign investors would be unambiguously expansionary, raising output and employment in nations like the United States, the United Kingdom, and Japan. Many people will, I know, object to this conclusion, which seems very counterintuitive—even though it is derived from a standard, off-the-shelf model—and is very much at odds with what almost

every policymaker and influential figure has been saying. [*Crisis*, caused by *collapse of confidence* and *monetary dependence*]

9) The question we need to ask here is why, exactly, we should believe that a sudden stop leads to a banking crisis. The argument seems to be that banks would take large losses on their holdings of government bonds. But why, exactly? A country that borrows in its own currency can't be forced into default, and we've just seen that it can't even be forced to raise interest rates. So there is no reason the domestic-currency value of the country's bonds should plunge. [*Bank undercapitalisation*, caused by *monetary dependence*]

10) Fear of a Greek-style fiscal and financial crisis has loomed over much of our policy discourse over the past four years, and has played a significant role in shaping actual policy, constituting the principal argument for austerity in countries that don't face any current difficulties in borrowing. However, despite repeated warnings that crises of confidence are imminent in floating-rate debtors—mainly the United States, the United Kingdom, and Japan—these crises keep not happening. Part of the explanation for the failure of disaster to strike on schedule lies in the DeGrauwe point: countries that borrow in their own currencies are simply not vulnerable to the kind of self-fulfilling liquidity crises that have afflicted euro debtors. [*Collapse of confidence*, caused by *monetary dependence*]

## CRISIS OF GREECE OF CRISIS OF THE EURO? A VIEW FROM THE EUROPEAN 'PERIPHERY' (MILIOS AND SOTIROPOULOS, 2010)

1) The problems that soon appeared, for example, in the UK, Spain, Iceland, Ireland, Russia, Hungary, not to mention Greece, have little to do with the 'toxicity' of the specific American CDOs. To put it in the most general terms, capitalism internationally went into a phase of re-pricing of risk, with everything entailed by that process (that is to say, into new arrangements for pricing financial instruments). [*Collapse of confidence*, caused by *financial crisis*]

2) The symbiosis of economies with different development levels under the same currency (and the same monetary policy) was responsible for the striking different rates of growth and profitability. The relatively fast growth of the 'periphery' (combined with the moderate growth in the European 'centre') reduced remarkably the 'developmental' gap between European regions. [*Lack of competitiveness*, caused by *monetary dependence*]

3) At the same time, the higher growth rates in the 'peripheral' economies were accompanied by both a fast reduction in cost of domestic borrowing and a significant

inflow of foreign savings (of various forms). This caused lasting surpluses in the financial accounts. The concomitant deficits in the current accounts mirror exactly this increase of the domestic demand and the inflow of foreign investments. [*Current account deficit*, caused by *Capital influx*] ALSO [*Capital influx*, caused by *EMU membership*]

4) In the case of Greece, the very same form of symbiosis allowed for remarkable tax reductions and tax evasion favouring capital and all those social strata that supported the capitalist strategy of neo-liberalism and the EMU. Yet, all these were taking place before the collapse of Lehman Brothers. In what follows we shall attempt to explain further the above points that comprise our argument. [*High debt*, caused by *poor revenue* and *corruption*]

5) To answer this question we must first investigate another more fundamental question that has repeatedly been posed, and with some urgency, in the relevant discussions: why should a social formation with a lower level of productivity 'want' to enter into an economic and monetary union with more developed social formations? The answer is complex but is to be sought in the Marxist argument according to which, for the developed capitalist countries, the strategy of exposure to international competition (promoted on a variety of bases and with various divergences, depending on the corresponding national vested interests) is the strategy par excellence of capital. [*EMU membership*, caused by *capitalism*]

6) This means that if a capitalist country has entered into the phase of developed or developing capitalism, the route of exposure to international competition is the most appropriate strategy for organizing bourgeois power (as a model for continuing reorganization of labour and elimination of non-competitive individual capitals to the benefit of overall social capital). [*Lack of competitiveness*, caused by *EMU membership*]

7) Member countries accordingly relinquished the exercise of autonomous monetary policy. It is in any case well known that liberalization of capital movement in conjunction with fixed exchange rates (or alternatively abandonment of the national currency) necessarily amounts to loss of control over monetary policy [10]. The procedure in question represents a certain way of dealing with what has come to be called the 'trilemma' of economic policy and amounts to an extremely aggressive capitalist strategy. In particular, the 'needs' of labour are sacrificed to satisfaction of the demand for capital mobility (i.e., capitalist competition) and exchange rate stability. Indeed the celebrated or notorious Delor's report, which takes for granted and regards as 'natural' the specific power plan of the single market, saw monetary union as something self-evident and inevitable. In reality the institutional framework of the EMU is interpretable as systematic organization of the specific way of solving the policy trilemma. [*Lack of competitiveness*, caused by *monetary dependence*]

8) This is an economic environment that crushes traditional welfare-state policies, imposing the harshest demands of capital over labour. The increase in productivity in relation to real income of labour (the 'terms' of labour, as it were) is the variable that is

called upon to bear the burden of adjustment to new capitalist conditions and in particular to the environment of the EMU. [*Lack of competitiveness*, caused by *low productivity* and *high wages*]

9) In this manner, the same argument continues, they have improved their exports within the eurozone forcing the less-competitive economies of the 'periphery' to 'underdevelopment' and causing 'destruction' of their 'productive base.' The persistent current account imbalances are thought to be the immediate results. [*Current account deficit*, caused by *EMU membership*]

10) The current account deficit, in other words, may not be simply the immediate result of a corresponding 'deficit' in competitiveness. On the contrary, it is quite probable that both will be the outcome of another deeper cause. Namely, of the considerable differences in the level of capitalist growth and of the specific mode of 'symbiosis' within the euro. Let us be more precise. On the one hand, the higher rates of profit at the 'periphery' boosted financial yields as a whole, with the result that international investors became ever keener to finance the high rates of growth at the 'periphery', particularly now that they had been granted dispensation from a number of significant risks in the environment of the euro, such as that of exchange rates, for example. The countries of the 'periphery' thus recorded strong surpluses in their financial account balance. [*Current account deficit*, caused by *Capital influx*]

11) On the other hand, the member countries of the eurozone with their different rates of growth and different rates of profit were without exception incorporated into the same monetary policy regime, that is to say, the regime of uniform nominal interest rate from the European Central Bank. These interest rates were considerably lower for the countries of the 'periphery' than they had been prior to the introduction of the single currency (see below). This fact, in conjunction with the higher rates of inflation prevailing in these countries, translated into even lower real interest rates for the local banking sector. These are the conditions that laid the groundwork for the explosion of (private and public) borrowing. As was to be expected, the two above-mentioned factors strengthened the potential for borrowing and contributed to a further heating up of the 'peripheral' economy. [*High debt*, caused by *access to cheap debt*] ALSO [*Excessive private credit extension*, caused by *Capital influx*]

12) The causal chain is therefore as described above. From this viewpoint countries like Greece, Spain and Portugal can be characterized as 'peripheral', not because of their geographical position but because of their mode of integration into the eurozone, registering: first, higher rates of accumulation (reduction in the 'developmental' gap between themselves and the competitive countries of the European centre) and profitability (thus becoming net capital importers), and second, deterioration in their balance of goods and services, as an immediate consequence. Development at the 'periphery' attracted 'savings' from the 'centre', financing increased demand. In this respect, and on the basis of the above-mentioned reasoning, it can be argued that financial

account surpluses at the 'periphery' are responsible for the ballooning of current account deficits. [*Current account deficits*, caused by *Capital influx*] ALSO [*Capital influx*, caused by *EMU membership*]

13) In many cases access to cheap loans contributed to a revival in the housing market [16]. Between 1999 and 2005 house prices in the eurozone increased at around the same rate as the corresponding figures for the USA (moving around levels approximately 40 per cent higher than the corresponding average for the last 30 years), while in specific areas such as, for example, Ireland and Spain, The rapid increase in household debt in the case of Greece, Spain and Portugal was accompanied by substantial falls in savings rates over the last decade, mainly after 2004. This means that as individual incomes are shrinking and unemployment increasing there will be a corresponding increase of difficulties in debt repayment, exacerbating problems for the already overexposed extended local banking systems. [*Bank undercapitalisation*, caused by *high debt* and *excessive private credit extension*]

14) We saw previously that the strategy of the euro corresponds to a mechanism for continuously exerting pressure for reorganization of labour in the various member countries. In this respect working people are being systematically attacked both at the 'centre' and at the 'periphery' of the eurozone. And if Germany has succeeded in keeping labour costs low, primarily through squeezing wages, this may be attributed both to the relatively low rate of growth and to the competitive pressures to which their individual capitals are subjected through the self-same mechanism of the euro. [*Lack of competitiveness*, caused by *monetary dependence*]

15) When the sovereign bonds of a country with a high level of debt and inside the euro are subjected to repricing, and this moreover in a period of recession, then the bankruptcy scenario cannot be excluded. In such a contingency the increases in the spread of sovereign and CDS (credit default swap) securities impel the decision-maker in the direction of the 'required' governmental strategies: austerity for Greece and specific interventions on the part of the EU (mechanisms for defending the euro along with the political framework necessitated by this). [*Collapse of confidence*, caused by *High debt* and *monetary dependence*]

16) Although the support mechanisms move the discussion into a specifically political framework, the strategic dilemma around the euro remains basically unsolved, and the cost of borrowing is not expected to fall anytime soon to lower levels. Supervision by the markets will continue to lend supplementary assistance to whatever support mechanisms are implemented and so will continue to produce political results. [*Collapse of confidence*, caused by *political instability*]

## Blame and Punishment: The Electoral Politics of Extreme Austerity in Greece (Karyotis and Rudig, 2015)

1) Despite general strikes bringing life to a halt and demonstrators rioting in front of the parliament building, the Greek government appeared to have done rather well in its first electoral test in the form of local and regional elections that took place in November 2010 [1]. Prime Minister George Papandreou had attempted to turn the elections into a referendum on his austerity policies. With overall results showing that PASOK lost support but remained the strongest party, he was able to claim victory and a renewed mandate for his policies. Nevertheless, this apparent electoral success in 2010 did not prevent the eventual fall of the Papandreou government, the formation of a coalition involving both major parties, and the collapse of PASOK's poll rating, leading to major losses in the general elections of 2012. [*Political instability*, caused by *political opposition to reform*]

2) A particularly potent strategy for governments to minimise electoral costs at times of crisis is to attribute responsibility for economic conditions to exogenous factors ('tHart and Tindall, 2009; Powell and Whitten, 1993). Barbara Vis and Kees van Kersbergen, writing several years before the Eurozone crisis, suggested that the removal of control over monetary policy from the nation state to the European level offers a new opportunity to pursue such a strategy: 'The European Central Bank emerges as the cause of tied hands and consequently blame can be shifted' (Vis and van Kersbergen, 2007, p. 167). More recently, Marina Lobo and Michael Lewis-Beck (2012) showed that the perception of the EU rather than national governments as being responsible for economic problems led to reduced levels of economic voting in Southern Europe. [*High debt*, caused by *EMU membership*]

3) In evaluating the role of economic assessments, blame attribution and the acceptance of government discourses, we face the challenge of endogeneity. Economic assessments could be expected to be influenced by party choice (compare Anderson, 2007; Tilley et al., 2008). PASOK voters may express a more hopeful view of the economic future of Greece as a way to provide a justification for their continued support of the party. Blame attribution and evaluation of discourses could also be expected to follow partisan cues (compare Malhotra and Kuo, 2007; Malhotra and Margalit, 2010). In the absence of a panel design, which constitutes one of the main attempts to control for endogeneity (compare Fraile and Lewis-Beck, 2010), we use a number of strategies to assess the extent to which our results might be affected by this problem. [*High debt*, caused by *poor governance*]

4) Related to this is the question about the electoral relevance of involvement in trade unions and anti-austerity protests. Despite PASOK's historically strong ties with the trade unions, more so than any other party in Greece (Mavrogordatos, 1997), the central involvement of trade unions in the organisation of a series of general strikes and demonstrations against the government's austerity measures could be expected to have undermined their loyalty to PASOK. We would thus expect that voters who position themselves ideologically on the left, participated in protest actions and are trade union members would be more likely to vote for parties to the left of PASOK. [*Political opposition to reform*, caused by *strong PS unions*]

5) Three factors were identified from this. The first factor mainly loads on allocating blame to foreign economic and political actors, such as the European Union, Germany, foreign investors and 'globalisation' generally. Forty-two per cent of respondents (moderately or extremely) blamed the EU, 50 per cent Germany, 66 per cent foreign investors/speculators but only 34 per cent the euro. The second factor is mainly defined by blame attached to Greek governments. About 41 per cent (moderately or extremely) blamed the PASOK government that came into power in 2009, and 64 per cent blamed the ND government that was in office from 2004 to 2009. The third dimension of blame attribution is mainly defined by reference to corruption in Greece and the responsibility of individual Greek citizens. Seventy-four per cent of respondents blame corruption as 'extremely' responsible for the economic crisis, while the perception of the blame attached to 'each and every one of us' is rather more varied, with just 20 per cent placing everybody in the category of those 'extremely' responsible. [*High debt*, caused by *poor governance*, *EMU membership* and *corruption*]

6) The results show that Greeks are deeply divided: 46 per cent of the population agree that the austerity measures are necessary for the country's survival but 41 per cent disagree. [*Political instability*, caused by *political opposition to reform*]

7) This analysis also resulted in three factors. The first factor appears to be a good measurement of the level of agreement (or disagreement) with the government discourse. The main elements the factor loads on are the reference to 'national survival' and the lack of any alternative course of action for the government. Thirty-nine per cent agree that the government had no option but to introduce these measures; 54 per cent state that the crisis can be seen as an opportunity to move forward. A negative attitude to protest also loads on this factor but only 24 per cent of respondents disagreed with the statement that people should protest against austerity measures. Two-thirds of respondents agreed that people should protest, which also includes some of those who considered the austerity policies as unavoidable. [*Failed austerity*, caused by *political opposition to reform*]

## ANALYSIS AND OUTLOOK OF THE GREEK FINANCIAL CRISIS (ABBOUSHI, 2011)

1) To overcome the consequences of the global financial crisis of 2008/09, many governments relied on debt to stimulate their economies out of recession, maintain domestic spending, and to service old debt. Special attention though focused on Europe and the euro zone in particular because member governments piled up debt that exceeded the limits they agreed to in the Maastricht Agreement which founded the euro zone. [*High debt*, caused by *financial crisis* and *non-enforcement of EU treaties*]

2) Data published by the OECD show that the Greek government spent close to half the country's GDP every single year between 1995 and 2008, and in 2009, it spent more than half of the GDP. Furthermore, a significant portion of the spending went not to stimulate the economy out of recession, but to pay for social welfare programs with questionable return on economic growth and vitality. Table 3 offers a brief comparison between Greek and OECD governments' spending on social programs. The data clearly shows that Greece over-spends in this area. Not only does the Greek government spend more than half the economy, but more than half the spending is for welfare programs. [*High debt*, caused by *large welfare state*]

3) The Greek government had a huge entitlement program and a stagnant economy and dysfunctional tax collection system; the government looked to sovereign debt to generate liquidity to pay for social entitlements and other fiscal obligations. [*High debt*, caused by *poor revenue collection*, *large welfare state* and *poor governance*]

4) As the details of this situation began to emerge, bond markets raised the yield on new Greek government bonds to levels the government could not afford. When 10-year old bonds were due in the second quarter of 2010, the government did not have the money to repurchase the bonds, nor could it afford obtaining new debt at punishingly high yield. Greece appeared on the brink of sovereign default. Prior to joining the euro zone, when Greek government faced the prospect of default, it devalued the local currency, the drachma, to ease the burden of debt and reduce deficit. But after adopting the euro, devaluing the currency was no longer an option. [*Collapse of confidence*, caused by *high debt*, *financial crisis* and *monetary dependence*]

5) Persistent over borrowing and over-spending aggravated Greek government deficit, which climbed higher every year. As Table 4 shows, Greek government deficit to GDP ratio was higher than the euro zone average every year since the introduction of the euro, and in 2009, it was more than double the average. Following the global financial crises of 2008, many governments introduced economic stimulus programs and ran a deficit in their efforts to stimulate their economies. [*High debt*, caused by *poor governance* and *financial crisis*]

6) Embarrassingly, it was the discovery that the government misrepresented (and possibly falsified) the data it disclosed about its public finances in an attempt to stay within the monetary guidelines of the euro zone. The EU's statistics office in Luxembourg, Eurostat, cited irregularities in Greek economic data and revised upward its estimate of Greece budget deficit more than once. In January 2010, the European Commission, the highest executive council in the EU, cited "severe irregularities" in the country's data (Davis, 2010). [*Collapse of confidence*, caused by *poor stats* and *upward revision of debt*]

7) Olli Rehn, the EU's Economy Commissioner, spared no words by stating that "Greece has had particularly precarious debt dynamics and is the only member state that cheated with its statistics for years and year" (Willis, 2010). In January 2010, the European Commission published a report about the Greek government's handling of deficit and debt statistics. The report affirmed that in October 2009, the Greek government revised its deficit for 2008 from 5.0% to 7.7% of GDP and revised thc 2009 deficit from 3.7% to 12.5%, which was revised again to 13.6%. [*Collapse of confidence*, caused by *poor stats*]

8) These disclosures spooked the bond markets and the credit rating agencies who decided that Greece was not trustworthy and not credit worthy. [*Downgrades*, caused by *high debt* and *collapse of confidence*]

9) It appears that Greece is not a particularly business-friendly country and seems to hinder entrepreneurship and capital investment. Researchers at the World Bank survey countries of the world to evaluate their environment for doing business and publishes the survey findings in a report titled Doing Business. The countries are evaluated and rank ordered on ten dimensions measuring a country's business environment. The dimensions include "starting a business," "employing workers," "protecting investors," and "registering property." Table 4 shows the ten dimensions, a summary assessment, and Greece ranking among the surveyed 183 countries. [*Lack of competitiveness*, caused by *regulatory burden*]

10) Actually, Greece has the lowest rank among OECD countries, and with an overall rank of 109, Greece ranks below such countries as Egypt, Zambia and Kazakhstan. In Greece, it takes 19 days to register a new business, and a business firm needs 224 hours to file taxes. The swelling civil service in Greece, employing an ever-growing segment of the labor force, all part of the social protection society mentioned earlier, managed to impose complex networks of fees, red tape, and taxes. [*Lack of competitiveness*, caused by *regulatory burden* and *large welfare state*]

11) Early in 2010, the Greek government approached global debt markets to generate funds to meet €8.5 billion debt obligation that was due in May. The markets were jittery because of the massive debt and deficit ratios. To complicate matters, the European Union's statistical authority announced in April that Greece national debt is wider than originally reported. Moody's Investors Service downgraded Greece's debt rating, and

shortly afterwards, Standard and Poor's downgraded Greece debt to "junk" status. [*Collapse of confidence*, caused by *high debt*, and *downgrades*]

12) First, these plans circumvented the Stability and Growth Pact rules that prohibit bailouts within the euro zone. Second, they weakened the market incentive for governments to get their debt situation in order. [*High debt*, caused by *access to cheap debt* and *non-enforcement of EU treaties*]

## A Fragile Eurozone in Search of a Better Governance (De Grauwe, 2011)

*Special Note: Due to the format of the academic article, it was not possible to copy and paste content from it into this document. The relevant concepts are captured in the points below, and the corresponding paragraph is noted in each case.*

1) P2 P1: [*Lack of competitiveness*, caused by *EMU membership* and *poor governance*]
2) P2: [*Collapse of confidence*, caused by *monetary dependence*]
3) P9 P2: [*Collapse of confidence*, caused by *monetary dependence*]
4) P9 P3: [*High debt*, caused by *access to cheap debt*] ALSO [*Access to cheap debt* caused by *EMU membership*]
5) P15 P1: [*Bank undercapitalisation*, caused by *collapse of confidence*]
6) P16 P1: [*Political opposition to reform*, caused by *EMU membership*]
7) P16 P3: [*Lack of competitiveness*, caused by *monetary dependence*]
8) P17 P1: [*High wage costs*, caused by *excessive private credit extension* and *Capital influx*]
9) P17 P1: [*Lack of competitiveness*, caused by *high wages* and *low productivity*]
10) P19 P1: [*Internal devaluation*, caused by *lack of competitiveness* and *monetary dependence*]
11) P20 P1:[*High debt*, caused by *poor governance*, *monetary dependence* and *access to cheap debt*]

## What Next in the Greek Crisis? (Finger, 2015)

1) The "institutions" will only equip the Greek economy with enough operating funds to manage a bare-bones operation. And they will begrudgingly accede to this only if Syriza maintains a primary surplus and the neoliberal labor market reforms that the Troika judges necessary to keep the Greek economy, and other eurozone economies,

competitive in the global market. [*Lack of competitiveness*, caused by *regulatory burden* and *destructive institutions*]

2) Bailout of the private and national central banks, which had or still hold sovereign Greek debt on their balance sheets, is, in any case, now being internalized by the ECB by means of quantitative easing. These toxic assets have been swapped out for euros at terms far in excess of their actual market values. [*Bank undercapitalisation*, caused by *collapse of confidence*]

3) This power asymmetry was baked into the EU framework. All nations, upon joining the eurozone, ceded their fiscal autonomy to an unelected banking technocracy. Unlike the consolidated federal banking system in, say, the United States, England, China, or Japan, the ECB exists by mandate solely to maintain price stability. It does this by setting key interest rates and by, supposedly, controlling the money supply—neither of which, incidentally, are directly meaningful in stemming state-induced inflation. [*Poor governance*, caused by *monetary dependence*]

4) Countries that issue their own sovereign currencies, in contrast, are never revenue-constrained. Such governments are themselves the sources of the money needed to pay for their own expenditures. They are not revenue-dependent on their populations, either as sources of taxes or of loans. Taxes, under such circumstances, exist first to drive state-issued monies, by defining the medium under which government liabilities can be law fully extinguished. They then exist as tools for siphoning off inflationary (excessive) demand, for redistribution, for carving out additional fiscal space to expand the public sector, and for discouraging activities deemed detrimental to the public welfare. [*High debt*, caused by *monetary dependence*]

5) Countries that issue their own sovereign currencies cannot suffer sovereign debt crises. It follows from this that anything that a currency-issuing economy is capable of producing, given the limits of its accumulated capacity, it also can fully afford to produce. And until the point of full capacity utilization is reached, no nation can be justly said to be living beyond its means. [*Collapse of confidence*, caused by *monetary dependence*]

6) The architecture of the European Union has quite simply robbed the constituent nations of this autonomy. It has created debt colonies subject to perpetual domination at the hands of an autonomous, unshackled, central banking system. That banking system has appointed itself, by dint of prior social engineering, the executive committee of Europe's ruling classes. And its agenda is clear. The Troika is prioritizing, for the moment, rent seeking and national exploitation over jump-starting the productive sectors of capitalism until the latter is drained of its social-welfare legacy and overhead. [*Destructive institutions*, caused by *EMU membership*, *capitalism* and *monetary dependence*]

7) Or it can prepare for as orderly an exit from the zone as it can negotiate and go it—for the moment—alone. It can repudiate its external debt or write it down and

redenominate the remainder of that debt in its own newly defined currency. Greek socialists can choose, in other words, to operate on the political terrain that they have already "hegemonized" and which plays to their acquired strengths. By so doing, Syriza can regain Greece's fiscal autonomy on a national basis. [*Collapse of confidence*, caused by *possible EMU exit*]

8) What is even more worrisome than a planned and orderly exit, however, is indecision and drift. For there is certainly a yawning gap between Germany's hysterical demonization of Syriza, and Syriza's actions. If, for instance, the Greek banks, unfettered by capital controls, are permitted to become insolvent in a prolonged impasse, Greece would be compelled to print its own currency under conditions not of its own choosing and under ad hoc circumstances for which it had not adequately prepared. [*Possible EMU exit*, caused by *lack of competitiveness* and *political opposition to reform*]

9) France and Italy, for instance, have already set precedence by missing deficit and structural adjustment targets, suffering little or no consequences for having done so. Germany violated the limits on its external balance. The Greek finance minister, Varoufakis, failed to convince the Troika to swap out existing debt instruments for perpetual interest bonds that would not add to the public debt for lack of a principal repayment obligation. [*High debt*, caused by *non-enforcement of EU treaties*]

10) They have already committed themselves to ramping up the intensity and efficiency of tax collection. This is probably the one place where Syriza and the Troika agree. When the necessary institutional changes are implemented, the Greek government can begin to securitize future taxes and issue scrip based on revenue anticipation. [*High debt*, caused by *poor revenue collection*]

## The Greek Economy and Banking System: Recent Developments and the Way Forward (Provopoulos, 2014)

*Special Note: Due to the format of the academic article, it was not possible to copy and paste content from it into this document. The relevant concepts are captured in the points below, and the corresponding paragraph is noted in each case.*

P2 P3: [*Collapse of confidence*, caused by *high debt* and *current account deficits*] ALSO [*High debt*, caused by *poor governance*] ALSO [*Lack of competitiveness*, caused by *high wages* and *low productivity*]

P2 P4: [*High debt*, caused by *EMU entry* and *access to cheap debt*] ALSO [*Collapse of confidence*, caused by *financial crisis*, *high debt* and *current account deficit*]

P2 P5: [*Collapse of confidence*, caused by *financial crisis* and *upward revision of debt*]

P4 P1: [*Collapse of confidence*, caused by *high debt*, *current account deficit* and *bank undercapitalisation*]

P5 P1: [*Lack of competitiveness*, caused by *EMU entry* and *monetary dependence*]

P5 P1: [*Current account deficit*, caused by *high debt*] ALSO [*Current account deficit*, caused by *high debt*]

P5 P2: [*Bank undercapitalisation*, caused by *collapse in confidence*]

P6 P1: [*Failed austerity*, caused by *poor governance* and *political opposition to reform*] ALSO [*Collapse of confidence*, caused by *failed austerity*]

## GREECE IN THE EUROZONE: LESSONS FROM A DECADE OF EXPERIENCE (OLTHETEN, SOUGIANNINS, TRAVLOS & ZARKOS, 2013)

*Special Note: Due to the format of the academic article, it was not possible to copy and paste content from it into this document. The relevant concepts are captured in the points below, and the corresponding paragraph is noted in each case.*

P3 P4: [*Lack of competitiveness*, caused by *regulatory burden*, *poor governance* and *EMU membership*]

P3 P5: [*High debt*, caused by *poor governance*, *large public sector* and *political opposition to reform*]

P3 P6: [*Current account deficit*, caused by *high debt* and *Capital influx*]

P4 P1: [*Monetary dependence*, caused by *EMU membership*] ALSO [*Access to cheap debt*, caused by *EMU membership*]

P4 P6: [*High debt*, caused by *non-enforcement of EU treaties*]

P5 P4: [*Capital influx*, caused by *EMU membership*]

P6 P1: [*Current account deficit*, caused by *EMU membership*]

P6 P3: [*Capital influx*, caused by *EMU membership*]

P7 P2: [*Current account deficit*, caused by *Capital influx*]

P11 P1: [*High wages*, caused by *EMU membership*] ALSO [*Lack of competitiveness*, caused by *high wages* and *low productivity*] ALSO [*High debt*, caused by *EMU membership*, *access to cheap debt*, *non-enforcement of EU treaties* and *poor governance*]

P12 P3: [*Collapse of confidence*, caused by *downgrades*]

P13 P3: [*High debt*, caused by *corruption*, *poor governance* and *STATS*]

P14 P6: [*Lack of competitiveness*, caused by *monetary dependence*, *regulatory burden*, *large public sector*, *low productivity* and *corruption*]

P14 P6: [*Lack of competitiveness*, caused by *poor governance*, *corruption*, *poor revenue collection* and *destructive institutions*]

P15 P6: [*High debt*, caused by *poor revenue collection*, *poor stats* and *poor governance*]

P15 P5: [*Poor governance*, caused by *regulatory burden*, *destructive institutions* and *corruption*]

P16 P3: [*Lack of competitiveness*, caused by *destructive institutions* and *regulatory burden*]

## GREEK CRISIS AND ITS IMPACT ON THE WORLD ECONOMY (REDDY, 2011)

1) Greece adopted the euro as its currency in January 2002. The adoption of the euro provided Greece (formerly a high inflation risk country under the drachma) with access to competitive loan rates and also to low rates of the Eurobond market. This led to a dramatic increase in consumer spending, which gave a significant boost to economic growth. [*High debt*, caused by *access to cheap debt*]

2) Key economic challenges with which the government is currently contending include a burgeoning government deficit (13.6% of GDP in 2009), escalating public debt (115.1% of GDP in 2009), and a decline in competitiveness. The EU placed Greece under its Excessive Deficit Procedure in 2009 and has asked Greece to bring its deficit back to the three percent EU ceiling by 2012. [*Collapse of confidence*, caused by *high debt* and *lack of competitiveness*]

3) In late 2009, eroding public finances, misreported statistics, and inadequate follow through on reforms prompted major credit rating agencies to downgrade Greece's international debt rating, which has led to increased financial instability and a debt crisis. [*Collapse of confidence*, caused by *high debt*, *poor stats*, *upward revision of debt*, *failed austerity* and *downgrades*]

4) Under intense pressure by the EU and international lenders, the Greek Government has adopted a three-year reform program that includes cutting government spending, reducing the size of the public sector, tackling tax evasion, reforming the health care and pension systems [*High debt*, caused by *poor governance*, *large public sector*, *large welfare state* and *poor revenue collection*]

5) Improving competitiveness through structural reforms to the labor and product markets. [*Lack of competitiveness*, caused by *regulatory burden*]

6) Unfortunately, foreign direct investment (FDI) inflows to Greece have dropped, and efforts to revive them have been only partially successful as a result of declining competitiveness and a high level of red tape and bureaucracy. [*Collapse of confidence*, caused by *lack of competitiveness* and *regulatory burden*]

7) EU transfers to Greece continue, with approximately $24 billion in structural funds for the period 2000-2006. The same level of EU funding, $24 billion, has been allocated for Greece for 2007-2013. These funds contribute significantly to Greece's current accounts balance and further reduce the state budget deficit. [*Current account deficit*, caused by *influx of capital*]

8) But as per the revised Statistics in 2009, the budget deficit is estimated to have been more than 13% of GDP, and many attributed these high budget and current account deficits to the high spending of successive Greek governments. [*High debt*, caused by *poor stats* and *poor governance*]

9) But this High Level of Budget deficit & Current account deficit are well above those permitted by the rules governing the EU's Economic and Monetary Union (EMU). Even though the US financial crises led to Liquidity problems in most of the world economies, the Greek government managed to raise the funds from international markets [*High debt*, caused by *the non-enforcement of EU treaties*]

10) The financial crises which led to global economic slowdown placed a lot of pressure on the governments of various economies including Greece, resulted in increases in Government expenditure & decrease in Tax Revenues. [*High debt*, caused by *financial crisis*]

11) The whole problem started during late 2009 when the new socialist government, led by Prime Minister George Papandreou, released the revised estimates of the government budget deficit for the year 2009 from the existing estimate of 6.7% of GDP to 12.7% of GDP6. Subsequent to this three main credit rating agencies downgraded the Greek bonds, which actually made investors to lose the confidence on Greek Economy. Countries with large external debts, like Greece, were of particular concern for investors. Allegations that Greek governments had falsified statistics and attempted to obscure debt levels through complex financial instruments also contributed to a drop in investor confidence. [*Collapse of confidence*, caused by *downgrades*, *upward revision of Greek debt* and *high debt*]

12) Domestically, high government spending, structural rigidities, tax evasion, and corruption have all contributed to Greece's accumulation of debt over the past decade. Internationally, the adoption of the euro and lax enforcement of EU rules aimed at limiting the accumulation of debt are also believed to have contributed to Greece's current crisis. [*High debt*, caused by *poor governance*, *regulatory burden*, *poor revenue collection*, *corruption*, *EMU membership* and *non-enforcement of EU treaties*]

13) Over the past six years, however, while the central government expenditures increased by 87%, revenues grew by only 31%11, leading to budget deficits well above the EU's agreed-upon three percent of GDP threshold. Observers identify a large and inefficient public administration in Greece, costly pension and healthcare systems, tax evasion, and a general "absence of the will to maintain fiscal discipline" as major factors

behind Greece's deficit. [*Poor revenue collection*, caused by *corruption*, *large public sector* and *large informal economy*]

14) According to the OECD, as of 2004, spending on public administration as a percentage of total public expenditure in Greece was higher than in any other OECD member, "with no evidence that the quantity or quality of the services are superior." In 2009, Greek government expenditures accounted for 50% of GDP. Successive Greek governments have taken steps to modernize and consolidate the public administration. However, observers continue to cite overstaffing and poor productivity in the public sector as an impediment to improved economic performance. An aging Greek population — the percentage of Greeks aged over 64 is expected to rise from 19% in 2007 to 32% in 2060 — could place additional burdens on public spending and what is widely considered one of Europe's most generous pension systems. [*High debt*, caused by *large public sector*, *large welfare state* and *ageing population*]

15) Weak revenue collection has also contributed to Greece's budget deficits. Many economists identify tax evasion and Greece's unrecorded economy as key factors behind the deficits. They argue that Greece must address these problems if it is to raise the revenues necessary to improve its fiscal position. Some studies have estimated the informal economy in Greece to represent between 25%-30% of GDP. Observers offer a variety of explanations for the prevalence of tax evasion in Greece, including high levels. [*Poor revenue collection*, caused by *large informal sector*]

16) Observers offer a variety of explanations for the prevalence of tax evasion in Greece, including high levels of taxation and a complex tax code, excessive regulation, and inefficiency in the public sector. [*Poor revenue collection*, caused by *regulatory burden*, *poor governance* and *corruption*]

17) Economists cite high relative wages and low productivity as a primary factor. According to one study, wages in Greece have increased at a five percent annual rate since the country adopted the euro, about double the average rate in the Euro zone as a whole. [*Lack of competitiveness*, caused by *high wages* and *low productivity*]

## IS THE GREEK CRISIS IN THE EMU CONTAGIOUS? (MICHAELIDES, PAPAGEORGIOU AND TSIONAS, 2014)

1) However, as a result of international and local factors, the Greek economy faced a severe crisis and austerity measures have been implemented. Greece is the first country of the economic and monetary union (EMU) where a sovereign debt crisis made its appearance after the introduction of the common currency. In this article, we examine whether EMU countries suffer from the fact that Greece is in distress. [*Crisis*, caused by *collapse of confidence*]

2) The various debt variables (banks' debt, government debt and monetary authorities' debt) express the various forms of the Greek crisis. [*Collapse of confidence*, caused by *high debt* and *bank under capitalisation*]

3) The Greek economy has a high convergence rate towards short-run equilibriums (alpha), with the Italian and the Spanish economy (0.52 and 0.33). Also, the Greek economy has lower convergence rates with the locomotives of the EU, i.e., France and Germany (0.14 and 0.15), indicating a limited connectivity of the peripheral countries with the core of the EU (Table 1, first column). [*Lack of competitiveness*, caused by *EMU membership*]

4) The empirical evidence shows that the GDPs of Finland, Germany, Luxembourg, Netherlands and Portugal are affected by the accumulation of banks' debt in Greece. [*Collapse of confidence*, caused by *bank undercapitalisation*]

5) In this article, we employed various techniques in order to examine the transmission of fluctuations between Greece and other EMU countries, after the introduction of the common currency during the period 2001–2012, which fully captures the recent crisis. Our main finding is that Greek economic activity and structural debt are, indeed, transmitted to several of its EMU counterparts, especially due to its various forms of debt, but cannot Granger cause their economic activity except for in the short-run. [*Collapse of confidence*, caused by *high debt* and *bank undercapitalisation*]

## The Financial Fragility and the Crisis of the Greek Government Sector (Argitis and Nikolaidi, 2014)

1) They have also argued that within the current institutional structure of the Eurozone the non-sovereign government spending depends on the perceived credit risk of government bonds in the financial markets. If this risk is conceived to be high, then the financing of government expenditures and debt commitments can be disrupted. [*High debt*, caused by *EMU entry*]

2) Moreover, the institutional framework of the European Central Bank (ECB) which does not authorise the latter to function as 'lender of last resort' to the government sector of the Eurozone countries is the major reason that the sovereign bonds of these countries face default risk [2] [*Collapse of confidence*, caused by *monetary dependence*]

3) As long as the ECB does not guarantee the non-default of the euro states, the debt-financing of the government deficits is susceptible to financial perceptions, the judgments of credit rating agencies and the speculation of investors, especially when these deficits are higher than the percentage defined by the Maastricht Treaty [3] [*Collapse of confidence*, caused by *downgrades* and *monetary dependence*]

4) As the recent sovereign debt crisis has indicated, a government sector with increasing financing needs is susceptible to potential changes in financial perceptions. The latter may lead to its incapability to borrow, with devastating effects on the implementation of fiscal policy as well as on the financial and macroeconomic stability. [*Crisis*, caused by *collapse in confidence*]

5) The willingness of both the government and its lenders to engage in financial relationships that rely on refinancing is a function of financial markets' institutional structure and country's previous fiscal and growth performance. Furthermore, this willingness depends upon government's and lenders' perception of the appropriate margin of safety and the conceived assuredness of future cash inflows. [*Collapse of confidence*, caused by *high debt* and *lack of competitiveness*]

6) Since a higher net debt implies more debt commitments and less financial assets in the future, the more a government remains in the Ponzi or ultra-Ponzi regime, the more difficult it is to improve its liquidity position. This may give rise to problems of debt sustainability, insolvency and loss of credibility. On the contrary, if the government is hedge or speculative its net debt declines. Thus, the risks of illiquidity and insolvency are lower. [*High debt*, caused by *poor governance*]

7) Figure 1 displays the liquidity index for the Greek government sector over the period 1988–2012 [13]. We observe that before 2001 the Greek government was either in the Ponzi or in the ultra-Ponzi regimes. More precisely, the Greek government was ultra-Ponzi in the 1988–1993 period and Ponzi over the years 1994–2000. This implies that in the pre-EMU period there was a significant accumulation of debt commitments. [*High debt*, caused by *poor governance*]

8) After the adoption of the euro in 2001, the Greek government sector remained in the Ponzi finance regime only for two years, shifting to the ultra-Ponzi regime in 2003. As a result, the government debt in absolute terms increased substantially over the period 2003–2009 and so did the need for debt refinancing. The surge in debt did not initially lead to a much higher debt-to-GDP ratio since the growth rate of the economy remained till 2007 higher than the real interest rate (see Appendix 2) [14]. [*Poor governance*, caused by *access to cheap debt*]

9) The rise in the debt-to-GDP ratio combined with the increasing financing needs rendered the Greek government sector extremely vulnerable to the expectations of the sovereign bond holders and the speculation in the global financial markets. [*Collapse of confidence*, caused by *high debt*]

10) An important message from the evolution of the liquidity index after the adoption of the euro in 2001 is that the Greek government made no effort to increase tax revenues and curtail tax evasion during a period of high growth. [*High debt*, caused by *poor revenue collection* and *corruption*]

11) The easiness to roll-over debt via the financial markets motivated the Greek government to rely more on new borrowing. [*Poor governance*, caused by *access to cheap debt*]

12) This rise in the principal repayment put substantial pressure on the financial position of the Greek government, since it coincided with the outbreak of the global financial crisis, which generated financial turbulence and conservative perceptions of risk by investors. In addition, the Greek economy shifted to a recessionary process in 2008, triggering negative effects on the liquidity index. [*Collapse of confidence*, caused by *financial crisis* and *high debt*]

13) This reveals that the Greek governments did not hold a sufficient amount of cash and deposits as a margin of safety against unforeseen contingencies that could potentially arise as a result of an unexpected fiscal or financial shock. Arguably, this might have been the result of the financial euphoria that Greece experienced after the country's entry into the EMU, which prevented the governments from paying enough attention to the creation of a sufficient amount of liquidity. [*High debt*, caused by *access to cheap debt*]

## Greek Public Sector Wage Premium Before the Crisis: Size, Selection and Relative Valuation of Characteristics (Christopoulou and Monastiriotis, 2014)

1) The issue of public sector premia and public–private differences in wage structures has recently gained prominence in Greece, albeit in a rather unfortunate conjuncture. The debt crisis has necessitated severe pay cuts in the Greek public sector, in the first instance (measures taken in 2010) to the tune of 12 per cent (NBG 2010), but more recently rising up to 30 per cent for specific worker categories — following the introduction of a universal public sector pay scale (Law 4024/2011). [*High debt*, caused by *large public sector*]

2) Although the need for curbing current public expenditure in the pursuit of fiscal consolidation is indisputable, it is important to stress that very little is known about the public and private pay structures in the country. [*High debt*, caused by *large public sector*]

3) The existence of a sizeable public sector wage premium in Greece is of course well known. It was reported to range between 25 and 40 per cent in the 1970s and 1980s (Kioulafas et al., 1991), while estimates for the 1990s are nearer 50 percent (Papapetrou 2006a)—although the results of these studies are not directly comparable due to their differences in data sources and measurement. [*Large public sector*, caused by *strong PS unions*]

4) Since the late 1990s, Greece has followed an extensive privatization programme and has taken continuous steps towards labour market deregulation (Ioannou 2000; Monastiriotis and Pissarides 2012). Coupled with pressures applied to its labour market from membership in the Eurozone (Featherstone 2003), these development sought to have altered significantly the valuation of skills and the appropriation of rents in the private and public sectors. By implication, they are also likely to have altered the relative and absolute wage premia there — rendering the available evidence less relevant or suitable for policy analysis. [*Lack of competitiveness*, caused by *large public sector*]

5) The Greek public sector has traditionally enjoyed high employment protection and premium pay. In theory, a number of factors may be responsible for this, including the typically higher union power in the public sector (leading to rent appropriation by insiders); incomplete information about average worker productivity (leading to wage setting above the 'prevailing' market wage — Fogel and Lewin 1974); or imperfect monitoring of individual workers' effort (leading to efficiency wages in the public sector). [*Large public sector*, caused by *large public sector unions*]

6) In practice, however, the reason is more political than economic: it concerns clientalistic government–voter transactions and the use of the public sector as a reserve for political favours. [*Large Public Sector*, caused by *destructive institutions*, *political opposition to reform* and *corruption*]

7) Union power has of course played an important role in maintaining this political exchange. Greek unions are openly politicized (with, often, direct links between their leadership and the parties in government), while the institutional architecture of the labour market affords much monopoly power to public sector unions (centralized representation by a top-level confederation that excludes private sector unions; union coverage effectively at 100 per cent; union density over three times higher than in the private sector — Matsaganis 2007). Thus, while formally public sector wages are set unilaterally by the government (Ioannou 2000), in practice unions exert a strong influence on public sector pay. [*Corruption*, caused by *strong PS unions*]

8) Owing to this, governments have traditionally looked for the least costly ways to satisfy unions and maintain industrial peace. In this process, they have occasionally favoured some segments of the public sector over others, causing basic pay to become rather disparate (for example, basic pay in publicly owned utilities is over twice as high as that in central government). To contain wage costs, such disparities were often addressed by the introduction of a range of horizontal (not performance related) pecuniary benefits specific to the disadvantaged segments. [*Large public sector*, caused by *corruption* and *large PS unions*]

9) In the wake of an alarming sovereign debt crisis, in early 2010, the Greek government was forced to implement a radical austerity programme with unprecedented reductions in public sector pay. In March 2010, it announced a headline 20 per cent cut in benefits in the so-called 'narrow public sector' (mainly, civil servants) and a two-year pay

freeze (excluding seniority pay rises). In May 2010, it further announced the replacement of the 13th and 14th months of salary with a flat payment of €1,000 (which was later abolished for high-wage earners). These cuts had a slightly progressive character, representing a reduction in annual pay that ranged from 8 per cent for civil servants earning less than €14,000 pa to over 13 per cent for those earning over €27,000pa [*High debt*, caused by *large public sector* and *large social welfare system*]

10) We find that prior to the crisis, public sector wages were considerably higher (by some 32 per cent) than private sector wages. We also find that significant differences existed between the two sectors in the structure of characteristics and in their returns. Conditional on the structure of characteristics and the average returns, the public–private wage gap was significantly smaller but still large, with a net premium of over 11 per cent. [*Lack of competitiveness*, caused by *large public sector*]

11) These findings suggest that despite offering a high premium on aggregate, the public sector has not been the sole source of labour market inefficiency in Greece. Labour market inefficiencies in the country are also evident in the private sector, concerning problems both of valuation (underpay of women and low returns to key labour force characteristics, such as education for men and experience for women) and of job quality (below average workforce endowments and an overall low level of pay). [*Lack of competitiveness*, caused by *regulatory burden* and *large public sector*]

## The Impact of the Fiscal Crisis on Greek and Portuguese Welfare States: Retrenchment Before the Catch-Up? (Zartaloudis, 2014)

1) The recent financial crisis of 2007 and the subsequent sovereign debt crises in Greece, Ireland and Portugal put cohesion counties along with Italy at the centre of a borrowing cost upward spiral. [*High debt*, caused by *financial crisis*]

2) After the restoration of democracy in 1974, Greece maintained its longstandingmodelofstatism–stateinterventionineconomicandsocialactivities – accompanied by clientelism, which marginalized any autonomous political expression of disadvantaged classes or groups (Diamandouros 1983). [*Poor governance*, caused by *destructive institutions* and *corruption*]

3) After 1974, however, monetary and fiscal stability were largely ignored by the post-dictatorship governments (Pagoulatos 2005). Hence, from 17.6 percent of gross domestic product (GDP) in 1970, public debt increased to 28.3 percent in 1981 and reached the level of 112 per cent in 1986 (Ioakimides 2001: 77). [*High debt*, caused by *poor governance*]

4) Additionally, the 1980s were characterized by government intervention that resulted in minimum wages that were not always in line with changes in productivity or levels of employment, but rather with the political promises and ideological convictions of the Pan-Hellenic Socialist Movement (Greek acronym: PASOK) governments. This policy, however, had a negative effect on unemployment, which became an acute problem especially among the young and women (Katrougalos and Lazaridis 2003: 59) as the country's competitiveness declined considerably (Venieris 2006). [*Lack of competitiveness*, caused by *regulatory burden*, *low productivity* and *high wages*]

5) Moreover, pay rises and generous pensions along with early retirement schemes continued unabated (Tsakalotos1998:121). Additionally, Greece had been traditionally plagued by low tax revenues, which had been consistently lower than the EU and the Organisation for Economic Co-operation and Development (OECD) average (Meghir et al. 2010: 10–13). The latter is not only related to public sector inefficiency and corruption, but also to the structure of the economy, as the country's unofficial sector is larger than the EU average and self-employment and/or family businesses are more common than in the rest of the EU (Katrougalos and Lazaridis 2003). [*Poor Governance*, caused by *poor revenue collection* and *corruption*] ALSO [*Poor revenue collection*, caused by *corruption* and *large informal sector*]

6) Despite media coverage of public sector profligacy (cf. Featherstone 2011; Verney 2009), clientelism did not lead to an overstaffed public sector, but one plagued by persistently low efficiency despite gradual improvement during the period 1990–2000 (Afonso et al. 2005). [*Poor governance*, caused by *corruption*]

7) Moreover, Greece was one of few EU countries providing pay rises to public (and private) sector employees until 2008 (cf. Kapsalis 2011). Despite some very minor pension reforms (cf. Featherstone and Papadimitriou 2008), Greece continued to provide generous pensions to public sector employees along with various formulas for early retirement (Tsakalotos 1998: 121). Consequently, public sector personnel outlays (including pensions), despite a temporary slowdown in the mid-1990s, constitute the principal expenditure item in the budget (Papapetrou 2006: 451; OECD 2002). [*High debt*, caused by *large welfare state* and *large public sector*]

8) Additionally, although Greece faced a number of Excessive Deficit Procedures, high growth rates and the notorious 'Greek statistics', which systematically under-reported Greek debt and deficits, 2 allowed Greek governments to avoid electorally painful reforms that required the reduction of public expenditure (see tables 1 and 2). [*High debt*, caused by *political opposition to reform*, *poor stats* and *poor governance*]

## THE MOTHER OF ALL SUDDEN STOPS: CAPITAL FLOWS AND REVERSALS IN EUROPE 1919-1932 (EICHENGREEN AND ACCOMINOTTI, 2013)

1) From 2001 through 2008 one half of Europe received enormous capital inflows from the other half of Europe and the rest of the world. Starting in 2009, the recipients then experienced a sudden stop, a capital-account reversal, and an economic and financial crisis. [*Crisis*, caused by *collapse of confidence*]

2) In both periods there was a flood of capital from one half of Europe to the other, as well as to the continent's recipient half from the rest of the world. There was neglect by lenders of public debt burdens and their implications for credit worthiness during the boom and then the sudden rediscovery of sovereign risk once capital dried up. [*Access to cheap debt*, caused by *capital influx*]

3) In both periods, countries that imported foreign finance most liberally during the boom suffered the largest reversal and most serious dislocations when the surge of capital inflows came to an end. [*Collapse of confidence*, caused by *high debt*]

4) At least as important were conditions in international capital markets. Among the important factors there was the level of interest rates, as emphasized in a host of earlier studies, but also perceptions of the riskiness of the investment environment, as captured by the volatility of equity prices, the same proxy utilized in studies of the recent period. [*Capital influx*, caused by *EMU membership*]

5) Interwar experience thus underscores the extent to which global factors largely exogenous to conditions in the borrowing countries shaped the capital inflows and outflows to which European countries were subject. This was a precedent of which European countries in the period leading up to subprime/global credit crisis of 2007-8 could have usefully taken heed. [*Collapse of confidence*, caused by *financial crisis*]

## AN EMPIRICAL STUDY ON FISCAL SUSTAINABILITY IN THE EUROZONE (YILDIZ AND YILDIRIM, 2014)

1) The recent financial and economic crisis has put a heavy burden on public finances in euro area countries. This resulted from three main factors. First, in some countries, capital injections for financial institutions created large fiscal costs. Second, the economic down turn had an immediate impact on tax receipts and unemployment-related spending. Third, discretionary measures adopted to compensate for declining private demand in the economy had an adverse impact on fiscal positions (ECB, 2011). [*High debt*, caused by *financial crisis*]

2) Deterioration of fiscal discipline caused an increase in public debt and deepening in budget deficits of countries. Union counties combating the crisis are trying to catch the sustainable growth by taking extraordinary measures as well as achieving a reliable structure of financial markets by eliminating vulnerabilities in the financial markets. [*High debt*, caused by *poor governance*]

3) Another application that is implemented into force on 13 December 2011 for financial stability is called "six-pack". This package aimed to improve the co-ordination and supervision of the economic policies of the EU. The pack was introduced in order to ensure the financial stability, aimed at more powerful preventive and corrective implementation and through these mechanisms to decrease macroeconomic imbalance and increase competitiveness. [*Lack of competitiveness*, caused by *EMU entry*]

4) On the other hand, according to the Panel VECM analysis results, there is not a relationship between series neither in the short or long-run. In this context, policy-makers may provide the fiscal sustainability through primary surplus by fiscal policies. [*High debt*, caused by *poor governance*]

5) Union countries were noticed to apply many Short-term policy implementations over their economies in order to eliminate the destructive effects of the European crisis, sustainable growth and well-functioning of financial markets. [*Lack of competitiveness*, caused by *EMU membership*]

6) We analyzed the relationship between debt/GDP and primary surplus for panel causality covering EMU 12 (1995-2011) using annual data. The result on the panel co-integration tests, Pedroni (1999) and Fisher-type cointegration test by Maddala and Wu (1999) revealed that the variables are co-integrated which means statistical significance long-run relationship among the variables. The direction of relation is that primary surplus causes financial sustainability. [*High debt*, caused by *poor governance*]

## ESTIMATING SOVEREIGN DEFAULT RISK (BI AND TRAUM, 2012)

1) Since 2009, mounting fears over a eurozone sovereign debt crisis have heightened risks of sovereign debt restructuring and outright default. [*Collapse of confidence*, caused by *financial crisis*]

2) Using rational expectation models, theoretical studies show that the government's willingness/ability to service its debt depends on the underlying macroeconomic fundamentals and therefore is country specific; see Bi (2012), among many others. [*Collapse of confidence*, caused by *lack of competitiveness*]

3) Turning to the Greek estimates (Table 3), we see that the data are informative about ˜ b * for all δ A calibrations. 2 The estimates of ˜ b * suggest that if agents expect a

37.88 percent annualized default rate, there is a 30 percent probability of default when the debt-to-GDP ratio is between 1.58–1.78. [*Collapse of confidence*, caused by *high debt*]

4) Interestingly, the ˜ b * estimates for Greece are virtually identical for the high and mid-range default rate calibrations. Holding ˜ b * constant, a higher default rate implies a larger risk premium in the model. In order to avoid this, γ g, L, the response of government spending to debt, adjusts. In the high δ A calibration, the posterior for γ g, L has more values concentrated at higher levels than the posterior for the mid δ A calibration. Ceteris paribus, a larger γ g, L implies a stronger response of government spending to debt, which lowers the risk premium. Thus, the two estimated specifications still imply similar risk premia overall. [*High debt*, caused by *access to cheap debt*]

5) Looking across countries, we find that the debt level associated with a 30 percent probability of default is higher in Greece than in Italy. This is due to the fact that over the sample period, Greece is estimated to adjust taxes and expenditures more systematically with fluctuations in its debt (that is, γ g, L and γ τ, L are higher in Greece). [*High debt*, caused by *poor governance* and *poor revenue collection*]

6) Although we find that Greece historically had a lower probability of default for a given level of debt, our estimates suggest that the Italian government is more willing to service its debt than the Greek government. [*Collapse of confidence*, caused by *lack of trust*]

7) This implies that, were both Italian and Greek governments willing to tax at the peak of their Laffer curves, the latter would be able to service a higher level of debt; we assume the average levels of government spending and transfers in the future are the same as the historical levels, which are higher in Italy than in Greece. [*High debt*, caused by *poor revenue collection*]

8) One interpretation is that the market perceives the Italian government is willing to raise taxes to the peak of the Laffer curve with a probability of 62 percent to 65 percent, while the Greek government with a mere 45 percent to 50 percent. In other words, the political willingness to service debt is 12 percent to 20 percent higher in Italy than in Greece. [*Collapse of confidence*, caused by *political opposition to reform*]

## LEAVING EMU: A REAL OPTIONS PERSPECTIVE (STROBEL, 2005)

1) The European Monetary Union (EMU) has only been in operation since 1 January 1999, yet some of the current member countries may already be considering whether or not a return to monetary independence might be preferable. Policymakers are concerned about inflation performance, possibly because a time inconsistency problem in monetary policymaking can cause an undesirable inflation bias to persist. [*Lack of competitiveness*, caused by *monetary dependence*] ALSO [*High wages*, caused by *capital influx*]

2) The present paper builds on and applies the theoretical model of Strobel (2005) in examining the real option implicit in a country's decision of whether or not to leave a monetary union when the costs of later rejoining it are considered prohibitively high and there is uncertainty over the future benefits of such a move. [*Collapse of confidence*, caused by *EMU exit*]

3) It is shown that a country perceives exercises of this option of monetary disintegration as desirable only when the current value of relative inflation preference parameters is larger than a specific trigger value; intuitively, the lower a country's inflation preference relative to the existing union's, the more it stands to gain from returning to monetary independence. [*EMU exit*, caused by *lack of competitiveness*]

4) For the unemployment rate proxy, it is observed from Table 1 that a core group of countries comprising Belgium, Finland, France, Germany, Greece, Italy and Spain would prefer to remain within EMU irrespective of the time horizon or reference period considered; this criterion provides a certain degree of robustness. [*Capital influx*, caused by *EMU membership*]

5) Results somewhat change when the debt-to-GDP ratio proxy is used. Table 2 indicates that for this measure the robust group of countries preferring to stay within EMU irrespective of time horizon or reference period now consists of Belgium, Finland, Greece and Italy only. [*Access to cheap debt*, caused by *EMU membership*]

6) Across the two proxies used, a robust group of countries was observed that would choose to remain within EMU consisting of Belgium, Finland, Greece and Italy; France and Spain loosely also belonged to this core. [*Capital influx*, caused by *EMU membership*]

## THE EURO: WILL IT STILL BE AROUND FIVE YEARS FROM NOW? (BRITTAN, TIETMEYER, BERGSTEN, EICHENGREEN AND MELTZER, 2010)

1) The big weakness of the project was seen to be the lack of a common fiscal policy to support it. This in turn reflected the fact that it was a currency with a central bank but without a government. Previous so-called currency unions were all ultimately based on a precious metal such as gold or silver. The euro is unique, backed neither by precious metals nor by a political authority. What is surprising is thus not the weaknesses brought to light by the Greek crisis, but that its market performance was above expectation for so long. [*Access to cheap debt*, caused by *EMU membership*] ALSO [*Crisis*, caused by *high debt*]

2) The ungainly acronym PIGS has been invented for the members most at risk—Portugal, Italy, Greece, and Spain. Portugal has already suffered a credit rating

downgrade. The stakes are so high that the euro is likely to survive the present turmoil with Greece remaining a member. [*Collapse of confidence*, caused by *high debt* and *downgrades*]

3) And there is not enough discussion of how far Greek costs have risen above the level of its euro partners. An "internal devaluation" involving a slashing of nominal wages by up to 20 percent, on Latvian lines, is difficult to imagine in the Greek case. [*Lack of competitiveness*, caused by *monetary dependence*] ALSO [*Political instability*, caused by *internal devaluation*]

4) True, during the past months the euro has faced some serious difficulties. In particular, news of the long-running fiscal misbehavior in Greece has fostered mistrust in the markets for fiscal financing there and in other euro countries. [*Collapse of confidence*, caused by *high debt*]

5) It is also critical that the common rules, established in the Maastricht Treaty and the Stability and Growth Pact, not be undermined or eroded by misguided political decisions. [*High debt*, caused by *non-enforcement of EU treaties*]

6) The other oft-mentioned problem for the euro is the divergence in the current accounts of some euro member countries. This development, obvious for some time, reflects mainly a growing divergence in the members' international competitiveness politics. To address this problem, some politicians are arguing for the establishment of an "economic government" for the eurozone. I am skeptical of such an idea. [*Current account deficits*, caused by *monetary dependence* and *lack of competitiveness*]

7) A bottom-up revolt against bailing out profligate Greeks, Portuguese, Spanish, and maybe even charter-member Italians challenges the primacy of the cooperative outcomes of the past. The historical glue that held Europe together may no longer prevail. Given the rise of populist referenda, it may no longer be possible to move European integration forward through the will of political elites—even if that will still exists, which is uncertain. [*High debt*, caused by *poor governance* and *corruption*] ALSO [*Lack of competitiveness*, caused by *political opposition to reform*]

8) We saw a hint of this in the first week of April, just before the terms of the EU-IMF rescue package for Greece was announced. If talk of abandoning the euro and reintroducing the drachma ever got serious, Greece would experience the mother of all banking and financial crises. And that's precisely why abandoning the euro and reintroducing the drachma will not happen. [*Collapse of confidence*, caused by *possible EMU exit*]

9) The Greek crisis brought forward latent fears that the fixed exchange rate system, based on the euro, cannot survive. Like much policy discussion, this concern reflects media bias toward the very near term. The euro solves an ever-present problem faced by principal European countries. Most of their trade is with each other, so they prefer fixed exchange rates. Further, exchange rate changes disrupt their common agricultural policy

by requiring price adjustments that governments have difficulty resolving. [*Lack of competitiveness*, caused by *monetary dependence*]

10) The Greek crisis, and problems in Portugal, Spain, and Italy, show that the fiscal rules that limit deficits to 3 percent of GDP are not observed. Bailing out the miscreants creates the European version of too-big-to-fail, creates moral hazard, and pushes the European Central Bank toward the mistakes that the United States has made: rescuing failed institutions is hard to limit once it becomes established. Good answers do not stop political pressures for poor policies. [*High debt*, caused by *non-enforcement of EU treaties* and *destructive institutions*]

11) Greece, Portugal, and others understood when they joined the European Central Bank that a fixed exchange rate system eliminates one adjustment mechanism. That leaves only fiscal restriction and real wage reduction as the adjustment mechanisms. [*Internal devaluation*, caused by *monetary dependence* and *lack of competitiveness*]

## WAS THE EURO GOOD FOR GREECE? (HAMILTON AND OLSON, 2014)

1) High levels of sovereign debt in southern Europe have hamstrung policy-makers from using fiscal policy to aid growth. Austerity measures demanded by international creditors have thus far only exacerbated employment problems in southern Europe leading to political instability, especially in Greece. [*Political instability*, caused by *high debt* and *internal devaluation*]

2) As such, the opinion regarding the role monetary policy should play in the crisis varies widely across the continent. Low interest rates and unconventional measures (i.e., sovereign bond buying program, long-term refinancing operations) taken to avoid a second financial crisis have been heavily criticized by the Bundesbank, whereas southern European central banks would prefer more pro-growth policies. [*Collapse of confidence*, caused by *monetary dependence*]

3) Historically, southern European economies were able to monetize sovereign debt and devalue their currencies in exchange for higher inflation rates during times of crisis; however, the adoption of European Central Bank (ECB) policy eliminated the option of this adjustment mechanism. As such, adoption of ECB policy that is chartered to maintain inflation of 2% resulted in southern European governments (particularly Greece) losing the ability to collect revenue through an inflation tax. [*High debt*, caused by *monetary dependence*] ALSO [*Internal devaluation*, caused by *monetary dependence*]

4) The current debt crisis in Greece brings to light the difficulties monetary authorities face in conducting monetary policy in an optimal currency area. Moreover, it raises the question as to whether the benefits from joining the Euro area for Greece outweighed the costs associated with surrendering control of monetary policy. [*Monetary dependence*, caused by *EMU membership*]

5) To preview our results, we find that joining the European Monetary System (EMS) greatly improved macroeconomic stability in Greece during the 1990s but at the expense of monetary policy efficacy [*Access to cheap debt*, caused by *monetary dependence*]

6) As a preliminary, Figure 1 displays the first and last Taylor curves estimated in our sample period. Clearly, the Taylor curve has shifted through inward since 1980 suggesting macroeconomic stability in Greece has dramatically improved. [*Access to cheap debt*, caused by *monetary dependence*]

7) Fiscal deficits and inflation were substantially higher than the average of other EU countries which was primarily the result of expansionary fiscal and monetary policies in the 1980 [*High debt*, caused by *poor governance*]

## The Price Effect of Joining the Euro: Modelling the Greek Experience using Non-Linear Price-Adjustment Models (Arghyrou, 2007)

1) The accession of Greece to the European Economic and Monetary Union (EMU) in January 2001 was followed by a noticeable increase in the level of Greek consumer prices. This has given rise to a widely-held hypothesis according to which the euro has caused a structural shift in the Greek price level. [*High wages*, caused by *EMU entry*]

2) Such a hypothesis can theoretically be supported by the price-transparency properties of the single currency. These are typically regarded to be among the benefits of the latter, as they are expected to promote price competition in the traded sector, reduce price differentials associated with exchange rate variability; and limit the ability of firms to follow pricing-to-market policies. [*Lack of competitiveness*, caused by *EMU entry*]

3) In the case of Greece, the above imply that by making comparisons of non-traded prices more transparent (contributing to upward rather than downward price equalization), and by providing domestic firms with an extra motivation to increase their productivity due to the loss of the competitiveness-inducing option of currency depreciation (giving rise to a Balassa–Samuelson type of effect), accession to the euro may have caused a structural increase in Greek consumer prices. [*High wages*, caused by *EMU entry*] ALSO [*Lack of competitiveness*, caused by *monetary dependence*]

4) The second is a demand-based hypothesis according to which the increase in Greek prices beyond their equilibrium level in 2003 reflects an incompatibility between the domestic requirements of the Greek economy and the monetary policy followed by the European Central Bank. [*Lack of competitiveness*, caused by *monetary dependence*]

5) Instead, Greece experienced, along with the rest of the EMU members, interest rate reductions, aiming to revive economic activity in the face of subdued economic

growth in the EMU area (see European Central Bank, 2004, pp. 91–92) [18]. This incompatibility hypothesis has been tested in another paper, belonging to the same research project that the present paper belongs, and have found significant econometric evidence in support of it. [*Access to cheap debt*, caused by *EMU entry*]

## Greek Labor Market, the Euro and the Current Crisis (Papanikos, 2014)

1) Many thought that by joining the EU and later the eurozone, Greece would be forced to modernize its economy and implement the necessary structural reforms for economic growth. Political decisions would be taken easier and most importantly their implementation would come faster because certain deadlines had to be met at each stage in the process of European integration [*Lack of competitiveness*, caused by *EMU entry*]

2) Furthermore, its structure of production was such that the benefits of the common currency might not have been sufficient to compensate the costs. As it turned out during the current crisis, these studies needed to be taken more seriously. In this study, we adopt these arguments as being long-term arguments: Greece's participation in the euroland would most probably have negative macroeconomic impacts, particularly in periods of country specific disturbances [*Internal devaluation*, caused by *monetary dependence*]

3) Despite this objective handicap, up until 2008, the Greek economy was performing very well relative to the other EU members. Similar to the political goals of stability and democracy, the goal of economic growth was also accomplished. Greece's economic growth rate was one of the highest in the eurozone up to the beginning of the recent crisis. [*Capital influx*, caused by *EMU membership*]

4) The most important of them is the lack of any institutional provision for a common fiscal, wage and international trade policy, deemed necessary to complement the common monetary and exchange rate policy. [*Lack of competitiveness*, caused by *monetary dependence*]

5) The current institutional set up of the euro requires member countries to give up their monetary policy, losing an important economic policy tool to accommodate country specific shocks, whenever the latter might arise [6] [*Internal devaluation*, caused by *monetary dependence* and *financial crisis*]

6) Fiscal policy, wage policy and international trade policy have remained as a national priority but within the targets set by the EMU: the ratio of deficit (debt) to GDP should be less than 3% (60%). If monetary policy is set according to a conservative rule, then asymmetric shocks can be accommodated only via a flexible wage rate policy [7]. [*High debt*, caused by *non-enforcement of EU treaties*] ALSO [*Internal devaluation*, caused by *monetary dependence*]

7) If nominal wages and prices are rigid (presumably because of trade unions and other institutional settings), then there is a hysteresis in real wage rate adjustments, thereby increasing the level of unemployment. [*Lack of competitiveness*, caused by *regulatory burden*] ALSO [*Regulatory burden*, caused by *strong public sector unions*]

8) The purpose of this paper is to look at the current Greek economic crisis by examining both the historical developments in Greece's labor market and in eurozone's common monetary and exchange rate policy. The symptoms of this crisis have been the so called twin deficits8: budget and trade deficits. Both deficits have increased the Greek sovereign debt. [*Lack of competitiveness*, caused by *regulatory burden* and *monetary dependence*]

9) They designed a program of drastically reducing government expenditures and nominal wages. During the euro years, both have increased at record high levels because it is alleged that Greek trade unions were demanding nominal wages to catch up with the other eurozone countries, without taking into consideration productivity differences. [*High wages*, caused by *EMU entry* and *strong PS unions*]

10) Since most unionized workers are employed in the public sector and in state controlled enterprises, these nominal wage increases were mainly financed by running government budget deficits. [*High debt*, caused by *large public sector* and *strong PS unions*]

11) The exogenous economic crisis that hit Greece in 2009 exacerbated the situation because government revenues (taxes) were decreasing and government spending was increasing. [*High debt*, caused by *financial crisis*]

12) This segment is also characterized by tax avoidance and corruption. It constitutes the greatest share of the Greek labor force. Another common characteristic is their mobility. [*Poor revenue collection*, caused by *corruption* and *large informal sector*]

13) It is the nominal wage growth which workers, employers, government and public opinion (press) are looking at with great interest. Trade unions want to improve the economic conditions of their members, employers want to preserve their profits, and the government wants to keep wage inflation down but also reduce unemployment, and promote economic growth with a fair distribution of income. [*High wages*, caused by *political opposition to reform*, *strong PS unions* and *EMU entry*]

14) The arguments in the actual bargaining process are debated on issues that are captured by the right hand side variables. It is common for trade unions to emphasize the gains in productivity and the growth in consumer prices (inflation) to demand higher nominal wages. On the other hand, employers' associations emphasize the economic

conditions captured by unemployment, sluggish economic growth and loss of external competitiveness (captured by the exchange rate changes) as arguments in support of their refusal to yield to higher nominal wage increases. [*Lack of competitiveness*, caused by *EMU entry* and *high wages*]

15) The symptoms of the current Greek economic crisis are known as the twin deficits: the budget and trade deficits. In the euro years (after 2001), both have reached unprecedented levels for a non-war period and have contributed to an unparalleled accumulation of sovereign debt [*High debt*, caused by *current account deficit*]

16) In 2001, the Greek public debt was 152 billion euro or 105% of the Greek Gross Domestic Product (GDP) (see Table 2). In 2012, it reached 426 billion euro or 198% of the GDP. This was made easier by the historical declines in the nominal and real cost of borrowing, both private and public. [*High debt*, caused by *access to cheap debt*]

17) The current account deficit followed a similar trend. Up to 2009, the annual trade deficit was above 9% of Greek GDP. It reached record high levels in 2007 and 2008 before it was forcefully reduced by the austerity measures in 2010. These twin deficits are further discussed below in this section. [*Current account deficit*, caused by *lack of competitiveness*]

18) What is less documented is that trade unions and their members were now able to compare their nominal wages expressed in Euro with those of the other eurozone countries' wages and salaries. In absolute levels, Greek wages and salaries were the lowest in the eurozone (see Figure 2). They were lagging behind. Only Portugal of the 12 eurozone countries had a wage level lower than Greece's. This has put an upward pressure on Greek nominal wages. [*High wages*, caused by *strong PS unions*]

19) Nominal and real wages were increasing at an exceptional rate. The public employees and the workers in the public enterprises were pioneers in demanding higher nominal wages. The weak and in many ways the corrupted Greek political system could not refuse to go along with it. [*High wages*, caused by *strong PS unions*, *political opposition to reform* and *destructive institutions*]

20) As mentioned above, with the introduction of the euro, Greek political parties and trade unions aimed at increasing their nominal wages as fast as possible in order to reach the 80% of the average nominal wage of the Eurozone [24] Figure 2 shows that they were very close in achieving it. In 2009, the ratio of Greek nominal wages to the average of the 12 eurozone countries reached its ever highest proportion of 72%. From a very low share of 32% in 1991, Greek nominal wages almost doubled their share in 2002 reaching 62%. It is not shown in the graph, but Greece had the highest nominal wage increases relative to any other of the initial 11 countries of the eurozone. [*High wages*, caused by *strong PS unions* and *destructive institutions*]

## Why Did Forceful Internal Devaluation Fail to Kick-Start Export-Led Growth in Greece? (Mitsopoulos and Pelagidis, 2014)

1) The official creditors initially sanctioned an implementation of the agreed conditionality program, which principally focused on increasing taxes and reforms facilitating a sharp fall in private sector wages. [*Lack of competitiveness*, caused by *high wages*]

2) During the third year of the program's implementation (2013), they complemented these with cuts in pensions, medical benefits, and public sector wages (Pelagidis and Mitsopoulos 2014), further weakening an already falling domestic demand [*High debt*, caused by *large public sector* and *large welfare state*]

3) Growth-enhancing progressive structural reforms to fight the oligopolistic closed markets of the country were not deemed a priority and at the time were basically off the agenda, with the exception of a few half-hearted and therefore incomplete attempts. [*Lack of competitiveness*, caused by *regulatory burden* and *destructive institutions*]

4) In addition, since 2010 there has been, with the troika's approval, a policy to reduce general government employment by encouraging early retirement (Figure 3). This policy helps to meet the target reduction in the number of public sector employees in Greece while avoiding outright layoffs, but it burdens the budget with increased pension payments that largely match any decline in public sector wages. [*High debt*, caused by *large public sector* and *large welfare state*]

5) While the rapid and forceful decline of wages was a stated objective of the internal devaluation policy, the breakdown of the compensation of employees to GDP for the total economy in the ratios of the compensation of employees from corporations, and compensation of employees from the rest of the economy (essentially, an indirect way to estimate the general government wage bill), reveals the large decline in the compensation of employees to total GDP from corporations (Figure 5), and the relative persistence of the government's wage bill (Figure 6). [*Internal devaluation*, caused by *high wages*]

6) In that sense, the way the "internal devaluation" has played out in Greece during the first years of the adjustment program not only seems to have "internally devalued" the tax base as an aggregate, but also has undermined the sustainability of the public finances by shrinking the tax base of the economy faster than the cost of key expenditure items such as the government's wage and pension bill. [*Failed austerity*, caused by *large welfare state* and *large public sector*]

7) Since early 2012 regular earnings have started to fall rapidly, which can be attributed to the changes in the labor laws, the introduction of a reduced minimum wage, and in particular the increased flexibility to determine wages above the minimum wage

without the constraints introduced by sectorial and professional wage agreements [2]. [*High wages*, caused by *regulatory burden* and *destructive institutions*]

8) While the reaction of the domestic clientelistic politics can be explained, it remains an unanswered question why the troika failed to assess these facts and to insist on a more constructive qualitative composition of the "internal devaluation" strategy designed to address the budget and current account deficits of –15 percent of GDP in 2010. [*Failed austerity*, caused by *destructive institutions* and *corruption*]

9) The neglect becomes even more striking when one considers the lack of progress on growth-enhancing reforms and taking into account that Greece really stood out, before the crisis, as the eurozone country with the lowest ratio of private sector wages to GDP and the highest estimated administrative cost to GDP (Figure 9). [*Lack of competitiveness*, caused by *large public sector* and *regulatory burden*]

10) That is, it stood out as the country with the smallest potential to improve cost competitiveness through the reduction of the productive sector wage bill, and the country with the largest potential to improve cost competitiveness through the reduction of red tape and waste, as depicted in Figure 9 [*Failed austerity*, caused by *regulatory burden* and *destructive institutions*]

11) However, the main issues that held back the competitiveness of the private economy—like rent-seeking regulation that preserves oligopolistic structures in product markets and stifles competition creating rents, which increases the cost of introducing innovations in production to streamline and increase the efficiency of supply lines and that would allow productive ecosystems to evolve and research based innovation to increase (Pelagidis and Mitsopoulos 2014, chap. 3) were not addressed. [*Lack of competitiveness*, caused by *regulatory burden* and *destructive institutions*]

12) But the failure of the internal devaluation to improve the export performance of the Greek economy ultimately did not follow from the combination of a failure to reduce existing costs and inefficiencies at the same time wages fell. It was rather a result of further increasing costs and introducing new risks and burdens on the productive economy that more than overcame any competitiveness gain from the fall in labor costs. [*Regulatory burden*, caused by *failed austerity* and *internal devaluation*]

13) For example, as part of the adjustment program, Greece had proceeded to significantly increase excise taxes on energy that is used in productive activities (Figure 10) [3]. After over 60 percent increases in energy prices for industrial use since 2009, according to Eurostat data, now Greece has a combination of high prices in both electricity and natural gas for industrial use, as a result of the unique combination of high taxes (Figure 11) and the politically sanctioned price increases of the state-controlled dominant electricity producer. [*Regulatory burden*, caused by *failed austerity* and *internal devaluation*]

# Monetary Policy Before and After the Euro: Evidence from Greece (Arghyrou, 2009)

1) This shift is well-founded as the ECB is now the exclusive interest-rate setting authority within the EMU. [*Monetary dependence*, caused by *EMU membership*]

2) The potential costs of a single monetary policy that is incompatible with domestic economic conditions have been highlighted by the theory of optimum currency areas as early as the 1960s (see e.g., Mundell 1961). Perhaps surprisingly, however, the recent literature has largely overlooked the compatibility issue. [*Lack of competitiveness*, caused by *monetary dependence*]

3) In addition, since 2001 the process of inflation convergence towards the EMU average observed throughout the 1990s has been discontinued and the inflation differential has slightly increased. As a result, in contrast to the high real interest rates observed in Germany, since 2001 Greece has experienced real interest rates significantly lower than the EMU average (see Sect. 2). [*Capital influx*, caused by *EMU membership*]

4) The difference between the actual ECB and projected Greek target interest rates may reflect two potential effects. According to the first, Greece needs a monetary policy tighter than the one followed by the ECB. This may be so because in 2001–2005 the Greek economy grew significantly faster than the EMU average, in which case Greece needed higher nominal interest rates to control inflation more effectively. [*Capital influx*, caused by *access to cheap debt*]

5) Instead, according to this argument, the low interest rates set by the ECB over-stimulated Greek domestic demand, fuelled inflationary pressures, increased real exchange rate overvaluation and, ultimately, resulted in historically high current account deficit levels. [*Current account deficit*, caused by *EMU membership* and *capital influx*]

6) The second effect may be the elimination of the risk premium embodied in Greek interest in the 1990s caused by the replacement of the Greek drachma by the euro. This would imply that the forecasts reported in Table 5 are driven by the high constant coefficients reported in Table 2, which are now not applicable due to the change in the monetary policy regime. In that case, the difference recorded in Table 5 would reflect the credibility gains caused by EMU accession. [*Access to cheap debt*, caused by *monetary dependence*]

7) Such credibility gains may in the short-run result in excessively low interest rates, an increase in inflation and higher-than-normal current account deficits (see e.g., Giavazzi and Spaventa 1990). [*Current account deficit*, caused by *access to cheap debt*]

## The U.S. Dimension of the Euro Zone Debt Crisis (Arestis and Karakitsos, 2012)

1) The purpose of this paper is to argue that although the United States poses a far greater risk than the European Union in terms of budget deficit and federal debt, a sovereign debt crisis has emerged in the euro zone rather than in the United States. This paradox is due to the different policies pursued in the European Union and the United States and their monetary union structure. [*Collapse of confidence*, caused by *high debt* and *monetary dependence*]

2) Large budget deficits and high public debt are a threat to long-term inflation expectations as there is always the risk of monetizing the debt. Accordingly, the priority after the worst recession in living memory has been to curb budget deficits and public debts. [*Collapse of confidence*, caused by *high debt*] ALSO [*EMU exit*, caused by *high debt*]

3) As labor mobility is hammered by language and cultural differences, while capital mobility is hindered by the lack of harmonized bureaucratic structure, capital transfers should have played a major role in defending the monetary union in its infancy. [*Lack of competitiveness*, caused by *regulatory burden*]

4) The emphasis even in the exchange rate mechanism (ErM) convergence process to monetary union was on nominal (e.g., inflation, nominal long-term interest rates) rather than real magnitudes (e.g., growth, productivity). Post-EMU, there was divergence in real magnitudes, which is at the root of the current EU debt crisis. The combination of the types of policies pursued in the European Union with its peculiar monetary union structure implies that a debt crisis (sovereign or banking) in the periphery was an accident waiting to happen. [*Lack of competitiveness*, caused by *monetary dependence*]

5) The global credit crisis and the subsequent "great recession" are the adverse shocks that triggered the current EU debt crisis. [*Collapse in confidence*, caused by *financial crisis* and *lack of competitiveness*]

6) Budget deficits widened as governments bailed out their financial system and/or as they pursued easy fiscal policy to combat the worst recession in living memory. Although this trend was witnessed in the entire European Union and the United States, in some periphery countries it was more astute than anywhere else. But even within the periphery group, the causes and symptoms of the sovereign debt crisis are different. [*High debt*, caused by *financial crisis*]

7) Greece is the only country in the world where a state bubble was created. Successive governments in the past 30 years came to office on the pledge of enhancing the social, welfare, and even productive role of the state; state pensions, welfare provision, and most importantly, permanent jobs were offered to supporters of the party in the wider public sector, although there was no real need for such jobs. [*Poor*

*governance*, caused by *destructive institutions*, *political opposition to reform* and *large public sector*]

8) The provisions of subsidies or the grant of special tax status to the private sector, whether it was the agricultural sector, manufacturing, construction, or tourism, was the norm [*Poor revenue collection*, caused by *poor governance*]

9) The infamous cheating on the public deficit at the time of the EMU entrance was, after all revisions, 3.1 percent, while it was reported at 2.9 percent at the time, hardly a difference to deserve the characterization of cheating. At any rate, the tiny divergence was due to a difference in reporting military expenditure. But this characterization that has stained Greece came from Greek political parties in office at the time to gain popularity within the Greek electorate—it was the old government that is to blame. [*Lack of trust*, caused by *poor stats*]

10) This was a theme that was repeated by New Democracy (the conservative and right wing party) in 2004–9 and Pasok (the socialist and centre political party) when they took over from the previous government in the 2009. Thus, Greece has no one else to blame for its international reputation as a "cheat" than its own political parties. [*Lack of trust*, caused by *poor stats* and *upward revision of debt*]

11) Once the goal of joining the EMU was achieved, successive governments resumed their old pre-1990s habits. the higher than the EU average growth rates in the 2000s were not exploited to curb the public debt, and take measures to make the economy more competitive, but to make sure that the government of the day remained in office. [*Poor governance*, caused by *access to cheap debt*]

12) The crisis ballooned because the European Union procrastinated in coming to the rescue of Greece in a convincing manner to choke off speculators, thereby spreading the crisis to other EU countries and creating what we now call the "EU debt crisis" that threatens the viability of the euro as a single currency. [*Collapse of confidence*, caused by *slow EMU response*]

13) The divergence of real magnitudes between periphery and core was not unexpected, but it was regarded as a country-specific problem rather than an EMU problem, and accordingly, it required a change of policy in the country concerned to enhance its competitiveness [*Lack of competitiveness*, caused by *regulatory burden* and *monetary dependence*]

## A New Global Financial Architecture: Lessons from the Greek Crisis (Papandreou, 2010)

1) The case of Greece — which accounts for just 2 percent of Europe's gross domestic product (GDP) — demonstrated how financial markets can destabilize entire

economies if safety nets are not in place. Although Greece is now well on the road to recovery, the dangers for the eurozone are still present, as European and global economic recovery remains fragile and the flawed systems that created this crisis remain very much intact. [*Collapse of confidence*, caused by *financial crisis* and *monetary dependence*]

2) The recent crisis in Greece has provoked painful austerity measures but also critical structural reforms that were long overdue. The Greek case also provides useful lessons about the need to reform regional and global economic governance. The global financial crisis in 2008 found Greece in a very vulnerable position, unprepared to face the challenges ahead. When my government took office in October 2009, we discovered that the deficit presented by the previous government as 3.7 percent was in fact more than 12 percent of GDP. Public debt was more than 110 percent of GDP, and state institutions were suffering from chronic mismanagement and endemic corruption. [*Lack of competitiveness*, caused by *regulatory burden* and *poor governance*] ALSO [*Collapse of confidence*, caused by *high debt* and *upward revision of debt*]

3) To put Greece back on track, we introduced a number of recovery measures designed to cut the deficit and reduce national debt, in addition to launching deep structural reforms to make our economy more competitive and productive in the long term. Unfortunately, the markets did not respond positively to these bold reforms. [*Lack of competitiveness*, caused by *regulatory burden*]

4) Market skepticism can be attributed partly to a history of unreliable accounting; the previous conservative government saddled us with not only a huge fiscal deficit but also an enormous credibility deficit. [*Collapse of confidence*, caused by *high debt* and *lack of trust*]

5) Many countries have taken on high levels of debt in order to prevent the crisis from escalating. Even without such countervailing actions, deficits would have grown because downturns inevitably lead to lower tax revenues and greater government expenditures. [*High debt*, caused by *financial crisis*]

6) At the root of all these problems is a breakdown in trust in our financial and political institutions. [*Collapse of confidence*, caused by *lack of trust* and *destructive institutions*]

## GREECE IN CRISIS: AUSTERITY, POPULISM AND THE POLITICS OF BLAME (VASILOPOULOU, HALIKIOPOULOU AND EXADAKTYLOS, 2014)

1) The global financial crisis that started in 2008 has significantly impacted on European economies. Greece has been particularly affected by the profound global transformations associated with the crisis. In comparison to other eurozone countries

facing similar external financial pressures, such as Ireland, Portugal, Spain, Cyprus and Italy, Greece has presented the most problematic case. [*High debt*, caused by *financial crisis*] ALSO [*Collapse of confidence*, caused by *financial crisis*]

2) These agreements have entailed the imposition of severe fiscal and economic adjustment measures with paramount socio-political implications, including a significant strain on the provision of welfare – for example, health and education. Large sections of the Greek population have been disadvantaged by a series of pension and benefit cuts, salary reductions, redundancies and tax increases. [*Lack of competitiveness*, caused by *regulatory burden* and *high debt*] ALSO [*Political instability*, caused by *Internal devaluation*]

3) The political dimension of these social problems has manifested itself through a series of strikes, protest and mass demonstrations, often paralyzing the country. [*Political instability*, caused by *political opposition to reform*]

4) Greece's sovereign debt crisis, and the paramount domestic socio-political dimensions it has assumed, have even made euro exit a possibility, threatening the very foundations of the eurozone. More than any other Member State, Greece has exposed the deficiencies and systemic weaknesses inherent within the European integration project and the broader crisis it currently faces. [*Fears of EMU exit*, caused by *high debt* and *political instability*]

5) These range from taking into account the international dimension of the crisis itself and the institutional weaknesses of the eurozone model of governance to Greece's domestic institutional make-up and its cultural and historical experiences. [*Crisis*, caused by *EMU membership* and *destructive institutions*]

6) On the other hand, however, these exogenous factors notwithstanding, the Greek predicament may also not be fully understood without a reference to Greece's endemic problems: essentially the paradox of sustaining a democratic institutional system while not progressing beyond the entrenched and deeply embedded clientelistic and rent-seeking networks that permeate Greek political culture (Featherstone, 2011; Mitsopoulos and Pelagidis, 2011). [*Poor governance*, caused by *destructive institutions* and *corruption*]

7) The coexistence of these contradictory systemic features during the post-dictatorship era has facilitated the establishment of a 'populist' democratic system (Pappas, 2013a), which has allowed Greece to develop politically and economically during periods of international financial stability, but at the same time has rendered the country unable to withstand external shocks. [*Collapse of confidence*, caused by *destructive institutions*]

8) As the theory places populism at the heart of Greece's endemic domestic weaknesses, if it is correct and populism is a defining feature of the Greek political system, then we should expect populism to constitute a master political narrative. In other words, if populism as an ideology is the bedrock of the Greek political system, it is likely

to be expressed through the narratives of political actors. [*Lack of competitiveness*, caused by *political opposition to reform*, *poor governance* and *destructive institutions*]

9) Given that Greece has an adversarial and clientelistic political system and that access to political power has tended to imply varied access to rents, then we may expect that the rhetoric of blame-shifting populism is likely to differ depending on party position in the system. [*Corruption*, caused by *destructive institutions*]

10) This system developed on the basis of Greece's deeply embedded clientelism (Featherstone, 1990) and the polarization of its party system strategically rather than ideologically (Pappas, 2013a, p. 40). More specifically, the emergence of Greek populist democracy took place in three stages: the rise of a strong populist opposition party; populism's rise to power; and a populist contagion to other major parties (Pappas, 2013b, pp. 7–8). The platform on which the [*Corruption*, caused by *destructive institutions*] ALSO [*Poor governance*, caused by *destructive institutions*]

## IS GREECE AT A TURNING POINT? (THIEMANN, 2013)

1) However, the first austerity package failed to tum Greece around, and the country has now experienced the longest and steepest recession anywhere in Europe in recent times, with real GDP contracting for the sixth consecutive year in 2013-by 3.8%, according to the OECD's latest economic survey of Greece. The consequences for the Greek people have been dire. Salaries have fallen by over a quarter on average, though retail prices kept rising in early 2013. Pensions were reduced by nearly one-third, too, but prices of heating fuel skyrocketed because of tax increases. The unemployment rate now exceeds 26%, and more than half of those under 25 years old are out of a job. Little wonder the Greeks regularly take to the streets to protest against this daily reality. [*Political instability*, caused by *failed austerity* and *political opposition to reform*]

2) But they have nonetheless pushed on ninth structural reform to redress the imbalances and put Greece on a more sustainable growth path. [*Collapse of confidence*, caused by *high debt* and *current account deficit*]

3) In addition, among several specific measures, such as a project with the OECD to tackle red tape and reduce the administrative burden on businesses, in November 2012 the OECD and the Greek government signed an agreement whereby the OECD would screen the Greek economy for regulatory barriers to competition. Four sectors were chosen-food processing, retail trade, building materials and tourism-which accounted for 21% of GDP and 26% of employment in 2011 (most recent comparative data). The project was supported by the Hellenic Competition Commission. [*Lack of competitiveness*, caused by *regulatory burden*]

4) Over an 11-month period, the OECD found a total of 555 restrictive provisions that could potentially lead to market distortions, and made 329 individual

recommendations for amending or abolishing specific legal provisions. [*Lack of competitiveness*, caused by *regulatory burden*]

5) To this effect, the government must resist pressure from interest groups intent on protecting their own status quo rather than the well-being of the wider population, and carry on with the necessary reform to the benefit of everyone, including those who need it the most, such as young people and the unemployed. [*Regulatory burden*, caused by *political opposition to reform* and *destructive institutions*]

6) While 329 reform proposals seems like a big mouthful to swallow for a government that has already been in the international wringer for some time, the nature of the pro-competitive recommendations is very different from anything that has been attempted before. Each of these recommendations refers to a specific legal provision that is holding back competition and that not only affects markets but undermines people's welfare. [*Lack of competitiveness*, caused by *regulatory burden*]

7) Cleaning up this legislative archipelago will make for a better overall investment climate as legal uncertainties are removed and the economic and administrative machinery is oiled. Improving the ability of Greek businesses to compete will benefit not only firms but also consumers, by boosting efficiency, turnover and job creation for years to come. [*Lack of competitiveness*, caused by *regulatory burden*]

## HOW TO AVOID A EUROZONE BREAKUP (KOO, 2011)

1) The fact that the European Union had to offer financial support to Greece instead of collecting fines from the country for going over the 3 percent Maastricht limit on budget deficits also suggests that the current rules are not working. [*High debt*, caused by *non-enforcement of EU treaties* and *poor governance*]

2) In particular, they wanted to make sure that member countries would not run profligate fiscal policies by taking advantage of the ease in attracting foreign funds in a single currency arrangement. This concern led to the limit on budget deficits of 3 percent of GDP. Recent events in Greece and Ireland, however, have proven that this limit not only failed to prevent problems from happening, but is also making the situation worse for many countries. [*Access to cheap debt*, caused by *monetary dependence*]

3) The problem that was anticipated was the problem of profligate fiscal policy financed by foreigners. This is the problem Greece has created for itself. [*High debt*, caused by *poor governance* and *Capital influx*]

4) The problem of profligate fiscal policy requires fiscal discipline. But the problem of the balance-sheet recession needs fiscal flexibility. This time around, however, the first problem triggered the contagion, forcing the countries facing the second problem into premature fiscal consolidation. That, in turn, brought their economies far worse trouble. [*Collapse of confidence*, caused by *high debt*]

5) This means those protesting in the streets of Athens are no longer able to blame everything on rich, fat, foreign bankers. Instead, protestors must redirect their energy toward convincing their neighbors, relatives, and friends to buy more Greek government bonds or face further cuts by the government. [*Political instability*, caused by *EMU membership* and *high debt*]

## CRITICAL REVIEW: THE POLITICS OF SOVEREIGN DEBT (HEMBRUFF, 2013)

1) In the media the proximate cause of the Greek sovereign debt crisis is not difficult to locate: fiscal irresponsibility by the past several Greek governments. 'In October 2009, the new socialist government, led by Prime Minister George Papandreou, revised the estimate of the government budget deficit for 2009, nearly doubling the existing estimate of 6.7% of GDP to 12.7% of GDP'.1 Lenders, already spooked by the 2007–08 subprime financial crisis in the USA, were no longer willing to lend money to the Greek state at the low rates to which the Greek government was accustomed. [*Collapse of confidence*, caused by *high debt*, *financial crisis* and *upward revision of Greek debt*] ALSO [*High debt*, caused by *access to cheap debt*]

2) facilitating expanded accumulation in the debtor state (through privatisation and financialisation), and maintaining investor confidence in debt repayment (generally with bureaucratic reforms, spending cutbacks and investment-friendly policies). [*Failed austerity*, caused by *capitalism*]

3) Political elites in debtor states, then, also have a vested interest in staying within the golden noose, given that economic and social stability is dependent on the continual refinancing of maturing loans. This highlights an important power imbalance between lenders and debtors that is often obscured in dominant interpretations of sovereign debt; debtor states need to follow the prevailing development orthodoxy (generally prescribed by the IMF and World Bank) because to deviate is to risk losing access to new loans, leading to default. [*Political instability*, caused by *failed austerity*] ALSO [*Destructive institutions*, caused by *high debt*]

4) In this narrative Greece has long been plagued by a dysfunctional, patrimonial political system, out-of-control spending, and a weak social safety net.5 Greece promised European leaders it would fix these problems if it were allowed into the European Union, and was granted transitional loans that would allow it to undertake the macroeconomic reforms necessary to reduce patrimonial corruption, reform the state administrative capacity, and improve tax collection. [*Poor governance*, caused by *poor revenue collection*, *destructive institutions* and *corruption*]

5) Private investors flooded the country with money, believing that reforms would be carried out and that the EU as a whole would take responsibility for any potential problems. Sinn, as quoted by Young and Semmler, has claimed that capital outflows to peripheral states such as Greece 'deprived Germany of necessary investments and led to the lowest growth rates—second only to Italy—between 1995 and 2005'.6 Peripheral countries such as Greece experienced a demand-driven boom, with a current account deficit financed by cheap core-provided credit. [*Capital influx*, caused by *EMU membership*] ALSO [*Current account deficit*, caused by *access to cheap debt*]

6) As the story goes, Greece abused the 'privilege' of EMU membership and deserves to be punished for its profligacy in order to be put back on track. [*High debt*, caused by *poor governance* and *access to cheap debt*]

7) This group of theories, of which the 'blame Greece' narrative is a part, is unable to capture the dynamic interplay of social forces that either support or oppose various aspects of austerity measures and privatisations by dramatically underestimating the relative fixity and entrenchment of social structures such as professional groups, unions, class fractions, supranational institutions, patronage networks, and so on. [*High debt*, caused by *strong PS unions*]

8) The reverse of the above argument blames Germany for its artificially competitive labour productivity and pathological obsession with maintaining a current account surplus at the expense of the eurozone periphery. According to this narrative, Germany (and to a lesser extent other 'core' states such as France) has been the main beneficiary of the EMU at the expense of the eurozone periphery. [*Lack of competitiveness*, caused by *high wages* and *low productivity*]

9) According to this perspective, the root of the problem lies within divergent labour competitiveness, compounded by differences in the real rate of inflation. Germany achieved its export boom (and associated current account surpluses) through a policy of wage moderation. These reforms focused largely on reducing non-wage labour costs and increasing flexibility in labour markets in order to achieve fiscal consolidation.1 [*Lack of competitiveness*, caused by *regulatory burden* and *Capital influx*]

10) Because the member states of the EMU share the same monetary policy—one aimed at inflation targeting and price stability, with Maastricht criteria limiting the freedom of fiscal policy—pressure is forced onto labour markets as a lever for increasing competitiveness.14 [*Internal devaluation*, caused by *high debt* and *monetary dependence*]

11) According to the final set of dominant approaches, the crises of the EMU have been presented as a failure of surveillance and incentive mechanisms amid the rush to lower barriers to capital circulation, as well a failure of macroeconomic coordination resulting from a conflict between the emu's single monetary policy (exercised by the European Central Bank, ECB) and the independent fiscal policies exercised by member states. This tension creates an incentive towards chronic deficits, since excess spending does not cause a change in a country's interest rate or exchange rate, and states need to

use fiscal rather than monetary policy to offset temporary economic weakness [26]. [*High debt*, caused by *access to cheap debt*]

12) Because EU member states do not control their currency (and so cannot devalue to make exports cheaper), they should have become more competitive by putting pressure on labour costs in order to increase relative productivity. However, in the run-up to the crises states papered over these imbalances by borrowing rather than implementing the necessary neoliberal reforms. [*Poor governance*, caused by *access to cheap debt*] ALSO [*Lack of competitiveness*, caused by *access to cheap debt*]

## INFURIATED WITH THE INFURIATED (THEODOSSOPOULOS, 2013)

1) During that time we have seen many citizens in Greece disapproving of the financial restrictions imposed "on their lives" by others: their government, European Union (EU) officials, or the world's financial establishment (to mention only some recipients of local blame). [*Political instability*, caused by *political opposition to reform*]

2) The adjective has grown to become a noun: the "indignants" *(oi aganaktisménoi)* in Greece are those who challenge the proposition that the nation's citizens have to pay the cost of financial mismanagement and corruption. [*Political opposition to reform*, caused by *corruption* and *poor governance*]

3) The Spanish message to the Greeks was circulated through television channels and Internet blogs, and the first mobilization of the Greek movement of the indignants: (or Indignant Citizens Movement) was organized through Facebook. Its followers protested in major Greek squares but primarily in Syntagma Square (Constitution Square), in front of the Greek Parliament in Athens. [*Failed austerity measures*, caused by *political opposition to reform*]

4) Many protesters in Greece chose to camp in Gonstitution Square itself (from the end of May to the end of July 2011), thus creating a physical manifestation of their :imagined: community of discontent—one that the members of Parliament convening next door could not easily ignore: their campsite was the starting point of dynamic protest but also worked as a communication station, a forum of debate, and space for socialization more generally (frequented by citizens who did not necessarily participate in the protest). [*Political instability*, caused by *political opposition to reform*]

5) In this generalized context of discontent I discovered that some Greeks citizens were critically predisposed toward—or even infuriated—with their infuriated compatriots. Some of them referred to themselves, with self-inflicted irony, as "indignant with the indignants" *{aganaktisménoi me tous aganaktisménous)* and clarified that they were equally outraged with the crisis and its effects on their lives but upheld serious reservations about the expressive infuriation (or lack of systematic political orientation)

of their more vocal—"self-pronounced infuriated"—fellow citizens. [*Lack of competitiveness*, caused by *political instability*]

6) For many Greek migrants in Panama the austerity measures introduced recently in Greece represent a sense of poetic justice. The Greeks of Greece, their argument goes, have lived in a state of affluence for the last 20 or 30 years, working less, having more leisure, relying on subsidies—and bureaucratic machinations—to eat/swallow *(natron)* European or government money.* [*Lack of competitiveness*, caused by *low productivity* and *large public sector*]

7) The familiar rhetoric about laziness and corruption in Greece was more unforgiving toward laziness in particular, as it reflected the point of view of men who sweat to earn a living, working hard away from their country, deprived of comfort, but succeeding in acquiring financial opportunities that Greece had previously denied them. From their point of view, the Greeks living in Greece do not work as much, and many do not work at all, living on their parents' money or government benefits. [*Lack of competitiveness*, caused by *low productivity*, *large public sector*, *large welfare state* and *corruption*]

8) Many Greeks in Patras, for example, maintain that their fellow citizens who complain passionately in public about the austerity measures are serving their personal or trade-union interests {prosopika or syntehniaka symferonta). [*Political opposition to reform*, caused by *strong PS unions*]

9) In May, June, and July 2011 the protesters in Gonstitution Square voiced their defiance toward the austerity measures imposed by the Greek government and requested by the European Union. For many this was also an expression of discontent with the economic system that led Greece and other European countries into debt. [*Political opposition to reform*, caused by *EMU membership*, *high debt* and *capitalism*]

10) The protesters with whom I talked highlighted that they were paying the consequences of the mismanagement of others: Greek and foreign politicians, bankers, speculators^, multinational banks, and corrupted civil servants. [*Political opposition*, caused by *Capital influx*, *EMU membership*, *poor governance* and *corruption*]

## THE BAIL OUT! POSITIVE POLITICAL-ECONOMICS OF GREEK-TYPE CRISES IN THE EMU (FAHRHOLZ AND WOJCIK, 2012)

1) We demonstrate that, conditional on the present political-economic set-up of EMU, the bail-out was inevitable, i.e., a threat of default by one member that creates a negativity externality for the whole monetary union must (under identifiable conditions)

result in sharing the costs of fiscal adjustment by the rest of the members. [*Collapse in confidence*, caused by *high debt* and *EMU membership*]

2) One of the key novelties in our work is that we formally take account of the negative externality problem that has been central to policy debates related to the EMU's institutional design since the very birth of the euro (see, for example, Gros et al. (2005) and de Haan et al. (2004) for early contributions within this debate) and played an important role in the specific case of the Greek crisis. [*Access to cheap debt*, caused by *EMU membership*]

3) (ii) the role of political factors such as voters attitude towards fiscal retrenchment and their support for the European integration process, (iii) how the risk of contagion to other weak members, the perceived risk of

EMU break-up or the possibility of coalition-building between groups of euro area members can affect the negotiation outcome. [*Failed austerity measures*, caused by *political opposition to reform* and *slow EMU response*]

4) The political-economics setting of our analysis resembles that of Alesina and Drazen (1991) who argue that domestic fiscal reforms may have significant distributional implications, so that societal groups may seek to pass the burden of fiscal adjustment costs onto other groups at the national level. [*Political opposition to reform*, caused by *strong PS unions*]

5) This "two-level metaphor" postulates that national executives intermediating between the national and the European level have to craft ratification within the domestic arena. The latter process can also be traced to a permissive consensus of voters and lobbies that can enforce substantial political conflict potential. [*Political instability*, caused by *political opposition to reform*]

6) First, the main basis of the game is the negative externality problem arising from the fact that an unsustainable fiscal position and a threat of default by one EMU member is likely to spill-over on the rest of EMU members. As indicated earlier, since the birth of the euro the negative externality problem has been central to all policy debates related to EMU's institutional design. In fact, it has been one of the key arguments in favor of the Stability and Growth Pact: Imposing fiscal rules on EMU members would — as it was hoped — counter the tendency for fiscal bias and free riding. [*High debt*, caused by *EMU membership* and *non-enforcement of EU treaties*]

7) Also in the context of the recent euro area crisis Baldwin et al. (2010) point out that "(…) in a monetary union without a fiscal union governments might be tempted to run up unsustainable debts and push the ECB to inflate them away or run up high levels of debts that would create negative spillovers for others. [*Collapse of confidence*, caused by *high debt* and *EMU membership*]

8) However, it is important to stress that the results are conditional on the present political-economic set-up of the EMU. In other words, the EMU problems do not only ensue from the Greek fiscal problems alone, but from the interactions of these problems

with the actual political economic configuration of the EMU. [*High debt*, caused by *access to cheap debt* and *non-enforcement of EU treaties*] ALSO [*Lack of competitiveness*, caused by *EMU membership*]

9) The weakness of the current EMU set-up is that it neither provides sufficient incentives for curtailing excessive lending and indebtedness (de Haan et al., 2004), nor secures the degree of political integration necessary to attain a sufficient degree of policy coordination. [*High debt*, caused by *access to cheap debt* and *non-enforcement of EU treaties*]

## LEADING REFORM AMIDST TRANSBOUNDARY CRISES: LESSONS FROM GREECE (ZAHARIADIS, 2013)

1) Deteriorating Greek public finances have triggered a European financial calamity that threatens the stability of the eurozone and the future of the euro. Greece's economy is only 2 per cent of the European economy. But its inability to respond on its own, the European Union's (EU) hesitation, and vulnerabilities in the euro's financial architecture helped morph the crisis into a systemic catastrophe, posing major leadership challenges. [*Collapse of confidence*, caused by *high debt* and *monetary dependence*]

2) Political leaders face the challenge of urgently needing to respond while being tempted by the opportunity to implement long-awaited reforms. Response is defined as the short-term effort to reduce damage and is measured as the ability to stem capital flow and balance the government's books. [*Failed austerity*, caused by *political opposition to reform*]

3) Greece's two bailout packages demand a fundamental restructuring of public revenues and expenditures. Tax collection illuminates revenue dilemmas imposed by macro-political conflict. [*High debt*, caused, caused by *poor revenue collection*, *poor governance* and *political opposition to reform*]

4) Labour reserve policy examines the politics of spending cuts in light of declining revenues. The argument has implications for political leadership and EU crisis management [*Lack of competitiveness*, caused by *destructive institutions* and *regulatory burden*] ALSO [*High debt*, caused by *lack of competitiveness*]

5) The nature and instruments of response to financial crises are likely to be coloured by policy legacy and political gain (Haggard 2000; Bermeo and Pontusson 2012). Because of the urgency and high degree of turbulence permeating the sovereign debt crisis, leaders are likely to rely on familiar instruments to deal with it. There is little time to create new tools which may be more effective but also politically more costly. On the one hand, there is an obvious need to stop the pain caused by prolonged economic and social damage. On the other hand, information uncertainty creates a need for

experimentation, possibly prolonging pain. [*Failed austerity*, caused by *political instability* and *political opposition to reform*] ALSO [*Collapse of confidence*, caused by *failed austerity*]

6) Effective reforms are difficult to implement because they require sustained mass arousal and support for major change. If leadership benefits from the current system, it has little political incentive to engage in such reforms. However, if the crisis is severe and reforms can be attached to creating a rosier future in the face of an economically bleak present, as is the case with Greece, leaders have a strong incentive to urgently commit to reform. [*Failed austerity*, caused by *political instability* and *corruption*]

7) The Greek debt crisis is multidimensional. It involves high public and private debt, heavy borrowing from external sources, and rampant corruption. Saddled with too much debt, the government is asked to raise revenues and cut expenses during economic recession, which cause uncertainty and reduce economic activity [*Collapse of confidence*, caused by *excessive private credit extension*, *high debt* and *poor revenue collection*]

8) The Greek government was hard pressed by creditors to shore up revenues and slash expenditures. However, electoral concerns impeded its ability to deliver on both fronts. Both bailout packages reduced short-term capital flight by insulating Greece from higher premiums demanded by creditors to refinance its public debt. But aid came with strings attached. Eventually the government found itself having to do too much too soon. [*Failed austerity*, caused by *political opposition to reform*]

9) However, higher taxes proved highly unpopular, creating incentives for more, rather than less tax evasion. Affected groups vehemently protested the loss of disposable income while voters fled *en masse* from the governing party. Electorally, the cards were stacked against reform. [*Poor revenue collection*, caused by *failed austerity* and *corruption*]

10) Electoral concerns limited the appetite for reform. The government simply feared the political cost of pushing through harsh reforms, while opposition parties stoked the flames of discontent, demanding new elections and an end to austerity. Within the first two years, a number of socialist (PASOK) MPs resigned or were kicked out of the party because they disagreed with the imposed 'neoliberal' austerity. Consequently, the government's majority in parliament shrank from 160 seats (out of 300) after the 2009 elections down to 155 seats, a number which fluctuated depending on the measure debated. [*Failed austerity*, caused by *political opposition to reform*]

11) Tax measures create greater scope for political favouritism (and hence more electoral gains), but they lead to lower revenues by amplifying incentives for tax evasion. By definition, the size of the underground economy is contested; some estimate it to be around 25 per cent of GDP, 12 per cent above the OECD (2011, p. 84) average. Tax receipts lag, especially in personal income taxes, with the greatest incidence occurring among the self-employed (Matsaganis and Flevotomou 2010). Greece has almost twice as many self-employed professionals as the eurozone average. [*Poor revenue collection*,

caused by *corruption*, *destructive institutions*, *poor governance* and *large informal economy*]

12) Without appropriate reforms, higher taxation increases tax evasion for two reasons (De Santis 2012). Producers evade taxes to continue financing their operations. Consumers simply seek to maintain the same lifestyle in light of nominally lower disposable income. Both may estimate that the drawback of penalties does not outweigh the benefit of avoiding bankruptcy, especially when administrative capacity is lacking. The vicious cycle of lower revenues leading to less economic activity and more austerity has not gone unnoticed. But the obligation to meet short-term targets has increased tax evasion, fueling public discontent and increasing the political cost of reform. [*Poor revenue collection*, caused by *corruption*, *poor governance* and *political opposition to reform*]

13) The case of labour reserve policy replicates the point of quick fixes standing in the way of reform that could deliver long-term prosperity. Following the path of least resistance, Greek leaders refused to reduce the public sector wage bill until they were forced by external actors. Creating a downward spiral, the severity of the crisis stiffened resistance to structural change, amplified blame avoidance, and lowered political resolve for long-term labour reforms. [*Poor governance*, caused by *access to cheap debt* and *political opposition to reform*]

## AN UPDATE ON EMU SOVEREIGN YIELD SPREAD DRIVERS IN TIMES OF CRISIS: A PANEL DATA ANALYSIS (GOMEZ-PUIG, SOSVILLA-RIVERO AND RAMOS-HERRERA, 2014)

1) Figure 1 shows that from the start of the European Economic and Monetary Union (EMU) and before the financial crisis, spreads on 10-year sovereign bond yields relative to the German benchmark moved in a narrow range with only very slight differences across countries. [*Access to cheap debt*, caused by *EMU membership*]

2) Nevertheless, with the financial crisis the picture changed completely; after the outbreak of the Greek sovereign debt crisis in late 2009, sovereign risk differentials rose sharply and then continued to fluctuate strongly. Indeed, the financial crisis put the spotlight on the macroeconomic and fiscal imbalances within EMU countries which had largely been ignored during the period of stability1 when the markets had seemed to underestimate the possibility that governments might default. [*Collapse of confidence*, caused by *financial crisis*]

3) Likewise, Favero and Missale (2012) find that the credit risk component has increased in importance as a determinant of sovereign bond spreads because of the

adverse market sentiment conditions after the global financial crisis. [*Collapse of confidence*, caused by *financial crisis*]

4) Specifically, it is striking that between the introduction of the euro in January 1999 and November2009, when it became clear that the Greek economy was unable to finance its sovereign debt, spreads on bonds of EMU countries moved in a narrow range with only slight differentiation across countries. In fact, the stability and convergence of spreads was considered a hallmark of successful financial integration (see, e.g., Abad et al., 2010) inside the euro area (neither the subprime crisis nor the collapse of Lehman Brothers bit significantly into euro sovereign spreads). [*Access to cheap debt*, caused by *EMU membership*]

5) Nevertheless, once the global financial crisis began to affect the real sector, the imbalances within euro area countries were plain to see. Spreads, which had reached levels close to zero between the launch of the euro and October 2009 (the average value of the 10-year yield spread against the German bund moved between 10 and 47 basis points in the cases of France and Greece, respectively), have risen ever since. Indeed [*Collapse of confidence*, caused by *financial crisis*, *high debt* and *current account deficit*]

6) Specifically, according to Dornbusch, Park, and Claessens (2000), reasons that may explain the evolution of sovereign yields spreads can be divided into two groups: fundamentals-based reasons on the one hand, and investor behaviour-based reasons on the other. While the former works through real and financial linkages across countries, the latter is more sentiment-driven. Following the literature, in order to measure the impact of fundamental variables (at both local and regional level) on sovereign spread behaviour, we use instruments that gauge not only each country's fiscal position, but the market liquidity in each country, its foreign debt, its potential rate of growth, and the loss of competitiveness as well. The private sector level of indebtedness has been added in the analysis of the effect of local fundamental variables and, finally, we have included foreign claims on sectoral private debt and cross-border banking system linkages as measures of the degree of crisis transmission through the financial system (see Gómez-Puig & Sosvilla-Rivero, 2013). [*Collapse of confidence*, caused by *high debt*, *lack of competitiveness*, *excessive private credit extension* and *bank undercapitalisation*]

7) Besides, the current-account-balance-to-GDP ratio is the instrument used as a proxy of the foreign debt and the net position of the country vis-à-vis the rest of the world. Note that this variable is defined as the difference between exports and imports. Therefore, an increase would signal an improvement in the net position of the country towards the rest of the world, reducing sovereign spreads. The importance of this variable has been underlined by the IMF (2010) and Barrios et al. (2009). In view of Mody (2009)'s argument that countries' sensitivity to the financial crisis is more pronounced the greater the loss of their growth potential and competitiveness, we include instruments that measure these features [*Collapse of confidence*, caused by *current account deficit*]

8) To assess the role of private debt in the euro area sovereign debt crisis, we also incorporate instruments that capture the level of indebtedness of each country's private sector in the analysis8. To this end, we make use of a single dataset on private debt-to-GDP by sector in each EMU country. In particular, we apply three variables: banks' debt-to-GDP, non-financial corporations' debt-to-GDP, and households' debt-to-GDP, constructed with data obtained from the European Central Bank Statistics. Since high leverage levels in the private sector have a negative impact on the public sector's sustainability, an increase in these three variables would positively affect sovereign yield spreads9. [*Collapse of confidence*, caused by *excessive private credit extension*]

9) The credit rating has been included as a proxy of the market perception of default risk in each localmarket13. [*Collapse of confidence*, caused by *downgrades*]

## BUSINESS CYCLE SYNCHRONISATION IN EMU: CAN FISCAL POLICY BRING MEMBER-COUNTRIES CLOSER? (DEGIANNAKIS, DUFFY, FILIS & LIVADA, 2015)

1) Since the launch of the Euro currency in 1999, the European Monetary Union (EMU) has experienced a short but turbulent history. The knock on effects of the 2007 economic and financial crisis has led to an "existential" crisis for the Eurozone. The root cause of the current difficulties for the Eurozone lies in the inherent contradiction between a single, supra-national currency and the maintenance of nation-based fiscal policies and financial regulation (see Lane, 2012 and Shambaugh, 2012 for a review). [*Lack of competitiveness*, caused by *regulatory burden* and *EMU membership*]

2) To ensure that supra-national ("one size fits all") monetary policies are appropriate in individual national economies and thus ensuring that the union-wide monetary policy can effectively substitute national monetary policies, business cycle synchronisation is of paramount importance. If business cycles are not synchronised, national fiscal policies take on an additional importance as a tool for macroeconomic stabilisation policy. [*Lack of competitiveness*, caused by *monetary dependence* and *pro-cyclical fiscal policy*]

3) However, when a country is impacted by an asymmetric shock (thus, its cycle becomes de-synchronised with the union-wide business cycle), or impacted asymmetrically by a common economic shock (once again, this will lead to a desynchronisation of its business cycle with the union-wide cycle), independent fiscal policy can be used as a macroeconomic stabilization tool. As such national fiscal policies in the Eurozone take on an additional role in promoting the cyclical synchronisation of Eurozone economies with the aggregate Euro-wide business cycle. [*Collapse of confidence*, caused by *pro-cyclical fiscal policy* and *financial crisis*]

4) Applying fiscal policy to dampen fluctuations in output in a monetary union will involve reacting to asymmetric shocks, as well as, reacting to symmetric shocks with asymmetric impacts. [*Collapse of confidence*, caused by *financial crisis* and *pro-cyclical fiscal policy*]

5) The ability of any country's economy to react to either shock, without fiscal policy intervention, will differ due to heterogeneous structural factors across countries, such as the degree of wage and price flexibility and the degree of labour mobility across countries. Such structural differences promote the need for and use of fiscal policy (Van Aarle and Garretsen, 2000). Along [*Lack of competitiveness*, caused by *high wages* and *regulatory burden*]

6) A political economy approach to fiscal policy emphasises that policy makers may not always use fiscal policy in a countercyclical fashion. Thus, the outcome of fiscal policy may be a deficit bias (Persson and Svensson, 1989; Tabellini and Alesina, 1990), a procyclical fiscal policy (Lane, 2003) or even a business cycle driven by fiscal policy shocks (Fatás and Mihov, 2008; Drazen, 2000). Due to such potential outcomes, the institutions of EMU have constrained the use of fiscal policy through the Maastricht Treaty, The Stability and Growth Pact and more recently through the Fiscal Compact Treaty. [*Pro-cyclical fiscal policy*, caused by *political opposition to reform* and *non-enforcement of EU treaties*]

7) However, Candelon et al. (2010) claim that there is an increase in the procyclical behaviour of fiscal policy during the post-Maastricht period. They interpret this as evidence of the constraints tying the hands of fiscal policy makers. Thus, Bearce (2009) argues that greater flexibility is required under the Stability and Growth Pact in order for the EMU member-countries to achieve greater macroeconomic synchronisation.

Furceri (2009) and Fatas and Mihov (2003, 2006), on the other hand, suggest that unconstrained idiosyncratic fiscal policy is often a source of macroeconomic destabilisation and increased business cycle volatility, which in turn leads to the reduced synchronisation between business cycles. Thus, fiscal policy constraints could be useful in avoiding such destabilisation. [*Pro-cyclical fiscal policy*, caused by *political opposition to reform* and *non-enforcement of EU treaties*] ALSO [*Lack of competitiveness*, caused by *pro-cyclical fiscal policy*]

8) Concerning the fiscal deficit, the descriptive statistics shown in Table 2 demonstrate that Greece, Portugal, Italy and Belgium experience significantly higher deficits compared to the average EMU12 and those of the core EMU countries, such as Austria, Germany and Netherlands. It is interesting to note that Finland has, on average, a fiscal surplus. Furthermore, the high standard deviations of Belgium, Greece, Ireland and Italy imply a more active fiscal policy in these countries. [*High debt*, caused by *pro-cyclical fiscal policy*]

9) On the other hand, in the cases of Greece, Germany and the Netherlands, fiscal policy had a detrimental effect on business cycle synchronisation. This is especially

evident in the case of Greece, where the difference between ρi,12,t and ρi,12,t ∗ was more than 40%. [*Lack of competitiveness*, caused by *pro-cyclical fiscal policy*]

## BUSINESS CYCLES AND ECONOMIC CRISIS IN GREECE (1960-2011): A LONG RUN EQUILIBRIUM ANALYSIS IN THE EUROZONE (MICHAELIDES, PAPAGEORGIOU AND VOULDIS, 2013)

1) For instance, the origins of the Greek financial crisis are manifested in the growing imbalances, primarily fiscal and current-account deficits, since euro-area entry in 2001 (Gibson et al., 2012). [*Current account deficit*, caused by *monetary dependence*]

2) The current economic crisis started, at least partly, in the US and is now behaving as an autonomous European crisis. [*Collapse of confidence*, caused by *financial crisis*]

3) The macroeconomic policies of the 1980s are related to this slowdown and most authors stress the absence of long-term planning. A common point of the analyses is the concentration of macroeconomic policies on the demand side and more specifically on consumption, neglecting both investments and the supply side of the economy. [*Lack of competitiveness*, caused by *large public sector*, *large welfare state* and *regulatory burden*]

4) More precisely, in a number of studies where Greece is included explicitly it seems that a lack of synchronicity of the national business cycle with that of the Eurozone emerges. For instance, Montoya and de Haan (2007) pointed to the existence of a 'national border' effect. In a similar vein, Gallegati et al. (2004) found weak links among Mediterranean countries, including Greece, and the European continental area. [*Lack of competitiveness*, caused by *pro-cyclical fiscal policy* and *monetary dependence*]

5) Papageorgiou et al. (2010) found that whereas in the post-Maastricht period synchronization among the EMU counterparts seems to increase, in the period after the introduction of the common currency, divergence has increased especially for Greece and Ireland. [*Lack of competitiveness*, caused by *non-enforcement of EU treaties* and *EMU membership*]

6) Now, let's turn to the transmission of U.S. shocks to Europe. In this context, the IMF (2007) found that spillovers coming from the U.S. have significant effects on the rest of the world if the disturbances are global, correlated across countries or characterized by global movements is asset markets. [*Collapse of confidence*, caused by *financial crisis*]

7) The interpretation of the negative deviation of the profit rate from its trend due to the underlying social conditions as was put forward in the examination of the GDP evolution is an alternative. As is the case with most other macroeconomic indices, clear

upward movements appear in the beginning both of the 1990s and the 2000s. [*Capital influx*, caused by *EMU membership*]

8) Furthermore, in the 2001–2011 time-span, after the implementation of the common monetary policy the Greek GDP is found to be caused at the same time by the EMU GDP and the U.S. GDP. This finding may be evaluated either as evidence of the transmission of the crisis to the EMU as a whole from the U.S. economy and as a shift towards increasing openness of the Greek [*Capital influx*, caused by *EMU membership*] economy.

9) We found that during the 2000s the Greek economy entered into a period of decoupling from the core EU countries, in contrast to the 1993–2000 time span during which a process towards convergence seems to have taken place. In particular, after the implementation of the common monetary policy, the Greek GDP is found to be synchronized to the U.S. economy. [*Lack of competitiveness*, caused by *EMU entry*]

## CONTAGION EFFECTS DURING FINANCIAL CRISIS: EVIDENCE FROM THE GREEK SOVEREIGN BONDS MARKET (PRAGIDIS, AIELLI, CHIONIS AND SHIZAS, 2015)

1) Since the inception of the common currency, European Monetary Union (EMU) countries have experienced a convergence of their long-term interest rates. [*Access to cheap debt*, caused by *EMU membership*]

2) The single currency implied a common monetary policy with very low interest rates set by the European Central Bank (ECB) that would be based initially on low German inflation rates. Thus, the countries with high inflation rates at that time (Greece, Portugal, and others) gained credibility from this. [*Access to cheap debt*, caused by *monetary dependence*]

3) However, this loose monetary policy prevented the inflation rates of these countries from converging with the EU average inflation rate over time (Gibson et al., 2014). This situation created problems such as a lack of competitiveness and the deterioration of their fiscal balances. [*Lack of competitiveness*, caused by *high wages* and *Capital influx*] ALSO [*High debt*, caused by *access to cheap debt*]

4) In 2007, after the bursting of the subprime mortgage bubble, the world long-term interest rates increased. As some authors (see Gartner et al., 2011; Chionis et al., 2014) claim, the fundamental macroeconomics of each country were the primary reason for this increase. [*Collapse of confidence*, caused by *financial crisis*, *high debt* and *current account deficit*]

5) This was hypothesized because Greece was the first country that claimed financial support from the EU and the IMF, in May 2010 (see Table 1). Greece's twin deficits,

macroeconomic imbalance, and its unsustainable debt path were the main concerns of the international financial community due to a possible contagion to other European countries. [*Collapse of confidence*, caused by *high debt* and *current account deficit*]

6) On the contrary, it is evident that there is a decoupling in the correlation dynamics between the yields of the PIIGs (Portugal, Ireland, Italy, Greece, and Spain) and the yields of the core eurozone. This results in line with previous findings of the bond determinants literature that, for the first time since the inception of the euro currency, market practitioners began to pay attention to the macro fundamentals of each country and separately evaluate each EU country's sovereign debt market. [*Collapse of confidence*, caused by *high debt* and *current account deficit*]

## CREDITOR MORAL HAZARD DURING THE EMU DEBT CRISIS (BRATIS, LAOPODIS AND KOURETAS, 2015)

1) The US subprime loan crisis of 2007 and the subsequent credit crunch of 2008 eventually led to the global financial crisis of 2007–2009 and the ensuing Eurozone debt crisis. Both the financial and debt crises had far reaching implications for the global and domestic financial system and even more for the real economy of a great number of countries, and in particular the Eurozone and the European Union (EU). [*High debt*, caused by *financial crisis*]

2) Thus, the financial crisis revealed that the current regulatory framework was insufficient to provide the correct signals to the governments, the central banks and the financial market regulators about the severity of the crisis and its systemic nature. [*Poor governance*, caused by *access to cheap debt*]

3) With respect to the subsequent European debt crisis there was also a need for the implementation of several memorandums with provisions for fiscal consolidation and structural changes. Additionally, with respect to the banking sectors of these countries an enormous program of refinancing was formed and the European Central Bank (ECB) had to implement on-conventional monetary policies to avert the collapse of several European banks which had no access to the international money markets to obtain the required funds or to avert a sovereign default over public debt [*High debt*, caused by *bank undercapitalisation*]

4) The situation in the Eurozone became more severe with Greece and Portugal facing a dramatic increase in their public debts and with Greece being on the verge of sovereign default. At the same time, the yield spreads of the sovereign bonds of all European periphery countries including Italy spiked. [*Collapse of confidence*, caused by *high debt*]

5) Our analysis focuses on the European debt crisis which is set at 2009:11, the date when Greece officially reviewed government debt data and its resolution setting [*Collapse of confidence*, caused by *upward revision of debt*]

6) Specifically, bond spreads tend to be lower in the pre-crisis period due to the adoption of the euro's absence of currency risk. [*Access to cheap debt*, caused by *monetary dependence*]

7) Post crisis, the pricing of sovereign bonds returns to rational grounds leading fiscal and key macroeconomic factors to be the determinants of spreads. The latter phenomenon is recognized as "return on market discipline" in the bond market. [*Collapse of confidence*, caused by *high debt* and *current account deficits*]

8) Our analysis is con-ducted for Greece (the zero-ground country), Ireland and Portugal for the period January 2001 to December 2012. The overall precrisis results reveal that international factors exert a greater influence on bond spreads than macroeconomic/fiscal variables do. By contrast, the findings for the post-crisis period show that macroeconomic/fiscal variables are more significant than international factors. [*Access to cheap debt*, caused by *EMU membership*]

## EMU and the Greek Crisis: The Political Economy Perspective (Katsimi and Moutos, 2010)

1) The metastasis of the Greek crisis from a peripheral incident involving a fiscally irresponsible government to a systemic crisis threatening the euro was for many a surprise. [*High debt*, caused by *poor governance*]

2) The announcement by the newly elected Greek government in October 2009 that the projected budget deficit for 2009 was 12.7% of GDP [1] (rather than the 5.1% projection appearing in the 2009 Spring Commission forecast) was initially met with shock and opprobrium in Brussels and euro area capitals. The opprobrium may well be what Greece deserved. The "shock" (especially expressed by EU officials) was not due to the economic significance of the situation but rather to the fact that a Greek government had lied to its euro area partners [*Lack of trust*, caused by *upward revision of debt*]

3) Although one can have doubts about how truly "shocking" were the revelations of the Greek authorities for the EU officials, [2] the key issue is that the systemic implications of the revelations were ignored – the fears of contagion were underplayed and the prevailing feeling was that the correct way to deal with the situation was to let Greece "swing in the wind". [*Collapse of confidence*, caused by *slow EMU response*]

4) Nevertheless, we argue that, beyond the imprudence displayed by successive Greek governments, the EMU and the attendant Stability and Growth Pact (SGP) were imprudently designed in being based on the supposition that the main threat to the EMU

is irresponsible behavior by member state governments only; the consequences of private excessive borrowing and lending, and accompanying moral hazard and deficient corporate governance, were ignored. [*Poor governance*, caused by *non-enforcement of EMU treaties*]

5) In contrast to the output-driven, "hard-conditionality" of the pre-accession period, the EMU period was characterized by the "soft-conditionality" of the SGP, which allowed Greece (even more than other governments) to breach both the letter and the spirit of the Pact (von Hagen, 2005). In fact, as shown in Figure 1, for all 9 years between 2000 and 2008 Greece violated in every year the 3% limit on budget deficits [*High debt*, caused by *non-enforcement of EMU treaties*]

6) (The decline in debt interest payments after EMU was considered by the Greek governments as a permanent windfall – due to their thinking that there is an implicit guarantee of a no-strings-attached bailout by the rest of euro area in case of a problem – a miscalculation that most Greeks have come to regret.) [*Poor governance*, caused by *access to cheap debt*]

7) The unwillingness of Greek policymakers to undertake expenditure cuts reflects the lower political cost of raising tax revenue compared to expenditure cuts. This has occurred for various reasons. First, the increase in revenue was mainly achieved through increases in indirect taxation, which is less 'visible' to voters compared to direct taxation and so is a source of fiscal illusion. Second, although the cost of an increase in taxation is spread among voters/consumers, the political cost of expenditure cuts mainly affects the constituency of the party in power, since a large proportion of government expenditure is targeted towards specific interest groups (e.g., public employment). [*High debt*, caused by *political opposition to reform* and *strong PS unions*]

8) Third, given that in Greece rent seeking [6] and tax evasion are endemic, [7] the beneficiaries of these practices have used their political power to minimize the reduction in public spending (their main source of pilfering) and to shift the burden of budget consolidation to increases in taxation (that they are adept at avoiding or evading). [*High debt*, caused by *destructive institutions*, *poor revenue collection* and *corruption*]

9) But why did the restoration of democracy in 1974 fail to reduce the outright corruption, nepotism and tax evasion that have characterized modern Greece? [*Poor revenue collection*, caused by *destructive institutions* and *corruption*]

10) The capture of the public administration by the political parties was cemented by the fragmentation of the unions representing public-sector workers along party-political lines, and by their overwhelming influence on personnel choice and promotion to potentially lucrative posts. [*Poor governance*, caused by *destructive institutions* and *strong PS unions*]

11) First, Greece's large fiscal deficits until 2008 were not incurred for economically sound reasons; they were neither a deliberate macroeconomic response to the dangers of serious recession nor were they associated with an increase in the quality of publicly

provided goods and services. Rather, the budget deficits of the previous decade must be seen as reflecting either lack of ability (or complicity) among governments to stem the predatory behavior of powerful elites to raid the state coffers [*High debt*, caused by *poor governance*]

12) Third, only if citizens receive the expected quality of services from the public sector – and thus do not have to source some of these services at a fee from the private sector – may it be possible to adjust wages by the amount required to address the loss in competitiveness and the extremely large current account deficits that Greece has been running for many years. In this respect, the rise in unit labour costs in Greece relative to the other eurozone countries may appear to reflect an inherent inability of the Greek trade union movement to accept real wage increases for private-sector workers in line with productivity developments. [*Poor revenue collection*, caused by *poor governance*] ALSO [*Lack of competitiveness*, caused by *high wages*, *low productivity* and *strong PS unions*]

13) Fourth, the large increase in taxation (since 1975, tax revenue have increased from about 25% to about 40% of GDP) without an equivalent increase in the provision of public services has discouraged tax compliance. [*Poor revenue collection*, caused by *poor governance*]

14) Increases in public employment and tax rates, without attendant increases in publicly provided goods and in tax revenue, along with the shouldering of the financial obligations of inefficient private-sector firms, led to both public debt accumulation and increased wage demands by private-sector workers and a weakening of private-sector performance and employment opportunities, which in turn induced the "nanny" state to intervene (as an employer and lender of last resort) in order to alleviate what it was co-responsible for creating in the first place, thus leading to further debt accumulation and providing new impetus to the vicious circle. [*High debt*, caused by *lack of competitiveness*, *poor governance*, *poor revenue collection* and *large welfare state*]

15) The Greek crisis, mainly government-induced, provides prima facie evidence in favor of the SGP's focus on government balances. Nevertheless, the Greek case also highlights that the interdependence between government and current account imbalances can create a semblance of fiscal prudence when none exists; [*Collapse of confidence*, caused by *high debt* and *current account deficit*]

## Fundamentally Wrong: Market Pricing of Sovereigns and the Greek Financial Crisis (Gibson, Hall and Tavlas, 2014)

1) In the run-up to Greece's entry into the euro area in 2001, the 2-year spread between Greek and German sovereigns fell precipitously, from about 500 basis points in

the late 1990s to about 40 basis points at the time when Greece became a member of the single-currency area on January 1, 2001; during that period, the spread on 10-year sovereigns fell from about 600 basis points to about 50 basis points. Over the following years, both the 2-year and 10-year spreads stabilized within a fairly narrow range of 10–50 basis points until the end of 2008, despite Greece's large and growing fiscal and external deficits (as we explain below). [*Access to cheap debt*, caused by *EMU membership*]

2) Then, in October of 2009, a newly-elected Greek government stunned the markets with news that the fiscal deficit for 2009 would likely turn out to be more than twice the outgoing government's projection of 6% of GDP. [*Collapse of confidence*, caused by *upward revision of debt*]

3) That news set-off a relentless upward rise of spreads and a succession of ratings' downgrades of Greek sovereigns and Greek banks (which held large portfolios of sovereigns), resulting in what appeared to be self-reinforcing feedback loops between ratings and spreads. The increases in spreads contributed to a sharp contraction of real output, which had a negative impact on the debt-dynamics, a process which itself contributed to rating downgrades, further rises in spreads, and, ultimately, an increase in political uncertainty [*Collapse of confidence*, caused by *downgrades*] ALSO [*Political instability*, caused by *collapse in confidence*]

4) Relative prices. With Greece's nominal exchange rate fixed against those of the other euro-area countries, we use the Greek consumer price level relative to that of Germany as a measure of the change in competitiveness. The top part of Figure 4 displays this variable. As shown in the figure, Greece's competitiveness deteriorated markedly throughout the sample period. [*Lack of competitiveness*, caused by *monetary dependence*]

5) Fiscal news. Since Greece's entry to the euro area in 2001, Greek fiscal data have been subjected to a number of revisions, sometimes several years after the initial (real-time) release of the data. These revisions have often involved upward revisions of the fiscal imbalances, generating negative surprises. In order to capture the news (or surprise) element that has figured prominently in the Greek experience, we construct real-time fiscal data. [*Lack of trust*, caused by *poor stats*]

6) For the 10-year spread equation, seven variables are correctly signed and significant – the debt-to-GDP ratio, fiscal news, real growth, oil prices, political uncertainty, the SMP program, and the residuals of an equation in which the economic fundamentals are used to determine ratings (see Appendix A) [9] T [Collapse of confidence, caused by high debt, upward revision of debt, political instability and downgrades]

7) First, to the extent that ratings were determined by the existing fundamentals – and not the expected future fundamentals – ratings downgrades appear to have played a very

important effect on spreads, over-and-above the impact of the economic fundamentals. [*Collapse of confidence*, caused by *downgrades*]

8) First, the time-varying results indicate that the coefficients on most, if not all, of the variables were near zero until 2008–2009. Attention to the deteriorating Greek economic fundamentals in pricing spreads. [*Access to cheap debt*, caused by *EMU*]

9) Second, sovereign downgrades and political uncertainly appear to have been drivers of the sharp rises in Greek sovereign spreads from 2008 to 2009 onwards, over-and-above the impact of the economic fundamentals. [*Collapse of confidence*, caused by *high debt*, *current account deficit*, *downgrades* and *political instability*]

10) Fourth, our time-varying results provide support for the view that once markets reassessed their pricing of Greek credit risk, the change in the influence of the fundamentals came swiftly and abruptly, exhibiting overshooting characteristics, thus suggesting that market psychology played an independent role in the pricing of spreads. [*Collapse of confidence*, caused by *high debt* and *current account deficits*]

## HOW THE EURO CRISIS EVOLVED AND HOW TO AVOID ANOTHER: EMU, FISCAL POLICY AND CREDIT RATINGS (POLITO AND WICKENS, 2014)

1) The contention of this paper is that the euro crisis originated in the introduction of a single currency which set a common monetary policy for countries with different initial inflation rates. [*Crisis*, caused by *EMU membership*]

2) The expectation was that inflation rates would converge making a single monetary policy for all countries viable. The outcome, however, was that countries with the highest inflation rates – which were also the crisis countries – had too low official interest rates, negative real rates, rapid output expansion which fuelled continuing higher inflation, and caused a loss of competitiveness compared with low inflation euro countries. Depending on the crisis country, the negative real interest rates and strong economic activity encouraged excessive private or public borrowing which led to banking and debt crises. [*Lack of competitiveness*, caused by *Capital influx* and *monetary dependence*]

3) Is striking that, following the introduction of the single currency, governments were able to borrow at the same short interest rate. As previously noted, this resulted in negative real interest rates for high inflation countries. Even the private sector was able to borrow at negative real rates in most of the crisis countries. [*Access to cheap debt*, caused by *EMU*]

4) It is widely accepted that the euro zone was not an optimal currency area prior to its inception. Of particular significance was the difference in member-countries inflation rates. It was thought that these would converge over time but having a single monetary

policy based, in effect, on low German inflation rates prevented this. The consequence was that countries with the highest inflation rates – what turned out in 2008 to be the crisis countries: Greece, Ireland, Italy, Portugal and Spain – suddenly had negative real interest rates. As a result, borrowing increased dramatically. [*High debt*, caused by *access to cheap debt*] ALSO [*Excessive private credit extension*, caused by *Capital influx*]

5) In the case of Greece and Italy this was public borrowing; [*Current account deficit*, caused by *high debt*]

6) The upshot was that economic activity in the crisis countries was strongly stimulated, inflationary pressures mounted instead of lessened and competitiveness was lost. [*Lack of competitiveness*, caused by *EMU entry*]

7) Again, as predicted, in Greece prices increased by 38% and output by 47%, the corresponding numbers for Ireland are 41% and 63%, and for Spain are 44% and 41% while those for Germany are 9% and 16%. Thus, comparing the price levels, Greece lost 29% of its competitiveness against Germany, Ireland 32% and Spain 35%. Not surprisingly these countries experienced growing current account deficits. [*Current account deficit*, caused by *lack of competitiveness*]

8) Taken together this evidence provides strong support for the argument that EMU, with its one-size-fits-all monetary policy, is likely to have been a major contributor to the crisis due to causing in the crisis countries low real interest rates which encouraged borrowing and led to strong but unsustainable economic growth, a failure of inflation rates to converge, a loss of competitiveness and current account deficits. [*Crisis*, caused by *EMU membership*]

9) The fiscal stance of EU countries plus the US is shown in Figure 6 which reports government expenditures, revenues and debt 1999–2012. It is clear that there was a deterioration in the fiscal stance of most countries from 2008. This was largely due to rising expenditures as a proportion of GDP, while tax revenues, although falling in absolute terms, were fairly constant as a proportion of GDP. [*High debt*, caused by *poor governance*]

10) All countries show a decline in the ability of governments to meet their debt obligations following the crisis in 2008, reflecting the loss of output mentioned above. Of the crisis countries, Greece, Ireland and Spain show the greatest fiscal deterioration. Prior to the crisis Italy, Ireland, Portugal and Spain had viable fiscal stances, but Greece did not. [*High debt*, caused by *financial crisis*]

11) As noted, prior to EMU most of the crisis countries faced much higher borrowing costs than they did afterwards as governments could borrow close to the official ECB interest rate before 2008 and private sector interest rates were similarly low. In principle, there is no reason why markets should not adjust rates to reflect the risk of default. After the crisis this is precisely what they did, but they failed to do so before the crisis. [*Access to cheap debt*, caused by *financial crisis*]

## THE PARLIAMENTARY ELECTION IN GREECE, OCTOBER 2009 (KOVRAS, 2010)

1) However, ND's meagre parliamentary majority, coupled with public dissatisfaction with the government – for various reasons, notably a string of corruption scandals and its perceived inadequate response to the calamitous forest fires around Athens during the summer of 2009 – significantly decreased the ''moral support'' available to the administration in its push for economic reforms. [*Lack of trust*, caused by *corruption*]

2) The need for such reform, in particular to narrow the fiscal deficits which had caused an enormous increase in the level of public debt, was even more pressing given that the global financial crisis, and its knock-on impact on the real economy, had further worsened the country's public finances. [*High debt*, caused by *financial crisis*]

3) The campaigns of both parties revolved primarily around the economy and institutional reforms. In line with the official justification of the early elections, ND's campaign focused on the critical decisions facing the country and on the painful measures that the new government should take over the next two years in order to revitalize the Greek economy. The phrase 'responsible and painful decisions' was repeated by Karamanlis, ND's leader, in every single campaign speech. [*Failed austerity*, caused by *political opposition to reform*]

4) Papandreou promised to revive the stricken economy with a V3bn stimulus, to raise education expenditure to 5% of GDP, and – in perhaps the most ambitious pledge – to hunt down the tax evaders that were claimed to be costing the Greek economy approximately V20bn (Stevis, 2009). [*High debt*, caused by *poor revenue collection* and *corruption*]

5) The other major point of contention was the need for extensive political reforms, a need inferred not only from the recent experience of scandals and corruption but also from wider problems as diverse as the wildfires that destroyed the area around Athens and the unprecedented youth riots in the capital and other major cities in December 2008. [*Corruption*, caused by *destructive institutions*]

6) While the global economic crisis triggered electoral collapse for several European social democratic parties in the EU, PASOK bucked the trend with a landslide win. Although the outcome was not surprising, the margin of victory – more than ten percentage points between the two leading parties – exceeded most expectations. With 43.9% of the vote, PASOK took 160 seats and thus a fairly comfortable majority, while the ND's 33.5% meant a meagre harvest of just 91 seats – compared to 152 in the previous election – and hence defeat on an unprecedented scale. [*Failed austerity*, caused by *political opposition to reform*]

7) The comfortable majority won by PASOK, in combination with the fact that its main opponent spent the election campaign pointing to the necessity of painful measures, legitimizes the new government to push for much-needed economic and institutional reforms. Provided that PASOK can maintain its lead over ND, the new electoral rules will give it a significant benefit because the next election will see the first party receiving a larger premium of 50 seats. Moreover, since the governing party has control over the timing of the elections – and early calls for elections are a tradition in Greek political culture – PASOK seems highly likely to be able to realise this advantage. [*Lack of competitiveness*, caused by *destructive institutions*]

8) Meanwhile, on the domestic front, PASOK has to govern the same distrustful and weathered society that punished Karamanlis's inability to deliver. In essence, the new Prime Minister has to face the two major problems that beset his predecessor: a large and inefficient state, heavily penetrated by partisanship and clientelism, and a significant section of support that is highly resistant to reforms. [*High debt*, caused by *large public sector*, *corruption* and *political opposition to reform*] ALSO [*Political Opposition to Reform*, caused by *corruption*, *lack of trust* and *institutions*]

## News Spillovers from the Greek Debt Crisis: Impact on the Eurozone Financial Sector (Bhanot, Burns, Hunter and Williams, 2014)

1) The crisis started when the Greek government announced that its debt service relative to receipts was much larger than previously acknowledged. Eurozone policymakers and multilateral organizations raised concerns that the Greek debt crisis could spread and impact Portugal, Italy, and Spain—countries viewed by many to have similar underlying weaknesses as Greece [*Collapse of confidence*, caused by *upward revision of Greek Debt*]

2) The crisis also caught the attention of the rating agencies who responded by adjusting their credit ratings for Greece and other countries, while multilateral organizations, such as the International Monetary Fund (IMF), urged Eurozone member nations to take collective action. [*Downgrades*, caused by *collapse of confidence*]

3) Second, investors possibly use the news to infer higher default probabilities of their own sovereign bonds as well as sovereign bonds in other Eurozone countries with high debt to-GDP ratios. [*Collapse of confidence*, caused by *high debt*]

4) A key implication of the above is that a bailout might be able to contain the risk of spillover from Greece via the banking sector, and to quarantine Greece from its impact on other Eurozone countries. [*Bank undercapitalisation*, caused by *collapse of confidence*]

5) We begin with an examination of the contemporaneous correlation between changes in Greek sovereign bond yield spreads and the abnormal returns on financial stocks in the Eurozone crisis countries, Greece, Italy, Portugal, and Spain, to determine if they are different in the pre-crisis and crisis periods. This provides preliminary evidence on the change in the relationship between Greek yield spreads and the abnormal returns during the crisis. [*Bank undercapitalisation*, caused by *collapse in confidence*]

## SHOULD GREECE ADOPT A DUAL-CURRENCY REGIME TO RESOLVE ITS ECONOMIC CRISIS? (KASIMATI AND VERAROS, 2013)

1) Concerns have been expressed about the ultimate ability of the country to avoid bankruptcy, or even more the viability of remaining within the eurozone given the serious deficit in the international competitiveness that has accumulated over time. [*Fears of EMU exit*, caused by *high debt* and *lack of competitiveness*]

2) A discussion has been initiated within both academic and political circles on the alternative approach of temporarily adopting a dual-currency regime, in order to restore international competitiveness and fiscal balances before being able to rejoin the eurozone at a later stage. [*Lack of competitiveness*, caused by *monetary dependence*]

3) Goodhart and Tsomocos (2010) together with Arghyrou and Tsoukalas (2010) are the two most prominent academic proposals for reintroducing a local currency for the period necessary to restore the country's international competitiveness, presumably through the gradual devaluation of the local currency as opposed to the euro. [*Lack of competitiveness*, caused by *monetary dependence*]

4) Goodhart and Tsomocos (2010), suggested that Greece and Portugal could re-introduce their own local currencies to be administered by their own central banks independently. Public debt would remain in euro, whereas the residents, although receiving their wages in the local currently, would still have to pay their taxes in euro. All external monetary transactions would remain unchanged and denominated in euro. All internal price/wage relativities, tax rates etc. would also remain unchanged. The local currency would be inconvertible and non-residents would not be allowed to borrow it. [*Lack of competitiveness*, caused by *monetary dependence*]

5) The result of Greece's accession to the EMU in January 2001 was a rapid deterioration in both its fiscal and current account deficits (Figure 1). The efforts by the Greek governments to curb government spending were abandoned sharply after the country succeeded in earning its place in the EMU. [*High debt*, caused by *EMU membership*]

6) The long nurtured anomalies of the Greek economic and political life exacerbated phenomena like tax evasion and corruption, and deteriorated the efficiency in producing public goods (Katsimi & Moutos, 2010). Sharing the common currency brought the benefit of increased mobility of international capital and reduced interest cost. However, at the same time, it annulled any ability of the country to restore its international competitiveness through currency devaluations. [*Poor governance*, caused by *access to cheap debt*, *corruption* and *poor revenue collection*]

7) Mounting losses in competitiveness were reflected in the significant appreciation of the real effective exchange rate and the purchasing power parity of Greece (Moschovis & Servera, 2009). The assumptions that the process of nominal convergence instigated by the treaty of Maastricht in the 1990s would lead to a convergence in productivity growth among EU members was proven fatally wrong for the Southern European countries, exactly the way Tsionas (1999) had predicted in his early paper. [*Lack of competitiveness*, caused by *regulatory burden*, *monetary dependence* and *low productivity*]

8) As a consequence, domestic savings in Greece failed to finance more than half of domestic investments throughout the period of EMU participation (Kasimati, 2011a). Increased international capital mobility allowed the domestic investment—saving gap to be financed via foreign savings (Christopoulos, 2007). Current account deficits never de-escalated, thus being the main contributor into bringing the country's net foreign debt from 3% of GDP in 1997 to 86% in 2009 (IMF, 2010b). [*Current account deficit*, caused by *Capital influx*]

## THE CAUSAL RELATIONSHIP BETWEEN DEBT AND GROWTH IN EMU COUNTRIES (GOMEZ-PUIG AND SOSVILLA-REVERO, 2015)

1) Shambaugh (2012) pointed out that the European Economic and Monetary Union (EMU) countries have faced three interlocking crises (banking, sovereign debt, and economic growth) which together challenged the viability of the currency union. [*Collapse of confidence*, caused by *bank undercapitalisation*, *high debt* and *lack of competitiveness*]

2) According to this line of thought, these crises connected with one another in several ways: the problems of weak banks and high sovereign debt were mutually reinforcing, and both were exacerbated by weak, constrained growth. [*High debt*, caused by *bank undercapitalisation*] ALSO [Bank undercapitalisation, caused by collapse in confidence]

3) In this regard, since low growth means lower government revenue, governments may be forced to increase their debt levels to maintain the welfare state, to stimulate short-term demand and to raise long-term growth (Feldstein, 2014). [*High debt*, caused by *financial crisis* and *lack of competitiveness*]

4) In turn, as economic growth decreases, since government revenues also decline, governments are forced to increase their debt levels in order to maintain the welfare state (the economy's "automatic stabilizers" may start to work, meaning an increase in public expenditure in social security transfers, for instance). [*High debt*, caused by *lack of competitiveness* and *welfare state*]

5) In contrast to Ireland and Spain, the origin of the debt crisis in Greece, Portugal and Italy was the structural deficit in the government sector. However, while Greek and Italian large fiscal deficit and huge public debt are the cumulative result of chronic macroeconomic imbalances, the case of Portugal illustrates the importance of external debt (specifically, that of its private sector: banks and enterprises). [*Collapse of confidence*, caused by *high debt*]

## THE EMU EFFECTS OF ASSET MARKET HOLDINGS AND THE RECENT FINANCIAL CRISIS (PALAIODIMOS AND TZAVALIS, 2015)

1) The establishment of the European Monetary Union (EMU) in the nineties and the introduction of euro in year 1999 in scriptural form (in year 2002 in fiduciary form) as a common currency has been among the most influential developments on the integration of the European financial markets. It has opened up possibilities for fully integrated financial markets of the same scale as those of the US. Financial integration is an essential precondition for a deeper and truly single European economy. [*Capital influx*, caused by *EMU membership*]

2) Competition intensification in the financial sector across the EMU member states, elimination of currency related investment constraints and reduction of costs for investors (i.e., pension, government and corporate debt, and mutual funds) and, finally, convergence of interest rates, equity returns, bond yields and inflation rates across the EMU countries. [*Access to cheap debt*, caused by *EMU*] ALSO [*Capital influx*, caused by *EMU*]

3) On the other hand, over the last decade, the global financial crisis and the subsequent governments' bail outs to restore financial market confidence reversed the previous decade financial market liberalization and integration effects, by creating concerns on the existing global financial architecture (see, e.g., Wolf (2009)). [*High debt*, caused by *financial crisis*]

4) First, they support that the establishment of EMU and the introduction of euro have indeed had important effects on the integration of financial markets, especially on the EMU bond markets. [*Capital influx*, caused by *EMU*]

5) Second, apart from the EMU integration effects, the paper shows that gravity-type of variables such as the size of markets, the capital market transparency, depth, and trade have affected positively bilateral bond and/or equity holdings between countries, since year 2001. Third, the integration effects of euro on the EMU financial markets, especially bond markets have considerably decelerated after the recent financial crisis. [*Collapse of confidence*, caused by *financial crisis*]

6) The EMU asset holdings by the non-EMU investors were reduced, especially the bond holdings. After year 2007, investors seem to consider typical gravity variables as less important when choosing their equity and bond holdings. Between the two groups of the EMU countries considered, our results indicate the strongest disintegration effects of the financial crisis on the bond markets were observed for the peripheral countries of the EMU. These effects became evident before the start of the European debt crisis in early 2010.

The paper [*Collapse of confidence*, caused by *financial crisis*]

## The Impact of EU/ECB/IMF Bailout Programs on the Financial and Real Sectors of ASE during the Greek Sovereign Crisis (Kosmidou, Kousendris and Negakis, 2015)

1) The sovereign debt crisis, which began in Greece, has been the first major test for the euro area (EA). The crisis is still unfolding, but it has already revealed that Greece is not the only country in the EA with an unsustainable fiscal position. [*Collapse of confidence*, caused by *high debt*]

2) The beginning of the crisis in Greece coincided with the election of the socialist government in October 2009. A few days after the new Minister of Finance took office, he announced a substantial revision of the previous government's projection for the value of Greece's budget deficit to ECOFIN, from 6% to 12.7% of GDP. Notably, this figure was four times higher than that permitted for EA countries. Moreover, given a 115% debt-to-GDP ratio and practically negligible growth potential, this announcement led market participants to wonder about the long-term sustainability of Greece's fiscal position. [*Collapse of confidence*, caused by *high debt* and *upward revision of Greek debt*]

3) This market nervousness reached a peak on December 8, 2009 when Fitch cut its rating on the Greek debt to BBB+. This was the first time in 10 years that a rating agency had rated Greek debt below A grade. [*Collapse of confidence*, caused by *downgrades*]

4) However, the first significant jump in the spreads occurred on January 8, 2010 when the European Commission condemned Greece for falsifying its public finance data. On that day, the spread rose by 170 bps and reached nearly 400 bps. [*Collapse of confidence*, caused by *poor stats*]

5) The response of the Greek Government was inadequate. First, in an attempt to reduce the fiscal deficit, it announced and implemented a number of austerity measures. However, these measures were insufficient to address the soaring budget deficit and to restore confidence to the markets. Moreover, with limited access to the financial markets, these measures simply accelerated the unfolding recession. [*Failed austerity*, caused by *poor governance* and *high debt*]

6) Moreover, the markets did not respond positively to the Greek bailout. In the next few months, all leading rating agencies downgraded the Greek government debt to junk status on the grounds of likely Greek default. Moreover, before the end of the year, the Greek public finance data showed a failure to meet the 2010 targets and signaled that the recession would be even more severe than originally anticipated. [*Failed austerity*, caused by *Collapse of confidence*]

7) To tame public unrest, the Greek Prime Minister announced a referendum on the bailout plan. However, EU leaders forced him to retract his announcement by threatening to withhold an allotment of 6 billion euros that Greece urgently needed by mid-December. [*Political instability*, caused by *failed austerity*]

8) However, market analysts did not share this enthusiasm about the effectiveness of the debt rescue plan. Indeed, the write-off of Greek debt was expected to only slightly improve the debt-to-GDP ratio for 2012 from a previous forecast of 198% to a new forecast of 160.5%. One reason for this mediocre improvement was that the restructured debt represented a small fraction of the Greek government's total debt. [*Failed austerity*, caused by *high debt*]

9) This negative attitude of international markets towards the debt rescue deal along with the failure of the major political parties to form a new coalition government after the May elections led to strong speculation that Greece would have to exit the Eurozone. [*EMU Exit*, caused by *collapse of confidence* and *political instability*]

10) The potential exit (broadly referred to as Grexit) deteriorated the behavior of domestic and international investors and resulted in a dramatic decrease in deposits into Greek banks. [*Bank undercapitalisation*, caused by *EMU exit*] ALSO [*Collapse in confidence*, caused by *EMU exit*]

11) The Troika decided to evaluate this request in light of an updated analysis of the sustainability of the Greek economy. This analysis showed that the bailout program was largely off track. [*Failed austerity*, caused by *poor governance*]

12) This period featured great economic and political instability, which was interpreted in the markets as giving rise to various types of risk. For example, in many cases the Greek Government was afraid to take on the political cost of unpopular austerity measures, leading it to display reluctance to fully comply with the directions of the troika therefore allowing for speculation that Greece was not committed to EA membership. [*EMU exit*, caused by *political instability*, *political opposition to reform* and *poor governance*]

13) Kutan et al., (2012) indicate that the public unrest caused by IMF-induced austerity measures could be relevant to value, while Hui and Chung (2011) suggest that the political instability of a country is closely related to its credit risk. [*Collapse of confidence*, caused by *political instability*]

14) Another interesting result is that type 3 events (public reaction) are found to have a significant negative effect (at the 5% level) on the HML slope dummy. It thus appears that high book-to-market (value) banking sector stocks are significantly affected by the reaction of the public to the application of austerity measures [*Collapse of confidence*, caused by *political instability*]

15) On the other hand, when government actions demonstrated reluctance to undertake the necessary reforms, the banking sector suffered significant losses. [*Bank undercapitalisation*, caused by *collapse of confidence*]

## 'DEBT CRISIS: THE PRICE OF CHEAP LOANS' (CREIGHTON, 2011)

1) The most remarkable aspect of the Greek debt saga is how a country so demonstrably profligate was able to borrow so much. [*High debt*, caused by *poor governance*]

2) The Hellenic Republic entered the twenty-first century in characteristic style: its net debt equalled 90% of GDP, the third highest level in the 30-country OECD. It had been consistently running large budget deficits from the mid-1990s. Between 1995 and 2008, the government's annual budget deficits exceeded 4% of GDP 10 times, including 7.4% in 2004 (the year Athens hosted the Olympic Games) and were at least 6% every year since 2006, [*High debt*, caused by *poor governance*]

3) And the country's labour productivity, hobbled by a bloated public sector, continues to decline, [*Low productivity*, caused by *large public sector*]

4) Greece's patchy fiscal record did not prevent its admission into the Eurozone, but it might have hampered its borrowing spree if lenders charged higher interest rates to lend to Greece, Creditors had ample reason to be cautious, as discussed. Yet Greek borrowing

costs fell substantially once it entered the European monetary union, [*Access to cheap debt*, caused by *EMU membership*]

5) Greece's fiscal excesses and ongoing contravention of the European Growth and Stability Pact did not appear to affect its perceived creditworthiness, [*High debt*, caused by *non-enforcement of EU treaties* and *access to cheap debt*]

6) Before the financial crisis prompted a re-evaluation of the riskiness of Greek debt in late 2008, the Greek government had been able to borrow at about 4%, the same rate as Germany, widely considered Europe's most creditworthy government,' Before entering the Eurozone, Greece paid around two percentage points more on its loans, which constrained borrowing. [*Access to cheap debt*, cause by *EMU membership*]

7) To the extent that suppression of independent Greek monetary policy reduced the likelihood of a Greek sovereign default, Greek borrowing costs should have fallen. [*Access to cheap debt*, caused by *monetary dependence*]

8) Global underpricing of risk, endemic throughout financial markets prior to the global financial crisis of 2008, facilitated Greece's borrowing. [*High debt*, caused by *access to cheap debt*]

## Rebalancing the Euro Area: The Costs of Internal Devaluation (Stockhammer and Sotiropoulos, 2014)

1) The Euro area is suffering from substantial internal trade imbalances [1]. These are widely recognized as important contributing factors to the crisis of the Euro system because persistent current account deficits come with increasing external liabilities. [*High debt*, caused by *current account deficit*]

2) The present economic policy regime essentially aims at rebalancing the Euro area by means of internal devaluation and/or by fiscal contraction in the deficit countries; in short, there would be a deflationary adjustment. [*Internal devaluation*, caused by *lack of competitiveness*]

3) The paper aims at estimating the costs of rebalancing via internal devaluation. This strategy tries to achieve the necessary adjustment via reduction of unit labour costs in the deficit countries. [*Lack of competitiveness*, caused by *high wages*]

4) We calculate how much output loss is necessary in order to eliminate the current account deficit for the GIIPS countries (Greece, Ireland, Italy, Portugal and Spain). [*Internal devaluation*, caused by *current account deficit*]

5) In one group of countries, growth was associated with increasing debt; this regime usually came with asset and/or property price bubbles. Typically these countries had

current account deficits and capital inflows. [*High debt*, caused by *Capital influx* and *current account deficit*]

6) Debt-led growth was made possible to a significant extent through European financial integration. The EU's policy (the Financial Services Action Plan) aimed at creating a single financial market for Europe (Grahl, 2009). In theory this means uniform interest rates across the Euro area; in practice it has translated into massive capital flows from Germany, France and the UK to the fast growing Southern European countries. [*High debt*, caused by *access to cheap debt* and *Capital influx*]

7) Given that Greece, Ireland, Portugal, Spain and Italy in 2007 had an average current account deficit of 8.4% of GDP, what is the GDP cost (on average) of eliminating this? Our estimates are 47.2% and 47.0% respectively, based on the results for the 1999–2011 and the 1990–2011 samples. [*Internal devaluation*, caused by *current account deficit*]

# APPENDIX 4.
# TABULATION OF CAUSAL CONCEPTS USED FOR CONCEPTUAL MAPPING

This appendix will follow the same structure as the analysis section and will therefore provide supporting evidence for each of the conceptual maps in step-wise manner.

## 4.1. POLITICAL SCIENCE

For each of tables below, the causal concepts for each of the most prevalent primary concepts identified in the political science is summarised.

| High Debt Causal Concepts | Count |
|---|---|
| Poor Governance | 20 |
| Corruption | 15 |
| Large Welfare State | 15 |
| Destructive Institutions | 12 |
| Large Public Sector | 10 |
| Financial Crisis | 9 |
| Political Opposition to Reform | 8 |
| Poor Revenue Collection | 7 |
| Access to Cheap Debt | 5 |
| Military Spending | 4 |
| Failed Austerity | 4 |
| Lack of Competitiveness | 3 |
| Current Account Deficit | 3 |
| Ageing Population | 3 |
| EMU Membership | 2 |
| Strong Public Sector Unions | 2 |
| Poor Statistican Services | 2 |
| Non-enforcement of EU treaties | 1 |
| Monetary Dependence | 1 |
| Regulatory Burden | 1 |
| Capitalism | 1 |

| Lack of Competitiveness Causal Concepts | Count |
|---|---|
| Regulatory Burden | 10 |
| Poor Governance | 9 |
| Destructive Institutions | 9 |
| EMU Membership | 8 |
| Large Public Sector | 7 |
| Political Opposition to Reform | 6 |
| Corruption | 6 |
| High Wages | 6 |
| Low Productivity | 6 |
| Large Welfare State | 3 |
| Strong Public Sector Unions | 3 |
| Capitalism | 3 |
| High Debt | 2 |
| Monetary Dependence | 2 |
| Access to Cheap Debt | 1 |
| Capital Influx | 1 |
| Political Instability | 1 |

| Political Opposition to Reform Causal Concepts | Count |
|---|---|
| Strong Public Sector Unions | 10 |
| Destructive Institutions | 8 |
| Internal Devaluation | 8 |
| Corruption | 7 |
| Poor Governance | 6 |
| Lack of Trust | 5 |
| EMU Membership | 2 |
| Capitalism | 2 |
| High Debt | 1 |
| Large Public Sector Unions | 1 |
| Large Welfare State | 1 |
| Capital Influx | 1 |

| Political Instability Causal Concepts | Count |
|---|---|
| Political Opposition to Reform | 13 |
| Lack of Trust | 2 |
| Collapse in Confidence | 1 |
| Failed Austerity | 1 |
| Corruption | 1 |
| Destructive Institutions | 1 |
| Internal Devaluation | 1 |

| Collapse in Confidence Causal Concepts | Count |
|---|---|
| High Debt | 5 |
| Financial Crisis | 5 |
| Political Instability | 5 |
| Fear of Possible EMU Exit | 4 |
| Upward Revision of Debt | 3 |
| Political Opposition to Reform | 3 |
| Downgrades | 3 |
| Monetary Dependence | 2 |
| Governance | 2 |
| Destructive Institutions | 2 |
| Failed Austerity | 2 |
| Lack of Competitiveness | 1 |
| EMU Membership | 1 |

| Poor Governance Causal Concepts | Count |
|---|---|
| Corruption | 5 |
| Destructive Institutions | 5 |
| Access to Cheap Debt | 2 |
| Poor Revenue Collection | 2 |
| Political Opposition to Reform | 2 |
| Poor Statistical Services | 1 |
| Large Welfare State | 1 |
| Monetary Dependence | 1 |
| Non-enforcement of EU treaties | 1 |

| Failed Austerity Causal Concepts | Count |
|---|---|
| Political Opposition to Reform | 9 |
| Political Instability | 2 |
| Destructive Institutions | 1 |
| Corruption | 1 |
| Capitalism | 1 |
| Poor Governance | 1 |
| Large Public Sector | 1 |

| Corruption Causal Concepts | Count |
|---|---|
| Destructive Institutions | 7 |
| Poor Governance | 2 |
| Large Welfare State | 2 |
| Political Opposition to Reform | 1 |

| Large Welfare State Causal Concepts | Count |
|---|---|
| Political Opposition to Reform | 6 |
| Poor Governance | 1 |
| Ageing Population | 1 |

| Fear of EMU Exit Causal Concepts | Count |
|---|---|
| Political Opposition to Reform | 4 |
| Political Instability | 3 |
| Internal Devaluation | 2 |
| Lack of Competitiveness | 1 |
| High Debt | 1 |

| Internal Devaluation Causal Concepts | Count |
|---|---|
| Monetary Dependence | 5 |
| Lack of Competitiveness | 3 |
| High Debt | 2 |
| Financial Crisis | 1 |
| Capitalism | 1 |
| Excessive Private Credit Extension | 1 |

## 4.2. Public Administration

The breakdown of causal concepts per primary concept follows below for the public administration literature:

| High Debt Causal Concepts | Count |
|---|---|
| Poor Governance | 19 |
| Poor Revenue Collection | 19 |
| Non-enforcement of EU treaties | 18 |
| Large Welfare State | 18 |
| Large Public Sector | 13 |
| Access to Cheap Debt | 12 |
| Financial Crisis | 9 |
| Political Opposition to Reform | 7 |
| EMU Membership | 6 |
| Corruption | 6 |
| Poor Statistical Services | 6 |
| Lack of Competitiveness | 4 |
| Regulatory Burden | 3 |
| Destructive Institutions | 3 |
| Failed Austerity Measures | 2 |
| Bank Undercapitalisation | 2 |
| Current Account Deficit | 1 |
| Strong Public Sector Unions | 1 |
| Large Informal Sector | 1 |
| Capital Influx | 1 |
| Pro-Cyclical Fiscal Policy | 1 |

| Lack of Competitiveness Causal Concepts | Count |
|---|---|
| Regulatory Burden | 18 |
| High Wages | 12 |
| Large Welfare State | 8 |
| Monetary Dependence | 7 |
| EMU Membership | 7 |
| Large Public Sector | 6 |
| Low Productivity | 6 |
| Political Opposition to Reform | 5 |
| Poor Revenue Collection | 3 |
| Access to Cheap Debt | 2 |
| Destructive Institutions | 2 |
| Strong Public Sector Unions | 2 |
| High Debt | 1 |
| Non-enforcement of EU treaties | 1 |
| Large Informal Sector | 1 |

| Collapse of Confidence Causal Concepts | Count |
|---|---|
| High Debt | 24 |
| Financial Crisis | 10 |
| Upward Revision of Debt | 10 |
| Slow EMU Response | 4 |
| Downgrades | 4 |
| Poor Governance | 4 |
| Current Account Deficit | 3 |
| Monetary Dependence | 3 |
| EMU Membership | 2 |
| Poor Statistical Services | 2 |
| Failed Austerity | 2 |
| Bank Undercapitalisation | 2 |
| Political Instability | 2 |
| Political Opposition to Reform | 1 |
| Access to Cheap Debt | 1 |
| Poor Revenue Collection | 1 |
| Excessive Private Credit Extension | 1 |
| Dubai World Default | 1 |
| Destructive Institutions | 1 |
| Fears of Possible EMU Exit | 1 |

| Current Account Deficit | Count |
|---|---|
| Lack of Competitiveness | 4 |
| Capital Influx | 3 |
| EMU Membership | 1 |

| Poor Revenue Collection Causal Factors | Count |
|---|---|
| Large Informal Sector | 9 |
| Destructive Institutions | 9 |
| Corruption | 8 |
| Poor Governance | 7 |
| Lack of Trust in Greek Government | 5 |
| Poor Statistical Services | 4 |
| Political Opposition to Reform | 1 |
| Failed Austerity | 1 |

| Poor Governance Causal Concepts | Count |
|---|---|
| Corruption | 5 |
| Institutions | 4 |
| Access to Cheap Debt | 2 |
| Poor Revenue Collection | 1 |
| Political Opposition to Reform | 1 |
| Non-enforcement of EU treaties | 1 |
| Strong Public Sector Unions | 1 |
| Poor Statistical Services | 1 |

| Failed Austerity Measures Causal Concepts | Count |
|---|---|
| Political Opposition to Reform | 8 |
| Lack of Competitiveness | 2 |
| Corruption | 1 |
| Slow EMU | 1 |
| Political Instability | 1 |

| Large Welfare State Causal Concepts | Count |
|---|---|
| Political Oppositon to Reform | 5 |
| Poor Governance | 4 |
| Ageing Population | 3 |
| Strong Public Sector Unions | 2 |
| Corruption | 1 |

## 4.3. Financial Economics

The tabulations of causal concepts for each of the identified prominent primary concepts in the financial economics literature follow below:

| Collapse of Confidence Causal Concepts | Count |
|---|---|
| High Debt | 38 |
| Financial Crisis | 15 |
| Downgrades | 12 |
| Upward Revision of Greek Debt | 9 |
| Current Account Deficit | 8 |
| Lack of Competitiveness | 6 |
| Monetary Dependence | 4 |
| Political Instability | 4 |
| Bank Undercapitalisation | 4 |
| Political Opposition to Reform | 3 |
| Poor Governance | 3 |
| Poor Statistical Services | 3 |
| Slow EMU Response | 3 |
| Fears of Possible EMU Exit | 3 |
| Lack of Trust in the Greek Government | 3 |
| Excessive Private Credit | 2 |
| Non-enforcement of EU treaties | 1 |
| Destructive Institutions | 1 |

| High Debt Causal Concepts | Count |
|---|---|
| Poor Governance | 9 |
| Financial Crisis | 7 |
| Access to Cheap Debt | 5 |
| Poor Revenue Collection | 4 |
| Political Opposition to Reform | 3 |
| EMU Membership | 3 |
| Large Welfare State | 3 |
| Lack of Competitiveness | 3 |
| Bank Undercapitalisation | 2 |
| Non-Enforcement of EU Treaties | 2 |
| Upward Revision of Debt | 1 |
| Large Public Sector | 1 |
| Corruption | 1 |
| Poor Statistical Services | 1 |
| Regulatory Burden | 1 |
| Failed Austerity Measures | 1 |

| Bank Undercapitalisation | Count |
|---|---|
| Collapse of Confidence | 5 |
| Financial Crisis | 2 |

| Access to Cheap Debt Causal Concepts | Count |
|---|---|
| EMU Membership | 12 |
| Monetary Dependence | 2 |
| Capitalism | 1 |

## 4.4. MONETARY ECONOMICS

The causal concepts for each of the prevalent primary concepts identified in the monetary economics literature are tabulated below:

| Collapse of Confidence Causal Concepts | Count |
|---|---|
| High Debt | 14 |
| Monetary Dependence | 13 |
| Lack of Competitiveness | 9 |
| Fears of Possible EMU Exit | 9 |
| Financial Crisis | 7 |
| Poor Governance | 4 |
| Slow EMU Response | 3 |
| Upward Revision of Debt | 3 |
| Political Opposition to Reform | 2 |
| Dubai Wolrd Default | 2 |
| Current Account Deficit | 2 |
| Non-enforcement of EU Treaties | 1 |
| EMU Membership | 1 |
| Regulatory Burden | 1 |
| Downgrades | 1 |
| Failed Austerity | 1 |
| Lack of Trust in Greek Government | 1 |
| Political Instability | 1 |

| High Debt Causal Concepts | Count |
|---|---|
| Poor Governance | 14 |
| Access to Cheap Debt | 9 |
| Non-enforcement of EU Treaties | 9 |
| Large Public Sector | 3 |
| Capital Influx | 3 |
| Destructive Institutions | 3 |
| Pro-Cyclical Fiscal Policy | 3 |
| Current Account Deficit | 2 |
| Large Welfare State | 2 |
| Monetary Dependence | 2 |
| EMU Membership | 2 |
| Political Opposition to Reform | 2 |
| Financial Crisis | 1 |
| Corruption | 1 |
| Lack of Competitiveness | 1 |

| Lack of Competitiveness Causal Concepts | Count |
|---|---|
| Monetary Dependence | 15 |
| Regulatory Burden | 8 |
| High Wages | 4 |
| Low Productivity | 3 |
| EMU Membership | 3 |
| Capital Influx | 3 |
| Political Opposition to Reform | 2 |
| Destructive Institutions | 2 |
| High Debt | 1 |
| Large Public Sector | 1 |
| Poor Governance | 1 |
| Access to Cheap Debt | 1 |
| Excessive Private Credit Extension | 1 |

| Current Account Deficit Causal Concepts | Count |
|---|---|
| Lack of Competitiveness | 5 |
| Capital Influx | 4 |
| EMU Membership | 3 |
| High Debt | 3 |
| Monetary Dependence | 1 |
| Access to Cheap Debt | 1 |
| Regulatory Burden | 1 |

| Access to Cheap Debt Causal Concepts | Count |
|---|---|
| EMU Membership | 26 |
| Monetary Dependence | 5 |
| Capital Influx | 1 |

| Internal Devaluation Causal Concepts | Count |
|---|---|
| Monetary Dependence | 5 |
| Lack of Competitiveness | 5 |
| Current Account Deficit | 2 |
| Hgh Wages | 1 |

## 4.5. ECONOMICS

The tabulations of all causal concepts for prominent primary concepts identified in the economics literature follow below:

| High Debt Causal Concepts | Count |
|---|---|
| Poor Governance | 22 |
| Access to Cheap Debt | 14 |
| Financial Crisis | 10 |
| Political Opposition to Reform | 9 |
| Non-Enforcement of EU Treaties | 8 |
| EMU Membership | 8 |
| Large Public Sector | 8 |
| Large Welfare State | 8 |
| Poor Revenue Collection | 7 |
| Current Account Deficit | 6 |
| Strong Public Sector Unions | 6 |
| Corruption | 5 |
| Poor Statistical Services | 4 |
| Lack of Competitiveness | 4 |
| Destructive Institutions | 4 |
| Pro-Cyclical Fiscal Policy | 2 |
| Excessive Private Credit Extension | 2 |
| Regulatory Burden | 1 |
| Large Informal Sector | 1 |
| Capital Influx | 1 |
| Military Spending | 1 |
| Ageing Population | 1 |
| Bank Undercapitalisation | 1 |

| Lack of Competitiveness Causal Concepts | Count |
|---|---|
| Regulatory Burden | 20 |
| EMU Membership | 16 |
| High Wages | 11 |
| Monetary Dependence | 10 |
| Low Productivity | 8 |
| Poor Governance | 4 |
| Pro-Cyclical Fiscal Policy | 4 |
| Corruption | 3 |
| Large Public Sector | 3 |
| Large Welfare State | 3 |
| Institutions | 3 |
| Poor Revenue Collection | 2 |
| Political Opposition to Reform | 2 |
| Non-Enforcement of EU Treaties | 2 |
| Capital Influx | 1 |

| Collapse in Confidence Causal Concepts | Count |
|---|---|
| High Debt | 22 |
| Financial Crisis | 12 |
| Current Account Deficit | 10 |
| Upward Revision of Greek Debt | 8 |
| Downgrades | 7 |
| Lack of Competitiveness | 5 |
| Poor Statistical Services | 5 |
| Poor Governance | 4 |
| Bank Undercapitalisation | 4 |
| Slow EMU | 3 |
| Monetary Dependence | 2 |
| EMU Membership | 2 |
| Political Opposition to Reform | 2 |
| Regulatory Burden | 2 |
| Failed Austerity Measures | 2 |
| Pro-Cyclical Fiscal Policy | 2 |
| Fears of Possible EMU Exit | 2 |
| Dubai World Default | 1 |
| Capital Influx | 1 |
| Lack of Trust in Greek Government | 1 |

| Capital Influx Causal Concepts | Count |
|---|---|
| EMU Membership | 8 |
| High Debt | 1 |
| Monetary Dependence | 1 |

| Current Account Deficit Causal Concepts | Count |
|---|---|
| Lack of Competitiveness | 10 |
| Capital Influx | 7 |
| High Debt | 5 |
| Monetary Dependence | 3 |
| EMU Membership | 3 |
| Excessive Private Credit Extension | 2 |
| Poor Governance | 1 |
| Political Opposition to Reform | 1 |

## 4.6. Cross-Disciplinary Analysis

Finally, the tabulations of all causal concepts for the most prominent primary concepts throughout the entire data set encompassing all five disciplines follows below. These tables were used to construct the final cross-disciplinary conceptual maps depicted in Figures 24 and 42.

| High Debt Causal Concepts | Count |
|---|---|
| Poor Governance | 84 |
| Large Welfare State | 46 |
| Access to Cheap Debt | 45 |
| Non-Enforcement of EU Treaties | 38 |
| Poor Revenue Collection | 37 |
| Financial Crisis | 36 |
| Large Public Sector | 35 |
| Political Opposition to Reform | 29 |
| Corruption | 28 |
| Destructive Institutions | 22 |
| EMU Membership | 21 |
| Poor Statistical Services | 13 |
| Current Account Deficit | 12 |
| Lack of Competitiveness | 11 |
| Strong Public Sector Unions | 9 |
| Failed Austerity Measures | 7 |
| Regulatory Burden | 6 |
| Pro-Cyclical Fiscal Policy | 6 |
| Military Spending | 5 |
| Bank Undercapitalisation | 5 |
| Capital Influx | 5 |
| Ageing Population | 4 |
| Monetary Dependence | 3 |
| Large Informal Sector | 2 |
| Excessive Private Credit Extension | 2 |
| Capitalism | 1 |
| Upward Revision of Debt | 1 |

| Access to Cheap Debt Causal Concepts | Count |
|---|---|
| EMU Membership | 43 |
| Monetary Dependence | 12 |
| Capital Influx | 1 |
| Capitalism | 1 |

| Collapse of Confidence Causal Concepts | Count |
|---|---|
| High Debt | 104 |
| Financial Crisis | 48 |
| Upward Revision of Greek Debt | 33 |
| Downgrades | 27 |
| Monetary Dependence | 23 |
| Current Account Deficit | 23 |
| Lack of Competitiveness | 21 |
| Poor Governance | 17 |
| Fears of Possible EMU Exit | 17 |
| Slow EMU Response to the Crisis | 13 |
| Political Instability | 12 |
| Political Opposition to Reform | 11 |
| Bank Undercapitalisation | 10 |
| Poor Statistical Services | 10 |
| EMU Membership | 6 |
| Failed Austerity Measures | 6 |
| Lack of Trust in Greek Government | 5 |
| Dubai World Default | 4 |
| Destructive Institutions | 4 |
| Excessive Private Credit Extension | 3 |
| Regulatory Burden | 3 |
| Pro-Cyclical Fiscal Policy | 2 |
| Non-Enforcement of EU Treaties | 2 |
| Capital Influx | 1 |
| Access to Cheap Debt | 1 |
| Poor Revenue Collection | 1 |

| Current Account Deficits Causal Concepts | Count |
|---|---|
| Lack of Competitiveness | 22 |
| Capital Influx | 14 |
| High Debt | 8 |
| EMU Membership | 8 |
| Monetary Dependence | 4 |
| Access to Cheap Debt | 2 |
| Excessive Private Credit Extension | 2 |
| Poor Governance | 1 |
| Political Opposition to Reform | 1 |
| Regulatory Burden | 1 |

| Lack of Competitiveness Causal Concepts | Count |
|---|---|
| Regulatory Burden | 59 |
| EMU Membership | 35 |
| Monetary Dependence | 35 |
| High Wages | 34 |
| Low Productivity | 23 |
| Large Public Sector | 17 |
| Political Opposition to Reform | 15 |
| Poor Governance | 15 |
| Destructive Institutions | 15 |
| Large Welfare State | 13 |
| Corruption | 11 |
| Capital Influx | 6 |
| Strong Public Sector Unions | 5 |
| Access to Cheap Debt | 4 |
| Poor Revenue Collection | 4 |
| High Debt | 4 |
| Pro-Cyclical Fiscal Policy | 4 |
| Non-Enforcement of EU treaties | 3 |
| Excessive Private Credit Extension | 2 |
| Capitalism | 2 |
| Large Informal Sector | 1 |
| Political Instability | 1 |

| Political Opposition to Reform Causal Concepts | Count |
|---|---|
| Strong Public Sector Unions | 13 |
| Destructive Institutions | 8 |
| Internal Devaluation | 8 |
| Poor Governance | 6 |
| Lack of Trust in Greek Government | 5 |
| Corruption | 5 |
| EMU Membership | 3 |
| Capitalism | 2 |
| Capital Influx | 1 |
| Large Welfare State | 1 |
| Large Public Sector | 1 |
| High Debt | 1 |

| Capital Influx Causal Concepts | Count |
|---|---|
| EMU Membership | 19 |
| Monetary Dependence | 2 |
| High Debt | 2 |
| Access to Cheap Debt | 1 |

| Failed Austerity Measures Causal Concepts | Count |
|---|---|
| Political Opposition to Reform | 18 |
| Poor Governance | 5 |
| Lack of Competitiveness | 3 |
| Corruption | 3 |
| Political Instability | 3 |
| Destructive Institutions | 3 |
| High Debt | 2 |
| Large Public Sector | 2 |
| Large Welfare State | 1 |
| Collapse of Confidence | 1 |
| Non-Enforcement of EU Treaties | 1 |
| Upward Revision of Debt | 1 |
| Capitalism | 1 |
| Fears of Possible EMU Exit | 1 |
| Slow EMU Response | 1 |
| Regulatory Burden | 1 |

| Poor Revenue Collection Causal Concepts | Count |
|---|---|
| Corruption | 16 |
| Governance | 13 |
| Destructive Institutions | 11 |
| Large Informal Sector | 11 |
| Lack of Trust in Greek Government | 5 |
| Poor Statistical Services | 4 |
| Regulatory Burden | 3 |
| Strong Public Sector Unions | 1 |
| Lack of Competitiveness | 1 |
| Large Welfare State | 1 |
| Large Public Sector | 1 |
| Political Opposition to Reform | 1 |
| Failed Asuterity Measures | 1 |
| Capitalism | 1 |

| Fears of Possible EMU Exit Causal Concepts | Count |
|---|---|
| Political Instability | 7 |
| Political Opposition to Reform | 7 |
| Lack of Competitiveness | 5 |
| High Debt | 3 |
| Internal Devaluation | 3 |
| Poor Governance | 3 |
| Collapse of Confidence | 2 |

| Poor Governance Causal Concepts | Count |
|---|---|
| Corruption | 13 |
| Destructive Institutions | 11 |
| Cheap Debt | 10 |
| Political Opposition to Reform | 5 |
| Poor Revenue Collection | 4 |
| Poor Statistical Services | 4 |
| Non-Enforcement of EU Treaties | 2 |
| Monetary Dependence | 1 |
| Large Public Sector | 1 |
| Large Welfare State | 1 |
| Regulatory Burden | 1 |
| Strong Public Sector Unions | 1 |

| Internal Devaluation Causal Concepts | Count |
|---|---|
| Monetary Dependence | 17 |
| Lack of Competitiveness | 12 |
| High Debt | 3 |
| Financial Crisis | 2 |
| High Wages | 2 |
| Current Account Deficit | 2 |
| Excessive Private Credit Extension | 1 |
| EMU Membership | 1 |
| Low Productivity | 1 |
| Capitalism | 1 |

| Political Instability Causal Concepts | Count |
|---|---|
| Political Opposition to Reform | 16 |
| Internal Devaluation | 5 |
| Failed Austerity Measures | 3 |
| EMU Membership | 2 |
| Collapse of Confidence | 2 |
| High Debt | 2 |
| Lack of Trust in Greek Government | 2 |
| Poor Governance | 1 |
| Destructive Institutions | 1 |
| Corruption | 1 |
| Strong Public Sector Unions | 1 |

| Large Welfare State Causal Concepts | Count |
|---|---|
| Political Opposition to Reform | 11 |
| Poor Governance | 5 |
| Ageing Population | 4 |
| Strong Public Sector Unions | 2 |
| Corruption | 1 |

| Corruption Causal Concepts | Count |
|---|---|
| Destructive Institutions | 9 |
| Large Welfare State | 3 |
| Poor Governance | 3 |
| Political Oppositon to Reform | 1 |

| Bank Undercapitalisation Causal Concepts | Count |
|---|---|
| Collapse of Confidence | 8 |
| Financial Crisis | 2 |
| High Debt | 2 |
| Monetary Dependence | 1 |
| Fears of Possible EMU Exit | 1 |
| Excessive Private Credit Extension | 1 |

| High Wages Causal Concepts | Count |
|---|---|
| EMU Membership | 5 |
| Strong Public Sector Unions | 5 |
| Capital Influx | 3 |
| Institutions | 3 |
| Political Opposition to Reform | 2 |
| Regulatory Burden | 1 |
| Excessive Private Credit Extension | 1 |
| Pro-Cyclical Fiscal Policy | 1 |

# Appendix 5. Dominant Discipline per Concept

This section includes two sections. Firstly, the tabulation of dominant discipline for those concepts that were prominently used as primary concepts. Secondly, the tabulation of dominant discipline for the relevant concepts that were only used in a causal manner as explained in Section 7 of the analysis chapter. These tabulations were used to determine the dominant discipline for each of the concepts depicted in Figure 42.

## 5.1. Dominant Disciplines for Concepts Used as Primary Concepts

| High Debt Disciplines | Count |
|---|---|
| Public Administration | 74 |
| Political Science | 64 |
| Economics | 63 |
| Monetary Economics | 33 |
| Financial Economics | 32 |

| Collapse of Confidence Disciplines | Count |
|---|---|
| Financial Economics | 76 |
| Monetary Economics | 47 |
| Economics | 46 |
| Public Administration | 40 |
| Political Science | 20 |

| Lack of Competitiveness Disciplines | Count |
|---|---|
| Economics | 49 |
| Political Science | 40 |
| Public Administration | 39 |
| Monetary Economics | 32 |
| Financial Economics | 6 |

| Access to Cheap Debt Disciplines | Count |
|---|---|
| Monetary Economcis | 31 |
| Financail Economics | 14 |
| Economics | 7 |
| Public Administration | 4 |
| Political Science | 1 |

| Current Account Deficit Disciplines | Count |
|---|---|
| Economics | 24 |
| Monetary Economics | 11 |
| Public Administration | 7 |
| Political Science | 5 |

| Political Opposition to Reform Disciplines | Count |
|---|---|
| Political Science | 32 |
| Public Administration | 3 |
| Monetary Economics | 1 |

| Failed Austerity Measures Disciplines | Count |
|---|---|
| Political Science | 12 |
| Public Administration | 9 |
| Monetary Economics | 6 |
| Financial Economics | 4 |
| Economics | 2 |

| Poor Revenue Collection Disciplines | Count |
|---|---|
| Public Administration | 20 |
| Economics | 6 |
| Political Science | 4 |
| Monetary Economics | 1 |

| Poor Governance Disciplines | Count |
|---|---|
| Political Science | 13 |
| Public Administration | 10 |
| Financial Economics | 5 |
| Monetary Economics | 3 |
| Economics | 1 |

| Internal Devaluation Disciplines | Count |
|---|---|
| Monetary Economics | 9 |
| Political Science | 8 |
| Economics | 7 |
| Public Administration | 1 |
| Financial Economics | 1 |

| Political Instability Disciplines | Count |
|---|---|
| Political Science | 17 |
| Economics | 2 |
| Financial Economics | 2 |
| Monetary Economics | 2 |
| Public Administration | 2 |

| Capital Influx Disciplines | Count |
|---|---|
| Economics | 9 |
| Monetary Economics | 8 |
| Financial Economics | 3 |
| Public Administration | 2 |
| Political Science | 1 |

| Fears of Possible EMU Exit Disciplines | Count |
|---|---|
| Political Science | 9 |
| Monetary Economics | 6 |
| Financial Economcs | 2 |
| Economics | 1 |

| Large Welfare State Disciplines | Count |
|---|---|
| Public Administration | 9 |
| Political Science | 7 |

| Corruption Disciplines | Count |
|---|---|
| Political Science | 10 |
| Public Administration | 4 |

| Excessive Private Credit Extension Disciplines | Count |
|---|---|
| Monetary Economics | 4 |
| Economics | 3 |
| Public Administration | 3 |
| Political Science | 1 |

| Bank Undercapitalisation Disciplines | Count |
|---|---|
| Financial Economcis | 7 |
| Monetary Economics | 3 |
| Economics | 1 |
| Political Science | 1 |
| Public Administration | 1 |

| High Wages Disciplines | Count |
|---|---|
| Monetary Economics | 7 |
| Economics | 6 |

| Lack of Trust in Greek Governments Disciplines | Count |
|---|---|
| Political Science | 5 |
| Monetary Economics | 2 |
| Public Administration | 1 |
| Financial Economics | 1 |
| Economics | 1 |

| Monetary Dependence Disciplines | Count |
|---|---|
| Monetary Economics | 5 |
| Economics | 2 |
| Financial Economics | 1 |

| Large Public Sector Disciplines | Count |
|---|---|
| Public Administration | 5 |
| Political Science | 4 |
| Economics | 1 |

| Large Informal Sector Disciplines | Count |
|---|---|
| Public Administration | 3 |
| Political Science | 2 |

| Destructive Institutions Disciplines | Count |
|---|---|
| Political Science | 5 |

| Upward Revision of Greek Debt Disciplines | Count |
|---|---|
| Financial Economcis | 13 |
| Public Administration | 12 |
| Economics | 10 |
| Monetary Economics | 5 |
| Political Science | 3 |

| Downgrades Disciplines | Count |
|---|---|
| Financial Economics | 4 |
| Public Administration | 1 |
| Economics | 1 |

| Regulatory Burden Disciplines | Count |
|---|---|
| Public Administration | 3 |
| Economics | 2 |
| Monetary Economics | 2 |
| Political Science | 1 |

## 5.2. Dominant Disciplines for Concepts Used Only as Causal Concepts

| EMU Membership Disciplines | Count |
|---|---|
| Monetary Economics | 48 |
| Economics | 47 |
| Public Administration | 26 |
| Financial Economics | 20 |
| Political Science | 19 |

| Financial Crisis Disciplines | Count |
|---|---|
| Financial Economics | 25 |
| Economics | 24 |
| Public Administration | 20 |
| Political Science | 16 |
| Monetary Economics | 8 |

| Strong PS Unions Disciplines | Count |
|---|---|
| Political Science | 16 |
| Public Administration | 15 |
| Economics | 7 |

| Non-enforcement of EU Treaties Disciplines | Count |
|---|---|
| Public Administration | 21 |
| Monetary Economics | 12 |
| Economics | 12 |
| Financial Economics | 3 |
| Political Science | 2 |

| Low Productivity Disciplines | Count |
|---|---|
| Economics | 9 |
| Political Science | 6 |
| Public Administration | 6 |
| Monetary Economics | 3 |

# APPENDIX 6. PRIMARY CONCEPTS PER YEAR (2010-2015)

**2010**

| 2010 Primary Concepts | Count |
|---|---|
| High Debt | 38 |
| Collapse of Confidence | 35 |
| Lack of Competitiveness | 27 |
| Current Account Deficit | 9 |
| Access to Cheap Debt | 9 |
| Internal Devaluation | 6 |
| Excessive Private Credit Extension | 5 |
| Poor Governance | 4 |
| Lack of Trust in Greek Government | 4 |
| Capital Influx | 3 |
| Failed Austerity | 3 |
| Monetary Dependence | 3 |
| Poor Revenue Collection | 3 |
| Political Opposition to Reform | 2 |
| Political Instability | 1 |
| Corruption | 1 |
| Bank Undercapitalisation | 1 |
| Downgrades | 1 |
| EMU Membership | 1 |

## 2011

| 2011 Primary Concepts | Count |
|---|---|
| High Debt | 51 |
| Collapse in Confidence | 43 |
| Lack of Competitiveness | 27 |
| Current Account Deficit | 12 |
| Access to Cheap Debt | 10 |
| Internal Devaluation | 6 |
| Failed Asuterity | 5 |
| Large Welfare State | 5 |
| Fears of Possible EMU Exit | 4 |
| Poor Revenue Collection | 3 |
| Political Opposition to Reform | 3 |
| Political Instability | 2 |
| Poor Governance | 2 |
| Regulatory Burden | 2 |
| Large Informal Sector | 2 |
| Downgrades | 2 |
| Excessive Private Credit Extension | 2 |
| Capital Influx | 2 |
| Bank Undercapitalisation | 1 |
| High Wages | 1 |
| Low Productivity | 1 |

## 2012

| 2012 Primary Concepts | Count |
|---|---|
| High Debt | 39 |
| Collapse of Confidence | 34 |
| Lack of Competitiveness | 12 |
| Poor Governance | 5 |
| Failed Austerity Measures | 5 |
| Access to Cheap Debt | 4 |
| Large Welfare State | 4 |
| Lack of Trust in Greek Government | 3 |
| Current Account Deficit | 2 |
| Poor Revenue Collection | 2 |
| Internal Devaluation | 2 |
| Large Public Sector | 2 |
| Bank Undercapitalisation | 1 |
| Corruption | 1 |
| Destructive Institutions | 1 |
| Military Spending | 1 |
| Non-Enforcement of EU Treaties | 1 |
| Political Instability | 1 |
| Political Opposition to Reform | 1 |
| Fears of Possible EMU Exit | 1 |

# 2013

| 2013 Primary Concepts | Count |
|---|---|
| High Debt | 53 |
| Lack of Competitiveness | 45 |
| Collapse of Confidence | 38 |
| Poor Revenue Collection | 18 |
| Political Opposition to Reform | 16 |
| Political Instability | 14 |
| Access to Cheap Debt | 12 |
| Poor Governance | 11 |
| Current Account Deficits | 11 |
| Failed Austerity Measures | 10 |
| Capital Influx | 8 |
| Corruption | 6 |
| Large Public Sector | 6 |
| Fears of Possible EMU Exit | 5 |
| Destructive Institutions | 4 |
| Lack of Trust in Greek Government | 2 |
| Large Informal Sector | 2 |
| Downgrades | 2 |
| High Wages | 1 |
| Excessive Private Credit Extension | 2 |
| Internal Devaluation | 1 |
| Regulatory Burden | 1 |
| Poor Statistical Services | 1 |
| Monetary Dependence | 1 |
| Large Welfare State | 1 |

# 2014

| 2014 Primary Concepts | Count |
|---|---|
| High Debt | 55 |
| Collapse of Confidence | 51 |
| Lack of Competitiveness | 33 |
| Access to Cheap Debt | 15 |
| Internal Devaluation | 11 |
| Poor Governance | 8 |
| Current Account Deficit | 8 |
| High Wages | 7 |
| Political Opposition to Reform | 6 |
| Bank Undercapitalisation | 6 |
| Excessive Private Credit Extension | 5 |
| Corruption | 4 |
| Failed Austerity Measures | 4 |
| Political Instability | 4 |
| Poor Revenue Collection | 4 |
| Fears of Possible EMU Exit | 4 |
| Regulatory Burden | 4 |
| Monetary Dependence | 3 |
| Capital Influx | 3 |
| Lack of Trust in the Greek Government | 2 |
| Large Public Sector | 1 |
| Downgrades | 1 |

## 2015

| 2015 Primary Concepts | Count |
|---|---|
| Collapse of Confidence | 27 |
| High Debt | 25 |
| Lack of Competitiveness | 24 |
| Failed Austerity | 7 |
| Access to Cheap Debt | 6 |
| Bank Undercapitalisation | 4 |
| Capital influx | 3 |
| Current Account Deficit | 3 |
| Political Instability | 3 |
| Fears of Possible EMU Exit | 3 |
| Political Opposition to Reform | 2 |
| Poor Governance | 2 |
| Pro-Cyclical Fiscal Policy | 2 |
| Destructive Institutions | 1 |
| Low Productivity | 1 |
| Poor Revenue Collection | 1 |
| Regulatory Burden | 1 |

# Glossary of Terms

**Austerity Measures**: Austerity measures are measures aimed at curbing excessive government expenditure and/or budget deficits.

**Capital Account:** An account that indicates the net movements in collective asset ownership of a country. A surplus on the capital account suggests that money is flowing into a country.

**Coding (codes):** A process whereby data is sorted into categories, where the categories are known as 'codes'. Codes are also referred to as 'concepts' or 'categories.'

**Conceptual Matrix:** A matrix showing the relationship between concepts identified in texts during the process of qualitative content analysis.

**Conceptual Model:** A model which visually represents the relationships between the concepts that make up a particular unit of analysis.

**Contagion:** The spread of financial market disturbances between countries.

**Content Analysis:** A research method used to summarise the aspects of chosen content.

**Current Account:** An account indicating the difference between a country's savings and investments.

**Deductive Research:** Research that develops hypotheses and then designs research approaches to test those hypotheses.

**Default Risk:** The risk that a country may not repay its debt.

**Expansionary Fiscal Policy:** Fiscal policy aimed at growing the economy through increasing government expenditure or lowering taxation.

**Fiscal Policy:** Economic policy that involves government expenditures and/or taxation.

**Floating Exchange Rate:** A currency regime where the value of a currency fluctuates based on global supply and demand dynamics.

**Grounded Theory:** A qualitative research methodology which aims to generate new theory by analysing data.

**Inductive Research:** Research that begins with observations, and concludes with attempted explanations of particular observations.

**Integrative Review:** A study that provides a synthesis of existing knowledge from a number of studies that can be applied in practice.

**Internal Devaluation:** A set of economic policies which aims to restore international competitiveness by lowering wages and lowering domestic demand.

**Labour Market Rigidities:** An inability of labour markets to adapt to market dynamics. Usually because of excessive regulation.

**Monetary Independence:** Countries are said to have monetary independence when they are free to set their own interest rates and exchange rate policies.

**Propositional Coding:** A more complex variation of coding, where content is not categorised in simple categories but rather into categories representing certain propositions (i.e., A caused B).

**Seigniorage:** The revenues that a government earns from issuing a country's national currency.

**Sovereign Bond Yield:** The return (interest) investors expect to receive on a government's bonds.

**Sovereign Debt Crisis:** When a country is unable or unwilling to repay its debts.

**Systematic Review:** A literature review which aims to summarise the content of all literature on a particular topic in a systematic manner.

# REFERENCES


Abboushi, S. (2011). Analysis and outlook of the Greek financial crisis. *Journal of Global Business Management*, *7*(1), 1-8.

Accominotti, O., & Eichengreen, B. (2013). The mother of all sudden stops: Capital flows and reversals in Europe, 1919-32. *National Bureau of Economic Research Working Paper No. w19580.*

Ali, T. A. (2012). The impact of the sovereign debt crisis on Eurozone countries. *Procedia Social and Behavioural Sciences, 62*(3), 424-430.

Antzoulatos, A. A. (2011). Greece in 2010: A tragedy without catharsis. *International Advances in Economic Research, 17*(3), 241-257.

Arestis, P., & Karakitsos, E. (2012). The U.S. dimension of the Eurozone debt crisis. *Journal of Post Keynesian Economics, 35*(1), 21-44.

Arghyrou, M. G. (2007). The price effects of joining the Euro: Modelling the Greek experience using non-linear price-adjustment models. *Applied Economics, 39*(4), 493-503.

Arghyrou, M. G. (2009). Monetary policy before and after the Euro: Evidence from Greece. *Empirical Economics, 36*(3), 621-643.

Arghyrou, M. G., & Chortareas, G. (2008). Current account imbalances and real exchange rates in the Euro area. *Review of International Economics, 16*(4), 747–764.

Arghyrou, M. G., & Tsoukalas, J. D. (2011). The Greek debt crisis: Likely causes, mechanics and outcomes. *The World Economy, 34*(2), 173-191.

Arghyrou, M. G., & Tsoukalas, J. D. (2010). The option of last resort: A two-currency EMU. *Cardiff Economics Working Papers E2010/14*.

Argitis, G., & Nikolaidi, M. (2014). The financial fragility and the crisis of the Greek government sector. *International Review of Applied Economics, 28*(3), 274-292.

Baele, L., Ferrando, A., Hördahl, P., Krylova, E., & Monnet, C. (2004). Measuring European financial integration. *Oxford Review of Economic Policy*, *20*(4), 509-530.

Balcerowicz, L. (2014). Euro imbalances and adjustment: A comparative analysis. *Cato Journal, 34*(3), 453-482.

Baltas, N. C. (2013). The Greek financial crisis and the outlook of the Greek economy. *The Journal of Economic Asymmetries*, *10*(1), 32-37.

Baskarada, S. (2014). Qualitative case study guidelines. *The Qualitative Report*, *19*(40), 1-25.

Belke, A., & Dreger, D. (2013). Current account imbalances in the Euro area: Does catching up explain the development? *Review of International Economics, 21*(1), 6-17.

Berelson, B. (1952). *Content analysis in communication research.* Glencoe, IL: Free Press.

Bhanot, K., Burns, N., Hunter, D., & Williams, M. (2014). News spillovers from the Greek crisis: Impact on the Eurozone financial sector. *Journal of Banking and Finance, 38,* 51-63.

Bi, H., & Traum, N. (2012). Estimating sovereign default risk. *The American Economic Review, 102*(3), 161-166.

Blanchard, O. (2007). Adjustment within the Euro: The difficult case of Portugal. *Portuguese Economic Journal, 6*(1), 1-21.

Bratis, T. D., Kouretas, G. P., & Laopodis, N. T. (2014). Creditor moral hazard during the EMU debt crisis. *Social Sciences Research Network Working Paper No. 2604909.*

Bremmer, I. (2015). A good government can beat bad debt. *Time Magazine.* Retrieved August 24, 2015.

Brittan, S., Tietmeyer, H., Bergsten, C. F., Eichengreen, B., & Meltzer, A. H. (2010). The Euro: Will it still be around five years from now?. *The International Economy, 3*(1), 6-10.

Buiter, W. H., & Rahbari, E. (2012). The ECB as a lender of last resort for sovereigns in the Euro area. *Centre for Economic Policy Research Discussion Paper 8974.*

Calvo, G., Leiderman, L., & Reinhart, C. (1994). The capital inflows problem: Concepts and issues. *Contemporary Economic Policy, 12*(3), 54–66.

Campos, N., & Kinoshita, Y. (2003). Why does FDI go where it goes? New evidence from the transition economies. *IMF working paper WP/03/228.*

Ca'Zorzi, M., & Rubaszek, M. (2012). On the empirical evidence of the intertemporal current account model for the Euro area countries. *Review of Development Economics, 16*(1), 95-106.

Cho, J. Y., & Lee, E. H. (2014). Reducing confusion about grounded theory and qualitative content analysis: Similarities and differences. *The Qualitative Report, 19*(32), 1-20.

Choupis, M. (2011). The crisis in the Greek economy and its national implications. *Mediterranean Quarterly, 22*(2), 76-83.

Creighton, A. (2011). Greece's debt crisis: The price of cheap loans. *Policy, 27*(3), 10-14.

Christopoulou, R., & Monastiriotis, V. (2014). The Greek public sector wage premium before the crisis: Size, selection and relative valuation of characteristics. *British Journal of Industrial Relations, 52*(3), 579-602.

Degiannakis, S., Duffy, D., Filis, G., & Livada, A. (2015). Business cycle synchronisation in EMU: Can fiscal policy bring member-countries closer?. *Economic Modelling, 1*(1), 1-29.

De Grauwe, P. (2011). A fragile Eurozone in search of a better governance. *The Economic and Social Review*, *43*(1), 1-30.

Dellas, H., & Tavlas, G. S. (2013). The gold standard, the Euro, and the origins of the Greek sovereign debt crisis. *Cato Journal, 33*(3), 491-520.

Dey, I. (1993). *Qualitative data analysis: A user-friendly guide for social scientists.* London, United Kingdom: Routledge.

Dimoulas, C. (2014). Exploring the impact of employment policy measures in the context of crisis: The case of Greece. *International Social Security Review, 67*(2), 49-65.

Dobrescu, P., & Durach, F. (2014). Euroscepticism - a sign of a Europe in distress. *Romanian Journal of Communication and Public Relations*, *16*(1), 25-40.

Doukas, J. (2013). Another Euro peril: EU current account imbalances. *European Financial Management*, *19*(1), 1-3.

Dullien, S., & Fritsche, U. (2009). How bad is divergence in the Eurozone? Lessons from the United States and Germany. *Journal of Post Keynesian Economics*, *31*(3), 431-457.

Duriau, V. J., Reger, R. K., & Pfarrer, M. D. (2007). A content analysis of the content analysis literature in organization studies: Research themes, data sources, and methodological refinements. *Organizational Research Methods*, *10*(1), 5-34.

Ebner, A. (2013). Capital inflows to Greece, Spain, Portugal and Ireland: A sector-level view. *International Finance*, *13*(3), 333-361.

Eby, L. T., Casper, W. J., Lockwood, A., Bordeaux, C., & Brinley, A. (2005). Work and family research in IO/OB: Content analysis and review of the literature (1980–2002). *Journal of Vocational Behavior*, *66*(1), 124-197.

Eichengreen, B. J. (2003). *Other people's money: Debt denomination and financial stability in emerging market economies*. Chicago, IL: The University of Chicago Press.

Elo, S., & Kyngas, H. (2007). The qualitative content analysis process. *Journal of Advanced Nursing*, *62*(1), 107-115.

Erlandson, D. A., Harris, E. L., Skipper, B. L., & Allen, S. D. (1993). *Doing naturalistic inquiry: A guide to methods*. Newbury Park, CA: Sage Publications.

Evangelopoulos, P. (2012). Rent seeking in the Greek economic drama. *The Independent Review, 17*(1), 95-98.

Fahrholz, C., & Wójcik, C. (2012). The bail-out! Positive political economics of Greek-type crises in the Emu. *Journal of International Commerce, Economics and Policy, 3*(2), 1-18.

Faisal, A., Arezki, R., & Funke, N. (2005). The composition of capital flows: Is South Africa different? *IMF working paper WP/05/40.*

Featherstone, K. (2011). The Greek sovereign debt crisis and EMU: A failing state in a skewed regime. *Journal of Common Market Studies, 49*(2), 193-217.

Featherstone, K., & Papadimitriou, D. (2008). *The limits of Europeanization: Reform capacity and policy conflict in Greece*. Basingstoke, United Kingdom: Palgrave Macmillan.

Finger, B. (2015). What next in the Greek crisis?. *New Politics, 3*(2), 55-61.

Fouskas, V. K. (2013). Whatever happened to Greece? *The Political Quarterly, 84*(1), 132-138.

Fouskas, V. K., & Dimoulas, C. (2012). The Greek workshop of debt and the failure of the European project. *Journal of Balkan and Near Eastern Studies, 14*(1), 1-31.

Furceri, D., & Zdzienicka, A. (2012). The consequences of banking crises for public debt. *International Finance, 15*(3), 289-307.

Georganta, Z. (2011). Greek fiscal and financial data: More than meets the eye. *Journal of Engineering Science and Technology Review, 4*(3), 209-217.

Georgoutsos, D. A., & Mitziakis, P. M. (2013). European sovereign bond spreads: Financial integration and market conditions. *Applied Financial Economics, 23*(20), 1609-1621.

Gibson, H. D., Hall, S. G., & Tavlas, G. S. (2010). The Greek financial crisis: Growing imbalances and sovereign spreads. *Journal of International Money and Finance, 31*(3), 498-516.

Gibson, H. D., Hall, S. G., & Tavlas, G. S. (2014). Fundamentally wrong: Market pricing of sovereigns and the Greek financial crisis. *Journal of Macroeconomics, 39*(2), 405-419.

Gibson, H. D., Palivos, T., & Tavlas, G. S. (2014). The crisis in the Euro area: An analytic overview. *Journal of Macroeconomics, 39*(2), 233-239.

Gibson, H., & Tsakalotos, E. (2001). The Euro, European Union enlargement and ERM 2. Paper presented at the *Conference on "Managing EU Enlargement", Munich, 14–15 December, 2001.*

Giordano, R., Pericoli, M., & Tommasino, P. (2013). Pure or wake-up call contagion? Another look at the EMU sovereign debt crisis. *International Finance, 6*(2), 131-160.

Glaser, J., & Laudel, G. (2013). Life with and without coding: Two methods for early-stage data analysis in qualitative research aiming at causal explanations. *Forum: Qualitative Social Research, 14*(2), 1-38.

Gómez-Puig, M., & Sosvilla-Rivero, S. (2015). The causal relationship between debt and growth in EMU countries. *Journal of Policy Modeling, 37*(6), 974-989.

Gómez-Puig, M., Sosvilla-Rivero, S., & Del Carmen Ramos-Herrera, M. (2014). An update on EMU sovereign yield spread drivers in times of crisis: A panel data analysis. *The North American Journal of Economics and Finance*, *30*(C), 133-153.

Gordts, E., & Robins-Early, N. (2015, July 5). Greece resoundingly rejects austerity in referendum on bailout deal. *Huffington Post.* Retrieved August 25, 2015.

Hamilton, E., & Olson, E. (2014). Was the Euro good for Greece?. *Applied Economics Letters, 21*(4), 248-251.

Hampl, M. (2013). The case of European monetary integration and its former hegemon. *German Economic Review, 14*(1), 2-14.

Hayes, A. F., & Krippendorff, K. (2007). Answering the call for a standard reliability measure for coding data. *Communication Methods and Measures*, *1*(1), 77-89.

Heikkilä, K., & Ekman, S. L. (2003). Elderly care for ethnic minorities: Wishes and expectations among elderly Finns in Sweden. *Ethnicity & Health, 8*(2), 135-146.

Hembruff, J. (2013). Critical review: The politics of sovereign debt. *Third World Quarterly*, *34*(4), 710-725.

Henning, C. R., & Kessler, M. (2012). Fiscal federalism: US history for architects of Europe's fiscal union. *Peterson Institute for International Economics Working paper 12-1.*

Houghton, C., Casey, D., Shaw, D., & Murphy, K. (2013). Rigour in qualitative case-study research. *Nurse Researcher*, *20*(4), 12-17.

Howard, M., La Foucade, A., & Scott, E. (2009). *Public sector economics for developing countries.* Kingston, Jamaica: University of West Indies Press.

Hsieh, H. F., & Shannon, S. E. (2005). Three approaches to qualitative content analysis. *Qualitative Health Research*, *15*(9), 1277-1288.

Kaplanoglou, G., & Rapanos, V. T. (2013). Tax and trust: The fiscal crisis in Greece. *South European Society and Politics, 18*(3), 283-304.

Karras, G. (2011). From hero to zero? The role of the Euro in the current Ccisis: Theory and some empirical evidence. *International Advances in Economic Research, 17*(3), 300-314.

Karyotis, G., & Rudig, W. (2015). Blame and punishment? The electoral politics of extreme austerity in Greece. *Political Studies, 63*(1), 2-24.

Kasimati, E., & Veraros, N. (2013). Should Greece adopt a dual-currency regime to resolve its economic crisis?. *Journal of Policy Modeling, 35*(4), 588-600.

Katsimi, M., & Moutos, T. (2010). EMU and the Greek crisis: The political-economy perspective. *European Journal of Political Economy, 26*(4), 568-576.

Kokkoris, I., Olivares-Caminal, R., & Papadakis, K. (2010). The Greek tragedy. *Journal of Banking Regulation, 11*(4), 257-259.

Koo, R. (2011). How to avoid a Eurozone breakup: Solve two key problems. *International Economy, 25*(1), 46-48.

Kosmidou, K. V., Kousenidis, D. V., & Negakis, C. I. (2015). The impact of the EU/ECB/IMF bailout programs on the financial and real sectors of the ASE during the Greek sovereign crisis. *Journal of Banking & Finance, 50*, 440-454.

Kouretas, G. P., & Vlamis, P. (2010). The Greek crisis: Causes and implications. *Panoeconomicus, 57*(4), 391-404.

Kouzis, Y. (2011). The impact of the crisis on labour relations and collective agreements in Greece. *International Journal of Labour Research, 3*(2), 245-257.

Kovras, I. (2010). The parliamentary election in Greece, October 2009. *Electoral Studies, 29*(2), 293-296.

Krajewska, A. (2014). Fiscal policy in the countries most affected by the crisis: Greece, Ireland, Portugal and Spain. *Comparative Economic Research, 17*(3), 5-27.

Kretsos, L. (2011). Grassroots unionism in the context of economic crisis in Greece. *Labor History*, *52*(3), 265-286.

Kretsos, L., & Vogiatzoglou, M. (2015). Lost in the ocean of deregulation? The Greek labour movement in a time of crisis. *Industrial Relations, 70*(2), 218-239.

Krippendorff, K. (1989). Content analysis. In E. Barnouw, G. Gerbner, W. Schramm, T. L. Worth, & L. Gross (Eds.), *International Encyclopedia of Communication*, Vol. 1 (pp. 403-407). New York, NY: Oxford University Press.

Krugman, P. (2014). Currency regimes, capital flows, and crises. *IMF Economic Review, 62*(4), 470-493.

Lapavitsas, C., Kaltenbrunner, A., Lindo, D., Michell, J., Painceira, J. P., Pires, E., Powell, J., Stenfors, A., & Teles, N. (2010). Eurozone crisis: Beggar thyself and thy neighbour. *Journal of Balkan and Near Eastern Studies, 12*(4), 321-373.

Leacock, C. J., Warrican, S. J., & Rose, G. C. (2009). *Research methods for inexperienced researchers.* Kingston, Jamaica: Ian Randle Publishers.

Leao, P., & Palacio-Vera, A. (2011). Can Portugal escape stagnation without opting out from the Eurozone?. *Levy Economics Institute, working paper No. 664.*

Lekakis, J. N., & Kousis, M. (2013). Economic crisis, the troika and the environment in Greece. *South European Society and Politics, 18*(3), 305-331.

Lincoln, Y., & Guba, E. G. (1985). *Naturalistic inquiry.* Newbury Park, CA: Sage Publications.

Major, I. (2014). A political economy application of the 'tragedy of the anticommons': The Greek government debt crisis. *International Advances in Economic Research, 20*(4), 425-437.

Malakos, T. (2013). Greece facing herself: The past and present as fate. *Journal of Balkan and Near Eastern Studies*, *15*(1), 1-15.

Malliaropulos, D. (2010). How much did competitiveness of the Greek economy decline since EMU entry? *Economy and Markets, 5*(4), 1-16.

Martin, F. M., & Waller, C. J. (2012). Sovereign debt: A modern Greek tragedy. *Federal Reserve Bank of St. Louis Review, 94*(September/October 2012), 321-339.

Matsaganis, M. (2011). The welfare state and the crisis: The case of Greece. *Journal of European Social Policy, 21*(5), 501-512.

Mayring, P. (2000). Qualitative content analysis. *Forum: Qualitative Social Research, 1*(2), article 20.

Merler, S., & Pisani-Ferry, J. (2012). Sudden stops in the Euro area. *Bruegel Policy Contribution (No. 2012/06).*

Michaelides, P. G., Papageorgiou, T., & Tsionas, E. G. (2014). Is the Greek crisis in the EMU contagious?. *Applied Economics Letters, 21*(1), 13-18.

Michaelides, P. G., Papageorgiou, T., & Vouldis, A. T. (2013). Business cycles and economic crisis in Greece (1960–2011): A long run equilibrium analysis in the Eurozone. *Economic Modelling, 31*(C), 804-816.

Milios, J., & Sotiropoulos, D. P. (2010). Crisis of Greece or crisis of the Euro? A view from the European periphery. *Journal of Balkan and Near Eastern Studies, 12*(3), 223-240.

Mink, M., & De Haan, J. (2013). Contagion during the Greek sovereign debt crisis. *Journal of International Money and Finance, 34*, 102-113.

Mitsopoulos, M., & Pelagidis, T. (2014). Why did forceful internal devaluation fail to kick-start export-led growth in Greece?. *Challenge, 57*(6), 85-102.

Morrow, S. L. (2005). Quality and trustworthiness in qualitative research in counselling psychology. *Journal of Counselling Psychology, 52*(2), 250-267.

Morse, J. M., & Field, P. A. (1995). *Qualitative research methods for health professionals.* Thousand Oaks, CA: Sage Publications.

Needleman, I. G. (2002). A guide to systematic reviews. *Journal of Clinical Periodontology, 29*(3), 6-9.

Nelson, R. M., Belkin, P., & Mix, D. E. (2010). Greece's debt crisis: Overview, policy responses, and implications. In *Report for Congress.* (Vol. 41167).

O'Donnel, O., & Tinios, P. (2003). The politics of pension reform: Lessons from public attitudes in Greece. *Political Studies, 51*(2), 262-281.

Oleinik, A., Popova, I., Kirdina, S., & Shatalova, T. (2014). On the choice of measures of reliability and validity in the content-analysis of texts. *Quality & Quantity, 48*(5), 2703-2718.

Oliveira, L., Curto, J. D., & Nunes, J. P. (2012). The determinants of sovereign credit spread changes in the Eurozone. *Journal of International Financial Markets, Institutions and Money, 22*(2), 278–304.

Oltheten, E., Sougiannis, T., Travlos, N., & Zarkos, S. (2013). Greece in the Eurozone: Lessons from a decade of experience. *The Quarterly Review of Economics and Finance, 53*(4), 317-335.

Ozturk, S., & Sozdemir, A. (2015). Effects of global financial crisis on Greece economy. *Procedia Economics and Finance*, *23*, 568-575.

Pagano, M., & Von Thadden, L. (2004). The European bond markets under EMU. *Oxford Review of Economic Policy*, *20*(4), 531–554.

Palaiodimos, G., & Tzavalis, E. (2015). The EMU effects on asset market holdings and the recent financial crisis. *International Review of Financial Analysis, 42*(xxx), 1513-161.

Papandreou, G. A. (2010). A new global financial architecture: Lessons from the Greek crisis. *Mediterranean Quarterly*, *21*(4), 1-6.

Papanikos, G. T. (2014). Greek labor market, the Euro and the current crisis. *The Singapore Economic Review, 59*(4), 1-27.

Pappas, A. P. (2011). The short-term determinants of capital flows for a small, open economy: The case of Greece. *Review of Development Economics, 15*(4), 699-713.

Petersen, M. A., Senosi, M. C., & Mukuddem-Petersen, J. (2012). *Subprime mortgage models.* New York, NY: Nova Science Publishers.

Petmesidou, M. (2013). Is social protection in Greece at a crossroads? *European Societies, 15*(4), 597-616.

Polit, D. F., & Beck C. T. (2004). *Nursing research: Principles and methods.* Philadelphia, PA: Lippincott, Williams & Wilkins.

Polito, V., & Wickens, M. (2014). How the Euro crisis evolved and how to avoid another: EMU, fiscal policy and credit ratings. *Journal of Macroeconomics, 39*, 364-374.

Pragidis, I. C., Aielli, G. P., Chionis, D., & Schizas, P. (2015). Contagion effects during financial crisis: Evidence from the Greek sovereign bonds market. *Journal of Financial Stability, 18*(1), 127-138.

Pronobis, M. (2014). Is the monetary policy of the ECB the right response to the Eurozone crisis? *Procedia Social and Behavioural Sciences, 156*, 398-403.

Provopoulos, G. A. (2014). The Greek economy and banking system: Recent developments and the way forward. *Journal of Macroeconomics, 39*, 240-249.

Psimitis, M. (2011). The protest cycle of spring 2010 in Greece. *Social Movement Studies, 10*(2), 191-197.

Rajan, R. (2010). *Fault lines: How hidden fractures still threaten the world economy.* Princeton, NJ: Princeton University Press.

Randolph, J. J. (2009). A guide to writing the dissertation literature review. *Practical Assessment, Research & Evaluation*, *14*(13), 2-18.

Reddy, T. K. (2011). Greek crises and its impact on the world economy. *The India Economy Review, 7*(1), 177-187.

Reinhart, C. M., & Rogoff, K. S. (2011). From financial crash to debt crisis. *American Economic Review, 101*(5), 1676-1706.

Robbins, P. (2015). The Greek debt crisis: The need for 'heroic' economic policy reforms in the European economic and monetary union. *Indiana Journal of Global Legal Studies, 22*(1), 175-199.

Sakellaropoulos, S., & Sotiris, P. (2014). Postcards from the future: The Greek debt crisis, the struggle against EU-IMF austerity package and open questions for left strategy. *Constellations, 21*(2), 262-273.

Schreier, M. (2012). *Qualitative content analysis in practice*. Thousand Oaks, CA: Sage Publications.

Scott, W. A. (1955). Reliability of content analysis: The case of nominal scale coding. *Public Opinion Quarterly*, *19*(3), 321–325.

Shambaugh, J. C. (2004). The effect of fixed exchange rates on monetary policy. *The Quarterly Journal of Economics, 119*(1), 301-352.

Shannon, P., & Hambacher, E. (2014). Authenticity in constructivist inquiry: Assessing an elusive construct. *The Qualitative Report*, *19*(52), 1-13.

Shapiro, G., & Markoff, J. (1997). A matter of definition. In C. W. Roberts (Ed.), *Text Analysis for the Social Sciences: Methods for Drawing Statistical Inferences from Texts and Transcripts*, (pp. 9-34). Mahwah, NJ: Lawrence Erlbaum Associates.

Shenton, A. K. (2004). Strategies for ensuring trustworthiness in qualitative research projects. *Education for Information*, *22*(2), 63-75.

Shirazi, B. A. (2015). Integrative research: Integral epistemology and integrative methodology. *Integral Review: A Transdisciplinary & Transcultural Journal for New Thought, Research, & Praxis*, *11*(1), 17-27.

Sklias, P., & Maris, G. (2013). The political dimension of the Greek financial crisis. *Perspectives on European Politics and Society*, *14*(1), 144-164.

Sklias, P., Roukanas, S., & Maris, G. (2012). Keynes and the fiscal crisis: Towards a fiscal union? *Procedia Economics and Finance, 9*, 66-73.

Steinberg, D. M. (2015). *The social work student's research handbook*. New York, NY: Routledge.

Stemler, S. (2001). An overview of content analysis. *Practical Assessment, Research & Evaluation*, *7*(17), 137-146.

Stewart, H. (2015, August). Memorandum of understanding: What exactly has Greece signed up for? *The Guardian.* Retrieved 22 August, 2015, from http://www.theguardian.com/world/2015/aug/12/memorandum-understanding-what-exactly-has-greece-signed-up-for

Stockhammer, E., & Sotiropoulos, D. P. (2014). Rebalancing the Euro area: The costs of internal devaluation. *Review of Political Economy, 26*(2), 210-233.

Strauss, A., & Corbin, J. (1994). Grounded theory methodology: An overview. In N. K. Denzin & Y. S. Lincoln (Eds.), *Handbook of Qualitative Research*, (pp. 1-18). London, United Kingdom: Sage Publications.

Strobel, F. (2005). Leaving EMU: A real options perspective. *Applied Economics, 37*(13), 1449-1453.

Sugawara, N. (2011). Fiscal adjustment in Greece under the financial rescue programme: The distributional effects on Greek households. *Applied Economics Letters*, *19*(11), 1071-1074.

Tagkalakis, A. (2013). The effects of financial crisis on fiscal positions. *European Journal of Political Economy*, *29*(3), 197-213.

Tamakoshi, G., & Hamori, S. (2013). Greek sovereign bond index, volatility, and structural breaks. *Journal of Economics and Finance, 38*(4), 687-697.

Theodossopoulos, D. (2013). Infuriated with the infuriated?. *Current Anthropology, 54*(2), 200-221.

Thiemann, A. (2013). Is Greece at a turning point? *The OECD Observer, 297*(4), 8-9.

Traynor, I., & Henley, J. (2015, August). Greece secures third bailout after Germany backs down on opposition. *The Guardian.* Retrieved August 20, 2015, from http://www.theguardian.com/business/2015/aug/14/greece-edges-third-bailout-positive-signals-germany

Turley, M. (2015, January 20). The year of austerity elections. *Public Finance International.* Retrieved August 16, 2015.

Vasilopoulou, S., & Halikiopoulou, D. (2013). In the shadow of grexit: The Greek election of 17 June 2012. *South European Society and Politics, 18*(4), 523-542.

Vasilopoulou, S., Halikiopoulou, D., & Exadaktylos, T. (2014). Greece in crisis: Austerity, populism and the politics of blame. *Journal of Common Market Studies, 52*(2), 388-402.

Verney, S., & Bosco, A. (2013). Living parallel lives: Italy and Greece in an age of austerity. *South European Society and Politics, 18*(4), 397-426.

Wakefield, A. (2014). Searching and critiquing the research literature. *Nursing Standard*, *28*(39), 49-57.

Wang, M. C., Haertel, G. D., & Walberg, H. J. (1990). What influences learning? A content analysis of review literature. *The Journal of Educational Research*, *84*(1), 30-43.

Weber, R. P. (1990). *Basic content analysis*. Newbury Park, CA: Sage Publications.

Williams, C. C., & Renooy, P. (2008). Measures to tackle undeclared work in the European Union. *European Foundation for the Improvement of Living and Working Conditions Policy Paper.*

Yfantopoulos, J. (2013). Dynamic aspects of the underground economy in Greece. *Journal of Economic and Social Measurement, 38*(1), 97-112.

Yildiz, H., & Yildirim, D. Ç. (2014). An empirical study on fiscal sustainability in the Eurozone. *Serbian Journal of Management*, *9*(1), 59-70.

Zahariadis, N. (2013). Leading reform amidst transboundary crises: Lessons from Greece. *Public Administration, 91*(3), 648-662.

Zartaloudis, S. (2014). The Impact of the fiscal crisis on Greek and Portuguese welfare states: Retrenchment before the catch-up?. *Social Policy and Administration, 48*(4), 430-449.

Zettelmeyer, J., Trebesch, C., & Gulati, M. (2013). The Greek debt restructuring: An autopsy. *Economic Policy, 28*(75), 513-563.

# About the Authors


## *Janine Mukuddem-Petersen, PhD*

Associate Professor in Economics at the University of Cape Town,
Graduate School of Business, South Africa
Email: janine.mukuddem-petersen@gsb.uct.ac.za;
jmukuddempetersen@gmail.com


*Professor Janine Mukuddem-Petersen* has served as a practitioner and an academic with teaching-learning, research and management duties. Janine has chaired several research related committees at various universities. She has experience in undergraduate and postgraduate lecturing and supervision as well as postdoctoral mentorship. She is a co-founder of the Economic Modelling and Econometric Research Group (EMERG) that later evolved into a registered company. She is a director of a non-profit company know as S.T.A.C. Foundation. Janine has published approximately 100 internationally peer-reviewed research outputs.


## *Dawie Scholtz*

Management Consultant and Independent Author
Johannesburg, South Africa


*Dawie Scholtz* is a South African researcher with a special interest in economic policy and electoral politics. Dawie worked as an economic researcher at a leading South African political party, has completed his MBA and is currently working as a full-time management consultant.

# INDEX

## D



## E



## F



## G



## H



## I



## J

## L



## M



## N



## O



## P



## Q



## R



## S

## T



## V



## W